passe... ... ... dans la
poêle et ... ... bouillant sur la préparation.

Gâteau praliné :

...ler un quart de pralines rosées, y ajouter 4 blancs
...œufs battus en neige très ferme et mettre ce
...élange dans un moule caramélisé, faire cuire
...bain-marie au four ou dans four de campagne
... fois la cuisson terminée, démouler et servir
... une crème faite avec les 4 jaunes d'œufs,
...uart de sucre et ½ litre de lait.

...de de bananes :

...es coupe transversalement en rondelles.
...oupoudre ces rondelles de sucre et on arro...
...kirsch ou de rhum.

...n doré :

...pez des tranches de pain d'un bon centimèt...
...aisseur environ. Faites les tremper dans du
...Passez-les ensuite dans des œufs bien battus.
...s fondre du beurre dans une poêle, lorsqu'...
...ien fumant, mettez y cuire les tranches de
..., qui doivent prendre une belle teinte
...Retournez pour qu'elles puissent cuire
...deux côtés. Soupoudrez de sucre et servez
...chaud.

A TASTE OF MY LIFE

www.**rbooks**.co.uk

Also by Raymond Blanc

Recipes from Le Manoir aux Quat' Saisons
Blanc Mange
A Blanc Christmas
Blanc Vite
Cooking for Friends
Foolproof French Cookery

A TASTE OF MY LIFE

Raymond Blanc

with James Steen

BANTAM PRESS

LONDON · TORONTO · SYDNEY · AUCKLAND · JOHANNESBURG

TRANSWORLD PUBLISHERS
61–63 Uxbridge Road, London W5 5SA
A Random House Group Company
www.rbooks.co.uk

First published in Great Britain
in 2008 by Bantam Press
an imprint of Transworld Publishers

This book is substantially a work of non-fiction based on the life, experiences and
recollections of Raymond Blanc. In some limited cases names of people, places,
dates, sequences or the detail of events have been changed. The author
has stated to the publishers that, except in such minor respects, the contents
of this book are true.

A CIP catalogue record for this book
is available from the British Library.

ISBN 9780593060360

Addresses for Random House Group Ltd companies outside the UK
can be found at: www.randomhouse.co.uk
The Random House Group Ltd Reg. No. 954009

The Random House Group Limited supports The Forest Stewardship
Council (FSC), the leading international forest-certification organization. All our
titles that are printed on Greenpeace-approved FSC-certified paper carry the FSC logo.
Our paper procurement policy can be found at
www.rbooks.co.uk/environment

Typeset in 11.25/16pt by
Falcon Oast Graphic Art Ltd.
Printed and bound in Great Britain by
Clays Ltd, Bungay, Suffolk

All photographs courtesy of the author and Le Manoir aux Quat' Saisons except
p. 3: RB with mother and RB's mother with tray of snails; p. 4: Paul Bocuse and RB; and
p. 6: RB with chefs and RB with chicken, all courtesy Network Lifestyle Publications.

2 4 6 8 10 9 7 5 3 1

Cook's Notes
- 1 teaspoon = 5ml
- 1 tablespoon = 15ml
- Use medium eggs, unsalted butter and whole
  (full-fat) milk unless a recipe says otherwise.

For Maman Blanc

CONTENTS

Acknowledgements   ix

Introduction: Madame, Monsieur   1

1   Taste: Tomato Essence   5

2   Saône: Village Life   21

3   Seasons: Maman Blanc's Tears   34

4   Christmas: Don't Mention the Boar   48

5   Fish: An Invitation to Provence   62

6   Soups: Know Your Onions   80

7   Le Palais: Frying Pan Fiasco   93

8   England: To the Rose (with Thorns)   110

9   Debut: I Spry   124

10   Hygiene: Half a Curried Mouse   136

11   Customers: From Little Acorns   143

12   The Buzz: The Heaven in Hell   160

13   Delicacies: Sex Appeal   165

14   Logos: The Smiling Apprentice and the Wretched
        Cockerel   181

15   Brasserie Blanc: Remind Me How to Laugh   189

16   Stocks: Taking Stock   203

17   Bread and Sweet Things: Crazy But True   209

18   Celebrity Chefs: Roux the Day   230

19   Nouvelle Cuisine: To Le Manoir Born   245

20   Molecular Gastronomy: The Professor   260

21   Japan: The Search for Kobe   274

22   Texture: The Return of the Chew   288

23   Le Soufflé: Rise Above It   296

24   Thought: The Salt Tests   311
25   The F Word: The Lost Secrets   322
26   The Smile: The Marseillaise with Ma'am   331
27   The Cookery School: A Perfect Coulis   348
28   The Future of Food: It's All in the Past   355

Further Reading   369
Index   373

ACKNOWLEDGEMENTS

Some compliments *from* the chef to . . . James Steen, my collaborator and companion at the computer, bar and table. James, thank you.

I pay a debt of sincere gratitude to my friends at Transworld Publishers: Doug Young, who was steadfastly confident and provided invaluable advice; Emma Musgrave, who edited with finesse and thoughtfulness; Daniel Balado-Lopez tidied up and saved blushes; Rebecca Jones brought the final bits and pieces together; Mari Roberts, the cookery editor, was utterly fantastic.

My agent Rosemary Scoular matched me with Transworld and deserves credit. And it would be entirely wrong not to acknowledge the team at Le Manoir, many of whom helped with this book and all of whom continue to inspire me. I am particularly grateful to Tom Lewis, the general manager, Anne Marie Owens, the head gardener, and, in the kitchen, Gary Jones, Benoit Blin, Andy Foulkes and Adam Johnson. I am also grateful to my assistant, Leanda Pearman.

I would also like to thank John Lederer and Clive Fretwell from Brasserie Blanc; my friends Jody Scheckter and Paul Levy for their invaluable advice and assistance: Caroline Drummond of LEAF; Rupert Howes of the Marine Stewardship Council; Sam Fanshawe of the

Marine Conservation Society; Charlotte and Jeanette of Sustain, and Patrick Holden from the Soil Association.

It goes without saying, but I will say it nevertheless, that I am eternally grateful to my wonderful family, especially Natalia.

A TASTE OF MY LIFE

INTRODUCTION

MADAME, MONSIEUR

THIS IS JUST A LITTLE BOOK ABOUT EATING AND COOKING AND LIFE. It has more pages than the publishers requested, but then there is so much to say about Eating and Cooking and Life.

Eating is extraordinarily easy. And Cooking is truly simple. To do it, all you need to do is connect all of your senses with your brain. That means you need to think. When you think, you have to reflect, and when you reflect, you have to take decisions. And there you have it: that's Cooking. Make good decisions and use great ingredients and there's every chance your food will be beautiful. What you present on a plate for your family and friends will be a culinary statement of love.

If only Life were so simple.

My existence, as you are about to learn, has been a series of decisions, some wise, others unwise. I'm sure yours is no different. *C'est la vie.* I have been in the right place at the wrong time, for instance when I was starting out in France and the head chef whacked me across the face. When I came to England back in the seventies I was convinced I was in the wrong place at the wrong time. On reflection, I was most definitely in the right place. I hung around, I'm still here, and I feel privileged to live in Britain. It has become my adopted country.

Within the pages that follow, I have set out to share the story of a life that has been propelled by a desire – no, more than that: a consuming, striving, self-set, never-ending requirement – to give excellence.

Sometimes people say to me, 'Raymond, you are a very lucky man.' No, no, no. I will be carrying a copy of this book with me at all times so that when that comment comes I can flick open the pages and show them the extensively highlighted passages that detail the struggles: the tough and gritty challenges of the self-taught chef; the dramas of opening Les Quat' Saisons, with my then wife Jenny; the traumas and madness of launching the patisserie and bakery Maison Blanc when I had only just mastered making pastry myself; the difficulties, immense beyond belief, of transforming a manor house in Oxfordshire into Le Manoir aux Quat' Saisons. You will discover in this book that I love difficulties and huge challenges! I live for them.

But the process of doing this book has encouraged me to do what the good cook does in the kitchen – reflect. Amid the difficulties, there have been many moments of bliss and lots of learning.

Shortly after opening Le Manoir, after a heavy service, I decided to treat myself. I looked in the cold room. There was a calf's head; it felt just right. I blanched the head for about five minutes and then cooked it with a stock of water, a splash of vinegar and a good half a bottle of white wine. In went onions, carrots, celery, leeks, a fat bouquet garni, a few pinches of salt and some whole black peppercorns. It cooked for about six hours, slow, slow, slow, with just a tiny bubble or two breaking the surface of the clear stock. I then lifted the head out of the stock, placed it on a beautiful dish and carried it into the dining room, which was now empty of guests. To accompany it I had made a lovely sauce of mayonnaise, gherkins and capers, and I'd also cut myself a good piece of bread.

I sat down on my own and ate . . . and drank a half-bottle of Brouilly. I grinned the whole way through. After a heavy service, the world now was just perfect.

Any nutritionist will tell you that you must never eat after eleven o'clock. I went to bed and a few hours later, and for a day or so afterwards, I was in severe pain. I felt as if I'd devoured a vat of fat that had congealed in my stomach – actually, that was exactly what was happening. Still, I can smile now because I don't remember the pain, just the taste. That is the great thing about looking back on the past: you can laugh about it.

And, on reflection, perhaps I should have shared that calf's head.

Voilà. Allow me now to share the stories and the knowledge distilled from a life spent on both sides of the kitchen doors. Along the way, I hope you enjoy the recipes.

This book is not the whole meal, so please don't treat it as such. It is a taste of my life, a taste which – let me think, let me reflect – has had a few bitter moments, but it has been deliciously sweet too.

Bon appétit.

ONE

TASTE

Tomato Essence

WHEN I WAS A CHILD AND IT WAS SUMMERTIME, MY MOTHER Anne-Marie would make a simple but delicious tomato salad. In the heat of the season it was a refreshing dish.

The children, five of us, would sit at the table and my father Maurice would open the proceedings. With the tip of a knife, he would make the sign of the cross on the crust of a massive loaf of bread. The bread was always a minimum of a day old, otherwise the five children would devour too much at once.

My father was an atheist – and not just an unbeliever; he really hated God – and for years I wondered why he performed this religious ritual. One day he explained to me that it was a mark of respect for the food, to show that he understood it was earned by hard work – most certainly not a mark of respect for God. In our village of Saône, perched above Besançon between two great food and wine regions of France – Burgundy below us and the rugged Jura mountains above us – food was worshipped.

Few salads could be easier to prepare than that one of tomato. The tomatoes, which were grown on nearby farms or came from our garden, were not just any tomatoes, but the Marmande variety, and were fat, meaty and juicy. They were picked when still firm, before becoming fully ripe, before they could fall to the ground and bruise. Then they were allowed to ripen further on the south-facing window sill in our kitchen. This sunlit line of tomatoes provided a colourful and scented still-life, the first thing you saw and smelled as you walked into the room. Some were big, others small, a mismatched assortment with bumps, lumps and humps. And they were just begging to be used.

When the tomatoes were perfectly ripened, my mother sliced them and arranged them in a dish with salad leaves, and finely sliced shallots scattered on top. If nothing else had been added to these two ingredients this book would have had to begin with a different tale. But over the salad she spooned the traditional Dijon mustard dressing. This she made using a generous tablespoon of Dijon mustard, two pinches of sea salt, ground black pepper, two tablespoons of red wine vinegar and then the same amount of water (which thinned the dressing by cutting down its oiliness and helped the emulsion). She then whisked in vegetable oil to finish the dressing. All these ingredients were at room temperature; if they had come straight from the fridge and been chilled it would have been difficult to create the emulsion.

Interestingly enough, she always made the dressing – almost to order – for each meal. We frequently ate salad from the garden, the varieties changing according to the month of the year, so why, I wonder, didn't she prepare half a litre of it in one go? Then she would have had enough to last the whole week. Maman Blanc is a great cook but not a chef.

The acidity of the vinegar and the salt combined and slowly drew out the juice of the tomatoes, changing both their taste and texture. Once the juice escaped from the flesh it settled as a light-red pool in the base of the dish. As children we loved this salad, and for me, without doubt the best bit was the juice, which I mopped up with chunks of bread. Unfortunately, my brothers and sisters also loved the juice, so I had to share it.

As chefs, too often we are encouraged to be complicated with our food, but in that dish on that dinner table in my childhood home was an example of the purest form of gastronomy. Simple ingredients – tomatoes, shallots, and the mustard dressing – produced a powerful impression on the palate. And they were ingredients that came from our own soil. A few decades on, the memory of the taste of that tomato essence had not faded.

———

At the age of twenty-seven I became a chef. I had never worked in a professional kitchen, except for a few months in a pub and a little bistro in Oxford. I was completely self-taught. I must say I was not great company when I was with friends and family because my mind was constantly besieged by ideas for recipes, or preoccupied by the scents and tastes of ingredients. As I was untrained I had so much to catch up with and a whole world of food to discover. How could I do *that* dish? What if I did *this* to *that*? I was a man obsessed, forever thinking of ways in which flavours could be mixed, seeking the ultimate taste experience.

I never knew when these ideas would come. There was no warning. Perhaps it was when I was in the kitchen, or taking a shower, or at a table with family and friends. One moment I'd be slicing a carrot, or washing my hair, or listening to a friend tell a story, the next I'd be gripped by images of ingredients, or the concept of a dish, and become entirely focused on something magical that could be done with food.

It can even get you in the middle of the night. There was a period in my life when I went to bed with a tape recorder, or pen and paper, on my bedside table. I might wake up two or three times with an idea for a dish, and make a note of it.

Come the morning, I'd refresh my memory by checking the notes or listening to the tape and sometimes I'd think, 'Where on earth did that idea come from? It's rubbish.' Other times I'd play back the tape and hear my voice telling me an idea that could grow into a dish.

Occasionally I knew I had a gem, an idea for something very, very special. At those moments I'd be the happiest man on earth.

Every now and again I would think back to my childhood and to the exceptional taste of that tomato salad. Passionate cooks are often a sentimental bunch who like to return to their roots. My mother's food has certainly been my inspiration. In fact, my mother has been my inspiration.

At the age of eighty-seven she stands four feet two inches high and is shrinking every day. Her skin is wilted like an old apple skin; her eyes are full of love and compassion for the world. Her hands are large and rough, from cleaning, washing, gardening and, of course, cooking. In her kitchen she does not walk, she runs. She will jump on to a chair and then on to the sink to reach essential ingredients on a high (for her) shelf. Or she will dive down to the lowest shelf to retrieve a specific spice. She is forgetful, just like me. And because of her absent-mindedness, when she is searching for an ingredient she'll cover as much ground as Thierry Henry on the pitch. My sons, Sebastien and Olivier, call her 'Mother Teresa on Speed'. She is a great cook and a truly loveable little woman.

So I found myself thinking back to that flavourful tomato salad juice, and at some point I started to contemplate recreating the taste of the liquid that settled at the bottom of my mother's dish. I reckoned that the liquid was a dish in its own right. It would not do simply to serve the salad and then while the guests were eating it emerge from the kitchen saying, 'Try the juice at the bottom of the dish. That's the best bit.' I wanted to serve the best bit in quantities that were large enough for the dish to feature on the menu as 'Essence of Tomato'.

But how could I reproduce a large quantity of the essence with the same strength of flavour? I couldn't just follow my mother's recipe as I would have needed a ton of tomatoes to achieve a few glasses of essence. My aim was precise: the primary ingredient was tomato, specifically a true summer tomato with its freshness and depth of flavour. The tomato would need the sweetness that comes with ripening and it would need acidity to give balance and length of flavour. So the first step was to find the best tomato. There were hundreds of varieties from which to choose, but only a few might provide the best dish.

I needed the assistance of Anne Marie Owens, the head gardener at my restaurant-hotel in Oxfordshire, Le Manoir aux Quat' Saisons. Anne Marie joined us as a young gardener a year after Le Manoir opened and she is still with us. How apt that she shares my mother's first and second names. Together we chose thirty-seven of the best-known varieties, from the large Russian Black to the Coeur de Boeuf and many types of cherry tomato. Then we grew them.

Very early in my life I was taught the importance of the variety of a vegetable. At home neither of my parents would use the general term 'potato' or 'salad', it was always by variety. The variety defined the experience and the cooking technique. Belle de Fontenay made the best French fries and the best potato purée; the Ratte were the best salad potatoes. In the case of the tomatoes, the trial was divided into three sub-trials: we wanted to find the tomato that was best for sauce, the tomato that was best for salad, and finally the tomato that would make the tastiest essence.

Oxfordshire is known for its apples but not for its tomatoes, so rather than try to defy the laws of nature we grew the tomatoes in large poly-tunnels whose sides could be lifted to create airflow and keep down the temperatures. For every trial we put together a group of tasters made up of chefs, waiters, gardeners, customers and whoever happened to be passing by when a tasting was taking place. These trials at Le Manoir were so important. They introduced the chefs to the garden, reconnecting gastronomy with its roots in the soil, in the seasonality, purity and nobility of the produce. They are the keys to the selection of particular varieties, not chosen for looks nor for abundance but for taste and texture. As it should be.

All the varieties were tasted first when raw, then when they had been cooked down. We made notes and rated each one. Eight out of ten tasters concluded that the best tomato for sauce was the classic Italian variety San Marzano and the Costoluta Florentina. The Black Russian, the black Japanese variety the Nyagon, the Saint Pierre and the Marmande won the day for the salad.

That left one dish that needed a tomato – the essence.

We worked our way through the varieties, discarding those that did not have the right balance of sweetness and acidity. Eventually, the winners were three varieties of cherry tomato called Nyagon, Petite San Marzano and Black Cherry. Maybe it was obvious that the cherry would be the best because it is packed with extreme flavour, sweetness and acidity. It would never work in a sauce because it would be too sweet, too concentrated for the human palate. But for essence it was unbeatable.

Having harvested the crop, I was overwhelmed by a sense of urgency to create the dish. At last we had the raw produce – the most important element.

There are times when I have an idea and within hours of being in the kitchen the concept has been transformed into a dish that is ready to put on the menu. That is rare. Then there are those ideas that hover in the background, coming forward every now and again so that I cannot forget about them. Alternatively, I'll see in my mind an image of how the dish should look and I will know precisely how it can be achieved technically, but still I can't get there.

Creativity comes from having an open mind to new ideas, from constantly questioning the established rules, though rarely does it come on those days when you set out to be creative. On those mornings when I awake and say to myself, 'Today I will create a new dish,' chances are what goes on to the plate will be a failure. That's the point at which your life, which yesterday was full of happiness, feels dark and empty. You panic and feel that God has abandoned you, snatched away your most valuable gift – creativity.

First, I tried to purée the raw tomatoes and put them through a *chinois* (conical) sieve, but the juice was disappointing, coarse and thick.

Then I tried to grind the tomatoes, but again the flavour was far from refined and delicate. I kept returning to the drawing board, or rather the chopping board.

Then I got it.

One day I was walking through the kitchen when I spotted a chef pushing a fruit purée through a *chinois* that was lined with a muslin cloth. I had a flashback to my childhood, a memory of my grandmother using a large cloth to make blackcurrant *gelée*. She used to cook down the fruit with sugar, add lemon juice and a little pectin towards the end, and then place this mixture into a large casserole lined with the cloth. The cloth was then tied up, lifted and hung above the pot in the kitchen. For the next few hours the clear ruby juices left the cloth, drop by drop, pushed through by the mixture's own weight, and collected in the pot. After that my grandmother would press the cloth to push through the fruit. The kitchen filled with the comforting scent of blackcurrant *jus*, and for a day or two my grandmother's fingers were stained red. The sweetened liquid was ladled into jam jars and would set to become a trembling jelly. My grandmother would not waste the pulp. Water was added to it to make fruit juice.

This memory told me how to make the essence.

I cut two kilograms of the perfectly ripe Petit San Marzano tomatoes into quarters. Then I added some herbs, which I wanted to include in the recipe because they give complexity and length of flavour, by which I mean a lingering taste in the mouth after swallowing. My mother hadn't used herbs, but for my dish they became a necessity. The first was tarragon, but only two leaves; any more and it would overpower the tomato flavour. Next came basil, but only three or four leaves, shredded. I also added a little finely chopped fennel, some sliced onion, and a few drops of Worcestershire sauce, Tabasco and Angostura bitters, though don't ask me why – it just felt right. I finished, just as my mother had done, with those two highly necessary ingredients: a few pinches of sea salt and a dash or two of red wine vinegar.

I took the whole marinating mixture, gathered it in a double-layered muslin cloth, tied it up tightly and hung it from a shelf in a fridge. Under its own weight the essence dripped overnight through the cloth into a basin, just like my grandmother had done with her *gelée*. The next morning that basin contained eight hundred millilitres of clear golden liquid, enough to serve four portions, each of two hundred millilitres.

It looked lovely, but I was apprehensive. Would it taste any good? I lifted a spoonful of it to my mouth. *Voilà!* I had captured the heart of the tomato, its very essence.

The dish is simple to make and requires little skill, though two rules must be obeyed: first, perfect, well-ripened cherry tomatoes should be used; second, don't chop them too finely otherwise you will lose the juice to the chopping board (though one way to chop them is to use the pulse of a food processor).

If the essence is frozen it becomes granita and will make a delicious appetizer. Or try it in a risotto, using half water and half essence when cooking the rice. The rice slowly fluffs into translucent whiteness, but don't be fooled by the colour: every grain holds an incredible burst of the red tomato. The vessel that carries the food is also important, remember. Please, do not serve the essence in a glass as it might look like a urine sample. Use the finest tureen or best china soup plates you have. I can assure you, you will have the best tomato experience.

Some might say that my obsession with this dish was a ludicrous time-wasting experience. Many would not say that. Essence of tomato has been much copied by chefs around the world, and hundreds of thousands of restaurant guests have enjoyed it. In America you will see it on menus as 'tomato water'. In fact, shortly after creating the essence I served it at a lunch in London for forty of the world's Michelin-starred chefs whose establishments were members of Relais & Chateaux. Most of them asked me for the recipe, which I handed over, feeling pleased that their interest was confirmation that the dish was special.

So I like to think that my curiosity and determination bore fruit, so to speak, or at least some very fine fruit essence. It tastes out of this world.

It is good to give some thought to taste. Taste is not elitist. Taste is not the preserve of a few. Most of us can do it, but too few do when it comes to cooking.

Many people go to the supermarket and buy the ingredients for a dinner-party dish. Back at home they open the cookery book on the relevant page and then peel, chop and cook. Five hours later they serve the dish. Then and only then do they taste. To me, this is not quite right. The cook has been so busy studying the fancy photograph in the cookery book he has completely forgotten to consider the most important element – taste, which at its best is the product of an ingredient that is seasonal, grown locally and of a good variety.

Forgive me if you think I am stating the obvious, but I have seen many cooks prepare a dish from start to finish without once dipping a spoon into the sauce and tasting before serving. So many chefs on television make a dish but forget to taste. Watching at home, you might think the dish looks fantastic. But what does it taste like? You simply don't know. Sometimes the credits roll without the dish having been tasted.

When new recruits join the kitchen brigade at Le Manoir – once they have managed to navigate the maze of kitchen corridors from the passe to Pastry without getting lost – I implore them to taste frequently. When fruit and vegetables arrive in our kitchens – 'Taste them.' When a sauce is simmering on the stove – 'Taste it, please.' Before plating up for the guest in the restaurant – 'Taste it again.'

There is much to be said for allowing your sense of taste to guide you to better food and a happier, often healthier life. Put the food in your mouth and taste it. Allow a few seconds for your senses to assess the flavours, the combinations, the acidity, the sweetness, the bitterness, the sugariness, the seasoning, the purity or even the vulgarity. Technique and presentation are important, but the ultimate truth of a dish is in its taste and texture.

It is crucial to dwell on taste for a moment or two because it is the first step on the path to connecting with food. Or should that be re-connecting with food, re-establishing the food culture that for many years has been largely forgotten in Great Britain, thanks in part to intensive farming and supermarkets?

I believe strongly that the character of an ingredient is not unlike the character of a person. Its growth and development will define its personality just as growth and development define ours. Think of a tomato that has been grown hydroponically in solutions of mineral nutrients as opposed to being grown in soil. It is fed numerous chemicals and stored in an environment in which the heat, light and humidity are controlled. This environment, which is hardly eco-friendly, is baking hot because heat promotes growth, of course. The growers want this tomato to grow as quickly as possible so that it can be picked and placed on the supermarket shelf, making way for another tomato that has been grown using hydroponics.

That fruit is like the child who has been born with a silver spoon in his mouth, the child who is given everything before he leaves his bubble and goes out into the big wide world where others discover he is not very nice. What makes us, what forms us and makes us better people, is partly the experience of meeting challenges. Picture the tomato that has grown – heavens above – in the soil. It has faced the cold of the night and the heat of the sun and taken in its nutrients from the chemical-free (or virtually chemical-free) ground. Surely it is going to be a happier, stronger tomato plant, and its fruit will taste damned good, better than the tomato that grew up in the bubble. It might even be good enough to provide essence of tomato.

And there is more to taste than meets the tongue. Taste, for example, has a wonderful way of jogging the memory. Sure, you might come across an old photograph that stirs sweet recollections. You might hear a Frank Sinatra tune (or indeed a Led Zeppelin track, or a Beethoven sonata) and the music instantly conjures up the face of a lover who has long gone. But if you ask me, taste – a mouthful of this, a spoonful of that – is a highly enjoyable mode of transport for a trip down memory lane. We've all been there. It could be a bite of cheese-on-toast that whisks you back to a moment in your childhood. Or a spoonful of apple crumble that instantly reminds you of cooking with your mother. Or maybe you taste a magnificent, earthy, succulent strawberry that has you remembering days when you went to the pick-your-own. You hear yourself saying, 'Now that's how strawberries used to taste.'

A couple of years ago I was staying at the Lanesborough Hotel, near Hyde Park, in London. It was a Sunday, I was alone, and I thought I would visit the bar for an early evening drink, and to see my old friend, the head barman Salvatore Calabrese, who is an acknowledged master of his trade. When Salvatore greeted me with a smile and a big hug I knew that nipping down to the bar was the right move. I should tell you that I rarely drink alone. In England the lone drinker is often a man who simply enjoys solitude and a crossword puzzle; in France the lone drinker is often considered to be a washed-up drunk.

I glanced at the bar and noticed the cognac list. Salvatore's finger zoomed in and hovered above the most expensive name on the list. He said, 'That is the best I have. Don't know who's going to buy it. It's £350 a glass.'

In that split second, as I spotted the age of the cognac and its potential taste, my memory took me back to one of my first jobs, when I worked at a restaurant called Le Palais de la Bière, in Besançon. I could picture myself, aged twenty, standing behind the bar of Le Palais, cleaning glasses. Not far from that bar area there was a special cabinet that contained a bottle of cognac of early 1800s vintage, and it intrigued me. All I could think of was that the bottle contained a liquid that was about 150 years old.

During the Second World War, Le Palais was the local headquarters for the German army. The soldiers ransacked local cellars to create their own magnificent cellar in Le Palais, and when the war ended this precious stash of alcohol remained in the bar. That's probably how the ancient cognac came to be at the restaurant.

One day at Le Palais, a customer ordered a glass of it. It was poured and carried over to him, and he savoured every drop and looked extremely happy. He drank the lot, but of course he couldn't drink the aroma, which remained in the balloon for me. When the glass was returned to the washing-up area I gently lifted it to my nose and inhaled. The smell, the perfume, was one I had never experienced. Until then I had known only distilled spirits made from berries and fruits. This cognac, however, was a sensational multi-layered blend of vanilla, sultanas, cardamom and roasted almond. There was a hint of coffee about it too, a delicate fragrance of citrus, and the smell of maple, and much more.

I am ashamed to say that a few days later I decided to risk my job at Le Palais by tasting some of the cognac for myself. Hell, I would do the same if I had my time again. My crime would have to be well conceived because the restaurant owner, Monsieur Spitz, was a strict man. He was in his mid-seventies but was a formidable force in his chalky pinstripe suits, with his square jaw, grey eyes and spiky hair. Monsieur Spitz not only looked streetwise and sharp, he was also shrewd when it came to keeping hold of his drink, his bottled profits: the labels of his prized bottles carried little notches where he had used his thumbnail to make a little scratch and thereby keep track of the volume. By contrast, his son, M. Bernard, who helped run the place, was considered to be the perfect gentleman and was popular among the staff – the best boss I ever had.

I sneaked up to that cabinet where Monsieur Spitz kept his ancient bottles, a treasure trove of old spirits and fortified wines, and gazed at the misshapen bottle containing my golden cognac.

My heart was beating fast. I could have been sacked just like that.

My drinking vessel was not a brandy balloon, but something not traditionally associated with drinking – it was a thimble, which I'd borrowed from my mother's sewing chest. Ever so carefully, I poured the cognac into the thimble, but did not fill it – to do so would have been far too risky. I put the thimble to one side, then replaced the bottle in exactly the same place.

First I looked, then I smelled. It was a miracle of complexity and seduction. Then I tasted.

The sip was only about five millilitres of liquid, certainly not even a mouthful. It was a shock. I was not prepared. The quantity was small, but large enough. I closed my eyes and concentrated, completely focused on memorizing every subtle layer. What I tasted was a revelation of the extraordinary beauty and purity that can be created when the genius of man combines with the passage of time. What's more, I also walked free. There was a crime, but no punishment.

So on that Sunday when I stood in the Lanesborough listening to Salvatore grumbling about who on earth would ever buy a glass of his old cognac, I thought about how everything was going right in my life at the time, and I silenced him.

'Please, quick, bring me a glass of it, Salvatore,' I said.

I had not previously spent £350 on one drink, and I doubt I will do it again. But while others spend their money on plasma televisions and flash clothes, this is how I chose to treat myself.

When Salvatore returned from the cellar he was carrying the most beautiful bottle, although about a third of its contents had evaporated with age. He poured into a measure, which slightly devalued the moment, but from my side of the bar I could already smell the aroma. Again, I was reminded of that sneaky experience at Monsieur Spitz's drinks cabinet, which had been marred by fear that my boss would catch me. This time I would have no such restrictions. I was free and happy.

That one glass took me three hours to drink. I sat there treasuring the layers of taste and aroma.

Did I have a second? No, I left it at one.

Autumn/Winter
Brasserie Blanc
Tarte aux Pommes 'Maman Blanc'
Apple Tart 'Maman Blanc'

Maman Blanc loves simplicity, and this tart is easy to prepare as the pastry case does not need to be pre-baked. Here, we have used apples, but plums, apricots or cherries make equally delicious alternatives. Use only the best seasonal fruits available.

Serves (Yield): 6
Difficulty rating: ● ○ ○
Preparation time: 15 minutes plus 45 minutes' resting time
Cooking time: 30 minutes
Special equipment: Tart tin 18cm in diameter, 2cm deep, with removable base

INGREDIENTS

For the pastry:
250g plain flour (*1)
125g butter, diced, at room temperature (*2)
1 pinch (1g) sea salt
1 egg

For the filling:
3 Cox, Worcester, Russet or Braeburn apples (*3)
1 tbsp (15g) melted butter, ½ tbsp (7g) lemon juice, 1 tbsp (15g) caster sugar, ½ tbsp (7g) Calvados (optional), mixed together (*4)
icing sugar for dusting

METHOD
MAKING THE PASTRY:

In a large bowl, rub together the flour, butter and salt using your fingertips until it reaches a sandy texture. (*5) Create a well in the centre and add the egg. (*6) Work the egg into the flour and butter mixture, then press together to form a ball. Line the work surface with cling film and knead the dough with the palms of your hands for 30 seconds, (*7) until you have a homogeneous consistency. Take off 20–30g of dough, wrap in cling film and store for later. Wrap the remaining dough in cling film and flatten it slightly to 2cm thickness so the dough can rest and refrigerate more easily. (*8)

LINING THE TART TIN:

Place a baking tray in the oven. Preheat the oven to 220°C.

Line the work surface with cling film. Take the pastry dough from the fridge, unwrap it and place it on a piece of cling film about 30cm by 30cm. Cover with another layer of cling film and roll the dough out to 2mm thick. Line the tart tin with the dough. (*9) Then take the piece of spare dough, wrapped in cling film, and press this into the corner between the base and side of the tin to ensure the pastry is neatly compressed and moulded to the shape of the tin. Trim the edges of the tart by rolling over it with the rolling pin. Now you need to raise the height of the dough 2mm above the tart tin. This is achieved by pressing and pinching the pastry gently all round the edge of the tin using your index finger and thumb. With a fork, prick the bottom of the tart. (*10) Allow to rest in the fridge for 20 minutes to relax the pastry.

MAKING THE FILLING:

Peel, core and cut the apples into 10 segments each. Lay the segments, closely together, in the base of the pastry case. Brush with the melted butter, sugar and lemon juice mixture, and dust liberally with icing sugar. Slide the tart into the oven, on to the preheated baking tray, and cook for 10 minutes. Turn the oven down to 200°C and continue to cook for a further 20 minutes until the pastry becomes a light golden colour and the apples have caramelized.

Remove the tart from the oven and allow to cool for a minimum of 1 hour. Remove the tart from the tin and slide on to a large flat plate.

Chef's notes: (*)

*1   Flour: for most pastry you do not need a strong (high gluten) flour; reserve strong flours for bread making.

*2   If the butter is cold you will have problems with mixing it. For a successful pastry you need to get the butter evenly distributed within the flour, which is why the butter needs to be at room temperature and pliable.

*3   Get to know your apples. Some are over-acidic and cook down too easily; others release water, or lack flavour, or do not caramelize because of the low sugar content. Or, indeed, sometimes they are too sweet. I have found that Cox, Worcester, Russet and Braeburn are delicious for baking or pan-frying.

*4   The butter, lemon juice and caster sugar mix: the butter will enrich, the lemon juice will bring acidity and more flavour, and the sugar will bring sweetness and browning. The Calvados will always add something!

*5   Do not try to gather the butter and flour together. Instead, work the flour and butter with your fingertips, ever so lightly. Do not try to work the mix through, but lift it, aerate it, until you reach fine crumbs – then it is ready to bring together.

*6   The egg will add richness, moisture, thickness and baking quality. It will also help bring the dough together.

*7   Gather the dough together and press it with the palm of your hand. If you overwork the dough, the pastry will lose some of its flakiness.

*8   The dough is elastic, and refrigerating it makes the dough easier to work with and more pliable when rolling. Flattening it to a 2cm disc before refrigeration enables it to cool faster and 'relax' more easily, and gives you a shape that's more easy to roll.

*9   Using cling film to roll out the pastry has two advantages. It means you don't need to use extra flour, which would otherwise be absorbed into the pastry. Secondly, the bottom layer of the cling film can be used to help transfer the rolled pastry into the tin. Once the pastry has been inverted into the tin, remove the film.

*10   Pricking the base aids the distribution of the heat and thus thorough cooking.

VARIATION

To finish with a custard topping, mix 1 whole egg with 50g sugar, then add 100ml cream. Pour over the top of the cooked tart and finish in the oven for 10 minutes.

TWO

SAÔNE

Village Life

I CANNOT DESCRIBE THE TASTE OF GRASSHOPPERS' LEGS, IT'S BEEN SO long since I ate them.

The grasshoppers were apparently at their best at the end of the summer, having spent the season growing big and fat. With my brother Gérard and my dear friend René I headed for the long grass to find the green insects. Grasshoppers were not ordinarily part of our diet but the three of us were desperate to be accepted into a gang of older boys, who told us that the initiation ceremony was to eat grasshoppers' legs. Just in case we were hesitant, the gang assured us that the legs were in fact a delicacy, which aroused curiosity about their taste.

I found a hopper and made a few attempts to catch it. If you have never held a grasshopper in your hand, they are quite frightening. They are pale green and about three inches long, their bodies lengthened by a long sabre-like protrusion. Finally I had it in a clenched fist and carried it to the older boys, who then told me how to eat it. Following their instructions, I held the body between finger and thumb of one hand and used the finger and thumb of the other hand to yank both sets of legs swiftly and simultaneously from their sockets. The body was discarded and the legs were munched.

The taste was mild enough to be uninteresting but the experience was disgusting. For hours afterwards I was pulling bits of grasshopper flesh from between my teeth (maybe I should have cooked them . . .). I shouldn't grumble, it was just another food experience. Some I had years later in Japan were much more extreme.

Now, whenever I smell recently cut hay I am zoomed right back to that initiation ceremony with Gérard and René.

———

My family was not well off but I would not have swapped my childhood for all the riches of the world.

I was born in 1949, in post-war France, and while many others in countries all over the world found it a difficult era, my childhood was one of utter happiness and excitement. Saône had some eight hundred inhabitants and the sort of landmarks you might find in any French village. There was the church opposite the school and a café nearby (if there is no bar near the church then you are not in France), the *mairie* (village hall), the café, a butcher and a *boulangerie* where people went to buy crusty baguettes and to exchange gossip, news and recipes. Then there was the *fromagerie*, where the cheese was made.

Within the village there were a dozen *paysans* – not what the British would describe as peasants, but farmers who worked the land, and worked hard. They were rugged men with shovel-sized hands. Each *paysan* family had perhaps a flock of chickens and ducks, a few pigs (pork was the traditional staple of the region) and a small herd of cows that tended to be called Marguerite or Cerise and were of the Montbeliarde breed. These were the best milk-producing cows in the whole of France. Their udders were enormous, heavily veined and bursting with milk – I was mesmerized. This reservoir of milk was also a way for me to earn a little extra cash, for I helped with the milking. Spring would yield the highest quantity and richest milk as the grass was lush and full of nutrients.

The *paysans* drove their little herds from the fields through the village. A trail of cow pats showed the route they had taken, and a few of the villagers would spade up the mess, dry it and use it as manure. The paysans more or less lived in the same accommodation as their animals; a wooden door separated the stables from the main dwelling. Though the heat from the cows kept the kitchen nice and warm, there was the distinctive smell of the beasts to endure as well as their manure.

Intensive farming, pesticides and fertilizers were pretty much unheard of. Farming, *paysan* fashion, was the perfect example of biodiversity and authenticity.

Every day the *paysans* would cart their fresh milk to the *fromagerie*. Some of the milk was bought by the villagers, the rest was transformed into cheese. Not just any cheese, but one of the world's best: Le Comté. My mother would send me to the *fromagerie* to collect milk in my *bidon à lait* (milk tin). I remember there were two separate and distinctive smells to the milk in the *fromagerie*. When it was fresh and being poured into my *bidon* it had the smell of a nursery school; the milk that was in a curd state had an acidic, sour smell.

For cheese-making, the milk was poured into huge copper vats and warmed up to the correct temperature. Then the *fromager* added the fermenting agent, the rennet, to the milk. The solid curd would separate from the whey and the long, muscular, hairy arms of the *fromager* would sweep through the curd, as the smell became more acidic and intense. Then two of the men would scoop up all the curds from the huge copper vat in an enormous muslin cloth. They would tie the ends, hoist the cloth containing the curds over the vat and allow the milk to drip through, just like my grandmother's *gelée*. Then the curd was collected and put into large circular wooden frames lined with muslin. It was pressed and more of the milk (petit lait) would escape. Lastly, the strong arms of the *fromager* would carry the frames down to the darkness of the cellar where the miracle of time and nature would take place. The flavour grew, the texture became firm and the curd changed in colour from white to cream. Slowly, the crust darkened and hardened. The cheese was then taken out of its frame and left for a year or so to mature.

A great Comté is packed with flavours and it also has pockets of crystals that are formed during maturation. The best Comté is up to two years old. It is the most renowned cheese of my region. In Franche-Comté, no meal is complete without a slice of Comté.

I could run from my home and within a few minutes I'd be in a large forest. Throughout my childhood this vast wilderness, an expanse of woods, was a hunting ground as well as a playground. It was also a battlefield. Although Saône was small, the children were divided into two camps, High Saône and Low Saône. The toughest kids were in Low, which was not so good because I was in High. Sometimes my brothers, friends and I were tied up and left in the woods by the tough nuts from Low Saône.

Like other children, we liked weapons (not that they did much to frighten the Low Saône gangs). We made catapults and used one another for target practice, and we found the hardest sticks to turn into swords and set about bashing one another. The craft of making bows and arrows required the most effort as the bows were intricately designed; for the arrows we used hollow dried stalks, and to give them weight and balance we inserted an eight-centimetre nail – sharp end in the stalk, of course. Come night-time, when I changed for bed, I'd examine bruises the size and colour of Victoria plums. OK, I wouldn't want to relive the bow and arrow battles today, but at the time it was great fun. I loved life.

And what of nature's food? I was surrounded by it. Each season brought its own wonderful fruits and glorious vegetables, delicious fish and succulent birds. In between bow and arrow battles we used the weapons to hunt birds, sometimes using arrows that had been made from spokes of bicycle wheels, sharpened to become lethal. We climbed trees and collected the eggs of magpies and crows. If there was a young crow to be had, we'd snatch it, because roasted baby crow was a delicacy.

In the summer months the woods, darkened by the shadows cast by high pine trees and ancient oaks, were like one of those forests in Walt Disney's *Snow White*. Completely unpolluted by fertilizers or pesticides, they overflowed with wild fruit. Raspberry and blackberry plants climbed tree trunks to create their habitat and cascaded down through the branches; other trees heaved with wild cherries, pears, crab apples and elderberries. All of this fruit was just waiting to be picked, and that's precisely what we did. We stuffed our bellies and we filled our buckets. The buckets were handed to my mother, and then she did her magic. The cherries became jam or were soaked in kirsch (the clear, slightly bitter brandy made from black cherries) or baked into the most delicious tart. The little pears were cooked in red wine and cinnamon; the crab apples made for the best apple *gelée*. Everything found its way into Maman Blanc's food chain.

For lunch every Saturday, my mother gave us steak accompanied by home-made French fries, and vegetables from the garden. It was just a simple steak, but thanks partly to the way it was cooked it remains among the best I have ever eaten. The quality of the steak is also crucial, as is the breed and how long it has been hung on the carcass.

Let us think for a moment about the hanging process, which must be done under controlled temperatures. I remember there was a time in England when after a pheasant shoot the birds would hang for about three weeks, and not in controlled temperatures. It was wretched. You'd arrive at a friend's home and he'd say, 'Watch out in the bathroom, the pheasants are in there.' There, above the bath, would be a dozen rotting birds, maggots crawling out of their backsides. The house would reek, and heaven knows what sort of food poisoning was passed on.

Often meat is hung for too long. You might, for example, have had venison and not enjoyed it because it tasted too gamey. Chances are it was overhung. But when food is hung in a controlled environment for the correct period of time, the meat becomes tender, tastier and more digestible. Three things happen in the hanging process. First, enzymes start their work, activating a slow decay of the meat. Second, the bacteria multiply. Third, moisture evaporates from the meat. These three events tenderize the meat and give it flavour, and in the case of beef this provides the true steak experience.

For years, British retailers have sold us meat that is vermilion red, a colour we have been encouraged to believe shows good quality and freshness. When a retailer hangs meat, he has to buy a large quantity, which is costly. All this stock will have to hang before being sold, therefore the money, if you like, remains hanging in the cold room. That is bad news for a retailer. The problem is compounded as the moisture evaporates from the meat. Moisture loss equals weight loss which in turn equals money lost. A whole carcass can lose up to 10 per cent of its body weight. There are other significant costs, such as buying the cold room in the first place, and paying staff to rotate the carcasses, control the temperatures and clean the cold room. So for many years retailers have made us think that a great steak is brilliant red in colour. Now, the darker appearance of well-hung meat is not so attractive to us.

To be fair to the retailer, for the best steak we must be prepared to pay more. In addition to its colour, when you buy steak, look for marbling, the tiny streams of fat that run across the face of the meat. It is a sign of good quality; the more of it the better. Also, when pressed with a finger the vermilion supermarket steak will often spring up (which may not be an advisable thing to do in a supermarket). On a proper steak a finger imprint will be left.

So to my mother's technique for cooking steaks. Let's say we're cooking for two hungry people.

Prepare your ingredients: two steaks, each weighing about two hundred grams (eight ounces) – remove the steaks from the fridge at least half an hour before cooking so that they have reached room temperature when it's time to go into the pan – twenty grams of unsalted butter, sea salt and coarse black pepper freshly ground from the mill, and a hundred millilitres of hot water. You'll also need a frying pan. A cast-iron frying pan will create more caramelization and pan juices, but in today's world most of us use a non-stick pan. Whatever the case, the pan should be just large enough to hold both steaks.

Just before cooking the steak, season both sides with the sea salt and black pepper. On a medium heat, melt the butter in the pan. Let the butter foam so that it becomes what is known as *beurre noisette* (hazelnut butter); it should be slightly brown with the smell of hazelnuts. At this stage the temperature will be about 160°C, the point at which the solid particles – the casein protein and the whey of the butter's milk content – start to brown through cooking and turn into scented foam. You must use unsalted butter rather than salted, and I refuse to use Anchor, which is not at all to my taste. It contains too much whey, which is prone to burning and will have a nasty farmyard scent.

Lay the two steaks into the foaming butter and turn up the heat (as you put an unheated mass into a hot pan it will cool the pan). The sizzling should be gentle rather than aggressive and fierce. If the heat is too high, the solids within the butter will burn, which is rather unpleasant, indigestible and carcinogenic. Too high a heat will also toughen the steak. If the heat is too low, the steak will not caramelize and will stew in its own juices.

Listen to the butter sizzling gently, creating the caramelizing effect. The wonderful juices will leak out and solidify on the bottom of the pan. Turn over the steak and to retain the temperature turn up the heat a little.

How do you like your steak? How long you cook it for depends on your pan and the thickness of the cut. But roughly speaking, for rare steak it should be cooked for one minute per side, medium rare is two minutes on each side, medium is three or four minutes on each side, and well done is four to five minutes per side.

When you have your steaks how you like them, add the hot water to the pan. The liquid will bubble, steam and spit. The miracle in the pan is simple: water and fat do not mix but under heat an emulsion is created between the fat and the water, giving a beautifully scented and textured *jus*.

Immediately remove the steaks from the pan and place them on a dish. Lower the heat and, using a spoon, scrape up all the caramelized deposits from the base of the pan to incorporate them into the *jus*.

This recipe can be used for cooking any other meat, especially veal and pork, and for game and fish. It is the most wonderful way to create a delectable *jus* and will take only four to eight minutes of your life. This technique of pan frying can also be used for caramelizing meat before slow cooking. It epitomizes the best of home cooking, producing a beautiful scented *jus* that to me is as great as any complex sauce.

All Year Round
Brasserie Blanc
Le Soufflé Franc-Comtois
Comté Cheese Soufflé

Comté is my home, my village, my county; it gives me a sense of place. Maman Blanc would not cook her soufflé in individual soufflé moulds, but in a large shallow earthenware dish. She would place the delicate dish on the table for all of us to help ourselves. Sometimes the soufflé mixture would fill a flaky pastry tart. Of course, only Comté would be used, never Gruyère or Emmental.

Serves (Yield): 4 to 6
Difficulty rating: ● ● ○
Preparation time: 20 minutes
Cooking time: 30 minutes
Special equipment: 25–30cm oval earthenware dish, electric whisk, pastry brush

PLANNING AHEAD
The soufflé base can be made up to 1 day in advance and covered with buttered paper to prevent crusting.

INGREDIENTS

For the soufflé base:
50g butter
50g plain flour
250ml whole milk
100g Comté cheese, grated
12g Dijon mustard
2 egg yolks
2 pinches sea salt
2 pinches white pepper

For the soufflé dish:
20g butter, softened
20g breadcrumbs, dry

For the soufflé mix:
6 egg whites
juice of ½ lemon
1 pinch sea salt (*1)

For cooking the soufflés:
20g Comté cheese

For the sauce (optional):
150ml double cream
70g Comté cheese, grated
4 turns freshly ground white pepper
dash of kirsch (optional)

METHOD
PREPARING THE SOUFFLÉ BASE:

Preheat the oven to 175°C. Place a baking tray on the middle shelf in the oven. On a medium heat in a small saucepan, melt the butter, add the flour and whisk until a smooth consistency; cook the roux to a blonde colour. (*2) Gradually add the milk little by little, whisking it to a smooth consistency. Lower the heat, add the cheese and mustard, and continue to cook, stirring from time to time, for 3–5 minutes. Remove from the heat and allow to cool a little. Add the egg yolks and stir until the mixture is consistent in texture. Season and keep warm.

LINING THE SOUFFLÉ DISH:

Line the earthenware soufflé dish with the softened butter and the dried breadcrumbs. Reserve.

WHISKING THE EGG WHITES:

Put the egg whites in a mixing bowl, add the lemon juice and salt and whisk until very soft peaks are formed, then continue whisking until you have firm peaks. (*3)

MAKING THE SOUFFLÉ MIX AND FILLING THE DISH:

For the soufflé mixture, place the warm soufflé base in a large mixing bowl and briskly whisk in a quarter of the whipped egg whites to lighten the base. Then carefully fold in the remaining egg whites; delicately cut and lift the mix to ensure there is a minimum loss of volume and lightness. Taste and adjust the seasoning if necessary. (*4) Pour the soufflé mixture into the dish, smooth the top with a long palate knife and push the soufflé mixture away from the side of the dish by sliding your thumb around the edge. (*5)

COOKING THE SOUFFLÉS:

Cook in the preheated oven for 21 minutes. Sprinkle the cheese on top of the soufflé and cook for a further 7 minutes. Remove from the oven and serve immediately.

MAKING THE SAUCE (OPTIONAL):

Whilst the soufflé is cooking, bring the cream to the boil and add the cheese and pepper, stirring continually. Once the cheese has melted, remove from the heat, taste. Of course, a dash of kirsch would not go amiss. Pour the sauce into a separate sauceboat.

SERVING:

Place the soufflé and the sauce in the middle of the table; let your family and friends help themselves.

Chef's notes:

*1   Salt does not help the coagulation of the egg white: it delays it. The salt helps to lengthen the whipping process. On the other hand, the lemon juice does three things: it helps the coagulation of the egg white, prevents graining, and makes the whipping of the egg white safe and easy. And it helps the flavour as well.

*2   By cooking the roux you make the flour much more digestible and you also get a wonderful nutty flavour. Cook the base for 3–5 minutes to break down the starch molecules in the flour, which in turn will thicken the base and leave a creamy taste and texture.

*3   For a savoury soufflé the egg white needs to be whipped a little firmer than for a sweet soufflé (in which the sugar helps stabilize the egg whites).

*4   The Comté cheese, like Parmesan, holds quite a lot of salt; you should need little or no additional salt.

*5   To achieve a tall, even soufflé, thumb around the edge of the soufflé dish just before placing it in the oven. This releases the mix and helps the soufflé rise evenly.

VARIATIONS

The list of different cheeses to use for soufflés is endless. Goat's cheese, Stinking Bishop, Stilton and Gruyère are just a few possibilities.

You can use individual moulds. Four moulds 9.5cm in diameter and 5.5cm deep would be perfect for this recipe. Preheat the oven to 200°C and cook for 10 minutes, then sprinkle the cheese and cook for a further 6 minutes for a great result.

All Year Round
Brasserie Blanc
Mousse au Chocolate Amer
Bitter Chocolate Mousse

———

This is the simplest and lightest chocolate mousse, with no cream and no butter. Yet it will be melting and completely delicious. Remember, the quality of the chocolate will define the quality of the taste. A home classic.

Serves (Yield): 4
Difficulty rating: ● ● ○
Preparation time: 15 minutes
Finishing time: 5 minutes
Special equipment: Electric mixing bowl with whisk attachment

PLANNING AHEAD

This recipe is best prepared 2–8 hours in advance and kept covered in the fridge. It will be at its eating best up to 1 day.

INGREDIENTS

*165g dark chocolate, 70% (*1), grated*
240g (8) egg whites
*40g caster sugar (or 20g fructose) (*2)*

METHOD

Melt the grated chocolate in a 20cm bowl set over a pan of simmering water, (*3) for 10 minutes or so. Then turn the heat off. In an electric mixer on medium speed, whisk the egg whites and sugar (*4) until they form soft but firm peaks. (*5)

Then, to make your work easy, place the mixing bowl with the egg white on your worktop with a large spatula by its side. Remove the bowl of melted chocolate from the bain-marie, place it next to the bowl of egg white and have a whisk ready by its side. Now you must work fast. Scoop a third of the egg white into the melted chocolate and abruptly and with no mercy whisk the egg white in; (*6) this will lighten the chocolate mixture for further incorporation of the egg white. Now you take your time. Delicately fold in the remaining egg white using the spatula. (*7) Your chocolate mousse is now ready. Pour into a serving bowl or individual glasses, as you wish, and leave to set in the fridge for 2 hours or until required.

Chef's notes:

*1   As we all know, 70% represents the percentage of cocoa solids in the chocolate. The remaining 30% is mostly sugar. So you have here a semi-bitter chocolate. But do not be mistaken: 70% does not represent the quality of the chocolate. The chocolate could have come from cocoa beans that have been badly fermented, badly dried and badly roasted, or indeed were of poor quality in the first place. So choose your chocolate well.

*2   You could replace the sugar with fructose (a fruit sugar). You will only need half the amount as it is much sweeter than sugar.

*3   Chocolate solids will start becoming grainy at 90°C.

*4   Normally when you whisk sugar with egg whites you lose a great deal of volume. But here the quantity of sugar is small so you will get an excellent yield.

*5   If you overbeat the egg white, into stiff alpine peaks, you will reduce the lightness: the mousse will be more compact and less melting. You need soft but firm peaks.

*6   Enemy number one of chocolate is water. Egg white is 90% water. It is also a cold mass, which you are going to mix with a warm mass. If you mix in slowly, the chocolate is likely to seize up and solidify. To prevent this, fast whisking is essential.

*7   Cut and fold delicately using the spatula in order to keep the maximum lightness and volume, wherein lies the success of a lovely chocolate mousse.

VARIATIONS

You could use this recipe for a baked chocolate fondant. Dilute 12g arrowroot (or cornflour) in 1 tbsp water and fold into the chocolate mousse. Fill small ovenproof moulds (buttered and lined with a mixture of half cocoa powder and half caster sugar) by two-thirds and bake in a preheated oven (170°C) for 6–7 minutes. The chocolate fondant should be cooked on the outside and melting in the centre.

THREE

SEASONS

Maman Blanc's Tears

A T AN EARLY AGE I WAS AN EXPERIENCED HUNTER–GATHERER WITH commercial nous.

On my tenth birthday my father presented me with a calendar he had made himself. It was handwritten and divided into two parts. Part one covered 'The Garden'. Alongside each month of the year, my father had written the corresponding vegetables, herbs and fruit that were in season. This part was the least exciting. It meant hard work, no friends and no football.

The second part of the calendar, however, was fascinating. It meant friends and adventure. It was a series of maps of the wild, each little drawing created by my father's own hand. The maps showed the secret places to go to for hunting, foraging and fishing. For example, one map illustrated which part of the stream had the best crayfish. Another map would direct me to the part of the river that was home to *goujons*, the tiny fish that the British freshwater fisherman knows as gudgeons. If I followed another map it would take me to colonies of mushrooms hiding in the forest. Some of these places had been discovered by my father; others were discovered by his father before him.

The calendar was the best gift I ever received from my father. These hand-drawn treasure maps led to scores of adventures, taking me into the forest to battle against the elements and to get lost. But there was no better place in which to be lost.

My friend René and I would go into the woods and forage for anything we could sell to the stallholders, shopkeepers and restaurateurs in my village and in Besançon. The restaurateurs were always the best payers. Mind you, knowing the prices they were charging their customers, I understood why they could afford to pay more than the stallholders. Anything I could sell I sold, from wild flowers to wild asparagus.

In fact, of all my hunting expeditions, those for wild asparagus were the most exciting. It grew in clearings in coombs (short valleys) because it needed moisture but it also loved light and warmth. René and I would wander for miles, searching for the coombs that also had a clearing. Our expeditions could last the whole day, but our parents didn't worry about us in the forest. When we saw a coomb in the distance we would run and run and . . . find that the coomb was dry and bereft of asparagus. But eventually, if we were lucky, we'd find them. It was an amazing sight, one of nature's most beautiful miracles: thousands or even tens of thousands of asparagus, their light green stalks and their heads stretching towards the sunlight. I knew then that I was a rich young man.

René and I would tie the asparagus into bundles, fix the bundles to two long sticks and carry them home stretcher-like, staggering under the weight of our haul, swapping between carrying on our shoulders and carrying in our hands as the long miles passed. It was a seriously large amount of asparagus.

The mushrooms, *petit gris de sapin*, were as good as wild asparagus when it came to hiding in the forest floor. Of all the mushrooms in the world, *petit gris* is the most perfumed, which is fortunate because I had to hunt them by smell as well as by sight. They love to grow near pine trees, but they also crave hilly areas with moss to give them moisture.

So I'd make my way towards the pine trees, then look for a hill, then for a mossy patch, and then . . . sniff, sniff, sniff. At times, my father's special map of the mushrooms' hiding places was invaluable. Once I had caught the fragrance, I would slowly walk towards the core of the smell. To the birds in the trees I must have looked an odd sight. Then, finally, I would spot the *petit gris*, their capped heads barely poking through the moss. I knew that if I rooted around I'd find dozens, sometimes hundreds, because like most mushrooms they grow in colonies.

At home, my mother would put her skills to use. If there were a few mushrooms she would do an omelette; if there were lots of mushrooms she would make a huge fricassee with a *persillade* made from butter, parsley, garlic, lemon juice and finely chopped shallots with a ladle full of cream from the top of the milk sprinkled over the dish (and a dash of white wine to give depth). Mushrooms that weren't used there and then would be preserved for the winter and kept in the cellar, which ran under the length of our house and contained my father's wine as well as hundreds of preserved foods, all pickled or cured, to see us through the harsh winter months.

Our food chain and lifestyles have changed so dramatically since my childhood that the idea of preparing yourself for the winter now seems laughable and very distant. For me, I can say it was the most treasured time of my life.

For a whole day we would think of nothing but the hunt or battling in the forest. We forgot parents, even food. But suddenly, at the end of the day, a primitive hunger would seize us. Desperately we would rush home, driven by visions of bread, saucisson, ham – all the contents of our mothers' larders. When we arrived we did not eat, we devoured, tearing through meat, fruit and bread.

Then there was the hunt for frogs, which I hazard to say was the most romantic of our expeditions. My father knew the best time to catch them. It was in early May, I think, but there were several other conditions that had to be observed. There had to be a full moon and it had to be a clear evening, with no rain or wind. Under such circumstances the frogs would mate, which enabled us to catch them unawares. If raindrops fell or the wind rose, the frog hunt was abandoned.

With our path lit by the moon, my brothers and I would follow my father through two or three miles of fields, carrying large bags in which to transport our catch. As we neared the lake we'd hear the frogs. The noise would increase to a huge croaking concert until finally we reached the water and there, in front of us, was the world's largest frog orgy, thousands of them copulating. In mid-pleasure we'd grab them by the handful, still attached to each other, and bag them. Then, for them, romance was halted abruptly. My job at home was to kill the frogs, cut off their legs, slip off the skin, and present the legs to my mother, who would go through the ritual of cooking and preserving them.

In those days no one felt there was anything wrong with killing frogs and eating them. It seemed perfectly normal, not in any way cruel. Now I look at it very differently. I feel sorry for the poor little sods. Although we ate everything that moved, my father always taught me that the killing itself should be swift and painless so as not to cause too much suffering to the animals. I have not served frogs' legs at Le Manoir for the last fifteen years because I don't approve of the way they are produced and processed. However, I confess to smiling a couple of years ago when a young English commis chef gave me a birthday present: a hand-drawn picture of six little frogs sitting on wheelchairs, a tiny blanket covering their legs, tainted with blood.

We had what I would describe as a balanced French diet. There were lots of vegetables, fruit, starches such as pasta, pulses, eggs in every permutation and, of course, plenty of cheese in dishes such as *tarte au fromage*, quenelle of semolina, a fondue of Comté cheese, and stuffed tomatoes with rice. Once every month when my father received his wages we had crushed bananas with crème fraîche. Meat was on the menu three to four times a week, and it was always served for Sunday lunch. On Friday we had fish, and cod liver oil most days . . .

When it was time for a chicken, my father would take me to a nearby farm. He'd point at the bird he wanted and I was the one who had to catch it, which was no easy challenge. These particular chickens were pretty wild, about the size of a small turkey. They didn't tend to run around on the ground but would invariably perch on the low branch of a tree. We're talking seriously free range here. I'd scare the bird out of the tree and the chase would begin. Eventually I'd make a successful rugby tackle on it.

At home, my father taught me to make a swift incision under the bird's neck and then let it bleed. The blood was kept for thickening and flavouring sauces. A little vinegar would be added to prevent coagulation. My job was to feather the bird, a chore that took a good hour of my time. (There was no such thing as a free lunch at Maman Blanc's.) Then I would slit the belly and remove the liver, the stomach and the heart; I gave the offal to my mother for use in dishes or salads. The chicken was then simply roasted, head on, of course.

Every other Sunday we would eat one of the rabbits we kept for the table. My father would pick out the big fat one and he taught me how to kill it using a large stick to give it a hefty knock on the base of the skull. One blow and the rabbit was dead – quick and fast. I would cut its throat, hold the body upside down and let the blood drain into a bowl. Then I'd take the rabbit down to the cellar to a wall where there were two large nails protruding. I tied some string around the rabbit's hind legs and then hung it from the nails so the rabbit's body was held in position while I skinned it.

First I made circular incisions around the tops of the legs; then I passed the small blade of my knife between the fur and the flesh, cutting down to the tail. After cutting off the tail I slowly pulled down the fur from the steaming body, making sure not to damage the head as this was the most prized piece. The skin was not tossed away: I stretched it on a plank of wood and dried it before selling it. The heart, kidneys and stomach were used for dishes. The liver was treasured: pan-fried and in a salad it is delicious. The fat, too, was used for cooking.

When it was time to turn the rabbit from a piece of meat into beautiful food, I watched my mother as she stood at the stove. She cut the rabbit into fourteen pieces (two pieces of thigh, the saddle into three or five, depending on the size), the rib cage into three, two shoulders, the belly made two pieces, and then there was the head and neck). After seasoning each piece with sea salt and black pepper and mustard, in a cast-iron pan on a medium heat she would caramelize the meat in foaming butter for about ten minutes. Then she would put in half an onion that was cut in six, six cloves of unpeeled garlic, a couple of leaves of sage, one bay leaf and one twig of tarragon. After adding vinegar she would reduce it down completely (and taste), add boiled white wine and then water, little by little. The pan was loosely covered and its contents slow-cooked in a preheated oven at 110°C for about an hour (with just a bubble or two on the surface). The meat would be turned and basted three or four times during this period.

The dish was served with French beans, Swiss chard, braised lettuce or whatever was in season. My father would serve at the table from the pot. Today, most people would want the fillet, but our favourite parts came from the head: the tongue, the cheeks and the brain, which is the most succulent piece.

I remember one of those rabbit meals when I looked up from my plate and stared at my mother. She had misty eyes, yet she had a smile on her face. The teardrops were there because she loved her rabbits. She adored them when they were alive, and it broke her heart when they were turned into a dish. The smile was there because, my God, the rabbit tasted superb. You could call it the French paradox. In France in those days, if a driver spotted a hare on the road he would, without hesitation, chase the animal in his car, if need be chase it across fields, and probably get nowhere. My point is that although animals were regarded as strokeable, they were primarily viewed as eatable. Invariably, the family pet ended up on the plate.

Years later I put Maman Blanc's rabbit on my brasserie menu and created a more complex dish using the same principles for Le Manoir. The brasserie dish was served this way: the rack of ribs was quickly roasted; the leg was confit but at a low temperature of about 80°C, and the fillet was wrapped in the belly and slow-cooked for a long time. Rabbits, just like us, tend to store fat in their bellies, but they don't have too much of it. If the rabbit is cooked too quickly, the meat will simply dry out. Every bit of the rabbit was served but I saved my British friends from the tongue and brain. I kept those for myself.

Again, the season determined which ingredients were cooked with the rabbit, and as the year progressed it brought wonderful new accompaniments. In early spring we had rabbit with field mushrooms and morels. In July it was cooked with girolles. Come August we had rabbit cooked with tomatoes, and in September and October those fragrant *petit gris* mushrooms were in the dish. We had it with all the vegetables from the garden. Season always defined what was on the table.

My mother often adopted the same method of caramelizing the meat, slowly, slowly, slowly in a casserole; fierce, aggressive cooking wouldn't have worked. You could hear the gentle bubbling of the butter coming from the kitchen stove. It was like a quiet song, and with it came the most incredible smell you could have in a kitchen.

———

It would be wrong to talk of childhood memories or indeed of my career as a chef without crediting my maternal grandmother, Germaine. I mentioned her briefly in chapter one. She made the raspberry *gelée* which helped me work out how to make essence of tomato.

Her culinary talents were renowned and respected throughout the region. She was known as La Mère Tournier, La Mère ('The Mother') being a title that was bestowed upon good women cooks. Les Mères were not professional chefs but would often be invited to cook for grand dinners in the big chateaux or for pillars of the local society. In fact, she was not a good cook but a magnificent one. I would go so far as to say that when it came to food, Mère Tournier was a genius. She knew food inside out. She didn't have all the gadgets of a modern cook, but she knew when the food was right, ready and perfect just from sight, touch, smell and sound. She passed on this cooking DNA to Maman Blanc who passed it on to me, the first male chef in the family.

My grandparents had been farmers but they lost the farm when all their animals died of a disease. They became keepers of a chateau, an imposing and beautiful eighteenth-century *maison bourgeoise* with ten acres of walled garden and a mini forest. It sat in its own micro-climate producing fruit and vegetables in abundance, even grapes, apricots and peaches. All the fruit that could not be eaten or bottled was distilled into alcohol in the cellar of their home.

I loved that cellar. A mossy staircase led down to large, weathered, creaking wooden doors that opened on to a room lit by a single electric bulb. The uneven floor was made of earth which had soaked up scents of distillation and cider-making. Wooden shelves were lined with straw upon which sat rows and rows of apples and pears that were being saved for the winter.

One day, when I was aged five or six, I went into the cellar when plum spirit was being made. At an earlier stage the plums had been put into a huge wooden barrel and left to ferment, creating a bubbly brownish surface. The fermented fruit was then poured into a copper pot which sat on an old rusty gas ring. A coiled copper tube ran from the top of the pot through a bucket of cold water and then a thin thread of alcohol flowed from the tube and was collected in a casserole. As I watched the men they seemed like Merlin, using magic to create alcohol from fruit.

As I was witnessing this process of distillation, I was also breathing in all the spillage, which had turned into alcoholic steam. Within a minute or two I was dizzy and sick. Drunkenly, I staggered out of the cellar and back upstairs. My grandmother happened to be at the top of the stairs, hands on her hips. I thought she would give me a kiss or a few words of kindness as clearly I was ill. Instead, she asked angrily, 'What did you drink?' Then I got a good spanking as she exclaimed, 'He is already drinking at the age of six!' She also gave my grandfather, Alfred, who thought it was extremely funny, a talking to. At least when she realized I had not done anything wrong I got my kiss.

As well as being a magician with alcohol, my grandfather had two beautiful Percheron horses, big, broad and chestnut-coloured. Even though he had lost his farm he still wanted to be in touch with the land so he would plough for other farmers. Why didn't he use a tractor? He wouldn't have wanted one. He loved his horses so much there was never a chance of them being turned into *steak de cheval*.

In the summer months I'd sit down on a hill and watch my grandfather ploughing the fields. On the stroke of twelve o'clock he'd come and sit down beside me for lunch. The horses had a bucket of cereal and water, and my grandfather and I would chat while he worked his way through a couple of glasses of wine, three or four bottles of water, a baguette, some bacon and a whole Camembert. Can you imagine? In the days when men ploughed fields without tractors they could eat like that. My grandfather lived to the age of ninety-two.

Every child was given alcohol, of sorts, from the age of about three. My grandfather would take a sugar cube, dip it into plum alcohol and then slip the cube from his fingers into mine, making sure my grandmother didn't see. At mealtimes in our house the children were also given wine, albeit heavily diluted with water and sweetened with sugar. The dilution decreased as we increased in age. I don't remember ever sitting at the table with just a glass of water. It was always a glass of water with a drop, or maybe a splash, of wine in it.

We always ate at the table, a large crowd of us. There was never a suggestion that we would eat in front of the television – not least because we didn't have a television! The children were not allowed to leave the table until the adults decided to go, and anyway, the best course was dessert. My favourite was chocolate mousse or *îles flottantes* (floating islands), made with poached meringue, real vanilla cream and topped with crunchy dark caramel, which is served as much in French homes as it is in the country's bistros and great Michelin-starred restaurants. When it comes to the dessert of a last supper, *îles flottantes* will be mine, I hope.

Our weekly get-togethers with extended family and friends were pretty similar to any get-together in any French home at that time. First there was chit-chat about family matters; then the alcohol started to take over and the topic of conversation would switch to the war and the army (my father was in the French Resistance). Then it heated up a bit and politics was fiercely debated. Invariably it would finish on the subject of sex, at which point my mother and the other women would leave the table and go into the kitchen.

I often think of that calendar my father made for me, and how wonderful it would be if everyone was given one. Like the other villagers, I worshipped the seasons, and when it was time to name my first restaurant it was so obvious: Les Quat' Saisons (The Four Seasons).

Today, seasons mean little, and we are missing out. If we buy food when it is in season we are ensuring that we have the best produce. It is fresh, full of flavour and texture and is nutritious. The consumer has been manipulated to believe that he should be able to have whatever he wants whenever he wants it.

Asparagus, for instance, is shipped from the other side of the world so that it can be on the supermarket shelves throughout the year. It's as if we can't wait for the best stuff. English asparagus and white asparagus are in season from April into June, while wild asparagus should be picked in April and May.

What about oranges? The tangerine is in season from October to

March; the satsuma from October to February; the clementine from November to February. Blood oranges are in season in February and March; Seville oranges are ready to eat in January and February. The seasonality of oranges dictates that the fruit is not available from April to September, during which period it is often stacked on supermarket shelves.

The season for raspberries – fresh, lush and British – is from the beginning of July through to September, but the supermarkets sell them in February. Strawberries, be they common, wild or *mara de bois*, are delicious from May to September. But low-grade, tasteless strawberries are shipped from afar and sold throughout the year. In the autumn months it breaks my heart to see shoppers buying Pink Lady apples imported from China when beside them are the far tastier British-grown Cox, Russet or Braeburn.

On the other side of the aisle, the shelves are stacked day in day out with numerous varieties of mushrooms. But mushroom lovers should know that April brings the first *mousseron miller* and the Saint George, and May the first morels. June brings lamb's feet, girolle, the giant puffball and the summer truffle, and July the first field mushrooms. In August we get the *trompette des morts* and ceps (porcini), and in September we start to see the bay boletus, the beefsteak fungus, the cauliflower fungus, the *pied bleu* (field blewit) and *pied de mouton* (hedgehog fungus), and the winter chanterelle. October heralds the arrival of the Alba white truffle. The year ends on a high when the famous and expensive Périgord truffle is pulled from the ground, in December.

Inadvertently, albeit once a year, we do still follow the seasons. The traditional British Christmas lunch includes roast parsnips and Brussels sprouts, both of which are seasonal in December. Cranberries, for the sauce, come into season in October and stay until the end of December. Turkey, as we all know, is bred specifically for the festive season, but if you want goose then again it is in season, from October to March.

All Year Round
Lapin à la Moutarde
Braised Rabbit with Mustard

It is probably the biggest divider between our two nations. The French see rabbits as food, the British see them as pets (non-edible). This dish was eaten every other Sunday. Remember, Maman Blanc had misty eyes as she fed her rabbits every day.

Serves (Yield): 4 to 6
Difficulty rating: ● ○ ○
Preparation time: 10 minutes
Cooking time: 45–60 minutes
Special equipment: 25–30cm ovenproof casserole with lid, 18–20cm saucepan

INGREDIENTS

1 whole rabbit (1.5kg), cut into 14 pieces: head, neck, 2 x shoulders, 2 x legs, 3 x saddle, 3 x ribcage, 2 x belly (*1)
4 pinches sea salt
2 pinches black pepper
1 heaped tbsp Dijon mustard
4 tbsp plain flour on a plate
3 tbsp butter
half white onion cut in 6, or 12 griotte onions
6 cloves garlic, skin on
1 tbsp white wine vinegar
1 glass white wine (150ml), boiled for 30 seconds (*2)
1 glass water (150ml)
6 whole black peppercorns
2 sage leaves
1 sprig of tarragon
1 bay leaf

For finishing:
1 tbsp chopped parsley or chives (optional)

METHOD
PREPARING THE RABBIT:

Preheat the oven to 120°C. In a large bowl, season the pieces of rabbit with the salt and pepper, then mix in the mustard until each piece is coated by a thin film. Dip each piece of rabbit into the flour. Pat off excess flour from each piece.

COOKING THE RABBIT:

In a thick-bottomed, 25–30cm ovenproof casserole dish on a medium heat, melt 2 tbsp of the butter, then sear and colour (★3) the rabbit pieces on each side for 7–8 minutes. Season a little after 2 minutes. Whilst the rabbit pieces are caramelizing, in a separate pan on a medium heat, sweeten the onion and garlic in the remaining butter for 10 minutes. (★4)

Add the vinegar to the rabbit and reduce down the liquor to a syrup, mix in garlic and onion, add the wine, water, pepper and herbs, cover with a lid and cook in the preheated oven for 45 minutes, stirring occasionally. Taste and adjust the seasoning.

FINISHING AND SERVING THE DISH:

When the rabbit is cooked, transfer to a serving dish for your guests to help themselves. Allow the liquid in the casserole dish to reduce on a high heat by a third, then stir in some chopped parsley, chives or your favourite soft herbs. Pour the sauce over the pieces of rabbit and serve with French beans, Swiss chard, braised lettuce or any other seasonal vegetables.

Chef's notes:

★1   First get to know your rabbit. Look for the best breed and quality, and ask your butcher to prepare it for you.

★2   I like to boil wine before adding it to the dish. It intensifies the desirable flavours and removes the alcohol, which can leave an unpleasant flavour in the mouth. If you over-reduce the wine, however, you will lose the freshness and acidity. See also page 85.

*3   This must be done on a medium heat: you can actually hear the gentle sizzling of the butter. Sure, I could easily cook it in hot oil, but it would not have the same colour, flavour or texture.

*4   Through heat, you are translating the carbohydrate and starch into sugar and flavour. I am sure you know the difference in taste between a raw onion and a cooked one?

VARIATION

Of course, any of your favourite herbs and vegetables can be added to the dish. Olives and wild mushrooms would be lovely. And once you understand the technique, you can use any type of meat you wish, from chicken to crocodile. (OK, not crocodile – it's an endangered species.)

FOUR

CHRISTMAS

Don't Mention the Boar

Y PARENTS CONTRASTED NICELY. MY MOTHER WAS A GUILTY
M Catholic while my father was an atheist communist who hated
God, which provided for lively and colourful debates at home. In fact,
even after so many years of marriage they still argue about religion,
albeit now in a somewhat more accommodating, battle-weary way.

My father earned his living as a skilled watchmaker, but at home he
was an expert gardener. When I was seven my father scooped out some
earth and showed it to me. He made me look at it, smell it, even taste it.
That way, he said, I would know how things would grow in it. Smelling
and looking would show whether it was a clay soil or limy; tasting . . . I
think my father got carried away. Have you ever tasted earth? Try it. It is
gritty, tannic, acidic, musty and so, so dry.

Most evenings my father turned into a project manager with an
amazing ability to delegate. I used to hate the garden. When my friends
were enjoying themselves playing football, my siblings and I were helping my father, and it seemed there was always something to be done. The
earth seemed never to rest. We dug stones from the ground, turned over
the earth, added the manure and turned it again. Then the great man

would spread the seed and water it, aerating the soil between the rows and removing the weeds; then, finally, came the harvesting and podding, topping and tailing of mountains of beans and peas for my mother.

It was as important to have a good garden as it was to have good food. The two are linked. Gastronomy often goes wrong when the chef or the cook fails to connect with this fundamental truth. Our garden was a typical French garden, about an acre in size with a tiny lawn, scruffy and overgrown with dandelions and buttercups. Exactly the reverse of an English garden. The rest of it was taken up by vegetables, fruit and herbs which would eventually make their way to our table. It was like a small industry, the garden produce in constant rotation.

The kitchen was Maman's domain, and I was her dogsbody. I never minded the chores as she was such lovely company and a good boss. My father would grow and harvest the fruit and vegetables, or hunt and fish, and the ingredients – the catch, the haul – would be passed to Maman, who would transform them into wonderful feasts for the five kids, the running order of which went like this: my older brothers Gérard and Michel, then me, followed by my younger sisters Françoise and Martine.

When Papa found the time to sit down and read the newspaper, he studied the political reports, shifting uneasily in his chair, hissing at views that did not suit his socialist outlook. When it was mother's turn for the paper, she immediately turned to the obituaries. She was always moved by what she read. Occasionally she would weep a little, sharing the grief of the deceased's widow and family. She carried the grief of the whole world.

She loves the whole world, and the world loves her back. I don't know of one single enemy. That's Maman Blanc. She is special and very dear to me, and she is dear to other villagers in Saône. She will probably end up canonized by the local priest and preserved in the tastiest jelly jar.

Her guilt about religion, as in not being religious enough, was never more prevalent than at Christmas. She believed strongly that Christmas was primarily a religious occasion. Mind you, once she had received communion, crossed herself at the doors and descended the church steps, psalms and sermons went out of her mind and she was a woman fixed on the kitchen stove that awaited her.

On Christmas Eve she took her children to Midnight Mass (when Midnight Mass was at midnight rather than the more sociable ten-ish as it is these days). We'd return home and gather round to watch my mother put baby Jesus in the crèche, then we'd have a light festive meal. With the help of a few women friends, my mother prepared salads, oysters, snails, hams, local charcuterie and cheese. A sumptuous *gâteau à la crème* might follow.

A crowd of us would sit down to eat, and when the meal was over the children would be sent to bed, after kissing goodnight my father and his friends, who remained at the table to play the popular (in France) card game *tarot*. It is played with the seventy-eight cards of a tarot card deck, which are divided into four standard suits (spades, diamonds, clubs and hearts), trump cards and *l'excuse* (the fool). It is a bit like the American card game Spades and requires skill, a mathematical mind and a good memory as the player has to keep track of the cards. Winters could last from November to April, and during those months men avoided the cold by huddling inside to play tarot.

Clutching a hot water bottle, I ran up to my bedroom, which was adjacent to the outside *grenier*, the hayloft where straw and wood was kept. Outside the snow was knee-deep and it was windy and cold. Inside it was still damned cold and there was no stove upstairs, so I ran upstairs just to keep myself warm. Then I climbed under the huge quilt on my bed, made by my grandmother from goose and duck down, and with my back on the mattress and my legs up in the air continued to run under the covers until I was warm enough to sleep. Running the equivalent of two miles on your back can tire you out, so I used to nod off easily.

Our house, incidentally, had five bedrooms and was built by my father and his friends. The men worked as if they were a co-operative, helping to build one another's homes. The task took them a total of six years. They didn't buy the breeze blocks, they made the blocks themselves, dynamiting and grinding the stone and moulding the blocks, which was an amazing feat. Of course the children also helped, with the smaller tasks.

The months of February and March were spent gathering fuel for the house. The local authorities allocated plots of forest to each family, and we would clamber on to a tractor and cart and drive two or three miles into the forest, through the snow, to reach our plot. Weather conditions were often dreadful, and to make things even harder we didn't have mechanical chainsaws. My father, grandfather and an uncle would fell a tree using large saws, one man at each end of the blade. Once felled, its largest branches would have to be removed. It was a military operation for the whole family. Then the wood was separated; the trunk, the large branches and the smaller branches were cut and lifted into the cart. My job was to help pick up the small pieces of cold wood and load them on to the trailer. It was all icy, heavy, slippery and rough. The wood was taken back to the house, day after day for about three weeks, until it had all been transported.

Once all the wood was piled up, *le scieur*, the woodcutter, came to cut the wood into blocks. Then, when you thought it was all over . . . oh no, it was not. The wood had to be chopped with an axe into pieces that were just the right size to fit into the oven. Then my brothers and I would form a chain to carry the wood upstairs and throw it into the loft beside my room. There it would dry and be ready for the following winter. Alongside the wood we kept the hay that made the rabbits' bedding. The lovely smells of wood and hay permeated the walls and came into my room.

The wood business took about two months, and there were only two wood burners to heat the whole house! We must have gathered around ten tons of wood each year. Between the garden and the wood gathering, there was barely time for football.

Christmas morning was the most beautiful of the year, and it was usually a white one. The overnight frost would have formed intricate patterns on my window. There was silence outside, created by the snow and the fact that there were few cars in the village.

The minute I stepped out of bed the cold would hit me. I'd dash downstairs, where my mother would be waiting. By then she would have lit the wood burners in an attempt to warm the house, and she would have lit the Christmas tree. Yes, *lit* it. She put real candles on the tree, which on reflection seems ridiculously dangerous but at the time we did not question such life-threatening decorating skills. The tree would also be hung with *papillotes*, my favourite fruit jellies wrapped in colourful paper (another fire hazard). The best were the jellies of quince, lemon and raspberry which had been rolled in caster sugar. My father would enjoy a lie-in; his tarot games with his cohorts would have finished with the last hand at about five in the morning.

Christmas breakfast was very special. We'd have the classic French breakfast of a large bowl of chocolate Banania and warm mik, followed by brioche, croissants and fresh crusty bread, toasted on the top of the stove and served with all the home-made jams you could wish for. Then, before Christmas Day Mass, we'd excitedly open the presents. We didn't receive scores of gifts like today's children. Mandarins, bananas and *papillotes* were used to pad out our small haul, and these edible gifts were gratefully received.

The best Christmas present I ever received was when I was seven years old. It was a mechanical Panzer tank I had previously seen in a shop but had never dreamt my mother would buy for me, or could afford. Perhaps she couldn't, but she must have seen my open mouth. My father had looked at the tank and didn't like it too much as it was a German design with the German cross on the top. That tank could move forwards and backwards and spit flames, and I played with it before heading off to Mass.

I couldn't wait to get home to play again with my best-ever present. I rushed through the door and to the spot where I had left the toy. I was horrified by what I saw. It was in hundreds of pieces – wheels and barrels all over the place. My brother, Gérard, had taken it apart.

Distraught, I jumped on him, but he was three years my senior and twice my size and he flicked me away. As I sobbed, Gérard said, 'Don't worry, I'll put it back together.' And he did. Quickly and with meticulous precision he rebuilt the toy, though once he had finished it would only reverse when I tried to make it go forwards.

Gérard's destiny was established at that point, when he was only ten years old and when my tank fell into his hands. You see, he went on to become an engineer, and an extremely gifted one at that.

Before lunch, the young ones (and that included me) would leave the house and, through a raging blizzard, we'd take our sledges and head for the peak of the hill that brought you into the village. Then we'd zoom down it, from the top of the village and right the way through it.

Christmas was magical, the greatest thing on earth.

After sledging we were ready for Christmas Day lunch, the proper feast of the festive period. Uncles, aunts, cousins and friends would arrive for the big meal. Kind uncles as well, the sort who would hand out ten-franc coins to their nephews. The guests usually included my maternal grandparents, the Tourniers. My grandmother would arrive with her Christmas present, a huge pot of tripe that had been sliced like thick lardons and marinated with onions, carrot, celery, cloves, garlic, tomato purée, white wine and a dash of Calvados. Then it was cooked slowly for up to twelve hours in its marinade. Still one of my favourite dishes.

The women, led by my mother, would busy themselves in the kitchen. If I entered I'd be ordered to help, be it chopping, cutting or preparing vegetables. Above the sound of kitchen work there was the continuous din of the women's chitter-chatter as they produced the meal.

We did not have canapés, except for a few salty savoury biscuits and maybe *gougère* (choux pastry with Comté cheese). Olives did not grow in Franche-Comté so they were not around, though if you were in the region today most likely they would be served before meals. Invariably, Christmas lunch would begin with white asparagus that had been preserved, served with mayonnaise. Crudités also came, comprising grated carrot, beetroot, slices of cucumber, celeriac, celery and hard-boiled eggs, all in a vinaigrette à la moutarde.

That was followed by *escargots*. You will have been to restaurants where the menu offers you a dozen snails. We ate substantially more than that. The snails, which had been gathered by me and my brothers, were finished off with parsley butter and garlic, lined on to huge trays and baked in the oven. No sooner were the trays removed and the contents put in dishes than the trays were refilled with more snails, and this new batch went into the oven. Between fifteen and twenty of us worked our way through maybe five hundred snails.

Then there were the terrines and pâtés, which were artistically con-structed and really showed off my mother and grandmother's true gifts. They would do a pâté of quail, or pheasant, or wild boar; the latter might contain a slice of the cheek, or an ear. Pâtés were served on a dish with gherkins and soused vegetables. The ideal mouthful gave you the sweetness of the pâté and the sourness of the gherkin. Here, the cellar came into its own. Preserved beans and mushrooms were unbottled for the table, all accompanied by persillade.

The dishes would keep arriving and we were yet to have the main course, which might be game, or a substantial plump goose with chest-nuts. Then the tripe would be served. Rarely did we have turkey, and if we did it was served with redcurrant jelly. We might have capons, each of them hefty, which came from the neighbouring farm and were selected by my father before I was sent in to grab them.

Apart from the crudités and salads, among the many dishes that were placed in front of us on Christmas Day there was infrequently a vegetarian option, but the mix of ingredients was healthy nonetheless. Coming from that cellar to accompany the meat were hearts of celery, peas and haricot beans. We'd have freshly picked Brussels sprouts, slowly cooked with bacon. A large tray of cheese was always served with salad. The cheese was the mild, creamy Comté from the *fromagerie* in the village; the Mamirolle came from the village next door. There was also Morbier, with its leathery rind, and home-made Cancoillotte, which was made of dried milk reconstituted with white wine and garlic – divine, but an acquired taste.

Dessert followed. It was often a fruit salad made with pears, apples, cherries and other berries, served with crème fraîche. These fruits would have been picked the previous summer and autumn and then bottled and jarred and stored in the cellar.

Then, finally, the long-awaited dish: *bûche de Noël*, or Christmas log, which I remember watching my mother create. First she made the sponge, spreading it thinly over a tray and baking it. Then she dabbed rum and syrup or kirsch on to the sponge with a brush. This moistened it, gave it flavour, and allowed it to roll more easily. She then pasted a rich chocolate butter cream on to the sponge, added chestnuts, and rolled the sponge into the shape of a log. She twisted it tightly in a cloth to give it shape, and let it rest overnight. The next day, with a palette knife she covered the log with Chantilly cream, and with a fork she scraped the top to create the effect of bark. To finish the log she sprinkled chestnuts and bitter chocolate powder over the top, and it was brought to the table with vanilla cream. It was truly beautiful, the way to a child's heart. The British may be accused of producing heavy puddings, but the French can rival the calorie count when they want to.

Lunch finished at about seven o'clock. As a child I felt that it went on a bit too long as we had to stay at the table all the way through. The reward was always the arrival of the *bûche de Noël*. Once that had been eaten the women headed back to the kitchen to wash up. The men remained at the table to talk more about sex and politics. Yes, from time to time the men entered the kitchen, but only to ask for more food.

I've experienced many English Christmases since those days, and I do not think they are so very different from the way we celebrate it all over Europe. It is true that there is not much spirituality left (apart from Maman Blanc), but it remains a great occasion for the meeting of the family around a table. And that is good reason enough.

Although Gérard broke both my tank and my heart when I was seven years old, we've since put that behind us. Sort of. I love him like a brother, but much more. When it came to hunting and fishing, he was always the most skilled of the Blanc children. By the age of twelve his knowledge was such that he could have been a professional poacher. In fact Gérard not only became an engineer but also a master huntsman. When the Blanc family gathers to spend Christmas at his home beside a forest in Franche-Comté, we feast on wild boar that has been shot by Gérard, or venison, served with chestnuts, root vegetables and Brussels sprouts.

He has seven hunting dogs, two of which are champions, and one of those is called Phoebus. The dog's copper-coloured hair is thick and it covers a thin, wiry frame. He is a shaggy beast but you can see his ribs through his skin, and the confident look in his eyes tells you he means business. When Phoebus is let out of his kennel for a hunt he is ready for action, but a sharp 'Quieten down' has a settling effect. While others put family photos in the post, Gérard frequently sends me snapshots of himself looking proud as he stands beside Phoebus and the rest of the pack. Gérard's wife and children stand behind, almost out of shot.

As I said, if he has been lucky enough to kill a boar before Christmas, then it will feature on the Christmas table. The dogs are trained to find the boar, but not to attack it. They will unearth the beast, probably a solitaire, an old wild boar that lives alone which can weigh a monstrous 120kg and has huge tusks and a foul temper. Once the animal is located, the hunt will begin, dogs and huntsmen working together to make the kill. That's how it always worked in the past, and that was how it was supposed to work when I joined the hunt for our Christmas lunch a couple of years ago. But on that particular day everything went wrong.

Gérard was there with his whistle, which he used to convey high-pitched instructions, and we were out with the seven dogs, which included three young ones who had never previously hunted. The hunt was an amazing experience. Boars like to inhabit the prickliest part of the woods where humans cannot tread.

The dogs found the boar, a monstrous animal, circled him, and then started to bring him out of the woods. We followed, running as well, across farms, fields and meadows. You have to be so fit; there are no horses in this hunt. Then the circle of dogs expanded and the boar spotted a gap. It escaped and started to make a run for it.

Actually, it started to run towards (or was it for?) me. I stood still in the middle of the field, and I must tell you I felt very alone at that point. I did not have a gun, and you know that I did not have a horse. As the beast charged towards me, looking angry, I was – yes, I'll admit it – petrified. I prayed.

I bent down and picked up a stone. It was not a rock or a pebble, it was a heavy stone, but still it would have been useless in a battle against the thick skull of the tusked boar. I was not in the kitchen with a dead boar but on his territory, and he was very much alive – perhaps bent on revenge for all the boar I had cooked. The stone remained in my hand as the boar charged past me, followed by the dogs, with no intention whatsoever of getting into a fight.

At the fence the beast was cornered, unable to escape. Then the three young dogs started to attack. They had been trained not to do so, but on this day they went for him. One went for the belly, another went for the tail, and the third dog went for the head. Phoebus was taken by the frenzy of the pack and, completely out of character, decided to attack as well. The boar responded, with force. By the time Gérard arrived on the scene Phoebus had been speared in the stomach by a tusk.

The boar escaped. Phoebus was rushed to the vet. He underwent treatment for a haemorrhage and has now recovered, but now he is certainly more sensible when he meets wild boar. I have never seen Gérard suffer with so much grief, afraid for the life of his best friend.

The wild boar that is sold in Britain is not what it is meant to be. It is a cross-breed of boar and other domestic pigs. Its flesh is whiteish compared with what you find on the other side of the Channel. In France, the wild boar has flesh the colour of blackcurrant and a scent that is rich and beautiful.

The boar is hung for up to three weeks. Then the coat is removed from the animal and the whole carcass is deconstructed – legs, loin, saddle, best end. But my favourite parts are the cheek, belly and shoulder, which are braised. The shoulder has to be cut into small pieces, which takes some strength and skill with a knife. Then braising pieces – cheek, belly and shoulder – these are marinated in a mixture of red wine (which has been previously boiled to remove the alcohol content, and to boost colour and flavour), diced celery and carrots, onion, juniper berries, whole black pepper, cloves, redcurrant jelly, sage and bay leaf. They sit in the marinade for about twenty-four hours, creating a wonderful exchange of flavours. The meat takes on the truly appetizing deep rich red of the wine.

After marinating, the meat is separated from the vegetables and herbs and caramelized in a huge cast-iron pot or casserole in a mixture of butter and oil. The fat is discarded and two tablespoons of flour are thrown over the meat, to create the liaison, and then it is covered with the marinade. It is slowly cooked for about six hours at a temperature of 90°C, which means the temperature in the meat will be about 80°C, just under simmering point, just enough for the fat and collagens to acquire a melting quality.

Sometimes pig's blood is used to finish the dish – and a dash of vinegar joins it to help prevent coagulation. I doubt you'll find it in any of our supermarkets (Waitrose, maybe?). The dish is finished with the blood and perhaps grated dark chocolate and redcurrant jelly, but importantly, the blood must not boil or it will coagulate. If you don't happen to have a pint of pig's blood, use a classic roux to bind the sauce. I fear that the suggested addition of blood will startle some, but it adds colour, depth and drama to the dish, as well as so much more flavour.

Blood has nutritional qualities too: it's a good source of iron and magnesium. After all, we eat black pudding, and it's delicious. The liver of a wild boar, however, is far too strong for the human palate. Gérard gives it to Phoebus as a tasty Christmas present.

My mother continues to try to run the kitchen at Christmas. When we were at Gérard's recently, the Blanc matriarch, in her mid-eighties, was still determined to cook the massive lunch for fifteen members of the extended family. I decided that she should at least take a day off once a year, and I used ultimate force. I strapped her into her chair with a scarf to prevent her from cooking, serving or, indeed, setting foot in the kitchen. It was useless: she broke free and headed for the cooker. Like many women of her generation, she is great at giving, and she knows that cooking is a big part of giving.

All Year Round
Les Tripes 'Grand-mère Tournier'
Tripe with Calvados

What a sight to see Grand-mère Tournier turning out on a late Christmas morning carrying a huge earthenware pot with its lid on. This was the most precious Christmas present. The pot contained a much-appreciated dish, *les tripes*. She had lovingly marinaded and then cooked them for twelve hours to get that special sticky, spicy *jus*, the prized gelatinized texture and, of course, that flavour we have come to love.

Serves (Yield): 6
Difficulty rating: ● ○ ○
Preparation time: 10 minutes
Marinade: 6 hours
Cooking time: 6 hours
Special equipment: 25–30cm earthenware casserole with a lid

PLANNING AHEAD

This dish can be cooked 1 day in advance.

INGREDIENTS

1.2kg tripe, blanched, cut into 3cm pieces (★1)
1 large white onion, sliced
8 cloves garlic
1 stick celery, cut into 2cm slices
4 carrots, cut into 2cm dice
300ml white wine, boiled for 30 seconds (★2) and cooled
1 bouquet garni consisting of a few sprigs of parsley, 4 sprigs of
thyme, 3 fresh bay leaves (★3) and 1 sprig of tarragon
4 cloves
3 pinches salt, plus 1 pinch later
6 whole black peppercorns
50ml Calvados, raw
1 chilli, deseeded and chopped
2 pinches cayenne pepper
1 tbsp butter
1 tbsp tomato purée

METHOD

Preheat the oven to 110°C. (★4)

Marinade all the ingredients (except the butter and tomato purée)
together for 6 hours. Drain the ingredients, reserving the liquor;
separate the vegetables from the tripe. Caramelize the vegetables
lightly in foaming butter for 10 minutes, season with a pinch of salt,
add the tomato purée and cook for 1 minute. Add the marinated
tripe, herbs and liquor, bring to a gentle simmer then transfer to the
oven and cook for 6 hours. Check and taste from time to time.

Chef's notes:

★1   Ask your butcher to prepare the tripe for you.
★2   See note 2 on page 46.
★3   Most dried herbs have a stronger, more pungent flavour than fresh.
So if you use dried, use half the amount.

*4   This low oven temperature will ensure the cooking liquor will reach 85–90°C, which is needed to give the tripe a lovely melting texture. You could also add a chopped trotter to give a more gelatinous texture to the braising liquor.

FISH

An Invitation to Provence

MANY YEARS AGO I EMPLOYED A COMMIS CHEF CALLED MARK Peregrine, who worked at my first restaurant, Les Quat' Saisons. I was very fond of him. He was a fine young Englishman with a good head, an intelligent mind and a passionate interest in cooking.

Mark has a special place in my heart because he was my first apprentice. For five years he shared with me the tough experience of starting up a restaurant and then trying to run it successfully. The two of us were unprepared for what lay ahead. I had never been a chef, never mind a mentor, but I did my best to pass on to him what I was learning myself.

When it was time for Mark to leave and gain more experience in other restaurants, I placed him in Burgundy with Monsieur Marc Meneau at L'Esperance. Mark was a keen fisherman, and he told me the story of what happened when he went coarse fishing in France.

As he was a skilled angler he reeled in one fish after another from the water. After each catch he removed the hook from the fish's mouth and then, holding the fish under its belly, placed it gently back into the water and let it swim away. A little crowd of French fishermen gathered around him, and Mark confidently felt that they were amazed by his talents with the rod. But then he noticed that the Frenchmen were smirking. They were nodding at him while pointing their fingers at their temples in complete incomprehension, grumbling and muttering, '*Ils sont fous, ces Anglais.*'

Mark got quite a lot of interest that day because he was doing something that no Frenchman would ever do. He was returning the fish to the water.

I learned to fish at an early age and there was never the suggestion that the fish, having been caught, should then be allowed to swim to freedom. Like the rabbits in my garden, the fish were destined for a dish. My father would take me fishing for *goujons* (gudgeons), those tiny fish that love sandy banks and shallow water with a gentle current. Back at home, my mother served them as *frittures*, or fritters, by quickly gutting the fish, flouring them and deep-frying them until brown and crispy. They were served with lemon and a lovely mayonnaise on the side.

My brother Gérard became my mentor (my other brother Michel much preferred to read a good book at home rather than join the hunts). Gérard would take me fishing for freshwater crayfish, which are a great delicacy in France. To catch them required a certain technique. A piece of very rotten cheap meat, perhaps ox heart, was wrapped into the middle of a bundle of sticks which were in turn tied up with string. The carnivorous crayfish were drawn to the meat. We had to wait a few hours for them to make their way along the riverbed to the bait, but on a good day we returned home with about three hundred crayfish, which we sold to restaurants, though we kept many for our own table of course. Their taste is sweet, succulent, far superior to their American cousins who have now eaten their way through the rivers and streams of Europe. My mother would boil them quickly and their shell was removed at the table. As with *goujons*, mayonnaise was the sauce to have with crayfish.

There were fishing expeditions to catch eels with my father, which bothered me for a while because I believed eels were evil serpents. My father taught me how to kill an eel quickly. Then it was hung up and the skin was peeled from its body, which takes some strength. The eel is like one large muscle.

Usually it was cut into two-centimetre pieces and pan-fried with a traditional *persillade*; sometimes it was filleted and smoked. As we were surrounded by pine trees we tended to smoke everything in Franche-Comté, or at least try it smoked. Yet I must admit that no nation does eels better than the British. In fact, jellied eels and smoked eels are among my favourite British dishes, along with potted shrimps, which I like to eat warm rather than cold (when cold, I find the butter is too rich) with toasted brown bread and a glass of Sancerre. At such moments the world is perfect. Alas, eels are now on the endangered list.

———

On my seventh birthday Life took on new meaning. I was given a fishing rod as a present. It was a gift from René Simon, who had been my best friend since we were both aged two.

I should quickly tell you a little about René. He was big and I was small, and we were comical with a slapstick edge. Our families saw us as Franche-Comté's answer to Laurel and Hardy. We'd spend days playing tarot with his mother, who was quite deaf. Her disability meant that we could cheat by telling each other what we had in our hands, safe in the knowledge that she could not hear us. Meanwhile, Madame Simon kept our plates piled high with cakes. I'd leave René's house, my pockets filled with his mother's money and my stomach filled with her wonderful gateaux.

On the day René gave me the rod, the pair of us scurried down to the river to fish and I caught a tench that was almost as large as me. I hauled it from the water, removed the hook, lifted it to my lips and gave it a big kiss. Maman slow-roasted the fish, on the bone, with butter, lemon juice and parsley.

I became hooked, so to speak, on fishing – a welcome addition to the hunting and the gathering.

It was not unusual to come home and see a pike in the bath. These fish can survive for four or five hours out of the water, so they were brought home and put in the bath. The water revived them and they remained in the bath for a few days. Pike are filled with riverbed dirt, so the bathing process was also designed to clean them inside before cooking. Thank God we had a shower as well.

My mother considered the pike-in-the-bath routine a terrible practice. Nevertheless, on feast days she would make quenelle of pike, served with freshwater crayfish. Alternatively, she would poach it with a celery stick and a bouquet garni, that traditional little bundle of herbs – usually thyme, bay leaf and parsley – which features in so much French cooking. Or she might poach the fish in a *court bouillon* made with a glass of dry white wine, water, diced onions, carrot, celery and leek, two or three slices of lemon, salt, whole peppercorns and, of course, the bouquet garni. Trout, meanwhile, was pan-fried in sizzling butter with lots of parsley and lemon juice on the side.

The Jura mountains were a good place to go for trout. For a month in the summer I was dispatched with Gérard and Michel to summer camp. The French government funded the camps and we would go to one that was high up in the Jura mountains, in the middle of a forest of pine trees. Our absence enabled my mum to have a bit of peace and quiet. We were always sad to say goodbye, knowing we would not see each other for a month, but on the other hand there were rivers and forests and adventures to be had.

The chalky mountains of my region were like a humungous Gruyère cheese from which streams and rivers gushed, and waterfalls cascaded into large pools. The average temperature of these pools was around nine to ten degrees – perfect for trout. These pools were also Nature's bathtubs carved from the stone (minus the hot tap) and could hold about ten shivering children. Every morning the chilly water numbed our bodies. There, a thousand metres above sea level, we splashed around, frantically trying to warm ourselves. Our skin resembled chicken skin. The moment when we leapt from the water and the warm rays of the sun hit our frozen bodies was blissful beyond words.

It was while at this camp that I tried the art of catching trout by hand. Gérard was well practised at it. He had taught me other fishing skills, of course, and I was a good student, but not the best. We spent up to two hours looking for the trout, which were well camouflaged among the stones of the riverbed, holding themselves on the spot with their heads into the current. First, Gérard tickled the fish gently on the tail. He then moved slowly up the body until he quickly grabbed the fish and lifted it out of the water. Gérard performed this trick regularly, pulling one fish after another from the streams. I could spot them and tickle them, but I never once managed to catch a trout in my hands. Maybe they smelled a cook . . .

I have conducted a number of little experiments with trout, trying to understand the different varieties. A few years ago I was fishing in the south of England and caught one rainbow trout and one brown trout. I thought I would cook both in the same way to compare them. Rainbow trout is a cross-breed, if you like, a breed that has evolved and is the product of mixed varieties. Brown trout, however, is the genuine article.

I put a good tablespoon of unsalted butter into a large oval pan and heated it until it foamed and was ready for the fish. I placed the two trout, both on the bone, into the pan and watched as they began to cook. I was fascinated by their different reactions to the heat. The rainbow trout remained completely flat in the pan, but the brown trout began to arch, and the more it cooked the more it arched. The white flesh started to break through the skin.

When I came to eat them, the rainbow trout had a pinkish flesh. There's nothing wrong with that, but it lacked both the flavour and the texture of the brown trout. And what did that tell me? It told me that while these two share a name, they could be entirely different fish. It is a perfect illustration of the difference between wild and farmed or organic and intensively reared animals. Their reaction in the pan was a result of their different muscle structure: the brown trout, which existed in the wild, had all the muscle fibres that come with such an existence; the rainbow trout, the descendant of farmed fish, might have looked good with its pink flesh but it lacked flavour.

Always go for the brown trout, which has more flavour. Then you have the true authentic taste of trout, a taste you will never get from intensively farmed fish. Of course, you will not find the wild brown trout in a shop, you'll have to catch it. And they are pretty rare; once again, they are threatened by pollution.

There were few sad moments in my childhood, but the one that sticks in my mind came at the age of fourteen. René announced that he and his family were leaving Franche-Comté. Shortly afterwards, the Simon family packed up and went to live in Provence.

René and I had such a close bond that I was devastated by his departure. In those days, people did not travel as they do now. To use planes and trains was expensive. So as far as I was concerned he may as well have been moving to another continent.

However, there was a silver lining to the grey cloud. Once René had settled he invited me to spend a few weeks with him. I was about to discover the magic, the glorious wonders of Provence, a new world with its own cuisine, new flavours, new tastes, new smells and new colours.

Until then I had spent my life in one region of France. I cannot underestimate how important the region is to the Frenchman. The majority of food that my family ate came from Franche-Comté. Had I lived in another region there is a good chance I would not have tasted food – the cheese, the wine, the vegetables, the fruit, the smoked meats, the wild mushrooms – specific to Franche-Comté. For example, as I have mentioned, olive trees did not grow in Franche-Comté. This meant that we did not have olives as a form of canapé before a meal. Now, yes; then, no. No olives also meant no olive oil. Yet there were plenty of cows which meant lots of milk and a good supply of butter and cheese. So there you have it: my mother cooked with butter, dishes were often creamy, and cheese was a staple dish.

The French are very protective of their regional cuisine. We all know that a Burgundy man would sooner succumb to death by dehydration than drink wine from Bordeaux, and vice versa. Ingredients from other regions rarely came into Franche-Comté. There was no demand, partly because our region supplied us with everything we needed and partly because we, like the inhabitants of other regions, would have been too proud of our produce to touch anything else. I suppose food is to France what football is to England. There is still extreme, almost tribal protectiveness over ingredients. The Italians have pesto, the sauce made from basil, pine nuts and olive oil. But be careful how you discuss pesto with the people of Provence. They will tell you that they have been making pistou soups since 1300, or some such date. Should you ever wish to be murdered by an inhabitant of Provence simply say to him that pistou is really pesto and was invented by the Italians.

Before meeting up with René I had yet to learn that Provence had its own ingredients, different from Franche-Comté's. My travelling experience was limited. When I was five or six we'd been on a Blanc family holiday to Switzerland. The journey was only about sixty miles, but for some reason my childlike mind convinced me that this country beyond the border would be like landing on a strange planet. 'The cows are green in Switzerland,' I'd told René, 'and the grass is blue.' It was a great disappointment when we crossed the border. I scoured the landscape for blue grass but, incredible though it might seem, there was none.

When I arrived in Provence and was greeted by the Simon family there were no green cows either, but I got my first sight of the blue sea. And there was more. There was the smell of fennel and lavender. There was the smell of old pine trees, different to the pines of the forest near my home. There was the lazy, repetitive sound of the cricket chorus, and the constant blue sky.

It was one big, refreshing, exciting, wonderful experience.

René's father, Monsieur Simon, drove us to the small port of Saint Cyr-sur-Mer where we met the fishermen. I was transfixed, first by the trawlermen in their salty blue overalls, then by the fish they were carrying in baskets. These were creatures, red, purple and green, I had never seen before, sea-fish that were not known of in rural Franche-Comté. There were little rock-fish, octopus and squid, tentacles galore. There were swordfish with their long, sharp noses, and monkfish with their grotesque heads. There were scorpion fish like *rascasse rouge*, better known simply as rascasse or *chapon*, which to my young eyes seemed like red monsters, with their large heads, protruding spiky teeth and spiny dorsal fins.

Monsieur Simon bought about three kilograms of small rock-fish, one large lotte and two large rascasse, and then we headed for the market. Every French town has had its market for hundreds of years. My home town Besançon had two markets, one covered and one outdoor, both vibrant and busy with an abundance of food; but at the market in Provence everything – the colours, the smells, the noise – was stronger. The market was a place to meet where everyone talked about and touched the food, planning the next feast. And to my great surprise, everyone bartered over the price. The food was also so different to what I had known before. There were hundreds of multi-coloured fish, yet so little meat compared to Franche-Comté. There were hundreds of goats' cheeses but no cows' cheese as we had at home. All the herbs were different, there were more varieties of vegetables, like the spiky purple artichoke and the bulbous fennel, and fruit to die for, especially the peaches and melons, the perfume of which dominated the whole marketplace.

Back at the Simon home, René and I were the minions reunited, gutting and cleaning the fish so it was ready for the soup – and, wow, what a glorious combination of flavours that was! To begin with, the cooking fat was different. In Franche-Comté my mother used butter, and sometimes vegetable oil. Here, in Provence, Madame Simon used olive oil, which went into the large casserole followed by chopped onions, garlic, bay leaf, thyme, celery, and was it fennel? At that stage of my life I often watched the cooking process, and I was certainly aware of the new smells. In Franche-Comté we had tarragon, chives, chervil, parsley, bay leaves and thyme. René's mother cooked with Provençal favourites like rosemary, fennel, basil, marjoram, coriander, star anise and saffron.

Once the vegetables and herbs were sweetened, she added the rock-fish and the saffron. The chopped tomatoes went in too, along with a generous splash of white wine. I remember being intrigued when she added a splash of pastis, the alcoholic aniseed drink, because although I had seen it drunk before I had absolutely no idea it could be used in cooking. Then the ingredients were covered with water and simmered for twenty or thirty minutes, just enough to cook them and create the exchange of flavours. After that she pushed the soup through a *mouli*.

While the soup was cooking Madame Simon made the aïoli, that delicious garlic mayonnaise made with the best extra virgin olive oil. If you add saffron and puréed potato you will have a *rouille*. Both reek of garlic, and you wonder why the French are in such rude health.

There you have your fish soup, which can be served with a spoon-ful of the aïoli and croutons rubbed with garlic. This soup was also a base to cook the fillets of rascasse and lotte. Then it becomes a bouilla-baisse, and it was this that Madame Simon made for us.

A bottle of rosé, the local Bandol, was uncorked to toast the reunion. What a feast. In one mouthful I discovered all these new flavours, as well as having my first taste of bouillabaisse.

There were more food treats. During my stay with René I saw and ate crayfish – the lobster of the Mediterranean, but without the claws.

Monsieur Simon took us to the fish market one morning and I gazed at the shellfish, which were handsomely presented by the stallholders, framed by onions, tomatoes and herbs – a colourful picture of abundance, designed to entice in a way French market stallholders have perfected.

In the sixties, crayfish were plentiful in the Mediterranean, but now pollution has seriously depleted their numbers. In fact, in April this year (2008) I went to Provence and visited the little town of Villefranche-sur-Mer, not far from Cannes. The first thing I did was head for the market. There I met a fisherman who told me that forty years ago the town had seventy fishermen. Today he is the only one. I also saw his catch displayed on the market stall: two crayfish, one John Dory, two rascasse and a couple of kilograms of small rock-fish. It told me a story, and I think everyone is aware of it. (It was also in this market that I was taught how to measure the freshness of white asparagus – make them sing. Of course, don't expect Maria Callas or the violin of Nigel Kennedy, but if the asparagus are truly fresh and you rub them against each other like a bow on a violin string, you will hear the beautiful music of ultimate freshness. Don't try it with green asparagus, though, it won't work.)

Back then, when I was a boy, the abundant crayfish at the stall were kept alive in a tank of water, and Monsieur Simon picked out two, which were a shiny pinkish colour. The creatures, with their long antennae, did not like this treatment, and they hissed. We returned home through the busy streets of the small town, and Monsieur Simon lit the barbecue. When the coals were white hot, René's father performed something akin to a culinary magic trick. He took a huge butcher's knife, placed it on the cross of the crayfish's head and quickly and masterfully sank the knife through the head and swiftly moved it downwards right through the tail so that the crayfish was cut cleanly in two. Using a spoon, he then removed the stomach and intestines and put them to one side, again with the utmost speed. Having prepared both crayfish in this way, he brushed them with olive oil, seasoned the surface of the flesh with *fleur de sel* and a few turns of pepper, and put them on to the grill of the barbecue, flesh side down. The entire process, from killing to putting them on the heat, took him just two minutes. After another two or three minutes the crayfish were turned over so that the shells met the heat and changed to an appetizing deep red.

Then we ate them, and more rosé wine was served. It was my first taste of crayfish from the sea – delicious, chewy, meaty and lightly smoky. Salad leaves and tomatoes were tossed together, dressed with olive oil and lemon juice, and placed on the table. A round of goats' cheese finished it off.

Monsieur Simon, incidentally, was three times the size of the Michelin man, and he had the most unsociable custom. Every morning he would peel a large onion and eat it raw. Now, raw onions are the single biggest producer of flatulence. A few hours after breakfast, the loud effects of his raw onion enabled you to pinpoint Monsieur Simon's location in the house. René and I would know then to get out into the garden. We cook onions to convert the rawness into sweetness – to make them tasty – but also to remove their flatulence-inducing properties. You needed nose-pegs and ear plugs to be near Monsieur Simon between breakfast and noon. But come lunch, if he was doing that crayfish barbecue, you'd pay to be there, plate in hand, right next to the man.

———

That memory of crayfish in Provence is bringing back other shellfish-related recollections, specifically one night at Le Manoir and the dish of lobster with chocolate sauce.

You need to know some essential background information. In my early days as a restaurateur I came up with a three-word rule for the Le Manoir team to follow: *never say no*. It could have been *always say yes*, which, granted, has a more positive ring. But on the particular day I made the rule it was *never say no* rather than *always say yes*. Whatever the wording, you get my drift. The point is, I love to say yes and hate to say no, and I have found it is so much easier to say yes. By doing so, an attitude of the warmest welcome is created on which the whole culture of a restaurant can grow. This simple philosophy is shared by every member of the team at Le Manoir and Brasserie Blanc. Inevitably, however, it raises a crucial question: at what point do you stop saying yes and find yourself saying no?

An American arrived at Le Manoir one evening. He was with a small group of friends, and before dinner he treated the crowd to a drink in the bar. He satisfied his own thirst with a tumbler or two of whisky. Good for him.

He and his group were shown to their table in the restaurant, where the American host ordered another whisky to see him through the ordeal of reading the menu. The maître d'hôtel went to the table, notepad in hand. For starters the American guest ordered Colchester oysters. 'And for a main course,' he said, 'would it be possible to have lobster with chocolate sauce?'

This request had the otherwise unflappable maître d' flapping, though very deep within; his anxiety was certainly not visible on the surface. Lobster with chocolate sauce? The dish was definitely not on the menu at Le Manoir. I am sure it was not on the menu at any other restaurant in Britain, maybe not on any restaurant menu in the world. Had the maître d' been working elsewhere he could have given a sniff of superiority and told the American to choose from the menu or drink up and leave. But the maître d' was not elsewhere. He was at Le Manoir, and he was aware of my never-say-no rule. This presented him with a problem. Was it time to break the rule?

To help find the answer, he came to see me and said, 'Chef, there is a pretty unusual request. An American guest wants lobster . . .' He could barely bring himself to finish the sentence. 'With chocolate sauce.'

I sent the maître d' back to the table, asking him to double-check the order.

'Sir, are you sure you want lobster with chocolate sauce?'

The American was polite but adamant. 'Yes, that is exactly what I want. If possible.'

When the maître d' relayed this news to me, I asked him, 'Is he serious about it, or is he taking the mickey?'

'He's had a few whiskies but he seems to be very serious.'

'Ask him what sort of sauce he wants. Does he want a sweet sauce, spicy, bitter?'

The maître d' checked with the customer once again and the message came back, 'He will leave it to you, Chef.'

'We will do it,' I said, without first pausing to consider the creation of such a dish, or that the service that evening was particularly busy. 'How could anyone eat lobster with chocolate sauce?' I thought. But I felt I had to adhere to my never-say-no policy, even if I was in danger of bringing down the evening's service. For a minute I wished I was my friend Marco and could throw the customer into the gutter, but my rule prevailed.

'Quick,' I told the maître d', 'hurry back to him and tell him yes. Don't say no.'

That bit was easy. All I had to do then was get my head around the bizarre order and work out how it would go from being a request to being on a plate placed in front of the guest.

I asked a commis to get all of the ingredients. I had to be fast because the pressure of service was increasing. First, I blanched the lobster for twenty seconds to release the flesh, then split it in two and removed the flesh from the tail and claws. I chopped the head and body into pieces and caramelized them. I deglazed the pan with a good splash of port and Pineau des Charentes, reduced the liquid, then added water and a tiny hint of vanilla seed. It simmered for a few minutes to infuse the flavours. Meanwhile, I cut the tail into segments, flash-fried them and put them to one side.

Then I returned to the simmering *jus*, where I had to work some magic. I pushed it through a *chinois* sieve, and what I had was a really good lobster *jus*. It had quite a strong lobster flavour, a lovely red sheen, but my sauce was lacking its primary ingredient – chocolate. I used a bitter chocolate with an 80 per cent cocoa content, which I grated and added to the *jus* so that the sauce acquired the black sheen the customer desired. I was trying to make something as good as I could but I took it light-heartedly. I was amused by the experience. I knew instinctively that lobster with chocolate sauce was a culinary aberration. Creativity in the kitchen is about combining ingredients that work; this one would never become a classic. It was a face-saving exercise for my rule.

I tasted it. Sure, it was a bit dodgy, but not that bad. It was as good as chocolate sauce with lobster could possibly taste.

I set it up on the plate and it was a magnificent picture. The red and pink of the lobster tail and legs against the black sheen of the chocolate sauce was seriously seductive. The dish was its own little drama of *rouge* and *noir*.

The plate left the passe and headed for the table. Chefs peeked through the swing doors to gauge the reaction. Waiters who were serving other tables glanced across the room to observe the American guest as the lobster was carried to him. Guests on other tables craned their necks to view the American and his unusual dish. We watched to see if he would enjoy it. And he did. He sent a message back to the kitchen: 'That was the best lobster with chocolate sauce I've ever eaten.' This suggested that he ate it on a regular basis, which I would not recommend. It certainly never made it on to my menu.

Recently I allowed (perhaps to the delight of my staff) the never-say-no rule to be bent. It now reads *never say no . . . unless you really, really have to*.

All Year Round
Soupe de Poisson, Sauce Aïoli
Fish Soup with Aïoli

When you think of fish soup, immediately the heady flavours of Provence spring to mind. On the Atlantic, we do not have as many rock-fish as there are in the Mediterranean, but you can still do a lovely fish soup.

Serves (Yield): 4 to 6 (1.4 litre)
Difficulty rating: ● ○ ○
Preparation time: 35 minutes
Cooking time: 45 minutes
Special equipment: Fine sieve, 30cm casserole, liquidizer (optional)

INGREDIENTS

For the fish soup:
1 large Spanish onion, finely chopped
1 bulb fennel, finely chopped
1 small stick celery, finely chopped
1 carrot, finely chopped
5 cloves garlic, crushed
2 sprigs thyme
1 bay leaf
100ml olive oil (*1)
1 packet saffron powder (0.25g)
500g gurnard fillets, chopped (*2)
500g grey mullet fillets, chopped
300g tomatoes, chopped
300ml dry white wine, boiled for 30 seconds (*3)
1.2 litres cold water (*4)
4 pinches sea salt
3 pinches cayenne pepper
1 tbsp Pernod

For the aïoli (all ingredients must be at room temperature):
>2 egg yolks (*5)
>3 gloves garlic, puréed
>1 pinch salt
>250ml extra virgin olive oil (*6)
>juice of ¼ lemon
>1 pinch cayenne pepper

For the garnish:
>30 toasted croûtons
>100g Gruyère cheese, grated

METHOD
MAKING THE FISH SOUP:

Sweat the onions, fennel, celery, carrot, garlic, thyme and bay leaf in the olive oil for 5 minutes. (*7) Stir in the saffron, add the chopped fish and stir again, then cook for another 5 minutes. Add the tomatoes, white wine and cold water and season with salt and cayenne pepper. Taste. Lastly add the Pernod, bring to the boil for 2 minutes, skim, then barely simmer for 20 minutes on top of the stove.

Take off the heat, then you can either strain the soup by passing it through a fine sieve, or you can give it more flavour and texture by lightly liquidizing it. (*8)

MAKING THE AÏOLI:

This is a simplified version of *rouille*, which normally contains potatoes or bread, but it is just as delicious. Aïoli is a mayonnaise with garlic and olive oil. This little sauce illustrates the magical power of egg yolks.

In a bowl, mix the egg yolks with the garlic and salt, then pour in the olive oil in a steady trickle, still stirring, until the oil is absorbed and thickens. Whisk in the lemon juice and cayenne pepper. Taste and correct the seasoning.

SERVING:

Heat the soup and serve the aïoli separately, or use a hand-held blender to liquidize the aïoli into the soup. Serve with the croûtons and Gruyère cheese. (★9)

Chef's notes:

★1   Don't use your best olive oil for this, as many molecules of flavour will disappear during cooking. Keep your extra virgin olive oil for warm or cold sauces.

★2   Gurnard is a good-tasting fish that will make an excellent soup, and our seas around Britain are full of this variety.

★3   See note 2 on page 46.

★4   The cold water will trap and coagulate some of the protein, which will rise to the surface as the water heats up. At full boil, skim off the surface froth, then immediately lower the heat to a mere simmer for 20 minutes.

★5   Egg yolks contain a protein called lecithin that will absorb the droplets of oil and emulsify the aïoli into a firm and smooth sauce. If the sauce is too stiff, thin it down with a bit of warm water. If the sauce starts to separate, pour a tiny amount of hot water down the side of the bowl and whisk it in; this will bind the sauce.

★6   Now is the time to use your extra virgin olive oil to get the best flavour from your sauce. If you find the olive oil too strong, replace some of it with a neutral oil such as rapeseed or sunflower. It is interesting to know that extra virgin olive oil (unrefined) can kill bacteria and salmonella.

★7   This must be done on a medium heat, without colouring the vegetables. The aim is to convert starches into sugars; this method will also add more flavour. Not so much 'sweated' as 'sweetened'.

★8   You can either serve this as a clear soup, or you can grind up the fish and the soup together, which will give you a richer textured and more flavoursome soup. When using the liquidizer, use the pulse button three times (for no more than 2 seconds at a time). Beware: you don't want to purée the soup, just break down a little of the fish and vegetables. Which way you choose to serve the soup is partly a matter of taste, and partly a matter of how much you have spent on the fish. If you've used expensive fish, you will not want to discard it in order to serve a clear soup.

*9   Gruyère cheese comes from Franche-Comté in the north-east of France and from Switzerland. Yet it works very well in this southern French dish.

VARIATIONS

By replacing the fish with fish bones, you will still have a very good soup and for a fraction of the price. Sieve it before serving.

By adding saffron to the aïoli sauce, you will create a *rouille*. Puréed potato is optional.

You can create a wonderful fish stew by poaching additional fillets of fish in the clear soup. A few saffron potatoes would be the right accompaniment.

SIX

SOUPS

Know Your Onions

Let's talk about onions and see where it leads us.

The onion, like garlic, plays a dominant role in many cuisines of the world, but is most important in French food. There are few savoury dishes in France that don't have a bit of onion, or indeed a bit of garlic. You might use it finely sliced in a tomato salad, or in a dressing, or whole in a *pot au feu*. Often the onion is the first building block in a dish, especially a rustic peasant dish. It brings acidity and sweetness – and taste.

When I think of this vegetable, onion soup invariably comes to mind. When I was growing up we would mostly eat onion soup in the winter months as it was seen as heart-warming. From November onwards it was a regular dish. Then, when I became a teenager and threw myself into a hectic social life, onion soup was the thing to have in the early hours of the morning as a pick-me-up after a night of partying. We'd sit around the table while one or two of us went into the kitchen to make the soup, which most of my friends could easily manage. Some of them made it well, and in typical Franche-Comté style, bread and cheese was added, making the soup extremely hearty.

Some of my friends, however, were not gifted soup-makers. They would head off to the kitchen and return with nothing more than bowls of burnt onion mixed with hot water.

Onion soup was a late-night treat when the old folks and the families in the village met up and the men disappeared into a room to play tarot. The women would go into the kitchen and start cooking for their husbands, and at ten o'clock the men would take a break from the game to have charcuterie, salads and cheese. Then they'd return to tarot. At four o'clock in the morning the onion soup would be ready for the men. Their game would finish and they'd enjoy the warming soup, their wives by then in bed. Maybe there was also time for one last drink – the Mirabelle or pear alcohol from my grandfather.

When done well, it is one of the best soups in the world. It is a perfect example of how you can make soup without stock – a subject to which I shall return.

The starting point has to be the onion itself, and it's worth experimenting with varieties. First, taste it raw. Slice it different ways to see how the structure is affected. You should get to know your onions by their colour, their shape and their variety, but mostly by their level of acidity and sweetness and flavour rather than their strength. The more flavour the onion has in its raw form, the better the onion soup will be.

Which type should be used? There are many varieties. The most well known are the white onion, which is quite mild and is the favourite of the French; then there are the Pink Roscoff and the Spanish onions, which are stronger; then come the red (purple) onions from Normandy, which are the strongest. Of these, my favourite is the white onion from France, which is the sweetest. It also contains less sulphur than the others, and it's the sulphur compounds in onions that cause tears when slicing. These compounds are fine when the onion is raw and unpeeled; it is only when you remove the outer layers and start slicing that a molecular cocktail is whisked up that begins to attack the eyes and nose.

In our taste tests at Le Manoir, we found that the Pink Roscoff and the white onion are the best for onion soup. And for salad, the red onion from Normandy.

I am sorry to say that if you are going to do a good onion soup you have to go through the pain of slicing the onion. By all means try all the tricks to stop the tears: bread in your mouth will make you look foolish; a wet towel over your head will hinder your vision and you might chop off a finger in your quest for soup; putting the onions in the freezer before slicing will indeed stop the tears but will also change the structure and the flavour of the vegetable, so I wouldn't recommend it. The sharpness of the knife is certainly important, so that you don't bruise the fibres. Equally, if you cut yourself, it will be a nice clean cut and the nurse will love you. I've seen too many horrendous cuts made by knives that were blunt.

The slice is important. Too thin and the onions will turn into a purée when cooked; too thick and there will not be enough caramelization when the onions are cooked and this will mean less flavour and a long cooking process. It is an easy soup but not a quick soup.

Then there are the other ingredients: a little garlic (because the French cannot help it), some thyme and bay leaf, and a splash of dry white wine. Don't buy expensive wine; a few pounds will get you the right bottle for this dish. The wine gives acidity, adds another element of structure and creates length of flavour so that the taste lingers in your mouth. You also need water for this soup, and unsalted butter. You can use olive oil but I find the best medium for caramelizing the onions is butter. If they ate onion soup in the South of France then perhaps they would use olive oil, but they don't.

And so to cook the soup, and let's say we are cooking for four people.

Many people make the classic mistake at this initial stage of using a pan that is too small. The sliced onions fill up to the top, the heat can't reach them all, and the onions don't caramelize. Ideally you should use a non-stick saucepan or casserole which is thirty centimetres in diameter. An anodized aluminium pan will also do the job, as will a stainless steel pan, as long as it has a thick bottom. The transfusion of heat must be medium and evenly distributed – that's when you know you have a good saucepan. In a thin-based pan the onions will burn and cook unevenly. So always look for the best equipment – it will make the job easier.

The saucepan goes on to a high heat. Once the pan has picked up some heat, add forty grams of butter. Let it melt, but don't allow it to brown. Then add the onions. For four people you should use two French onions per person (or if you are using Spanish onions, do one onion per person). These will have been sliced in half and then cut across into slices of about three millimetres in width (the depth of a pound coin). This means a lot of crying for some, but at least (you hope) it will be worthwhile.

Cover and cook at high heat for five minutes. The steam softens them, and partly cooks them. After five minutes, remove the lid and stir the onions. When making onion soup for the first time it is a good idea to watch the entire process because there is so much to be learned. This is your first good opportunity.

The soup needs between six and eight grams of salt, depending on your taste; don't forget you will be adding cheese, which is salty. Let's add three of those grams – three good pinches – at this stage to let the salt permeate the onion and intensify flavour. The remaining salt will be added at the end, and ground black pepper wouldn't go amiss.

As the heat permeates the onions it starts to draw out the water content of the vegetable. You will find yourself staring at a watery mess and saying aloud, 'This is never going to work. The onions will never caramelize. Raymond has got it all wrong. He is stupid. Why am I using two onions per person? It looks like too much.' Don't panic. Turn up the heat to speed up the evaporation of the water. Do not put a lid on the pan as this will only prevent the moisture escaping. The vegetables will then take too long to cook and could become a purée. Once the water has evaporated, lower the heat to medium low to ensure slow caramelization. Stir every five minutes or so.

Add a sliced clove of garlic and bay leaf, either two fresh bay leaves or one dry bay leaf, because the dry bay leaf will have twice as much flavour as the fresh as the drying process removes the moisture which in turn means a more concentrated flavour. (Experiment with a mushroom: slice it, dry it, then rehydrate it to discover that the flavour will be twice, sometimes four times the strength of the fresh mushroom.) If your bay leaves have been in a cupboard for ten years, throw them into the bin rather than the soup.

Should the bay leaf be torn? By tearing the bay leaf you will inject into the dish a flavour of raw bay leaf, and it will be harsh and strong. All the essential oils are immediately released rather than being slowly diffused.

You can gauge the difference in taste by putting two hundred millilitres of cold water into one pan and the same amount of water into a second pan. Into one pan add a bay leaf you have cut or torn into pieces. Into the second pan add an untorn bay leaf. Now cook them both in the same way, at a low temperature. When you see a bubble or two on the surface of the water, taste the liquids. The difference in flavour will be noticeable. After a further fifteen minutes the difference will be even more obvious. Give it another five minutes and you won't want to taste the water that contains the torn bay leaf because it will be too strong and coarse.

There are many herbs that should be added at the very start of the cooking process, and others that should go in right at the end. Bay leaf, rosemary, thyme, sage and marjoram are strong-tasting herbs best added at the very start. They diffuse their flavours slowly. Use them carefully – you can always add more. Basil, on the whole, gains from staying fresh and going in right at the end, as do chives, parsley and coriander. But the cook must be careful because although herbs enhance flavours, they can also murder a dish.

Listen to your onion soup. Smell it, watch it, taste it. It's a lovely process unfolding in front of you: the sugar within the onions caramelizes slowly, and the colour of the onion gradually changes. The process will take about twenty or thirty minutes. Stir occasionally to prevent burning.

Often cooks make the mistake of believing the onions are ready when they are slightly brown. I am afraid not. The great onion soup is achieved only when you completely caramelize the vegetable. And that is the stage at which you feel completely dismayed because the pile of onions that filled up your pan has now disappeared to become a brown mess at the bottom of the pan. One moment you thought you had too much onion, now you are convinced you have not cooked enough. 'Raymond is crazy,' you will say aloud. 'He doesn't know what he is doing.' Again, don't panic. It is quite a lot of onion and now you will be able to smell its wafting sweetness, the delicious result of the cooker's heat and your patience. Taste it and notice the ever-developing sweetness.

Now stir in a heaped tablespoon of flour. I like to use flour I have previously toasted under a grill and then stored in a jar. Toasting cooks the starches within the flour, making it more digestible and adding a nutty flavour. The flour also thickens the soup.

It is time to add the white wine. For four guests you would use a quarter of a bottle. Remember, the wine should be inexpensive and it should also be dry. Please, please, none of that sickly-sweet oaky New Age Chardonnay. It might be OK for a sip or to get wasted, but certainly not for your onion soup.

Elsewhere in this book I talk about how I like to boil wine before using it, and this is a worthwhile trick. Just cook a little in a pan and taste it every five seconds. Soon you will have cooked away the alcohol and you should taste some beautiful vinous flavours, along with acidity and tannins. When it is right, you will know it. By boiling the wine beforehand you will know precisely the amount of acidity you wish to add to the dish. But don't overboil. To do so will leave the wine with no acidity. The flavour will be flat and there will be no point in using wine.

If you have not followed my advice about boiling the wine in advance, then when you add it raw to the onions you must boil it. It might need thirty seconds, it could need forty seconds. Remember, cooking is an inexact science, and much depends on the alcohol content, age, acidity and tannins of the wine. The smell in the kitchen will become even more pleasant. Put a spoon in the pan and taste the wine. It is difficult to spoil the soup at this stage and it is better to boil the wine too much than not enough.

Now pour in two litres of cold water and bring to the boil. Why two litres? Because some water will evaporate (you should always take into consideration the potential loss). It is best to use five hundred millilitres of water per person which will leave you with about four hundred millilitres of soup per person. If you end up with too much soup you can keep it for the following day when it will taste better.

If you want your soup to have a stronger colour, simmer the onion peel in a little water for twenty minutes, then remove the peel and use the water, which will have taken on a rich brown colour, in the soup; add it at the same time as you add the cold water.

Why *cold* water to the hot mix? Because it brings down the temperature, and when the temperature begins to rise again the impurities will be trapped and promptly brought nicely to the surface. If you use boiling water the soup will be cloudy. It's a matter of aesthetics. Granted, perhaps a cloudy soup does not bother you. But if you are asking me about a good onion soup then I have to say, add cold water and then the finished product will look more appetizing than if you were to add boiling water.

Quickly skim the scum, those impurities, from the surface. Turn the heat down, taste and correct the seasoning, and taste again. In other words, don't oversalt. You can always add but you can't take away. Then let the soup simmer for ten minutes. So, in total it takes about forty minutes to achieve this fantastic bowl of delicious Frenchness.

I told you it was easy.

Serve it from the pan, or the way my mother used to do it – in a beautiful big tureen with dried bread and Gruyère or Comté cheese on top. The bread absorbs the soup and becomes doughy, giving a peasant quality to the soup. However, don't add too much bread because it will absorb too much soup and you will end up with a bread stew. And don't put the tureen in an oven to gratinate the cheese. This is very dangerous and at the very least will make the tureen unbearably hot for you to handle. You can put the tureen under a grill but please keep an eye on it and remember that the top will be hot. The classic accompaniment, you can serve a bowl of grated Comté and toasted croutons as a garnish on the side for your guests to add at the last moment if they so wish. Allow for twenty grams of Comté per person, but also take into consideration that it is a salty cheese and therefore you should be careful not to oversalt the soup. If the soup is too sweet, add a splash of white wine to enliven it.

When cooking, always try to think of the recipe measurements as if you were cooking for one. It will help to minimize waste and make cooking easier and more successful. For my onion soup I have considered one person and then multiplied by four. For example, I know that about two grams of salt per person is the right amount, and I know that about seven grams of butter per person will not be too much. Again, I have considered the amount of soup that will feed one person – about four hundred millilitres – and multiplied by four (and then added some to allow for evaporation) to get the correct servings. Likewise, two white onions per person will do the trick, though it is so good you might think I've underestimated.

In Normandy they make a very different, extremely good but far richer onion soup using milk as an ingredient – appropriately enough, as Normandy is another region of milk production. They sweat the onions, but only for about fifteen minutes, until they are light brown. Then they add a glass or two of cider, followed by milk, or a mixture of milk and cream, or indeed a mixture of water and cream. And there you have it, Normandy onion soup.

Pumpkin soup is another delicious dish that can be made with milk, and therefore has lots of richness. Its success depends very much on the variety of the pumpkin, and the best I have found is Potiron Muscade de Provence, which is large and quite flat with dark orange-brown skin and very pronounced curves. In England it goes under the name Iron Bark. I have tried many other varieties of pumpkin but they all seem average compared with this one. Prince of Wales is the next best I've found.

On a medium heat, and in a saucepan with a twenty-five-centimetre diameter, soften one small finely chopped onion for about five minutes. Add four hundred grams of diced pumpkin flesh and soften for a further six to eight minutes. Stir from time to time and season with eight pinches of sea salt, a pinch of freshly ground white pepper and six pinches of caster sugar. Then add six hundred millilitres of whole milk, bring to simmering point and simmer for ten minutes. If you boil the milk too long it will separate, so simmer.

Liquidize the soup with a blender stick until it reaches a smooth velvety consistency. Then taste. And there you have it, unless you want to add a tablespoon or two of crème fraîche. In fact, a couple of tablespoons of kirsch (which has previously been boiled for a few seconds) are a classic addition. Grilled croutons topped with grated cheese would be a delicious accompaniment, and toasted pumpkin seeds can also be added. Of course, you can use butternut squash rather than pumpkin. Jerusalem artichoke soup and parsnip soup can also be done in much the same way.

How bizarre that we head for the supermarket to buy cartons of soup when the homemade variety is cheaper, fast and enjoyable to make, and its taste and nutritional content are superior.

When I was young, it was normal to see my mother dash into the garden and return with her soup ingredients, picked a minute or two earlier. She might be carrying a pumpkin, or courgettes, or beans, or potatoes. Or maybe she'd have a bit of turnip, or some tomatoes or carrots. She would immediately boil some water. I would chop the vegetables. In a pan with butter she would sweat them, that simple but crucial cooking stage in which the starch element is converted into glucose and extra flavours. The British have a beautiful-sounding word for it, *sweetening*. She would sweat, or sweeten, them for three or four minutes, then pour in boiling water. She would simmer the vegetables for about five minutes, or longer if the vegetables were cut large. Then she would finish with a nice dab of sour cream, a good dollop of crème fraîche or a bit of butter, or add chopped herbs like chervil, or even a mix of chervil, tarragon and parsley. It was an incredible soup, all done in less than ten minutes. The taste of the garden – fresh, clean and lovely.

How much easier can cooking be? To create an entirely different texture you can purée the vegetables with a hand-held blender. If you want a bit of Thai, add coconut milk and a lime leaf. The technique remains the same. Once you know how to make one soup – and forget the stock – you can make thousands.

The French have their cherished *poule au pot*, where you drink the liquid first and then eat the chicken. Therefore, I consider chicken soup as being connected to the history of France because of our lovely king Henri IV, who decreed that each peasant family should have *poule au pot* every Sunday. *Poule au pot* may represent French values, but every Jewish boy can relate to a good chicken soup as a medicine during periods of ill health, a soup that is nurturing and reminds him of his mum. The Chinese also consider it to have healing properties; they add grated ginger to their version. Are the curative properties we ascribe to chicken soup a myth?

The British, meanwhile, prefer a dish of roast chicken.

Can we quickly talk about roast chicken? First, you must know that you cannot have a perfect roast chicken. The legs take longer to cook than the breast; you have to compromise. Also, you need a few extra pieces of chopped wing or neck: about 200 grams. This is to make the *jus*. This version involves about an hour's roasting time.

Then, go out of your way to find a good chicken, preferably organic – the real thing that you have to chew. The two best chickens I've found are from the Rhug Estate in Wales and Laverstoke Park Farm in Hampshire. I am delighted that at last we have found such good quality chicken in the UK, although of course it comes at a price.

An hour before cooking, remove the chicken (which weighs, let's say, 1.8kg) from the fridge, giving it time to reach room temperature. Preheat the oven to 230°C. Brush two tablespoons of soft unsalted butter over the chicken. Sear the chicken wings or neck in a little butter in the roasting pan. Place the chicken, breast up, in the tray on top of the chopped wings or neck in a heavy-duty roasting pan/tray that will comfortably accommodate the bird. Season with salt and pepper.

Roast the chicken in the preheated oven for ten to fifteen minutes to gain some colour, then baste. Basting is a term that refers to pouring hot cooking fat and juices over the roasting meat as it cooks. This accomplishes three things: it prevents the skin and meat from drying out; it assists with even browning as the coating of fat is a good conductor of heat; and it creates a tasty, golden skin. Turn down the oven temperature to 160°C and roast for a further thirty to forty-five minutes, with further occasional basting. The chicken should be golden brown all over.

Turn off the oven. Prop the chicken up on its breast and leave it to rest in the oven, with the door ajar, for another fifteen minutes before carving. It may be tempting to bring your chicken to the table immediately, but the resting time allows the juices, which during roasting are pushed to the outside of the meat, to redistribute themselves throughout the flesh, which will provide a more succulent eating experience. You will also find it easier to carve. Then transfer the chicken to a carving board, drain off any excess fat from the roasting tray and place it on the hob. Over a high heat, pour in a glass of water and scrape off any caramelized juices stuck to the bottom of the pan. If more body is required, thicken the *jus* with a quarter teaspoon of arrowroot, cornflour or potato starch dissolved in a teaspoon (15ml) of cold water.

Add whatever combination of herbs you like: rosemary, thyme, sage, marjoram, etc. The juice of a lemon could also be added, and garlic would make a delicious addition.

Now back to the *poule au pot*. A *poule* is an old hen chicken. When she is no longer any good at producing eggs she becomes redundant and finds a new place – in the pot. But where are they? I've looked low and high in supermarkets from Waitrose to Asda but there are no hens to be seen.

If you have a chicken carcass, use it for a soup. A carcass will give you a very nice soup. Simply add water and some seasoning, bring to the boil – skim again – and then simmer for twenty minutes, tasting every now and again. You just want a bubble or two on the surface. Slow, slow, slow. The secret is not to overboil. You want to facilitate a slow exchange of flavour. What you are doing is a sort of blanching process first, followed by a true cooking process in which the flavours will be drawn out. If you boil, the soup will be cloudy and the flavours will be unappetizing. The heat will also destroy many of the vitamins.

Use a whole chicken if you are looking for a soup that is more sumptuous, aromatic and rich in terms of depth of flavour. Again, simmer for about an hour. Look at your chicken soup closely. It's wonderful because you can see all these beautiful golden pools of fat changing shape on the surface.

Poule au pot has always appealed to me. I love the idea of a pot into which you throw your chicken, some big fat carrots, leeks chopped in half lengthways, halved onions, a couple of turnips, clove, a few black peppercorns and a bouquet garni. The ensemble is covered with water, brought to the boil, skimmed then gently simmered until a single bubble rises from the bottom of the pot to the surface.

With *poule au pot*, the chicken flavours grow more and more intense. Can chicken be swapped for belly of pork, knuckle of veal or salt beef? Of course. Whatever you have, throw it in (but if you use a cured meat, soak it first to wash away the salt). Every time you will get that glorious soup with the meat. Don't bother peeling and chopping carrots or, if you are using them, potatoes. Just give them a quick wash and throw them in. If you use non-organic vegetables, though, peel them first as the residues are more concentrated within the skin.

For me there are three types of fast food. There's the one you buy all prepared, whether fresh or frozen, but that doesn't bring you any great pleasure. This type of food tends to be thrown into the microwave and consumed alone in front of the television. The second involves cooking. It could be a quick salad, soup, pasta or a fluffy omelette, even a pan-fried lamb cutlet. Easy and rewarding and not too much washing up. The third one is less obvious, the one in which you need to invest a bit of time in the morning when you get up: slow-cooking. Get the leeks, carrots, onions, garlic and potatoes etc. out, whatever you like. Throw them in a pot or roasting tray, add a less expensive cut of meat, brush with a little olive oil or butter, season lightly with salt and pepper, cover loosely with tin foil and cook slowly for five to six hours at 90°C. Set your oven timer so that the oven switches itself off. When you come home from work your dinner will be ready; all the dish will need is a quick reheat before you eat it. Many underused cuts of meat – for example, belly and shoulder, neck, shins and knuckles – are made succulent by being cooked in this way. Herbs such as rosemary, thyme, sage, marjoram and bayleaf are also good added at the start of cooking. Food that cooks slowly while you are out of the house and is ready as soon as you step through the door is the real fast food.

SEVEN

LE PALAIS

Frying Pan Fiasco

AS A CHILD I HAD A PASSION FOR EATING FOOD BUT WAS NOT particularly interested in cooking it. That changed with age. I was fourteen years old when I progressed from kitchen minion to cook by making my first dish. Actually, the challenge was not entirely successful. It was my first humble pie.

It was a Sunday and, as was usual for the day of rest, a large crowd had come to the house to be fed by my mother, whose kitchen work ensured she did not have a day of rest. I said I'd make dessert: crêpes Suzette, thin pancakes in a sweet sauce of caramel and Grand Marnier.

My recipe drew on two sources. First, my grandmother's recipe for pancakes; second, the sizeable and well-respected cookery book *Larousse Gastronomique*, which told me how much liqueur to add, and when. The Grand Marnier came from my father's drinks cupboard, where cognac and Cointreau were also kept. My father, as you know, was good at carrying bottles up from the cellar but rarely set foot in the kitchen.

Making pancakes is simple. Making good pancakes is not so simple. I messed up one or two to start with, but I felt confident at the stove. I wanted to impress, and I felt intuitive. For instance, I knew I wanted the pancakes to be as light as possible, so I cut down on the suggested amount of flour and added an extra egg and milk. I also added the zest of lemon and orange to the batter for acidity, to balance the sweetness of the dish, and foaming butter, which served two purposes: as an anti-sticking agent, and the nutty flavour would add an extra dimension.

My pancakes were so light that when I tossed them from the pan they flew into the air and didn't want to come down. I was an extremely proud teenager. I made about forty of them which I folded and arranged on a big Pyrex dish. Then I made a light brown caramel, to which I added a knob of butter. I also added to the pan two glasses of orange juice and the juice of a lemon. It sizzled and boiled. I reduced it to the correct consistency – a light syrup – and added the Grand Marnier. The smell was unbelievable. I felt like an alchemist.

By this time the clan of good women cooks had formed a circle around me. They seemed impressed. I poured the sauce over the pancakes then decided to reheat the whole thing on a gas ring. I heated the cognac on the griddle and in an elegant movement a high flame wrapped around the pancakes. It was so perfect.

At that point catastrophe struck. The Pyrex dish exploded into millions of tiny pieces of glass wrapped in sticky Grand Marnier caramel. It was a good lesson in how Pyrex reacts to flames, but my confidence was severely knocked.

It may have been a blow to my ego (and French egos are quite large), but it didn't put me off cooking, or rather wanting to learn about cooking. Nowadays many men whip up the family meal, but back then it was unheard of. I would ask my mother plenty of questions about food and she would answer them, but there was never really a point at which she invited me to cook. On the other hand, it was assumed that my sisters, Françoise and Martine, would one day have to cook for their families, so for them it was a different story. My mother taught them how to make dishes. She didn't teach me, as such, because she would never have thought for one moment that I would end up cooking, let alone become a chef. If my father, brothers or uncles had been chefs I would have been encouraged in a different way. But there were never any male chefs in the family, just great women cooks. My role was to peel and chop and quickly move as my mother zoomed from stove to surface and back again.

It was decided – by my teachers – that I should be a draughtsman. This is the career I was set to follow, until I discovered that in order to draw plans there are two fundamental requirements: logic and a mathematical mind. I had neither. I also hated (I still do) squares, circles and triangles, upon which many designs are based. I much prefer asymmetrical objects, anything misshapen. So that particular career came to an end.

There was a moment in my life which, with hindsight, sent a clear message that my future lay in food. I was about seventeen years old and, having worked hard somewhere or other, I had about a year's savings in my right-hand pocket and was feeling rich. I was in Besançon and happened to stroll past a Michelin-starred restaurant called Le Poker d'As, as in the ace in a poker game. I'd never been into such a place; with our parents we had only been to small local bistros. I caught the cooking smells that were coming from the kitchen. At that precise moment the hunger clock that ticks in the belly of every Frenchman struck. It was twelve o'clock, the hour when tools are put down and the French head for the table. Layer upon layer of divine scents hit me, and there and then I knew that I would have to go into the restaurant.

The maître d' greeted me and I asked him, 'What are you cooking at the moment?'

'The special of the day is veal kidneys in Hermitage [red wine] sauce,' he said, and I ordered it.

There was even a wine specialist, a sommelier, and a kind one at that. He talked passionately about the wine he was about to serve me, explaining why it would be the best accompaniment for the dish. 'After this meal, Monsieur, you will feel richer rather than poorer.' Considering I was about to spend my year's savings on an expensive meal, I thought he was joking and I laughed nervously.

The sommelier brought me a lovely half-bottle of Guigal, the Côte rôtie from northern Rhone which is produced from two grapes: peppery Syrah mellowed by Viognier (if a third grape is added the wine cannot be classified as Côte rôtie). Along with Chapoutier, Guigal is one of the greatest wine-makers in the valley.

I sat there feeling extremely content. I had never been into such a classy restaurant. Le Poker d'As was rustic but elegant; the white table-cloths were cut from the finest cloth and well pressed, the carefully folded linen napkins were embossed with the restaurant's logo. I felt I was about to embrace a special moment in my life.

Then the food arrived at my table for one. The smell came from the plate to my nose and I knew I was about to enjoy what I had smelled being cooked when I was on the pavement outside.

I had never eaten veal kidneys before. My mother cooked pig and lamb kidneys, which are delicious but have a very strong flavour. What I ate at Le Poker d'As that day had a significant impact on me and my taste buds. The kidneys were so perfectly cooked, done by the hand of a master. Lightly caramelized on the outside, inside they were firm and pink, the taste delicate and refined. The sauce, as its smell suggested, was a collection of layers of flavour: the sweetness of the kidneys, the controlled acidity of sherry vinegar, the depth and richness of the wine, and the herbs I couldn't quite identify. I was in the presence of an artist and a magician. How could he create so many superb layers of flavour, all separate but fused into a long divine taste?

That day, not only did I taste a dish I had not tasted before, I also discovered haute cuisine. Not just a single taste, but layers of taste; and then the deliciousness of the wine complementing and enhancing the food. There was a completeness to the experience. Everything from the warmth and professionalism of the restaurant staff to the elegance of the room was so *right*. The sommelier had not lied. When I walked out of Le Poker d'As, and blown my year's savings, although I'd just settled the bill I felt richer than when I had entered the restaurant.

Maybe it's a mistake to compare haute cuisine to family cooking. My mother's food is delicious and wholesome and it has influenced many of my dishes. Haute cuisine has a more complex build-up, like those layers of flavour that stay on the palate, sometimes for a blissful minute, sometimes for hours, sometimes for years in your mind. Of course, both require a good cook or a great chef. I love Beethoven as much as I love Led Zeppelin and the Rolling Stones but I would never compare the composer to the bands. One day I might crave the Stones, another day I might want to listen to Beethoven. Likewise, there are times when I yearn for good home cooking, and other times when haute cuisine does the job.

Excuse me, please, I'm hungry and fancy some lunch. I'll come back to this.

It was around about this time, when I was seventeen years old, that I worked for the first time in a restaurant. I was so happy in the job that, coupled with my joy at dining in Le Poker d'As, I should have known I was destined for the restaurant business, but I saw it as nothing more than a summer job.

In order to earn some cash during the school holidays I had been to see the manager of a brasserie in Besançon to see if he had a vacancy I could fill for a couple of months. The brasserie, which was massive and situated within the town's well-used bus station, had about forty tables occupied mostly by customers who wanted a speedy something or other to eat or drink before boarding and heading off.

'You can be a waiter,' said the manager, before telling me what my salary would be – meagre, I am sure – and giving me an apron.

The brasserie had a long bar behind which two barmen whizzed. Its dining area was invisibly divided into four sections, each of which comprised ten tables; there were four waiters, and each of us was in charge of a section. It was not a grand place. In fact it was pretty cheap, though it did well at serving massive volumes of food. But I loved that restaurant. I loved the way its ambience changed as the day developed. I arrived at six every morning and turned the heating up, then the coffee machine on, and the staff began the shift with that wonderful French ritual of coffee into which croissant is dipped. We cleaned the room and dressed the tables, then dressed ourselves to look the part. I wore my black gilet with twelve pockets, a white shirt and a bow tie and a long white apron.

Then the first customers arrived for a kick-start. A few ordered a glass of wine as a pick-me-up; one or two went for the more alcoholic booster of schnapps made from Mirabelle plum or prune. Yes, that was France. But most wanted a *petit noir*, that enlivening shot of espresso, or a *petit crème*. Then their buses pulled into the terminal and the customers left to become passengers, some of them refreshed in a sober way, others a little tipsy and cheerful from the booze.

When the thin paper tablecloths were produced it meant it was lunchtime. The smell of cooked food now wafted from the kitchen and filled the dining room. Come noon, the atmosphere of the brasserie turned noisy as it became busier, and we had to work fast, pushing ourselves to cater for the traffic coming in through the three entrance doors.

There was no official training at the brasserie. It was in-at-the-deep-end teaching. I learned how to make an espresso, how to serve wine, and other basics of waiting. I realized the value of speed and became quick at the job, dashing from table to table with steaming cups of *café crème*, croissants and snacks.

I took considerable interest in the satisfaction of my customers. During my breaks I shined the glasses and polished the stainless-steel knives and forks. They were so ancient they had lost their shine but I polished with optimism nevertheless. While I prepared my section with enthusiasm, the other waiters would nip outside for a breather, to smoke Gitanes or Gauloises and squeeze in a coffee. They would peer through the window at me, giving me strange looks because they were puzzled by my devotion to duty. Yes, I was devoted. I loved it.

The chefs put the food as well as its garnish into serving dishes, which were then carried with plates to the table and placed in front of the customer so that he could help himself. Not in my section. Rather than plonking the dishes and plates in front of the customers I served *à l'Anglaise*, using a spoon and fork to put the food on to the plate at the table. The skill of this serving style is not to spill sauce on the customer's tie. I didn't simply plonk a glass and carafe of wine in front of the customer either. Instead, I elegantly poured the wine from the carafe at the table. Beneath the carafe I held a napkin to collect any spilt drops of the cheap wine. I'd seen this impressive napkin trick on television.

It was proper service with a great big smile, and it was lovingly done. I was well rewarded for it too as soon I became the waiter who received the largest tips, which made my smile even bigger. I also gained the loyalty of certain customers, who always came to sit in the section where I worked because they wanted to be served by me. Loyalty, I discovered, is crucial in this business. What a shame there were no flowers on the table to help along the romance and bring colour and fragrance.

Now, there was one particular customer, a middle-aged businessman, who would pop in for lunch twice a week. One day he appeared, took his seat, and I started to serve him stylishly, just as I'd done with him previously and just as I did with my other customers. However, this time when I arrived at the man's table with the dishes of food and began to serve on to his plate, he suddenly looked up at me, his face red with rage, and shouted, 'I don't come here for Michelin star bloody nonsense, OK?'

I stepped back, astonished. I could sense other customers looking up from their plates to watch the action from their ringside seats.

'I come here to eat,' the man continued, 'so just put the food on the table and let me eat . . . and go away.'

I got the message, obviously, and put the dishes on the table so that he could serve himself.

I found the incident traumatic, so much so that I remember it vividly some forty years later. The man was clearly irritable, but, with hindsight, his angry outburst could have killed my career there and then. I was shocked, offended and hurt. I had not yet decided to become a chef or a restaurateur, but that ticking off could have sent a message to my teenage brain: keep out of the restaurant business.

The way I worked in that brasserie was not really about service as such. It was connected to what I had learned from my mother: it was about giving the customer a special moment, doing my best for the guest, regardless of the fact that the environment was cheap. I tried to make my section as lovely as possible. If I was going to do something, I wanted to do it well. There may have been one ill-tempered customer who didn't like the treatment, but the customers on the nine other tables in my section were very pleasant that day. I made them feel damned important. They were appreciative that their average food was brought to them with attention and thoughtfulness. They admired the effort and the attempt at elegance. I am a people's person. I love to interact with others and to make them happy.

———

For a couple of years I moved from one job to another, never once contemplating a career in restaurants, just trying to find my little talent. For a while I was a trainee nurse at St Anne's Hospital in Besançon. I worked in the department that treated young sufferers of leukaemia. I started off by changing bedpans. When required, I would help turn the bedridden patients on to their sides. Often the patients had terrible bedsores and were so weakened they couldn't turn by themselves. I was motivated by a strong urge to be a Mother Teresa figure. I desperately wanted to help. I would form friendships with these kids who, God bless them, had come to the hospital to die. The nurses were tough, exacting and hardened by years of caring for dying young people, but the experience took its toll. Emotionally, I could not cope. I couldn't deal with it, and I left.

One of my many jobs was in a clothing factory. My role was to cut clothes, but I also became the factory's part-time catalogue model when a boss deemed me to be the perfect size to show off his garments. Factory work I found utterly demoralizing. Clock in, clock out. You're just a number. It was a low period of my life. It taught me a valuable lesson: mediocrity is probably the greatest evil of all. One has to find one's talent. Everyone has got one, I was convinced. I had to find mine.

It happened one summer night in Besançon when I was twenty years old. It was a perfect summer night: warm, a light breeze in the foliage, the moon and stars just right. It was late at night, about eleven o'clock, and I wandered into La Place Grandvelle. Right in the middle of the square was the best restaurant in Besançon, Le Palais de la Bière, and that night it was providing the setting for that clichéd picture of French life. Outside on the terrace couples were cuddling, holding hands and whispering, 'Je t'aime.' Other people were engaged in lively conversation. A few were heatedly debating politics, the state of the economy and football. Among the candlelit tables the waiters glided, dressed in immaculate Bordeaux jackets, attending to every guest's needs. The maître d'hôtel, dressed in black tie and a starched white cravat, was carving meat with precise and elegant strokes. Others flambéed crêpes Suzette in proper silver dishes.

Oh what a spectacle! I watched, mesmerized. At that moment I knew I wanted to be the chef who made this wonderful food. Not the waiter who gave it to the guests, but the craftsman who created these extraordinary dishes. The urge was powerful. At last I had found my *raison d'être*. I wanted to be in the business. Restaurants were the life for me.

Alas, my age was a hindrance. I was too old by a few years to become a chef's apprentice. Potential employers would have looked at my CV and concluded that I was the sort of person who had drifted from one job to another, when in fact the truth was . . . well, that I had drifted from one job to another. Nevertheless I applied in writing for a job at Le Palais and was asked to go for an interview with the owner, Monsieur Spitz.

I arrived at the restaurant as requested and waited at a table for the boss to find time to talk to me. As I told you at the beginning of this book, square-jawed, spiky-haired Monsieur Spitz was an impressive-looking man in his well-made pinstripe suits. He was all the more imposing surrounded by the many diplomas and awards that hung on the wall – a bastion of the French culinary establishment. The old school.

Eventually he joined me at the table but before he'd had a chance to say much my eagerness became uncontrollable.

'Monsieur Spitz, you must take me on,' I found myself telling him. 'I will be a great chef one day. Please, you must give me a job.'

He said nothing, just stood up and walked away from the table. I waited for him to return. He did not. I waited some more. Still he did not come back to the table.

I said to the manager, 'Why is monsieur not coming back?'

The manager said, 'Maybe you offended him.'

I left dejected and broken. I had just found my gift and my passion, only to be told to go away.

A day or so later a friend who knew Monsieur Spitz told me that the owner had been unimpressed because I was too intense and forthright. *Me?* I suppose I might have been a *little* over-exuberant. Of course I was, silly me.

I said to myself, 'Raymond, come on. Pluck up your courage and ask for a second interview.' I asked for it and got it. This time when I sat across the table from the imposing Monsieur Spitz, I tried to reason with him in a calm voice.

'Monsieur,' I said, 'please take me on. Just give me a chance to get into your industry. Please, I'll do anything.'

'OK,' he said, 'I'll give you a job as a cleaner. Understand, young man, you are too old to be a chef. Young people start at the age of fourteen in the kitchen. It would be too hard and you would never catch up.'

At twenty I was on the shelf, yet I was happy to be given this opportunity. I am telling you, I cleaned that place like it had never been cleaned. I buffed the gigantic mirrors until they gleamed like the *galeries des glaces* in Versailles. The toilets were perfect. My God, they were the reason to excuse yourself from the table. The bonus was that everyone loved me because the job was so well done it never had to be done twice. I gave my best and took pride in my work, gaining the trust and respect of the team. I became part of it.

After three months I was promoted to become a washer up of glasses. The idea of washing up might not thrill everyone, but I was so happy because it represented progression. It also meant I could increase my knowledge. The glasses were magnificent, all hand-blown in many shapes, specially designed around the characters of each region's wine. They were so delicate you could almost bend them. Each one was a precious and beautiful thing. As the glasses came back to be washed up I would smell the dregs of wine and learn about colour, grape variety and age. I tried to memorize everything and kept diaries of my olfactory experiences.

I developed a technique to polish the glasses using steam from a pot of boiling water, and then shining with a cloth. One part of my cloth held the base of the glass, the other was buried inside. Then, at great speed but with no pressure, I would let the cloth shine the glass, rotating in tiny concentric circles. In a few seconds the glass would come out shining. I cut down breakages by 40 per cent. The boss loved me, the maître d'hôtel loved me, the sommelier loved me. The other members of staff had never seen someone so dedicated.

I started to dream about food. I connected food with everything, not just instant gratification. I read books connecting food with science, politics, religion, history, gastronomy, sex, geography, farming and society; to me, food was linked to them all. After a twelve-hour service I would go back to my digs in the poorest part of Besançon (rue Battant) and there with two gas rings and a small oven I would cook for my friends.

My life became driven by an overpowering passion for food. I was compelled to catch up with the knowledge of this wonderful world, to immerse myself in it.

Eventually I was given a real break at Le Palais. I was made *commis debarasseur* – a runner. My new job involved carrying the silver dishes from the kitchen to the tables. At that time food wasn't served plated up but on silver dishes topped with bell-shaped silver lids which were lifted to reveal the food on the plates. I was not allowed to come into contact with the guests, though. This was the role of the chef de partie (that is, the chef in charge of a section, be it Meat, Fish, Starters, Garnish or Pastry). For twelve to fifteen hours a day I carried those heavy silver trays. The job was exhausting and very hard for a slight Frenchman.

In the factory where I had previously worked, we were treated like numbers. Here, at Le Palais, Monsieur Spitz actually addressed us by numbers rather than by our names. I was number two. The chef de partie might say to me, 'You can take a short break, number two,' or 'Take this to table twelve, number two.' (It would have taken much more than that to dampen my enthusiasm.) Every morning Monsieur Spitz would inspect our hands, the pleats of our trousers and the whiteness of our shirts. If you were one minute late you missed your break and worked an eighteen-hour day. So you learned to arrive clean, on time and perfectly prepared. It was at Le Palais that I learned about the importance of details. I had already learned that service, warmth and a welcoming smile are just as important as food. Not less, not more, but just as important. Few chefs knew that.

My new job meant that I could also taste the food and observe the chefs – a brigade of fifteen – as they worked away. Each morning had its own pace and rituals and everyone had a role, depending on his skills. The young apprentice would peel the potatoes, the commis would turn them and the chef de partie would cook them – there was a very strong hierarchy.

Soon I was promoted again, to commis, and was given my first Bordeaux jacket with red epaulettes. I was the proudest man on earth, and I was also closer to the kitchen.

The head chef at Le Palais was a truly gifted cook but he was also a giant of a man with a fierce temper. He had dark brown eyes which seemed to turn even darker when he was angry. The hairs on his moustache actually bristled when he was furious. Little things, harmless comments, could fill him with rage. He was a man who would not have done well under modern-day employment laws.

I would taste his sauces, and almost invariably they were superb. When they were not so good, I pointed out that it was too rich or that it might benefit from spice. 'Chef, it might be too thin,' or, 'Chef, it's a little too creamy.' I treated Chef as if he were my peer when of course he was my boss. When I voiced my opinions about his food I believed I was doing nothing more than simply sharing my thoughts with a colleague. I took it even further by asking him if he could please tell me when new menus were coming in, and I'd suggest some ideas for dishes. He would give me a dark look but no more. I didn't set out to upset him, I was not meaning to be impudent, I was just so excited and enthusiastic about the whole business of food.

He suffered my remarks until one lunch service, a busy one, when I tasted a sauce and said, 'Chef, I wonder if this is a little too salty. What do you think?'

His look darkened and his moustache bristled. The frying pan, which was an extension of his fist, hit me hard on the jaw, leaving me dizzy. Whoosh, and then whack. I fell.

Luckily it was not a hot pan or it would have left me with an odd-shaped scar. The pain was excruciating, as you can imagine. I can still feel it now, if I think too hard about the episode.

I went home to recover. Then I received a visit from Monsieur Spitz's son, M. Bernard, who helped his father run the restaurant. He offered words of sympathy. These were immediately followed by a real telling off. 'Raymond,' he said, 'how could you do it? Do you realize that Chef is the power behind this house? He is the man who made a name for the restaurant. He put a roof over my head. He paid for my children's education. He is the greatest part of Le Palais. He is the creative force, and you tell him that he doesn't know how to cook?'

I had not considered these things.

'You're out,' M. Bernard continued softly. 'You can't come back to Le Palais. But I will help you because I know you are a good young man. You are good inside, and I know you love what you are doing, and somehow I know you will succeed. I am going to help you find a position.'

He did find me a position, as a waiter, not in France but across the Channel in England, at the Rose Revived, an inn with a restaurant in the Oxfordshire village of Newbridge. M. Bernard certainly wanted to create some distance. It was hard to be expatriated; it was even harder at such a young age not to be able to get work in France. But my adventure was about to begin. It has yet to end.

Taste has its drawbacks, but I stand by what I said: Chef's sauce was a tiny bit too salty that day.

Although M. Bernard was getting rid of me, I had a great deal of admiration for him, which did not diminish. I felt that he was acting under his father's instructions. M. Bernard was a fair person, a good man and a good boss who cared for his employees. After all, he didn't have to help me. I still know him. I see him when I go back to Besançon. However tough this school of learning might have been, I was grateful. It has helped me through my life because it gave me discipline, will power, and an understanding of teamwork and the importance of precision and detail.

A few years after I opened Le Manoir I invited M. Bernard to come and stay. It was a thank you for what he had confidently said to me: 'I know you will succeed.' Even though I was nursing a bruised jaw, his words had been encouraging and uplifting. When M. Bernard arrived at Le Manoir he was impressed, to say the least. He could see for himself that I had moved on from the frying pan incident.

We ate, reminisced and laughed. He stayed at Le Manoir in the best suite. The next day we went to Brasserie Blanc, and then we ate some patisserie at Maison Blanc. I must admit I showed off a little bit.

All Year Round
Les Crêpes
Pancakes

Pancakes were my first attempt at cooking, and instead of impressing my mum, I turned this dish into a minor disaster when I chose a Pyrex dish to warm them up in. I put the dish over direct heat and it exploded.

Serves (Yield): 12 pancakes
Difficulty rating: ● ● ○
Preparation time: 15 minutes
Cooking time: 20 minutes
Special equipment: A cast-iron pancake pan is ideal, but a non-stick pan will do.

PLANNING AHEAD

The pancake batter can be prepared half a day in advance, and the pancakes can be cooked a few hours ahead.

INGREDIENTS

100g plain flour, sifted
110g (2) eggs
30g (2 tbsp) caster sugar

1g (1 pinch) sea salt
350ml whole milk
40g butter
½ orange or lemon
non-scented oil (such as sunflower or rapeseed) for greasing the pan
caster sugar and lemon juice, to serve

METHOD
MAKING THE BATTER:

Put the flour in a mixing bowl, make a well in the centre and add the eggs, sugar and salt. Whisk the milk in little by little, slowly incorporating the flour until you have a smooth batter. Strain through a conical sieve into a bowl. Heat the butter on a medium heat until it reaches foaming stage. (★1) When it is foaming, pour the butter into the mixture, whisking continuously. Finally, grate the zest of the orange or lemon into the batter. Leave the mixture to rest (★2) at room temperature for 30 minutes.

COOKING THE PANCAKES:

Lightly grease the pan with a tiny bit of oil. Place the pan on a medium heat, then, when hot, (★3) pour in a small ladleful of batter and rotate so that it covers the whole surface. Cook for 30–40 seconds, then turn over with a spatula and cook the other side for another 30 seconds. Reserve on a tray, overlapping the pancakes. (★4) Proceed with the remaining batter.

SERVING:

Sprinkle with caster sugar and lemon juice before serving to your guests.

Chef's notes:

★1   Butter starts foaming at around 155°C, at which point the solid particles start to turn golden, resulting in a wonderful nutty flavour. Whisk the foaming butter into the batter mixture. As well as adding flavour, it also helps stop the pancakes sticking.

*2   Whisking the mixture 'works' the gluten within the flour, which is perfectly correct. However, the gluten then needs to rest in order for your pancakes to have the perfect texture. If you cook the pancakes straight away, the recently developed gluten may give them a leathery texture.

*3   It is crucial to reach the correct heat. Too cool, and the pancakes will be pale and rubbery. Too hot, and they will spit and probably burn. The thickness of the pancake is equally important. Too thin and the pancake will have tiny little air holes. Too thick and the pancake will be dense.

*4   If you are cooking them in advance, cool them first on a pastry rack and then stack them. They will stick together if stacked up and then left to cool.

VARIATIONS

Of course, there are thousands of other ways to serve your pancakes: with honey, jam, fresh fruit, and so on. Caramelized apples with caramel sauce would also be delicious.

EIGHT

ENGLAND

To the Rose (with Thorns)

I LEFT FRANCE ONE DAY IN JUNE 1972. MY MOTHER HAD WITNESSED my driving skills (I'd pulverized two cars in eight months) so she gave me a St Christopher which I thanked her for and then pinned to the dashboard of my blue Renault Gordini.

Quite embarrassing really. The St Christopher, that is, not the car. In the early seventies, the Renault Gordini was considered *the* car to drive. Mine wasn't. I bought it cheap because it had been in so many accidents. I never asked for advice and I got what I deserved. The axle had twisted so I had to hold the steering wheel with all my strength to stop it driving to the left. The radiator was a sieve. Mr Clarkson would not have approved – well, maybe he might.

I was a crazy, carefree twenty-two-year-old driver who raced along the roads, recklessly overtaking anyone in my path. I would never allow myself to be overtaken. A few miles down the road, however, they would over-take me as I stood next to my car, bonnet up, trying to remove the scorching radiator cap to top up the steaming radiator with water. Other drivers won't leave home without a road atlas; I didn't embark on a journey without a canteen filled with five litres of water.

I was particularly proud of the eight lights that were attached to the front grille. They looked cool, I thought. Even when dipped they had the power to momentarily blind oncoming drivers, pedestrians and unblinkered horses.

I spilled my Renault on to the ferry at Calais and made my way up the ship's stairs and into the restaurant. As I sailed away from French shores, away from the gastronomic capital of the world, away from the land of sweet-smelling *boulangeries*, busy bistros and well-stocked charcuteries, as I sailed away and took a seat at a table I thought a meal would be the perfect way to congratulate myself for making it this far. What sort of food, I wondered, did Britain have to offer?

A grey-faced man with greasy hair, swamped in an oversized uniform – a waiter, but unlike any other waiter I had ever come across – asked what would I like. My English was poor. I pointed at the menu's picture of fish and chips – I had heard they were the gastronomic treat of Britain – and smiled inanely. Five minutes later the waiter returned with a plate. There was a smell on that plate unlike any other smell I had known. What worried me was that the plate was still a few yards away at the time.

Up until that point, when it came to vinegars my nasal senses had been treated to the perfumes of beautifully reduced white wine, cider and sherry vinegars. Here on the ferry I was hit by the sharp vapours of malt vinegar. A pool of the stuff had been used to drown my piece of fish. I started to cough.

It sounds ridiculous, but I have never quite recovered from that split second when malt vinegar attacked my senses. We all have food we cannot stomach. Malt vinegar is mine.

I stared at the plate and the ingredients on it: fish that may well have left the sea a decade earlier and spent the intervening years in a deep freeze; chips that had been cooked beyond crunch texture; and all of it made soggy by malt vinegar. Curiosity encouraged me to have a mouthful or two but the dish had been killed by the vinegar. I looked out to sea and as I watched the gulls swooping and diving for their lunch I decided I could go hungry.

What I later discovered was that, sadly, my pool of fish and chips was representative of the standard of restaurant food being served in Britain in the seventies. In fact, the food in post-war England was so bad that Raymond Postgate, the originator of *The Good Food Guide*, had founded a Society for the Prevention of Cruelty to Food. I was about to enter a culture that was so very different to the one I had known and adored.

Still, I remained upbeat as I left the ferry and began the drive to the Rose Revived. I zoomed through Kent, listening to Elton John singing 'Rocket Man' on the radio.

At that point Britain was not in a good way, economically fragile and run by the trade unions. Unemployment had topped one million for the first time since the 1930s. The nation, under the leadership of Conservative Prime Minister Edward Heath, was not in a hole, it was in an abyss. Yet the countryside was extremely pleasant. When I stopped every now and again to top up the radiator, friendly women smiled at me and called me 'love'. I thought, 'Fantastic, I'm going to be very popular here.'

Ordinarily, the drive from Dover to Oxfordshire would take a few hours. Mine lasted three days. The problem was that no one understood my accent when I asked for directions. I'd pull up and with a look of fear in my eyes I'd ask, 'Hoxfor, please?' I was intimidated by the British pronunciation of aitches, and in those early days I tended to add an aitch to words that began with a vowel. (Still do, in fact. While we're at it, for *the* I say *zer*. Don't get me on to *anger* and *hunger*. And I say *here* when I mean *there*, which over the years has confused staff and friends when I have told them I'll meet them *here* when I mean *there*, and vice versa.) The pedestrians, stunned by the glare of my eight headlights, just looked at me, baffled. They did one of three things: pretend they had not heard me and walk away; stare at me, then shake their heads before walking away; or try to give me directions that my very poor English could not comprehend.

The exhausting journey, combined with those hourly episodes when

I had my head under the bonnet, helped me build up an appetite. At one stage I promised myself I would find a bistro in the next town I came to. I believed that the big wide world was filled with little bistros. Sure enough, in the next town I spotted a restaurant that had a façade of red and white – the two colours that symbolize the bistro. I parked the car and eagerly hurried in for lunch. I could just make out the bistro's name: Wimpy.

'Wine list?' I enquired, thinking I would treat myself to a glass of something red.

Eventually reality kicked in: it was not a little bistro, I was in a burger bar. By the early seventies Wimpy had become an enormous chain with about two thousand outlets all over the world, but its global presence had passed me by. There may have been Wimpy bars in London, Paris (doubtful) and Amsterdam but we didn't have one in Besançon.

When I walked into the Wimpy I was happily convinced that I had found a comfort zone. At first I was mystified by the big plastic red tomato on the table. I studied it and discovered that it contained ketchup – another new experience for me as it did not exist in Franche-Comté. I ordered the fish, perhaps in an attempt to reassure myself that the ferry food was a one-off case of inedible mush. After all, I had good reason to be optimistic: Great Britain was surrounded by the sea.

Wimpy described my dish as 'battered fish'. I tell you, it was so battered you couldn't recognize it as fish. Then there was the shape of it. The malt vinegar on the ferry had been an alien smell; the shape of this fish was an alien sight. It was square! In France I had seen fish gutted and grilled and fried and chopped up. But in all my life I had never seen a square fish. Of course, as I ate I realized it was a piece of processed flesh. I tucked in gingerly while customers on other tables devoured gooey-bapped cheeseburgers.

———

I had been looking forward to seeing the centre of Oxford as I had read up on it before leaving France. I was by no means disappointed when eventually I got there. It is a beautiful city with a wonderful atmosphere. On the day I drove through, undergraduates filled the streets, milling around with big smiles on their faces – the end of term was near. I thought, 'Wow, what an elegant place.' I had a steak lunch in Le Mitre. In those days, steak (with a little Stilton to follow) was one of the few dishes you could enjoy in British restaurants. They were the only safe things on the menu. Then I set off on the last leg of my journey to the Rose Revived.

I remember fondly the evening when I arrived at Newbridge (which, I learned later, derived its name from when the town's bridge was rebuilt about five hundred years ago). In my little car I zipped over the ancient hump-backed bridge and there was the Rose Revived, a well-established inn and restaurant with six guest bedrooms.

On the lawn in front of the inn, customers were taking advantage of the summer warmth and the fading sunshine. They were sitting on the grass drinking pints of beer. There was the sound of laughter and clinking glasses. All in all, it was a happy picture. In France I had read up on England and the sight that greeted me now was what I had expected from my knowledge of the country through books. It was quaint. It was fantastic. I parked slowly as the car park was full, one eye on the merry people on the grass, another eye on my steaming bonnet.

As I entered the Rose Revived the sunlight cut beautiful shapes on the perfectly polished flagstone floor. The walls were painted red and there were red tablecloths on the tables. A few more people were sharing their first or last pint of the day around the beautiful inglenook fireplaces. Behind the customers' laughter and giggles of women a Carpenters track came rattling through the speakers. In time I would realize that there was always a Carpenters track rattling through the speakers. My arrival in Britain coincided with the pair's album *A Song For You*, and this was played over and over again. The album included the track 'It's Gonna Take Some Time' – a message perhaps to hungry customers who were waiting for their food. I would feel lost if I stepped inside there today and did not hear Karen Carpenter singing something like 'Bless the Beasts and Children'.

Lastly, there was the smell of the place. Kitchen odours, a layer of cigarette smoke, a layer of pipe smoke – in those days, the majority rather than the minority smoked – then, for a moment, another aroma, again an alien smell, this one a strong one. It was the whiff of Cona coffee. The machine went on in the morning and for the rest of the day the brew was kept on a steady heat so that the coffee evaporated and joined the smells of tobacco smoke.

I spotted a man in the corner of the room. He cut a strange figure. He was tall, with long blond hair descending to his shoulders, and he wore black trousers that stopped an inch or two above his ankles so that customers could get a good look at his socks. This was topped with a black jacket with sleeves rolled up. This man was called Robert, and he was the maître d'hôtel. When I worked at Le Palais de la Bière there was a morning ritual in which the staff stood to attention and underwent an inspection by the proprietor. Clothes, hair and fingernails. Robert would have failed.

As I tried to take in his appearance, I became gripped by what Robert was doing with his hands. He was so focused on this task that he had not yet noticed me. He had two bowls in front of him both of which contained remnants of what I failed to identify as trifle, and using his right hand he was scooping the contents of one bowl into the other. He was trying to make one trifle out of two. He created a great slop of custard and whipped cream. He then pressed the top with his two hands, added a layer of biscuits and soaked them with sherry, then piped on whipped cream, and finally he gracelessly lobbed on a few glacé cherries. For me, this grievous lack of respect for food was disturbing. He was to be my boss.

I smiled politely at Robert. He smiled back. But a voice inside my head was yelling, 'Oh my God. What's happening?'

The Rose Revived was owned by Mr and Mrs Colbeck and their

daughter Jenny. I felt that he liked me and she didn't. I had no clue what Jenny thought. Mr Colbeck was a lovely man, a *bon viveur* who wore trousers that clashed with his jacket. He was also very fair to his staff. Mrs Colbeck was not so popular; her style was distant. At times I felt she was almost autocratic and that I was the transparent waiter in her presence.

When Mr Colbeck shook my hand for the first time he said, 'Raymond, welcome to our place. We hope you enjoy it.' I presented him with a bottle of our local alcohol, which is made from the root of the *gentiane* flower. It is 60 per cent alcohol and a true digestif. It is bitter, certainly an acquired taste, and best taken in extremely small doses. A short while later he said, 'Let's open that lovely bottle of liqueur you gave me.' Before I could tell him it was not a liqueur he had poured himself a large glass, knocked it back and was coughing his heart out. This he followed with, 'Very nice. Lovely.' He was being dishonest but kind. It was hardly the most successful introduction.

The good news was that between the *bon viveur* Mr Colbeck and his frosty wife was their daughter Jenny. She was good to the staff, always the one who helped people out with problems and tried to create a good atmosphere. She helped her mother run the inn, its guest facilities and the restaurant.

I began, as M. Bernard had arranged, as a waiter at the Rose Revived. I would love to say that my time there was joyful beyond belief but that would not be entirely accurate. There were other members of staff who simply did not like the French, and I was the only Frenchman. Wages were bad and the accommodation was very poor. And there was a startling contrast between life at Le Palais and the Rose Revived because of the difference in attitude towards waiting staff.

In France, I had been proud to be a waiter. It was a profession that was by and large respected by the customer. If you chose to devote your life to serving people it was not frowned upon. However, I soon discovered that if you were a waiter in England you had no status. You had nothing. You were merely a servant, and service was something that was pretty bad in this country. If you were in service, you were entrenched at the bottom layer of society. You were irrelevant.

People were pushed into service; they took on the job reluctantly rather than with pride and enthusiasm. I had entered an industry that comprised servants, many of whom did not really want to serve.

It was an odd thing, to be a waiter in England. For the most part customers were pleasant and polite, but they were often dismissive. We were not meant to exist; we were certainly not supposed to enter into conversation with the guests. At Le Palais I had been told not to talk to the guests, but at least the guests gave me friendly smiles. In England there were customers who would not have stooped so low as to look at a waiter. My induction was downright peculiar because I felt transparent.

Moreover, although Great Britain produced world-class hoteliers, there were no great chefs as the restaurant was seen as merely an appendage. The profession was full of poor managers, bosses who couldn't communicate and were rarely trained. There was no passion in the kitchen and home-cooked food had disappeared. There was certainly no violence in the kitchen — such emotion had long ago disappeared. There was no proper structure either. Young people thought twice before becoming a waiter or a chef.

And what of the food at the Rose Revived? Aside from the dessert trifle, as manhandled by Robert, customers dined on prawn cocktail, avocado prawn, beef stroganoff and steak and chips (the safe option). Colman's sauces and stock cubes were relied upon in the cooking of the main dishes. Much of it was either frozen or came out of a bottle or jar. There was white sliced bread and white rolls, straight out of a factory. Curry, which had some years to go before it became Britain's most popular dish, also featured on the menu.

Yes, the food sold, but it was uninspiring. The Rose Revived was living perilously on its past reputation when the cook had been Jenny leading a small team of Cordon Bleu girls who understood and gave good home cooking from local ingredients. The kitchen was then handed over to the head chef David. After I watched and tasted I began to think that he either didn't give a damn or was blissfully ignorant of the joys of cooking, or maybe he had lost it along the way, defeated by the system. He prepared dishes days in advance and then froze them.

The kitchen at the Rose Revived was certainly not a place to inspire creativity. It was a sterile world, full of aluminium, white tiles and depressing neon lights. Passion had long since died in that kitchen. Day after day David went through a monotonous, mind-numbing ritual of reaching for a plate and plonking on top of it one ingredient next to another before handing the plate to a waiter. He had long ago lost all desire. Nearby, streams and rivers were filled with delicious trout and pike, but David served frozen fish. And he was no different from many other chefs of that era.

In those days, as I said, if I ever went out for dinner I tended to have just the steak and cheese. Although I could occasionally stomach bad food, the thought of drinking Cona coffee, simmered for hours, filled me with horror. So at the end of a meal I would ask the waiter for a pot of boiling water, claiming that I was ill and needed to make my own special brew of something or other for medicinal purposes. Once I had the hot water I would then produce from my pocket some decent filter coffee and make myself a cup of the real stuff.

In the kitchen at the Rose Revived I befriended David the chef. After the frying pan episode in France I'd learned how to treat chefs with utter diplomacy. I told him that I enjoyed cooking and he invited me to experiment by preparing one or two dishes when service was quiet. I made *coq au vin* using my mother's recipe, baby turbot grilled on a bed of fennel and *aromates* (herbs and spices) with essence of red wine and *beurre blanc*, and a good onion soup. They were good enough to impress Mrs Colbeck. It was a big moment for me to cook for paying customers, but it came to nothing. I was still just a waiter, albeit a good one.

In very little time Jenny became a friend, then a close friend, then so close we decided to marry. I felt that Mrs Colbeck was unimpressed that her daughter should marry a mere waiter, even if he was French. Although I had cooked one or two dishes at the Rose Revived which had seemed popular with the customers and even with Mrs Colbeck, I couldn't see how I could translate that into becoming a chef. I also profoundly disliked my future mother-in-law (I believe this is not uncommon). So, although there were many things I loved about England, not least the music, I could not deal with the English lack of food culture, and eventually we decided to leave. I could not be a chef, I accepted that, so I decided I would be a great director of a restaurant which required a good grasp of many languages. The first country would be Germany as I had some knowledge of that language, having studied it for five years at school.

Jenny and I went to Wiesbaden in the south-west of the country where I was to be a chef de rang (I was responsible for two commis) at the Hôtel de France. We lived in a single room above the restaurant and I worked six days a week. It was hard for both of us, especially for Jenny, as she had little Emma, her daughter, and was pregnant with our son Olivier. But after six months my German was good enough and we began to contemplate a move to Spain.

Out of the blue, a telephone call came from Mrs Colbeck. David the chef had gone, as had the whole kitchen brigade. She remembered the dishes I had cooked and had a proposal for us: would we return to the Rose Revived, would Jenny be front of house and would I be the chef? That kind of offer comes only once in a lifetime. In spite of the drawbacks, entering a kitchen as a head chef was all I had dreamed of, and more. We set off back to England.

Britain has many great desserts. Sure they usually have a high calorific content, but my God, they are delicious. Of all the desserts, such as steamed puddings and sticky toffee pudding, my favourite is the crumble. Any fruit will do – apricot, apple, summer fruits . . .

The French normally dismiss the possibility of good food in Britain. But lately they have stumbled on crumble. It was incredible – suddenly the whole of France was crumbling. When you went through the villages and the cities you heard French hands crumbling butter, sugar and flour softly, softly, as the scent of all the delicious seasonal fruits filled the streets. Crumble is even a bestseller at Brasserie Blanc.

So at this point I can't help giving you my favourite crumble recipe, from my friends Jody and Clare Scheckter, owners of the biggest small organic farm in Britain, where I get a great deal of my produce.

LAVERSTOKE PARK FARM

Autumn/Winter
Oonagh Fawkes's
Apple Crumble

Among the many visits to Jody and Clare's house and the many great meals and wine I have had there, one dish stands out: an apple crumble. I cannot claim to be a specialist in apple crumble but this is the best one I have ever tasted. Without shame I asked for the recipe, which Clare and Jody graciously gave me. Obviously, I have left the recipe untouched, as there is nothing to add or take away ... or maybe one thing. I often find when you cook a crumble that there is a gluey layer of uncooked flour caused by the steam rising from the fruit. So we precook the crumble, which prevents this little problem happening. If you like, adapt the recipe in this way.

INGREDIENTS

For the filling:
> 675g cooking apples
> 100ml fresh apple juice
> caster sugar, to taste

For the crumble:
> *290g self-raising flour*
> *175g butter*
> *290g Demerara sugar*

METHOD
PREPARING THE FILLING:

Peel, core and quarter the apples. Cut each quarter into chunks and put in a saucepan. Pour over the apple juice and sugar to taste. Allow to cook until almost soft, but not mush. Use a slotted spoon to lift out half of the apples and put into a baking dish. Add the juice, and use a potato masher to very gently mash the apple mixture. Then add the remainder of the semi-cooked chunks to the dish, leaving them whole.

MAKING THE CRUMBLE:

Rub the ingredients together as for pastry, and then squeeze gently to make it lumpy and sticky. Lay on top of the fruit – do not press it down – and cook for about 40 minutes at 180°C until lightly browned.
  Best served with homemade buffalo milk custard!

Iles Flottantes 'Façon Maman Blanc'
Floating Islands 'Maman Blanc'

A dessert from my childhood, and one of the most celebrated desserts of France, found in homes, brasseries and great restaurants alike. Specially for children, but grown-ups love it too.

> *Serves (Yield): 4*
> *Difficulty rating: ● ○ ○*
> *Preparation time: 30 minutes plus 4 hours' chilling time*
> *Cooking time: 20 minutes*
> *Special equipment: Electric mixer with whisk attachment,*
> *30cm shallow pan*

INGREDIENTS

Both the custard and the meringues can be made 1 day in advance.
You can add the caramel 1 hour before serving.

For the meringues:
> 1.2 litres milk
> 5g (1 tsp) vanilla purée (see page 202)
> 220ml (6) egg whites
> 160g caster sugar

For the custard:
> 150g (10) egg yolks
> 85g caster sugar
> milk used for poaching the meringue

For the caramel:
> 50ml water
> 100g caster sugar

METHOD

MAKING AND POACHING THE MERINGUE:

Pour the milk into a large saucepan and whisk in the vanilla purée.
Place over the heat, bring to the boil, then reduce heat to just below
simmering point.

Meanwhile, in an electric mixer on medium speed, beat the egg
whites to a light peak, add the sugar, increase to full speed and whisk
until firm peaks. (*1)

The meringues are now ready to cook. With a large spoon, scoop
out 12 meringues (*2) and poach them all in the simmering milk for
3 minutes on each side. (*3) Lift out the poached meringues with a
slotted spoon and transfer to a small tray. Reserve.

MAKING THE CUSTARD:

In a large mixing bowl, whisk the egg yolks with the caster sugar, then
gradually whisk in the hot milk. Pour the mixture back into the
saucepan. Cook over a medium heat for 4–5 minutes, (*4) until the
custard begins to thicken and coat the back of the spoon. Strain

immediately into a large bowl. Stir (★5) and allow to cool down. Pour the custard into a serving bowl and pile on the poached meringues. Chill for a minimum of 6 hours.

MAKING THE CARAMEL AND SERVING:

Put the water in a small heavy saucepan and scatter over the sugar. Let the sugar absorb the water. Then, on a medium heat, cook the syrup to a golden brown caramel. (★6) Stop the cooking of the caramel by putting the base of the pan in cold water for 3 seconds. Then pour over the custard and meringues.

Chef's notes:
★1   At this stage the sugar is not there to provide support, and the egg whites are prone to graining. So do not overwhip. When light peaks form, then slowly add the sugar, whisking until stiff peaks form.
★2   The meringues don't need to be quenelle shaped, just scoop them out. What is more important is that they are the same size.
★3   This process involves both steaming and poaching. If the heat is too high, the meringues will soufflé and then deflate. So a gentle heat must be applied to cook them.
★4   At this stage all sorts of small disasters can happen. The worst is that you will overcook the custard. To prevent this, a few steps must be taken.
   1) Before you start, ensure you have a bowl ready to transfer the hot custard into.
   2) Stir constantly to distribute the heat, and also to prevent burning on the bottom of the pan.
   3) The cooking process will be very short. What we want to achieve is to partly cook the egg yolks so they thicken the custard. If you cook them completely you will have scrambled eggs. The perfect temperature for making custard is around 90°C.
★5   Once you have transferred your hot custard into the bowl, go on to stir it for a minute or so. The residual heat could still scramble the custard.
★6   If blonde, the caramel will be too sweet. You need to cook the caramel to a dark colour to dissipate the sweetness and increase the caramel flavour.

NINE

DEBUT

I Spry

I T'S POSSIBLE THAT MRS COLBECK ASKED ME TO TAKE OVER THE kitchen at the Rose Revived in order to bring her daughter back to Britain rather than to ensure that her customers were served good food. Whatever the case, I was appointed head chef, and the way I remember it I fell in love with cooking the moment I picked up the frying pan.

I entered that kitchen disguised as a chef flanked by two English cordon bleu cooks to help me. It was probably the proudest moment of my life – and the most terrifying. I became both chef and apprentice. So, what do you do when you take over a kitchen? I did the sensible thing: I didn't change everything. I looked at the unfamiliar recipes for the curries and whitebait and scones and tried to learn how to do them first, then to do them better. But I was so eager to give the customers a taste of real Maman Blanc food that I couldn't keep it up for long.

But before I could stage a revolution in the kitchen, I had to revolutionize the garden. I picked a huge fight with the gardener Mr Lay as I wished to cook seasonally. I looked at his garden and didn't like what I saw. Everything was grown for size. But I needed small, delicate young vegetables, which Mr Lay vehemently disagreed with. I sometimes had to raid his garden at night to get the vegetables I wanted as there was no way he would part with them willingly.

What did I cook? I decided to do that frighteningly complicated, over-demanding dish that required serious knowledge: quenelles of pike. I was certain that I wanted fish as my debut dish, but it was difficult to find a good supplier.

When fish was delivered to the Rose Revived, and perhaps most other restaurants in Britain, the stench was so strong that you could smell the contents before the van doors were opened. In fact, you could be in the kitchen and get a whiff and think, 'Here comes the fish man.' Usually the fish had been frozen, thawed and refrozen several times. But my pike dish was OK because I gave up on the idea of locating a good supplier. Instead, I went fishing myself and caught a monster just by the bridge next to the Rose Revived.

Now I turned to the recipes of Escoffier, the French master whose cuisine was served during the early days of London's Savoy Hotel, as well as in many restaurants in France. In the restaurants of the early seventies in Britain Escoffier's recipes were still being followed, though the quality of the ingredients would have had him spinning in his grave.

I studied his recipe for quenelles of pike in lobster sauce. There were two problems. The first was the lobster, which was unavailable, unless I wanted the frozen-thawed-refrozen variety from the fishmonger (which I could do without). But freshwater crayfish were available in the nearby Cherwell, one mile away, so I caught some of them as well. The second problem was the recipe itself. As I read it and re-read it, I could hear myself saying, 'This must be a printing mistake.' I have immense respect for Escoffier but his recipe called for large quantities of flour and butter and cream. The dish would end up being far too heavy and rich. It didn't make any sense. I thought that anyone who ate it might die. So I changed the recipe.

With little pieces of the fish and other ingredients I began to experiment in an attempt to create the perfect quenelle. I knew I wanted it to be light so I omitted the flour. From my limited culinary experience I had noticed that the protein of fish will solidify when cooked and it will stick together, causing a natural coagulation. I had not worked out the science of it all, but I knew that flour would thicken and also add weight. The flour, therefore, was unnecessary.

I puréed the flesh of the fish, passed it through a sieve and put it on ice to cool it down: you cannot add cream to warm flesh. Once it had cooled sufficiently I added the salt and pepper, egg yolks, then an egg white, softened butter and some cream, but only a little. Then I had a beautiful, shiny, silky quenelle mixture. I refrigerated the mixture to let it get back some density. To shape it into a quenelle with a spoon at first I used a cold spoon but immediately the mixture stuck to it, so I used two large warm spoons to acquire the shape. I poached the quenelles so that the outside was sealed and stayed firm, but the inside was rare.

Then I made my first freshwater crayfish *jus*. I reduced Escoffier's butter content by three quarters, then I had a light *jus* into which I put two tablespoons of cream. I wanted the cream to give roundness, but I didn't want the gallon (or so) of cream Escoffier might have recommended.

I got the first ten quenelles wrong. The oven temperature was too high. The quenelles would puff up, then deflate miserably. Eventually I found the ideal temperature of my oven was 150°C. At this temperature the quenelles would cook slowly and at the same time the pike and the *jus* would swap flavours. When they emerged from the oven the quenelles had puffed out appetizingly, smooth and beautiful and magical, and the *jus* was perfectly reduced to the right texture.

Everyone said, 'Wow.'

That was the first one. It had seemed so easy and natural. Maybe I had been lucky. Probably I was. Yet during the whole lenghty process, I felt an immense joy, pride – and a real sense of belonging.

———

Apart from everyday conversation with Jenny, her parents and the British staff at the Rose Revived, I had two forms of English tuition. The first was a cassette called *L'Anglais Sans Peine*, which I bought because I thought it would teach me the language without pain, though I discovered pretty quickly that it was ambitiously titled. I'd do an hour in the morning and another hour at night, listening to the tape and writing out sentences in French and their translation in English. Then I would read the sentences out loud until I sounded like the man on the cassette. (Though I never did.) I can tell you, there was a hell of a lot of pain. Sometimes I'd take the tapes into the kitchen so that in between service I could get a quick blast. 'Shopkeeper, I would like it gift-wrapped, please . . .'

My other source of English was a cookery book. One day I wandered into the local library to look at the cookery books – nothing like the variety we have today – and picked up Elizabeth David. The librarian came up behind me and pointed at *The Constance Spry Cookery Book*. 'Constance Spry is the best you'll find,' he said. I think he was right.

Spry was a fascinating woman, and when you think that she wrote the book (with Rosemary Hume) in the 1950s, she was way ahead of her time. She had a true understanding of science and nutrition and she talked about her own world and the way in which her recipes played a part. I have just been looking at my well-thumbed copy of her book and have reminded myself that she opens with a chapter entitled 'The Cocktail Party', admitting that she does 'not set great store by cocktails or their accompanying savouries'. She adds, 'One never knows, indeed, what trifle may awaken the enthusiasm necessary to carry one beyond the early arduous tasks connected with cooking into those realms in which cookery is an art and a pleasure.' As true today as it was when she wrote it some fifty years ago.

One day I decided to follow a recipe for steak, kidney and oyster pudding from a book, *English Food*, written by Jane Grigson, who in turn had picked it up from a cookery book written in the previous century, when oysters were cheap and popular with the British. The recipe seemed odd, and very wasteful. Why on earth take the best oysters and prime steak and cook them for hours? It didn't make sense. But out of a sense of curiosity, and also to poke fun at British cusine, I made the dish. It used a kilo of rump steak, half a kilo of ox kidney and twenty-four oysters; it also required mushrooms, onion, beef stock, seasoned flour, butter and a bouquet garni. The suet crust was made with 150 grams of suet, 300 grams of self-raising flour, baking powder, white pepper, salt, thyme and cold water.

I followed the recipe precisely, cutting the steak into pieces and slicing the kidney. The meat was caramelized in a pan and then cooked with the mushrooms and stock for about an hour and a half. I made the dough and lined the basin before putting the filling of meat and oysters into it. The pastry lid, half an inch thick, went on top. The pudding went into a large saucepan of gently boiling water and it cooked for about two hours.

The smell that filled the kitchen told me another story. It was glorious, quite magnificent. I couldn't wait to try the dish. When it was finally done, I lifted the basin from the saucepan, cut the pudding open and tucked in. I ate and ate. It was delicious, but for the next three days I was so weighed down by suet and flour I couldn't move. Served me right. I got what I deserved. And what I got was, I believe, exactly what the dish was meant to deliver!

A few years after that Jane Grigson became one of my favourite customers at Les Quat' Saisons. She was a lovely woman and would come to eat with her young daughter Sophie, who also grew up to become a successful and well-known author of cookery books.

———

Once I had control of the kitchen at the Rose Revived, I thought it would be wonderful to serve some local produce. 'Enough of the frozen fish and meat that's being delivered,' I thought. 'Let's give the guests something special and at the same time support local producers.' After all, in France, when you wanted chicken or duck you simply went next door to the farm.

I had huge rows with the suppliers because I had my own idea about freshness, which was taught to me at a very early stage by my parents. And my idea of freshness was at odds with the suppliers' idea of freshness. 'Fresh,' I would tell them, 'means your red mullet doesn't arrive with dead eyes, dead teeth, dead scales, dead everything. It has to be fresh.' All I wanted was fresh produce, but behind my back the suppliers called me 'crazy Frenchman'. Actually, sometimes behind my back, sometimes not. But I didn't care. I was a man on a mission.

I had heard about Aylesbury ducks, with their pink bills and white plumage, and was intrigued. In the early eighteenth century, Aylesbury's farmers bred the birds and used to walk them to London to sell them in the capital's markets. With the introduction of railways, a station was built in the town and the ducks were transported by rail to the capital's gourmets. Aylesbury had its own cottage industry and the town, rightly so, had a duck as its heraldic emblem. 'Aylesbury duck should be on my menu,' I thought.

As I climbed into the car and zoomed off to Aylesbury I was already entertaining myself with thoughts of my famous wobbling duck, with the white plumage and the long thick breast underneath. My mind was whizzing through the different dishes that could be made. At the first butcher's shop I pulled up and nipped inside.

'Sir, do you have any famous Aylesbury duck?'

He shook his head.

'Could you please tell me where to go?'

'Of course,' said the butcher helpfully, and he pointed me in the direction of another butcher's shop.

The next butcher also shook his head. He did not have any Aylesbury ducks but he knew a man who might, and he told me to head off to another shop.

My search took me from one shop to another until one of the

shopkeepers insisted that I'd be able to find it at the first butcher's I'd stopped at. I returned to the original butcher and when I walked into his shop he was laughing. He tried to suppress his giggles as he explained, 'I'm sorry, young man, but Aylesbury duck doesn't exist any more.'

I was confused. He told me that, yes, it was true there had once been such a thing as Aylesbury duck, and very good it was too, but then it was interbred and factory-produced and the original duck was so rare I would never be able to find it. Apparently, every so often some fool like me would arrive in Aylesbury trying to find the duck and the shopkeepers would amuse themselves by giving him the same runaround. Not so much a wild goose chase as an Aylesbury duck chase.

I suppose this little story illustrates how Britain, sadly, has lost its way. It shows the loss of craft, the loss of regional produce. The Aylesbury duck saga is just one of many examples of how we became disconnected from food. Factory produce won the day!

When I was back at the restaurant and looked at the ducks that were available through suppliers I thought, 'My God, this can't be it!' They were the wrong shape, so thin I could barely see the breast. They were grey, they seemed to be lacking blood, and they had thick, white, fatty, shiny skin. When carved the breast had thin grey-pink flesh rather than the thick reddish meat I was dreaming of.

This meant I couldn't buy my local produce, which had been lost to the factory. So I had to buy ducks from the Bresse area of France, which had a shape I found pleasing and a taste I liked; its breast was thick, well-filled and oblong; the legs were perfectly shaped but small; its skin was yellowish and hand-plucked; and when carved, the meat was a beautiful plummy colour. Of course, it had run, laughed, run some more and eaten great food – maize and corn as well as all the tasty treats it could collect from the farmyard.

Laugh all you like at duck à l'orange or lemon, but done well it is a wonderful dish, and I used to serve it at the Rose Revived. The bird's flesh is quite sweet and rich so it goes well with sweet, tangy acid flavours, hence its combination with citrus fruits like orange and lemon, and also cherries or gooseberries.

If you were to taste the greatest dishes of the world you would identify a pattern: the majority of them, like duck à l'orange, are based on contrasts – sweet-sour, acid-sweet. If you don't have enjoyable contrasts then you have mono-flavour. What creates the build-up of flavours is contrast, and a great chef or cook who knows his stuff will do this.

You could look at it another way.

Think for a moment about an alcoholic cocktail where taste is so important (one sip and you know if you like it or not). Cocktail-makers, the good ones, will follow what is known as the 'Three S' rule. The first S is for Strength, i.e. the alcohol base, and you should never blend two spirits. Pick vodka, for instance, and make it your base. The second S stands for Sour, usually a fruit or a fruit juice. (While we are on the subject, you stir when there is no fruit juice, except lemon juice. Shaking leads to homogenization of the ingredients and chills the drink.) The third S is for Sweet, which is a liqueur, or perhaps something sweet and fizzy. These combinations, or contrasts, will result in a lovely cocktail.

So if we think of the margarita – and why shouldn't we? – we begin with Strength in the form of one and a half measures of silver tequila. Next comes lime juice – the Sour element. Lastly, you add Cointreau to give it a Sweet characteristic. Think of a gin and tonic. On its own it has the Strength of the gin and the Sweetness of the tonic. How different it becomes when you add that slice of lime or lemon, the Sour. (In fact, at Le Manoir we also serve a G&T with a slice of cucumber rather than lemon. The cucumber provides sweetness but brings out the bitterness of the tonic.)

So a good cocktail is a contrast of sweet and sour, just like thousands of great dishes. The only difference is the drink can hurt you the next morning.

Summer/Autumn
Brasserie Blanc/Raymond Blanc Cookery School
Epaule d'Agneau de Lait Rotie; Son Jus de Cuisson
Slow-roasted Shoulder of Lamb, Braised Summer Vegetables and Roasting Juices

To me, the tastiest cut of lamb is the shoulder. Slow-cooking is the best technique to give this cut of lamb melting quality and maximum flavour.

Serves (Yield): 4 to 6
Difficulty: ● ○ ○
Preparation time: 30 minutes
Cooking time: 5½ hours (*1)
Special equipment: Heavy-duty roasting pan of 36cm x 24cm, cast-iron pan of 25cm diameter with lid

INGREDIENTS

For the shoulder of lamb:
6 pinches Maldon sea salt
1 tsp freshly ground black pepper
1 sprig rosemary, finely chopped
3 leaves sage, finely chopped
2 tbsp olive oil
1.5kg shoulder of lamb on the bone (*2), new season, hung 10 days, skin scored

For roasting the lamb:
300g lamb bones and meat trimmings, (*3) chopped into 3cm chunks
45ml (3 tbsp) olive oil
1 onion, chopped into 2cm pieces
2 medium carrot, chopped into 2cm pieces
½ stick celery, chopped into 2cm pieces
½ bulb garlic, cut in half across

200ml white wine, dry (boiled for 30 seconds) (*4)
100ml cold water
2 bay leaves
3 sprigs thyme

For the braised summer vegetables: (*5)

30ml (2 tbsp) olive oil
30ml (2 tbsp) water
100g (12 small) new season Griotte onions, or 1 white onion, cut into 8 segments
200g (12 small) new season carrots, trimmed and washed
400g (4 medium) golden beetroot
160g (2 medium) turnips
100g (2 stalks) Swiss chard plus leaves, cut into 5mm batons
sea salt and freshly ground black pepper

METHOD

PREPARING THE LAMB:

Mix the ingredients together and rub all over the lamb; this can be done 30 minutes in advance.

ROASTING THE LAMB:

Preheat the oven to 220°C. In a large roasting pan on a medium heat, colour the lamb bones and meat trimmings in the oil for 5 minutes, then add the vegetables and continue to cook for a further 2 minutes. Place the seasoned shoulder of lamb on top of the bones and vegetables, transfer to the hot oven and roast for 30 minutes until golden brown. Lower the temperature to 120°C and cook for another hour, basting the shoulder of lamb every 20 minutes or so. (*6) Now take the lamb out of the oven and spoon out the fat, add the wine, water and herbs and bring to the boil on the hob. Cover loosely with tin foil (*7) and return the lamb to the oven. Cook for a further 4 hours at 110°C.

BRAISING THE SUMMER VEGETABLES:

Sweat the vegetables in the olive oil with a little seasoning in a large cast-iron pan over a medium heat for about 5 minutes until sweetened. Add the water and cook alongside the lamb at 110°C for the last 2 hours; taste and correct the seasoning.

SERVING:

Remove the lamb from the oven, strain the juices, spoon out any fat and serve in a sauceboat. Place on the table to be carved in front of your guests. Serve the braised vegetables from the cast-iron pan.

Chef's notes:

★1   5½ hours may seem a long time but we use a very low temperature, which lends the meat its tenderness, moisture and flavour. You could also apply a temperature of 65°C and a cooking time of 12 hours.

★2   We have selected three organic suppliers. Rhug specialize in highland lamb; the breeds we use are Beaulah, Cheviot and Ewe Rouge, which are all crossed with the Welsh lamb. Laverstoke Park, with whom I have worked for the past seven years, are organic, and currently converting to a bio-dynamic system. The breeds we have chosen are Lleyn and Hebridean. The third supplier is my dear Colin Ring, who has worked at Le Manoir for twenty years; his excellent breed of lamb used to graze on Le Manoir grounds. Early in the season, March and April, I use French lamb from the Pyrenees.

★3   The roasting and caramelizing of the bones and trimmings will provide a delicious *jus*; it will also provide a support for the meat, allowing the heat to circulate.

★4   See note 2 on page 46.

★5   Within the gardens of Le Manoir we grow many varieties of vegetables. For this dish, the carrots we use are Nantes and Rainbow; for the beetroot we use Rouge Crapaudines, Chioggia, Bull's Blood and Golden; for the Swiss chard we use Rainbow, Yellow and Rhubarb; and the only turnip we use at Le Manoir is the demi-long Blanc De Croissy.

★6   The basting will help provide colour and flavour, and some of the juices mixed with the fat will caramelize the meat.

*7 The foil is placed loosely on the shoulder of lamb to retain moisture and prevent drying out.

VARIATION

The cut of lamb can be replaced by any braising cut, such as shin of beef, silverside, brisket or blade. Mix in your favourite herbs. You could add parsnips, turnips and yellow beetroot; all perfect accompaniments to a roast. Some new season garlic simply roasted in a little olive oil would also be delicious.

TEN

HYGIENE

Half a Curried Mouse

THE BASIS OF GREAT FOOD IS HYGIENE.

If you respect food then it makes sense that you should care for it. If you buy, let's say, meat or shellfish and don't store it properly, your first dinner party might be your last. Similarly, if a cook fails to observe the correct period of conservation for ingredients and they become contaminated, he is in danger of quickly losing his dinner guests, perhaps to the graveyard. If you want to kill someone, serve him dodgy food. It's a surefire way of achieving your aim. Put some food into your fridge, forget about it for a couple of weeks, then bring it out and pop it in the oven.

The most frightening moment of my career involved hygiene, and it happened when I was cooking one evening at the Rose Revived.

I was mid-service when suddenly the entire restaurant was silenced by a woman's scream. A minute later a waitress was standing at the passe.

'Look,' she said to me.

I looked down at the bowl she had placed on the counter. It contained curry – nothing wrong with that. But there, in the middle of the bowl, semi-submerged in the brown, spicy sauce, was half a mouse, from its head down to its rib cage, including front legs. There was a stone-cold dead rodent in my piping hot curry. Curry was served at the table from a tureen, and while the waitress had been ladling the curry into the customer's bowl the mouse had been spotted.

'It made the lady scream,' the waitress said.

Yes, I heard her. It made me scream deep within too. I was disgusted and panicky but mostly concerned for the guest, even if she did have a good tale to dine out on, so to speak. I went to see the distraught lady and apologized to her. Then I apologized some more. I invited her to see the kitchen, the cool room, the plastic containers. I explained that hygiene was at the core of our business. I sent flowers for two weeks. I had not been in the job long and wondered if this was the end of my career. If you are a chef and you start poisoning guests, longevity is no longer an option. You are a dead man before you start. In addition, there are ways of poisoning someone and then there are ways of poisoning someone. The half mouse was the latter. Thank God, health and safety issues were not as stringent then as they are today. Nowadays you'd be closed down if you tried to pass a mouse, or even half a mouse, on to the guests.

Questions needed to be asked. How did this happen? How did the rodent get there? Everything I did was fresh. I was invested in every dish from beginning to end. I tasted each dish again and again at every stage of preparation, checking and rechecking. I sealed and dated every container. The dish would have been made and then allowed to cool before it was divided up into plastic containers. Its conservation time – the period of time it was at its best – would have been two days. How could this mouse have jumped into my curry? I was a man possessed, in control of every tiny step of the cooking, yet half a mouse was in my food? And, by the way, what happened to the other half?

I felt so ashamed. I was religious about hygiene, and rightly so. It was the first thing I had learned about the kitchen. Without such a rule you are dead as a chef, and it seemed I had broken the rule. I felt everyone was laughing at me.

The questions remained unanswered until some months later when one day a colleague took me to one side and whispered, 'It was him.'

'What was him?' I asked, confused.

'The mouse. The curry. It was him.'

My confidant pointed at a waiter, a man who despised me, possibly because I was engaged to Jenny. Or maybe because I had become a chef and he was still a waiter. Or was it because I was French? Apparently he had boasted to other members of staff that he was the culprit, the mouse-slayer. I wish I could have done to him what he did to the mouse, but he left the Rose Revived before I could exact revenge.

I had another frightening experience about ten years ago when I went to Scotland to cook for some two hundred guests. My team and I prepared a seven-course menu that was truly beautiful. One of the courses was *gelée* of oysters, using the best Scottish oysters, which were juicy and fresh; you smell them and you can smell the sea, sea lions and algae. The *gelée* was set in a trembling rectangular shape, like a little golden ingot, within which were trapped the oysters, slivers of wild salmon and the best beluga. Threads of sour cream and black pepper, cured cucumber ribbons and seaweed completed the dish. It was quite stunning, and I was very proud of it.

It was completely inspired by good home practice. Salmon bones were being thrown out – they were no good for fish soup or stock. As I hated waste (just like Maman Blanc) I had to use these fish bones. After many trials and errors I emerged with the most heavenly scented *gelée*, gold and melting with all of its flavour and character as I did not clarify it with egg white. It exuded spring when every flavour is young and delicate, a promise of their potential; it also trapped the very colours of spring – the pink of the blossom, the pale green of the newest leaves.

The cuisine I love is entirely structured on this principle of the seasons. After spring we move on to summer where the flavours are big, ripe and triumphant. In autumn the flavours of the harvest are richer, earthier and deeper. In winter there are gamey flavours, dark and intense.

In Scotland, the guests were suitably impressed. As each dish was carried from the kitchen to the tables it received a round of applause.

At the end of the evening I was nodding appreciatively as the departing guests paid compliments. 'Thank you very much,' I said, and beamed happily. 'What a magnificent success!' I thought, and I congratulated my brilliant brigade for their hard work.

I climbed into bed just after midnight, exhausted and run down but truly satisfied with the evening.

At one o'clock in the morning I was awoken by a phone call from the kitchen.

'Chef, someone's complained about food poisoning.'

That was the first call. Half an hour later there was another call to tell me of more complaints. Then came another call, followed by another. Symptoms ranged from violent vomiting to diarrhoea, or both. Not nice.

Soon there were twenty complaints from guests who were nursing their poisoned loved ones. The hotel was filled with the sounds of feet dashing from bed to bathroom, and toilets flushing. It seemed just a matter of time before a lynch mob banged on my door.

There was absolutely nothing I could do.

Inevitably, I got a call from a journalist at one of Scotland's news-papers. 'How did it happen?' he asked. I could not tell him.

The hotel was like a morgue the following morning. Then the paper hit the stands with a headline that read something like 'Raymond Blanc poisons two hundred Scots'. The accompanying article went on to ask, 'Does Mr Blanc like Scots or not? I thought there was an alliance between the French and the Scots against the English.'

At that stage I was not blaming the oysters, but myself. I started to feel sure that I was responsible. I felt bad, and my team felt as bad as I did. The oyster dish was the obvious concern and I tried to retrace every single step. The oysters were fresh and they were of the finest quality. When we had opened them they were tight and heavy with sea-water, looked beautiful and smelled clean. The dishes and utensils had been correctly sterilized. My kitchen brigade is a clean, well-trained, professional team. Each of us understands the consequences of poor hygiene. We had all washed our hands before and during cooking. It is a ritual. We'd taken all the right precautions, so how could it be that scores of guests were bedridden? I just couldn't work out how these people could be so ill.

Then a horrible thought crawled in. In one moment I had ruined my reputation, so hard won over so many years. Yes, you've guessed it, I can be dramatic. I am a worrier.

It just so happened that there were two portions of the dish left in the fridge. Thank God they were there. When the health and safety inspectors arrived they asked about all the safety procedures I had gone through. I explained everything and they couldn't find anything wrong. They left with the two portions of oyster *gelée*.

A couple of days later they got in touch to say that after carrying out tests they had discovered that the oysters had come from water contaminated with bacteria. This is what caused the mass food poisoning. Strangely, I had tasted the dish myself and had not suffered.

I was exonerated. The newspaper, of course, printed an apology of a single line.

HEALTH AND SAFETY

There is more food poisoning in private houses than in restaurants. You may argue that there are more houses than restaurants, which would be a valid argument, but none the less I give you these rules, which are the foundation of excellence, not just hygiene. You cannot have great food without a clean kitchen or good food hygiene practices.

FOOD SAFETY RULES

Many dos and don'ts apply to working within the kitchen. A professional kitchen requires a high level of food safety in order to create excellent food. By following these basic rules, you can sleep well in knowledge that your family and friends will also sleep well after your exquisite feast . . . rather than being ill.

1) Hand washing is one of the simplest and most effective ways of reducing the risk of contamination. It forms an important part of our hygiene policy and the rules for hand washing must always be observed.

ALWAYS WASH YOUR HANDS AFTER:

- **TAKING A BREAK AND RETURNING TO THE KITCHEN**
- **VISITING THE TOILET**
- **HANDLING DIFFERENT FOODS – BETWEEN RAW AND COOKED**
- **HANDLING CHEMICALS OR CLEANING MATERIALS**
- **TOUCHING HAIR, FACE, EYES, NOSE, MOUTH, ETC.**
- **BLOWING NOSE**
- **COUGHING (INCLUDING WHEN INTO A PAPER HANDKERCHIEF)**
- **SMOKING**

If these rules are not followed, potential food poisoning may occur with such bacteria and toxins as: *Clostridium perfringens* (symptoms: acute abdominal pains and diarrhoea); *Staphylococcus aureus* (symptoms: abdominal cramps, nausea, vomiting, some diarrhoea and subnormal temperatures), and *Escherichia coli* (symptoms: abdominal pains, diarrhoea, vomiting and fever).

2) All food must be stock-rotated effectively, using a first-in first-out procedure (FIFO for short). This ensures that food gets used in correct date order.

3) Whilst preparing and cooking, make sure you avoid cross-contamination of foods, especially the high-risk ones such as poultry, meat, dairy, fish and shellfish. Where possible, keep raw ingredients separate from cooked ingredients.

Cross-contamination can lead to infection by the food-borne disease *Campylobacter*, or to food poisoning, such as by *Vibrio parahaemolyticus* or *E.coli*, with symptoms of fever, nausea, headaches, diarrhoea and colicky abdominal pains.

4) Never wear jewellery or make-up as physical and chemical contamination could occur.

5) Always keep food covered both in and outside of the refrigerator. This prevents contamination and preserves foods to make them safer to consume.

HEALTH AND SAFETY RULES

1) Always wear protective clothing, such as a chef's jacket and apron. Not only will it protect you from foods such as beetroot juice that will stain your finest cashmere, but also from hot fats and oils that will burn you. It also makes a professional statement.

2) Never run in the kitchen. There are many hazards, such as wet floors or greasy surfaces. Avoid trips, slips and falls.

3) Always make sure your knives are sharp. Blunt knives cause more cuts, stabbings and lost fingertips than sharp knives.

4) Always make sure your chopping board is safe and secure. Use a board mat or rubber mat to prevent slips or movement – it might just save your little pinkies.

5) Always read the instructions before using any dangerous such as food processor or blenders.

6) Allow plenty of room to work in, so your creative genius has room to manoeuvre.

Remember, a safe and hygienic kitchen is a happy kitchen that creates beautiful food.

ELEVEN

CUSTOMERS

From Little Acorns

IT IS IMPORTANT TO ACKNOWLEDGE THAT IF YOU ARE ABOUT TO create your own business and it happens to be a restaurant, you might be frightened if you are not a trained chef and have absolutely no knowledge of accounting, management or training skills. Is passion enough to see you through?

Yet for me there was no real fear. Instead, I was filled with excitement when Jenny and I opened our first restaurant, Les Quat' Saisons, in September 1977, a couple of months before my twenty-eighth birthday. I had had just three months of cooking experience.

Today, the aspiring restaurateur would have a three-year business plan. He would have come up with pages detailing forecasts, growth, revenue and costs. Jenny had helped her mother with the finances at the Rose Revived so she had some of the required skills, and we put together some figures, but truth be known, we built the business on optimism and bags of energy rather than forecasts and numbers. Still, her knowledge was hugely relevant as I knew I could concentrate on the front of house, the wine and the kitchen.

We mortgaged our house to the hilt so that we could secure a bank loan. This presented us with another driving force: the knowledge, confirmed to us time after time by the bank manager, that if the restaurant went bust we would lose our home as well as our business. That's how most people start.

Every restaurateur has his own story of how it all began. This is mine.

I had attained my dream, but the building was cheap and uninspiring. But that was all we could afford. We would love it, and make it special and successful. The restaurant was in Summertown, which was the wrong part of Oxford, and it was on the wrong side of the road. It was hidden away in the most hideous sixties concrete shopping parade. Next door there was a shop selling ladies' underwear — not sexy Agent Provocateur-style garments but big pants and knickers that appeared to have been knitted out of wool. On the other side and above was Oxfam.

It had once been a Greek restaurant. It was a corridor twenty metres long and five metres wide, divided into two parts, restaurant and kitchen. On one side of the dining room there were four tables with booths: a wooden structure reaching behind and right up into the ceiling. They looked like stables and were very ugly. My God, were they ugly. But we had to learn to live with them. To remove the stables would have meant removing the ceiling, which would have meant putting in a new ceiling, which would have been too expensive. So the booths stayed. Jenny and I told ourselves they were there for customers who wanted privacy and intimacy. There were also seven tables without booths, and a little service bar, and we had enough seating to cater for forty guests.

Now, let's walk through the restaurant and down to the kitchen, which was built as a lean-to and about the size of a small caravan but felt more cramped and claustrophobic than that. There was the passe, and behind it the cooking area. To the left was a sink for washing up, a job which in the early days was mostly shared among the chefs as we could only afford a part-time washer-up.

On the day we got the keys and excitedly opened up I entered that kitchen, stopped and looked at the grey tiles covered with black grease after years of neglect. The tiny space, the smell, the cheapness of the appliances, the sight of the light bulb dangling on a wire – suddenly exhilaration was replaced by fear. This was my domain, where I would have to toil away and spend all of my time. Would I be good enough? I knew that the consequences if we failed would be dreadful. This cheerful little moment lasted a few minutes, then it was replaced by a huge urge to make the place mine. Chip away every bit of dirt; clean it, polish it and love it. In those days you didn't think of ringing a cleaning firm; that's a modern convenience. We worked through the nights trying to get that place into shape, aware that every day we weren't open was another day of no takings.

We discovered a dead rat in the fridge in a serious state of decomposition. We got rid of the rat, and we got rid of the fridge. There were more rats to come, many more. They had a nest in the roof. The place was infested with the rodents. If you want your restaurant to have a good reputation it is advisable to make sure there aren't rats in the kitchen, and I am pleased to say that we got rid of them long before serving our first customers.

Then there was that black dirt, in some parts compacted, in other parts greasy. It was dirt like you have never seen. It coated everything. In order to clean it off I used a spatula. One night I was in the poorly lit kitchen, perched on a ladder. There was so much grease still stuck to the wall I had to speed up, and my spatula slipped into an electric cable. I was sent flying across the room by a nasty electric shock. My life as a restaurateur could have ended there and then. Believe it or not, that was the last time I tried to clean in the near darkness with a spatula.

The kitchen's roof was made of sheets of corrugated iron so there was no insulation, except for where the rats lived, and there seemed to be no ventilation either. This meant that in the summer the kitchen was boiling and in the winter months the temperature in that part of the restaurant was as cold as it was outside. I had to scrape frost and ice off the work surface. Not that there was much of a work surface.

The enamel-topped stove, which had four gas rings, had started life in the fifties, or even the forties; I'd picked it up second, third or fifth hand. I thought I'd got a bargain, but it was cheap because it didn't have a bottom. It was a cube that was designed to hold heat but had only five of its six sides. I put two pastry trays side by side in order to create a bottom for the oven. When switched on, the heat would go into the oven and quickly leave it via the bottom. It would then rise up to the corrugated iron roof before disappearing into the skies above Oxford. I suppose it was a bit like cooking with the oven door open – impossible to achieve a really hot oven. But the four gas rings worked brilliantly.

As we were strapped for cash, we kept the design simple. Expensive white linen was not a consideration. We bought the cheapest red-and-white check tablecloths and we decorated the walls with inexpensive prints that depicted Paris life. Along with the name of the restaurant, customers were left in no doubt that we served French food. To make sure, we added a painting of a cockerel, that symbol of France, to the frontage.

Being obvious can be a virtue, and it worked for us. It certainly didn't look like the Ritz, but our little restaurant looked lovely . . . and very French.

———

If I had been a trained chef, I could have lessened my workload by a thousand times. I was learning all the basic techniques as I went along, whether it was trying to make puff pastry for the twentieth time, boning a leg of veal, cutting a piece of liver properly, or understanding the secrets of marinating or making stock. But the food discoveries were the most exhilarating part. Regardless of my many failures and how painful the journey of learning was, I was progressing. I was also enjoying myself. Any small success felt like a triumph.

The funny thing about being self-taught is that you feel you are inventing every minute of the day. I was doing things I had never seen done before. In reality, I was often 'creating' dishes which had been there for hundreds of years. We did wonderful dishes like quenelles of pike, Jerusalem artichoke mousse, *gâteaux de foie gras* and chicken liver, as well as big fat turbots with red wine *jus*, or maybe sea bass, which came from France (sold to them by the Cornish and Devonian fishermen as no one in England would pay the premium for such fish), with *beurre blanc* sauce and essence of red wine. We would also roast sea bass on the bone with the aroma of fennel, lemon and star anise coming through. Succulent best end of highland Welsh lamb with Provençal crumbs was another favourite. There was also that dish from my childhood, *lapin à la moutarde*, and a lot of offal – brain was popular. Offal, remember, was cheap in those days. Nobody wanted it, and no one knew how to cook it anyway. I particularly remember a classic dish we used to do called *medaillons de veau, ses beatilles et amourettes*, which demonstrated how completely integrated poetic ideas were with the French culinary language. Let me explain. *Beatilles* means 'little delicate things', like sweetbreads, testicles, brain, etc. As for *amourettes*, that means, a little more poetically, 'little loves'; it is actually the spinal cord from the veal calf. *Bon appétit*. Of course, all these delightful things were served in the days before BSE. I never translated these poetic thoughts for my English friends, unless they really probed. It was a stunning dish, and hugely popular.

For the first six months I served mostly food inspired by my mother and the chefs at Le Palais, like *îles flottantes*, iced biscuit with raspberries, *tarte Tatin* and the Maman Blanc tart. Once I had established the basics of the menu, I began to experiment. Through questioning and probing I looked for new techniques that would create lighter, sharper dishes. I constantly embraced new possibilities. I made kidneys with green chartreuse and *escargots*. Before long I started to look at flavours in other cuisines. But the first two years were all about survival, leaving the basics of food and wine, training, food cost, budgeting, marketing, setting up the neccessary systems. We were grateful the restaurant was full.

The quest for quality produce wasn't easy. In fact it was the biggest challenge. England had become an industrial intensive garden. Farmers had become solely dependent on pesticides, nitrates and fertilizers. Animals suffered the same fate. They produced pork without fat, veal in crates, fatty chicken fed on hormones and fish feed and routinely treated with antibiotics. So finding good quality products was hell, and I often resorted to placing advertisements in newspapers. I would get some responses, but mostly from journalists.

Yet of course there were some good products. My beef always came from Scotland. The lamb came first from France in March and April, from Devon in May, in June and July from Wales, in July/August from Oxfordshire and then from Shetland in November. Nobody truly understood freshness, they were only interested in buying and selling, so it was a constant fight. 'Fresh' fish was routinely four or five days old, but when we managed to get good fish it was great, from Dover sole to sea bass and turbot, Colchester oysters, hand-dived scallops, monkfish and Scottish langoustines. It took many years to secure a supply and initially we had to import a lot of produce from France – not by desire. Our veal and their kidneys came from Limousin, and all the other poultry was imported, from quails to Barbary ducks, Bresse chickens and guinea fowls. Yes, it was a gigantic struggle to get good quality ingredients, and great food can only be made from great ingredients.

Every minute of every day was another minute of progress, though. The learning curve was never invisible to my kitchen staff. In the morning I would prepare a dish a certain way and perfect the presentation. Five minutes before service I would then rearrange the ingredients, change the dish and say, 'OK, let's do it this way instead.' An hour later I'd be at it again, rearranging the plate, changing the garnish, adding and telling the cooks, 'From now on, let's serve it like this.' I might change a dish five times a day. It would drive the staff mad. Even today my executive chef, Gary Jones, laughs when I do it, but I know that he has caught the bug himself and he will constantly change dishes too. But I was not changing it for the sake of it, just always trying to improve and to give the guests the best experience. If you lose your curiosity about any dish, that dish will die.

At times I worked eighteen hours a day. I have never known exhaustion quite like it. And those long days would continue for the next thirteen years. When I slept, I was dead. When my wife Jenny woke me up, I was still dead. When I shaved in the morning, I would look at my reflection in the mirror and it was a daily reminder of the hardships of a restaurateur: the drawn complexion, the hollow look, the raw burns on my hands and wrists, the plasters on my fingers, covering the cuts caused by knives. Then off I'd go, a knackered young man in his late twenties, to face the first problems of the day – the ingredients not arriving, or arriving but having to be returned to the supplier because I did not consider them good enough for my wonderful customers, or perhaps a waiter had called in sick, or maybe it was Jenny telling me that we broke even this month, or worse, that we had lost money. I'd have a double espresso – OK, maybe it was a triple espresso – and then, wow! Maybe it was wow, wow, wow! Suddenly I could focus on the day ahead, replenished with the energy and the passion needed to deal with the numerous difficulties that would come my way. I could tell myself that everything made sense.

In the beginning there were only four of us staffing the kitchen and four in front of house. Of course, I couldn't call in sick, neither could Jenny. We knew we had to make it work because we had put our life savings into the venture. There was £10,000 and there were loans, and when that money was gone, that was it. To make matters worse, interest rates were 17 per cent. Make or break. Sink or swim. You get the picture.

Stamina, I must say, is essential for any successful restaurateur. Another requirement is the constant smile – the smile that hides the grief.

Perhaps because I am a Frenchman, and because the French are renowned for their restaurants, people assumed I knew what I was doing. Of course, I had the knowledge I acquired in Maman Blanc's kitchen and the knowledge of the garden, seasonal produce and varieties. But running a business, running a kitchen, following all the health and safety guidelines and employment laws, consistently giving the best food and training to staff and making money – it's a big ask. You had to be an expert in every field.

The truth is, I didn't have the faintest idea what I was letting myself in for. There was, for example, the question of compiling a wine list.

How many times have you been to a restaurant and studied the wine list, thinking you could do better? Let me tell you, creating such a list is not as easy as it might seem. It takes many years to acquire a good knowledge of wine and to master the skills of choosing wine. When I came to choose the wines for Les Quat' Saisons it would often create headaches (and not simply from the tasting). I worked with a wonderful English gentleman, Mr Tom Abel. He was my wine supplier but he also became my teacher, and I learned a lot from him.

And, as I said, the ingredients had to be the best. In the winter months I'd get an hour's sleep and then clamber out of bed. With my German Shepherd dog Prince as a companion I would head off to London to shop for fruit and vegetables in Covent Garden, then to Billingsgate to get the fish. (Prince loved me very much but hated my driving.) The summer months would allow me a little more sleep as the whole team would go to the local pick-your-own at about six in the morning for three hours of picking.

It wasn't just a case of me knowing what my philosophy was, I had to surround myself with people who could learn it, appreciate it and own it, be part of the culture. If you are the only person who owns the philosophy then your restaurant is going to the wall. A philosophy drives a restaurant, a vision established on a set of values that cover everything within your business.

One of the main things I learned early on is that concentrating on the artistic side of the food is not enough to bring success. You always have to think of the profits, without which you have no business. For an idealist like me, that was very difficult. When I meet aspiring restaurateurs – and I meet them for my BBC TV series *The Restaurant* – I am keen to know why they want to enter this industry. What drives them? What are their motives? The guy who talks only about the food and doesn't mention the service, or the wine, or the accounts, well, you know you have a dreamer. The guy who wants to be a celebrity or a millionaire overnight, please, don't bother. The guy who is totally business-led, who's going to tell you that he wants to make so much money, well, he might not have any charm with the customers – his table manner or personality might be cold – so he too is doomed. The guy who thinks it is nice to run a restaurant for the social status; the guy who believes he can do everything and can't accept help. You'll soon see that a building block is missing.

You need elements of leadership, teamwork, accounting knowledge, knowledge of food and service; you need to have the ability to delegate; you must be able to accept that you don't know everything. I have a good business vision but I'm not a businessman so I try to surround myself with dedicated, able people. If you are not a 'mein host', find the best maître d'hôtel who will nurture both your staff and your guests.

And again, to make a great place to eat you need to appreciate the importance of that smile, which must be constant. It must never drop.

But please, do not mistake me. It was hard, but there were also huge daily rewards, the first of which was meeting the guests. These people came in with huge expectations, and to see them leaving with a broad smile and words of thanks that I could pass on to my team was the very best tonic. It was hard, but I always felt privileged that I had what others only dreamt of.

I was the oddball chef because I left the kitchen to see the guests. Most chefs who open their own restaurant might have ten years' experience behind them; I had practically no experience, but I had front-of-house experience, and this would prove to be very important. My CV tells you that my first job was as a cleaner, and a good one at that. Then a glass washer. Then six years as a waiter. You might think that is hardly impressive – and you are right. But it gave me what most chefs don't have. Regardless of how beautiful the food may be, the service will define the experience for the guests. Whenever you go to a restaurant you know in a few seconds what kind of experience you are going to have and you will probably immediately identify the host – the maître d'hôtel. He radiates confidence; he is in control. He will pass on warmth and true hospitality to his guests. He is the embodiment of the restaurant's philosophy and culture, and his staff will be inspired by his leadership. He will also set up strong systems, service standards and knowledge of food. All that supported by good training will create the ultimate experience for the guests.

Of course the design, the environment you create, makes its own statement and will also define the atmosphere. We have all entered temples of gastronomy where the maître d'hôtel looks like a prime minister and you are surrounded by heavy chintz, plush carpet, gold taps and ancestors looking down at you in a disapproving manner. The protocol of the table will murder both the food and the special moment. Later this world was replaced by another fashion, for minimalist design, which made a statement with its prickliness, coldness and unwelcoming aura. For me, a great design and ambience in a restaurant or hotel is one that immediately tells you to relax. Time stops. It is quietly modern but warm. It doesn't actually make a statement, it simply works with the desired human experience. You sink into an arm-chair, for example, and you know you are in for a great experience.

Our food was bloody good and very affordable. When we opened, the average cost per head à la carte was £18, and the locals were pretty fast to come along and try it out. And when they came, they knew it was something special. We knew we would be able to hold on to our restau-rant – and our home.

Within a couple of months the local newspapers were giving us good reviews, and before long the national newspapers cottoned on to us. In 1979, Les Quat' Saisons was awarded its first Michelin star. There was more. We were named Restaurant of the Year by Egon Ronay, the man behind the guides that steered food lovers to the best restaurants in Britain. A dinner was held by Egon Ronay at the Dorchester Hotel to celebrate this accolade and I was cooking with three other chefs for seventy guests. The other three chefs were twenty years older than me and they were among the best in Britain. They took along their food already prepared. By contrast, look at how I prepared for this important dinner . . .

As Les Quat' Saisons could seat forty, and our customers did not all arrive and order at the same time, in reality I had never cooked for a table larger than eight. I misjudged the demands of cooking for seventy gourmets at the same time. I had only four chefs in my kitchen and we were working hard. Of course, now it would be easy after thirty years of experience and with forty chefs in my kitchen. I would be able to organize it with ease. After all, we have travelled the world with my casseroles and cooked in so many great kitchens, sometimes for up to eight hundred guests. But for that Dorchester dinner, not only did I not have the manpower, I was unprepared. We finished a service at Les Quat' Saisons at midnight. I had given a full list of ingredients to the Dorchester to prepare for me. We arrived at one a.m. and cooked through the night. Somehow I knew it would be a disaster.

First, I was over-ambitious. I planned to serve *coquilles St Jacques en croûte* (scallops in puff pastry) and a warm pâté of turbot. First, the puff pastry went wrong. I could see the streaks of butter through the door. I was horrified. I was also too proud to ask the Dorchester for puff pastry. Then I did the pâté of turbot. I should have tested the temperature of the oven first. But I didn't. I assumed the temperature corrosponded to the dial. Whatever the case, half of the fish was hot while the other half was uncooked.

The food was carried to the tables and guests were far too polite to say, 'The puff pastry was leaking and the turbot was raw.'

The other chefs must have been thinking, 'How did that guy achieve Restaurant of the Year?'

It was my Waterloo. My God, did I learn a few lessons that night. It was, in fact, the biggest learning experience of my life. It was just humiliating.

———

I have searched high and low to find a menu from Les Quat' Saisons so that you might have an idea of the starters and main courses on offer, *et voilà*! It's not from the very early days, but the spring of 1980. Dishes were listed in French, helpfully followed by a description in English. Incidentally, check out the regard for seasonality, as well as our prices . . .

HORS D'OEUVRES

◇◇◇◇

Terrine de Printemps, coulis de courgettes au jus de truffes *(£4.50)*
The generosity, the freshness, the colours and taste from spring – young pressed vegetables served with a courgette and truffle dressing.

Salade de caille tiède *(£5.80)*
Quail, roasted and served on a bed of spring salads, topped with a quail egg, croutons and lardons, the quail juice being reduced and seasoned with walnut oil acidulated with lemon juice.

Parfait de foie de volaille voilé de gelée au xérès et poivre vert *(£5.50)*
The lightest and tastiest pâté of goose and duck livers, with the subtle aroma of truffles, masked with a jelly made of sherry wine sharpened with green peppercorns.

Gâteau de topinambours au coulis d'asperges *(£4.50)*
Mousse of Jerusalem artichokes served with a coulis of asparagus.

POTAGES (SOUPS)

◇◇◇◇

Bisque d'ecrivisses *(£4.50)*
The lightest freshwater crayfish soup.

Potage Quat' Saisons *(£2.75)*
The flavour of spring vegetables and the aroma of garden herbs in a light veal stock.

ENTRÉES

◇◇◇◇

Emincé de volaille flanqué de morilles *(£9.50)*

Breast of chicken filled with quenelle of chicken, served with
a sauce made with Jura wine and Marc du Jura, bringing
out the beautiful flavour of these wild mushrooms.

Aiguillettes de canard aux trois fruits; salade à la peau *(£10.50)*

Breast of duck, cooked pink; the sauce made with
Monbazillac wine, apples and mangos, and a few
blackcurrants; the crispy duck's skin and confit of stomach
served on a bed of salads.

Tournedos grillé au sabayon de tomates et échalottes grises rôties *(£10.75)*

Aberdeen Angus fillet, grilled and served with a tomato
sabayon sauce sharpened with red wine vinegar and
garnished with roasted shallots.

Filet d'agneau rôti dans sa panouffle au basilica *(£9.50)*

It is the best time to do this dish. Welsh lamb, sweet and
tender, the basil fresh and scented . . . welcome, spring.

Côte de boeuf à la moèlle au vin de Chiroubles

(for two people, £10.50 each)
Grilled Scotch Angus wing rib of beef served with a sauce
of Beaujolais wine, meat glaze and marrowbone.

Specials on that particular day included a tomato sorbet on raw sliced artichoke hearts with basil (£4.50); lobster salad on a bed of spring vegetables (£7.50); fillets of sea bass and rock red mullet steamed with basil, pink berries and star anise, the juices enriched with a hazelnut butter (£10.50);

and a paupiette of wild salmon and quenelle wrapped in spinach and sorrel leaves, poached in vegetable stock, bound with a sabayon (£10.25).

The Michelin Red Guide was, and still is, a sort of bible for chefs across the world, probably because it has got international status. The guide's inspectors are hard to spot and you never know when they will come. They will arrive at the restaurant unannounced – not in disguise exactly but hoping that they won't be identified as inspectors. They might visit up to a dozen times a year to ensure that the restaurant's food is of a consistently high standard and therefore worthy of a star or three. One star denotes 'a very good restaurant in its category'. Two stars means 'excellent cooking and worth a detour'. Three stars equals 'exceptional cuisine, worth a special journey . . . one always eats extremely well here, sometimes superbly'. The guide is published annually, every January, and that's the time when chefs start to get nervous, dreaming that they might win a star, or maybe having nightmares that (God forbid) they will face the humiliation of losing a star and the dreadful consequences for their business.

To give you an idea of the food scene in 1982, the Republic of Ireland had four restaurants that each had one star, Scotland had just one restaurant with a star, and there was not a single establishment in Northern Ireland, Wales and the Channel Islands that was deemed good enough by Michelin to be awarded any stars. There were very few restaurants with two stars: Michel Roux's Waterside Inn in Bray, Berkshire, Pierre Koffmann's La Tante Claire in London's Chelsea, and the Box Tree, in Ilkley, Yorkshire, where Michael Lawson was head chef. In that year, there was only one restaurant in Britain that had achieved three stars: Le Gavroche, in London, where the chef was Albert Roux.

In that January of 1982, at eight p.m., in the middle of service, the phone in the kitchen rang. I was annoyed. You don't phone a chef in the middle of service, and this was a particularly tough one.

It was Albert Roux, and he gave me the incredible news: 'Tonight, Raymond, you will sleep on a two-star Michelin pillow.'

All my life I never really worked for stars, whether Michelin or AA. I much prefer to work for excellence. Excellence is enough for me. The by-products of that excellence are these stars. But on that night, of course, I was elated by the news. The team and I drank some excellent wine (beer for my British chefs), and lots of it.

Autumn/Winter
Les Quat' Saisons
Gâteau de Topinambours au Jus de Cerfeuil
Jerusalem Artichoke Mousse with Chervil Sauce

One of my oldest and most popular recipes from Les Quat' Saisons. The Jerusalem artichoke is an ugly duckling in the vegetable family, knobbly and awkward to cut and cook evenly. The quantity of artichoke in this recipe seems large. This is because much of the weight is water and will evaporate during the cooking process, leaving a wonderfully fragrant purée which gives the mousse its distinct flavour.

Serves (Yield): 6
Difficulty rating: ● ● ○
Preparation time: 35 minutes
Cooking time: 35–40 minutes
Special equipment: 6 ramekin dishes, 25cm thick-bottomed saucepan

PLANNING AHEAD
The mousse can be cooked 1 day in advance, then cooled, refrigerated and reheated in a bain-marie.

INGREDIENTS

For the mousse:

1kg Jerusalem artichoke, washed
juice of 1 lemon
3 pinches sea salt
freshly ground pepper
2 whole eggs
2 egg yolks
150ml whipping cream
150ml whole milk
1 tsp softened butter for greasing the ramekins

For the chervil jus:

20g shallot, finely chopped
20g butter
100ml water
1 tbsp double cream
10g chervil, stalks removed, chopped
1 tiny pinch sea salt
freshly ground white pepper
1 squeeze lemon juice

Garnish:

sprigs of chervil

METHOD

MAKING THE MOUSSE:

Peel and slice the artichokes. Steam for 20 minutes. In a liquidizer, purée the Jerusalem artichokes with the lemon juice. (★1) Taste and season. Pour the purée into a thick-bottomed saucepan. (★2) Over a high heat, whisk continuously until two-thirds of the water from the purée evaporates. You will be left with about 250g purée. Leave to cool, whisk in the eggs, yolks, cream and milk. Taste and correct seasoning.

COOKING THE MOUSSE:

Preheat the oven to 160°C. Brush the ramekins evenly with the softened butter and divide the purée between them. Place the ramekins in a deep roasting tin and pour in boiling water, three-quarters of the way up the dishes. Cover the ramekins loosely with greaseproof paper (★3) and bake for 35–40 minutes. (★4)

MAKING THE CHERVIL JUS: (★5)

In a small saucepan, sweat the shallots in half the butter for 1 minute. Add the water, cream, remaining butter and chopped chervil; boil for 10 seconds, taste, season and finish with a dash of lemon juice.

SERVING:

When the mousses are cooked, pass the blade of a small knife between the mousse and the side of the ramekin and turn each mousse onto a warm plate. Spoon the sauce around the mousse, decorate with a sprig of chervil and serve.

Chef's notes:

★1 Putting the lemon juice in the purée will do two things: prevent the discolouration of the artichokes, and lengthen and refresh the flavour.

★2 This stage is to evaporate the water from the artichokes as quickly as possible over a large surface area, so use a wide saucepan and stir constantly to prevent the purée from sticking and burning.

★3 The greaseproof paper will prevent any direct heat drying and forming a skin on the mousses. Ensure the sheet is loose so there is no build-up of heat or you will end up with soufflés.

★4 The mousses will be cooked when they are slightly convex on top and no depression in the middle.

★5 This will only take 3 minutes and can be done to order. The shortness of the cooking will ensure that the chervil retains its fragrance and colour.

VARIATION

If you want more colour in the sauce, add some finely diced tomatoes.

TWELVE

THE BUZZ

The Heaven in Hell

MY FIRST YEAR AS A CHEF–PATRON WAS HELL, ABSOLUTE HELL. BUT apart from the many lessons I learned, I also discovered the sheer joy – a unique feeling – of being a chef. I would like to tell you about that feeling because it might help to explain not necessarily why someone becomes a chef but possibly why he stays in the job.

First, as a young chef you can become so involved, so utterly immersed in the job because service, that compacted period of synchronization, is an experience unlike no other. The chef is under all sorts of pressures: there is money to be made, time to be saved, and you want to give the guest the best. Time. Heat. Proximity. Speed. Space, or lack of it. Exacting cooking and complete coordination of every part of the kitchen. And again, the guests' expectations for the best meal must be met. Two grains of salt may destroy a dish and it will have to be started again from scratch.

In a good kitchen, service is fast-paced and it is powerful. What if the starters don't come together at the same time? What if a main course dish has barely been started when all the others are ready to go? Maybe you cut into the meat and discover it hasn't rested long enough.

Perhaps a guest decides to go to the loo as the table's plates are about to be carried out to the dining room, which means you have to wait for the guest to return to the table before dressing the plates; maybe you'll even have to cook the food all over again. Or maybe a guest doesn't like a dish and it is sent back to the kitchen, throwing the whole service into a spin.

On those days when it goes wrong you are overwhelmed by a sinking feeling. You feel you are in a pit of failure. You know long before the guests do that the day is going to be bad. You sense the exhaustion, you know it is there within you, but if you give way to it then the job will not get done. The business is finished, the restaurant will close, and then you might lose your home and even your wife. So you keep moving. You keep pushing yourself to cook, plate up, cook, plate up.

Then there is the extreme sauna-like heat of the kitchen which batters your senses, along with the movement all around you. Other chefs are going through what you are going through but there is no time to stop and observe. A flicker of movement to your left; another to your right. As service progresses, as more orders come in, you cease to be completely human. You're now driven by adrenalin alone. There is pushing to get to the stove. Push, shove, push, shove. If you're the head chef then you shouldn't get pushed around, but the competitive element is always there. Nothing matters but the moment and being the best.

A sauce is spilt on the floor, which then becomes slippery. The noises of the kitchen are all around you: metal hitting metal; hissing and sizzling; chefs swearing at themselves for getting it wrong; chefs swearing at others for getting it wrong; chefs just swearing for the hell of it. Some chefs say nothing and just get on with it. I am not pretending it is a war zone. Others have far tougher jobs with real danger. But the professional kitchen brings out savage characteristics. The environment is so unyielding it will extract the worst out of anyone.

All the while a flurry of beautiful food is plated up, put on the passe and then whisked away by waiters. The first plate goes, then the second, then (if you are in a successful restaurant) the fiftieth.

Then the last plate goes, and that is the strangest part of all. It lasts for just a few seconds, and it is a few seconds of silence, but it is the best moment. During that period you have that look on your face, a stupid grin, because you got there, you made it. You are sweating like a pig, you are burnt out and you are pale, turned white by the sheer intensity of the heat and the pressure, but for those few seconds you grin away, completely dazed. You know you have done a great service. You are aware that you have achieved something that was close to perfection.

As I said, it is a feeling that lasts for only a few seconds. But for that brief period you feel you are in a different world, supremely floating about with your grinning friends. If you enjoy that buzz, if you get that kick, if you really want that adrenalin-induced grin again, then nothing will stop you being back in the kitchen for the next service.

Just a few seconds of bliss a couple of times a day. But what bliss!

That's why chefs are chefs.

———

These scenes I have described could easily be taken from any kitchen where quality and the guests matter, but I have learned that it doesn't need to be so. The problem with our industry in the past was that our chefs were trained to be craftsmen, not managers, and were ill equipped to deal with these pressures. When facing such extreme conditions often tempers would flare. Looking back, of course I have made those mistakes. Back at Les Quat' Saisons, as I was untrained and unprepared I had no idea what to do with my staff. But I learned from those mistakes and I have spent years now developing strategies for training the people who work for me.

I have placed training at the very heart of Le Manoir, Brasserie Blanc and Maison Blanc to create a respectable industry into which any parent would be happy to send their child. One is often led to think that roughness and chaos in the kitchen where verbal (and sometimes physical) abuse is common is essential to the creation of excellence, but this is wrong. Many hoteliers and chefs in England are now working very hard at creating a modern industry based on respect, in which excellence will thrive. If you come into my kitchen now, first it will be extremely clean, then it will be quiet. Even in full throttle during service, the chef, M. Gary Jones, or chef patissier Benoit Blin, will give his orders and they will be quietly observed. Each person will be passionately involved in his own tasks without the chaos and madness. So the chef has become not only a great craftsman but a manager of money, a manager of people, and a manager of a vision, a philosophy. It is a sustainable modern culture, a strong base from which to grow. I am not saying we are perfect, but we are working at it every day.

The average person who is not in the restaurant business will still be aware of the hardship of restaurants. And yes, it is a tremendously tough business, and the pressure takes its toll on marriage (I speak from experience) and personal relationships, especially when you are starting out. You have to be everything: the cook, the washer up, the cleaner, the accountant, the designer, the wine specialist, the PR man, the hygiene specialist, the human resources expert. You can easily burn out, and it was even easier to burn out in the seventies when there were none of today's work directives. I just worked and worked, and as I was a self-taught chef I worked even harder because I lacked the benefit of training and knowledge that could have been passed on to me. I was learning all the time. Jenny and I were saving constantly, for our next place, so if I fell, if I felt my spirits dropping, I just picked myself up because . . . well, because I had to. Anyone who has ever had to set up and run their own business will understand that feeling.

Although it was a challenging time of my life (and Jenny couldn't have found it easy either), I was immersed deep in the core of Food. As we progressed there were at most six of us in the brigade: I had five cooks, three English and two French, and four front-of-house staff led by the superb Alain Desenclos, who is still with me at Le Manoir today as the director of the restaurant. Emotions were raw, but my aim was always to cook my best. My life revolved around ensuring that Les Quat' Saisons was successful. I was just working to realize my dream and create something truly beautiful.

THIRTEEN

DELICACIES

Sex Appeal

IF I HAD OPENED A RESTAURANT IN FRANCE THEN MY MENU, AND indeed the wine list, would have been guided by what the region had to offer; my team too would have come from the surrounding villages. From canapés to desserts, customers would have been served many dishes made from ingredients that were to be found in that part of France. The wine of the region would have also complemented the food.

But I wasn't cooking in rural Franche-Comté, or in Bordeaux, Burgundy, Provence, Rhône or Reims. Les Quat' Saisons was in a shopping parade in Oxford. And here, as elsewhere in Britain, it was extremely difficult, as I have said, to find good regional produce.

Whenever possible at Les Quat' Saisons I tried to use ingredients that came from nearby farmers and suppliers, but I also dipped into other countries for my food. Gastronomically speaking, I knew very little and was keen to taste and work with ingredients I had never previously experienced. These new tastes included the Russian delicacy caviar and the French delicacy foie gras.

Of course, I had heard of caviar. I knew that it was the salted eggs of a sturgeon from the Caspian Sea and Black Sea. I was also aware that there were different types, each one the roe of a different species of sturgeon. There is beluga, the great sturgeon, which weighs about two thousand pounds and produces the largest eggs. Beluga caviar is widely considered to be the finest if you happen to be near the Caspian, though it is reckoned it doesn't travel well. A beluga takes up to twenty years to reach egg-producing maturity. The sevruga species, which is the main source from the Caspian Sea, takes about nine years before it produces eggs, while the oscietra species is an albino fish and will be about thirteen years old before it produces its golden-coated eggs.

I also knew – and this knowledge was in itself a problem – that caviar was considered to be a delicacy for only the very wealthy. My father's socialist principles had rubbed off on me. Caviar, he would have said, represented inequality in Food because it was available only to the supremely rich. It was elitist, and it was hard to argue against this. So when I first tasted the prized fish eggs, my father's voice was in my mind, nagging away about the immorality of it all. A spoonful went into my mouth and I thought, 'It's OK. The texture is interesting, but the flavour is a bit too salty.' I told the brigade at Les Quat' Saisons as they tasted it with me, 'This is gastronomy's overstatement. Such a fuss is made about this, and for what?'

I must admit I remained curious. The food that I had grown up with was big, wholesome and rustic. I thought I would educate my palate to like caviar, teach my taste buds to enjoy the renowned delicacy of these eggs.

New food takes a bit of time to come round to. Some food we instantly love, some needs to be discovered slowly. My palate education was achieved by tasting as often as possible, which was not often in the case of caviar as it was expensive.

I soon realized that what I enjoyed most about caviar was its texture. The salty eggs go into your mouth and you bite. For a split second you sense the resistance of the membrane around those bubbles of iodide liquid, then, puff! You feel and taste those little explosions.

So after much caviar tasting I have not only managed to overcome my father's socialist prejudice that caviar is food only for the rich, I have dealt with those preconceptions. Sure, you will have the initial expense when it comes to buying caviar, but you can use it maybe as a once or twice a year treat. I put it on to my menu at Les Quat' Saisons but it was never the primary ingredient. For instance, I served eel, which was cooked using different techniques – cured, smoked – and then a tiny spoonful of caviar went into the dish to provide that salty burst. I wouldn't keep it in the top drawer, so to speak. I don't rave about it, but I appreciate it, and there's no question it belongs to Gastronomy.

The woman in my life, my fiancée Natalia (I am sorry to say that Jenny and I have long since divorced; she is now running a very successful design company called Jenny Blanc Interiors), is half Russian, and we are lucky enough to receive supplies of caviar through people she knows in Russia. The tins find a place in our fridge at home in Oxford, and I occasionally have it on those nights when I return late from work. I reckon it has got to be the best fast food available. You need no culinary skills to enjoy caviar. I like it on its own, or with a fine slice of rye bread and soured cream, or with toasted croutons. You don't have to be a cook to slice rye bread and open a pot of soured cream.

The Russians drink vodka when eating caviar, which Natalia tells me works because caviar has a high fat content (73 per cent) and the vodka clears the palate. The French, maybe incorrectly, drink champagne with it.

If you are one of those privileged people with a tin of caviar in your fridge, I urge you to turn the tin upside down every now and again so that the oil is evenly distributed. And, pasteurized or unpasteurized caviar? The latter always. If you're going to treat yourself, take the best.

There is also a question of ethics to consider. The sturgeon has been decimated by pollution and over-fishing. Export of caviar from the Caspian is restricted, which has only increased its price for the consumer. In other words, caviar has become more of a food for wealthy gourmets than it was when my father said it was something only the rich could afford.

Many chefs are turning to farmed caviar, which is ethically produced and comes from . . . the Bordeaux region of France. *Caviar from France? Do not be so surprised.* We need to go back about ninety years when a Romanoff princess, having escaped the Bolsheviks, arrived in Bordeaux. She was horrified when she learned that while the region's fishermen caught sturgeon, the roe of the fish was discarded and never made it on to the plate. Come to think about it, this seems strange to me: surely my fellow Frenchmen, who eat anything, even snails' eggs, would have at least tasted the roe? But as the story goes, the princess encouraged the locals to try it and that is how the Gironde estuary became a caviar producer. The roe came from the sturio species, but by the nineties pollution and water dams had taken their toll. The species became endangered and the region's caviar production seemed doomed. But in recent years caviar farmers have stepped in, creating hatcheries in which the sturgeon – often the baeri species – are kept and will usually reach egg-producing maturity by eight years. One of the producers is an Englishman, Alan Jones, whose Caviar d'Acquitaine is considered good enough to be sold in Harrods and Fortnum & Mason, as well as Petrossian in Paris. We are considering buying it for Le Manoir.

———

Some people might be surprised that I managed to grow up on the other side of the Channel without once tasting foie gras. After all, what translates as the 'fatty liver' (less sexy-sounding than its French counterpart) of geese and ducks is renowned across the world as a French delicacy, a must-have dish on any menu serving haute cuisine. For me, a Frenchman, not to have had foie gras might sound as peculiar as the thought of a Briton never having eaten roast beef or apple crumble.

There is a good reason why I had not tasted it, not dissimilar to the reason why I had not had lobster, crayfish from the sea, scorpion fish, fresh almonds, fennel or melon before visiting my childhood friend

René in Provence. Foie gras is a delicacy from south-west France, and although it made its way into certain wealthy homes and had its place in certain expensive restaurants, I never saw foie gras, even at the Palais de la Bière and the Poker d'As. It goes back to that regional issue. You should imagine a border patrol checking that foods did not stray from one region to another. We had our food, they had theirs. It was certainly never cooked by my mother, and we did not go to expensive restaurants. When I came to Britain, even when I ate at the Sorbonne and the Elizabeth restaurants in Oxford (both Michelin-starred, as Oxford was the second gastronomic city after London) it was not on the menu. I had to wait until my late twenties before trying it. And when I did, wow!

Today, my opinion of foie gras is coloured by the controversy that surrounds its production. But for a moment, let's go back to the late seventies, when the arguments over the force-feeding of the fowl did not exist.

I was at Les Quat' Saisons and serving French food, therefore I reckoned foie gras would have to be on the menu. Money was tight so I ordered one liver. It was the best and was not intensively produced but came from a small farm in the south-west of France. To have ordered a larger quantity would have been too risky: if it did not sell it would have seriously affected our small profits.

The foie gras duly arrived, beautifully shaped and a creamy pink. I had seen many a duck liver in my native Franche-Comté, pinkish red and about a hundred grams; this duck foie gras was 550 grams. How could it have become so big? I was told the stories about the greedy geese in Egypt – but I would come back to that later. For now I was eager to prepare for my first foie gras experience.

I set to work. From the tip of the lobe, I took a slice and put it into a pan, on its own with no butter or oil. It does not need fat as there is enough in the liver itself. I did not season it with salt and pepper. Whenever I taste for the first time I do so without seasoning to get a good idea of what the food is like. As I quickly caramelized the foie gras my senses awoke to the treat that was coming. Oh my God, the kitchen was filled with an incredible new smell. The other chefs, both British, hovered, watched and sniffed the air. They too had never smelled (never mind tasted) foie gras. Stove-side there was an atmosphere of excitement and anticipation.

Soon it was a beautiful golden brown on the outside, amazingly tempting and appetizing to the eye. My gastric juices were running at a million miles an hour. The liver came out of the pan, went on to a chopping board, and I sliced.

Time to taste. I put the foie gras into my mouth, and for a few seconds allowed my taste buds to appreciate the beauty of the food. Everyone did the same, and there was absolute silence in the kitchen. How could food be that good? The complexity of flavours was in-credible. The taste was strong but it was also refined and elegant. Foie gras had sex appeal. I was shocked, taken aback by its deliciousness. You could not help but fall in love with it. It won over my taste buds and heart faster than any other food I have ever tasted. In terms of the delights of gastronomy, foie gras was *par excellence*.

I am reminded that not so long ago at Le Manoir a young guest, a six-year-old boy, came up to me after lunch and said that he'd had the foie gras. I asked him what he thought of it, and he said, 'It was like eating silk.' For a moment, his remark startled me. I'd conjured up an image of trying to chew through a silk curtain. But then I realized that the little boy was so right. Foie gras is silky, with a delicious melting quality – and it tastes much better than curtains.

Having tasted foie gras at Les Quat' Saisons, I knew that I had to use this wonderful ingredient in a dish. I wanted to bring it together with whole tiny shallots, which I soused so that they were sweet enough to complement the richness of the foie gras but also acid enough to balance the foie gras sweetness.

Sousing is much the same as pickling, but the former technique uses a smaller acid content and the acid is applied for a far shorter time than it is for pickling. The main objective is to give flavour to the food rather than to preserve it. Soused food will tend to keep for two or three days at most. To souse the shallots, I cooked them in white wine and vinegar, sugar and water, slowly, slowly, slowly. Cooking the shallot converts the fibres into sugar and slow cooking ensures that the sugar and acid permeates the vegetable, giving me those reliable contrasting sweet and sour flavours.

I also had some French beans which we had picked that morning from a nearby farm and which I thought would work well. (At the crack of dawn I was a regular at the pick-your-own farm.) The beans would bring freshness to the dish. I blanched them in boiling salted water until they were just medium – a bit of crunch, but not too much. Then I refreshed them in cold water to halt the cooking process and retain the vibrant green of the beans. (Many cooks choose to serve green beans rare. Personally I prefer medium as the flavour of the bean comes through better. On the other hand, mangetout, sugar snap peas and young peas love to be cooked rare.)

The dish came together *à la minute*. I pan-fried two or three small slices of foie gras, each weighing about sixty grams, and as soon as they were caramelized they came out of the pan and were put to one side. I spooned out most of the fat, leaving just a little. Then I deglazed the pan with, first, a dash of Jerez vinegar, which I reduced, then a splash of water. What did this do? The acidity of the vinegar removed the glaze (the cooking juices of the foie gras from the bottom of the pan), and the flavours of the vinegar would bring roundness to the overall taste of the sauce. The water rose in temperature, and as it boiled it mixed with the hot fat in the pan and an emulsion was formed. The liquid was glossy, clean and appetizing rather than greasy. Two flakes of salt and a touch of pepper went in. The beans joined the sauce, and now the sauce became a dressing. It had reduced to perhaps only a tablespoon but it embodied a superb combination of flavours.

Then to plating up: first the beans with their dressing; then the foie gras; then a heart or two of soused shallot, which I had previously placed on the lower shelf of the grill just to warm through. Crushed walnuts were scattered to finish.

It was one of the early dishes of Les Quat' Saisons.

Later on I discovered a lovely little technique to cook certain vegetables, easy and fast: the emulsion technique. It can also be done to order. Normally, especially in a professional kitchen, the vegetables are blanched – i.e. immersed in boiling water, then refreshed in ice-cold water and drained. In the case of spinach it would also be compressed in the hands to remove the juice and most of the taste and goodness. It would then sit around waiting for service. When an order came in from the dining room, the spinach was reheated with butter.

Now let's apply the emulsion technique to the cooking of spinach. In a pan, put the butter, water and spinach, a little salt and pepper, and garlic if you wish. The pan goes on to a high heat, lid on. The water steams the spinach and mixes with the butter to form a delicate emulsion, which will give flavour to the spinach. It takes only two or three minutes.

The method can be used with all vegetables: simply adjust the amount of water and the heat and cooking time. Cook peas, for example, for a very short time (30 seconds) in a little water over a high heat. Cook sliced carrots for ten to twelve minutes in slightly more water over a medium heat. Only a tiny amount of fat is required to create a fine layer that coats the vegetable. For me, the best fats to use are first butter, then olive oil, but you can use others. The advantages of the technique are that the vegetable is cooked to order, is light (because there's so little fat) and has double the flavour (because it is cooked largely in its own juices), has better colour and texture (because it is cooked quickly) and has better nutrient retention: all of which is good practice both in restaurants and at home.

I also did a terrine of foie gras at Les Quat' Saisons, following a recipe from Michel Gérard, a three-star Michelin chef whose roots lay in the south-west of France so he knew his stuff when it came to this delicacy. The terrine needed to be matured for two days in a controlled temperature, which gave it a superior flavour. It is a simple process, similar to hanging meat, which I have previously talked about. A great terrine or pâté improves significantly in flavour during maturation, though there is an exception: chicken liver pâté gains very little from the process and is more likely to oxidize and discolour.

Then I began to serve *parfait de foie gras*. It was the richest dish you can imagine, and one that was smooth as velvet (rather than silk). Its components included the magical foie gras, along with chicken and duck livers. It also had Madeira (which had to be dry rather than sweet), port (ruby rather than tawny) and cognac.

The parfait was cooled immediately and topped with duck fat to prevent oxidization and discolouration. I served it with ribbons of soused vegetables (and those soused shallots, again, served cold), wild mushrooms and a slice or two of sourdough bread, so that the parfait could be spread like pâté. This can be almost as good without the foie gras.

One of the loveliest dishes was *gâteau de foie gras*, which was devised by the acclaimed French chef Paul Blanc (no relation). He has a son, Georges, whose son Frederick I trained for three years. It was made with foie gras and chicken livers, milk, eggs (for binding), Madeira and port, and served warm. The trick, as with crème caramel, was to make sure it was barely set; it must tremble on the plate. This dish, interestingly, is still done beautifully at L'Atelier in London.

The trouble, the controversy, started a few years back. Animal rights activists began bombarding me with letters in which they complained about my use of foie gras at Le Manoir and my group of restaurants, Brasserie Blanc.

I did not see the evils of foie gras. When I started to investigate how the liver could come to be the size it is, I was told that extaordinary story which is supposed to illustrate that geese are greedy animals. For thousands of years the production of foie gras was based on the observation that geese stuff themselves before migrating in order to survive as they fly thousands of miles across land and over oceans. Like humans, they store fat to sustain them for their long journeys. Hence the tale of the Egyptian hunter many centuries back who shot a goose with an arrow. When he opened up the bird to prepare it, he was first alarmed to see that its liver was huge, but then delighted with the flavour after he had cooked it. At that moment foie gras was born, so the legend goes. Although there may be no truth in the story, it made sense to me that there was nothing too wrong with force-feeding geese and ducks.

Now, I'm a champion of ethically produced food. The process must care for the animals. That is my strongest principle. So as far as I am concerned every form of intensive farming is a cruel form of production. I would never think of using foie gras, chicken or duck – or any produce for that matter – which has been intensively farmed. I went to great lengths to ensure that the foie gras I served to my guests at Le Manoir was ethically produced. It took me months of research and I would have removed foie gras from the menu if there had been conclusive evidence that there was pain inflicted on the geese. I have letters from a reputable French professor, Dr Guénemé, stating that the stress level of geese while feeding is almost non-existent. And stress is easily measured. Like humans under stress, stressed geese and ducks release the cortisone hormone, levels of which can be assessed scientifically. Foie gras at Le Manoir comes from a few farms in south-west France's Communité de la Renaissance, a group that is a standard bearer for animal welfare and quality. Our foie gras at Le Manoir weigh a maximum of 550 grams and the animals are never caged. Of course, as a result it is significantly more expensive. And I still want to know more. I want to see records of the stress levels of the geese, before feeding, during feeding and after feeding.

I have always stood against any form of intensive farming, whether vegetable, fish or meat. Look at the way chickens and turkeys are farmed in this country, which caters for about 80 per cent of the poultry people eat. These chickens are raised in the worst possible conditions. There is no natural light, they are stuffed with antibiotics, and they are packed so tightly that when they grow they can no longer move around.

The controversy, however, has affected my taste buds. In the old days I wanted to incorporate foie gras in every dish, but less so now. I stopped using it long ago at Brasserie Blanc, as the group of restaurants is associated with my mother's food. The delicacy is also too expensive for a brasserie menu.

Grandmère Tournier had already sussed out how to give richness to the liver. She didn't use foie gras (of course) but she put in an equal amount of chicken or duck liver and lard. She probably couldn't afford butter, and lard was commonly used in the kitchen.

Truffles are a different story. The Périgord truffle, again from south-west France, would definitely feature somewhere on the menu for my last supper. As with caviar and foie gras, I used truffles for the first time at Les Quat' Saisons, but I had tasted them (just once) when I worked at Le Palais de la Bière in Besançon.

It was during the period when I was washing glasses at Le Palais and had started to read up on all things gastronomic. One of the first books I bought was ambitiously entitled (something like) *The History of French Cuisine* and it included pictures from the seventeenth and eighteenth centuries depicting the archetypal gastronome as an obese man with bulging eyes and saliva dripping from his fat red lips. The book was fascinating in that it revealed the evolution of gastronomy and restaurants, and truffles took up a sizeable chunk of the index.

I remember being in the kitchen at Le Palais when a chef passed nearby with a whole basket of truffles. A whole basket! Worth a fortune today. But before I saw what he was carrying my nose picked up the musty complex scent of the funghi, a smell that had filled the kitchen. Once the chef was at his station and seemed settled, I dashed over to him with the sole intention of tasting truffle. I complimented him on his new hairstyle – or was it his new shoes? – and then politely asked, 'Would it be possible to have a little taste of a truffle?'

He took a knife, cut a thin sliver and handed it over with this advice: 'Take it to the oven and warm it up slightly before you eat it.' I followed the instruction, placing it under the grill for just a second so that it was warmed through. It was sensational, quite something else.

Unlike caviar, truffle has got real power in its taste. You don't get what you smell, you get so much more, and it has a wonderful texture, which is destroyed if it is cooked for too long. If you are using truffle with pasta, rice, scrambled egg or in a *jus*, it should be grated and mixed at the last moment so that it can release its flavour. If they are sliced before cooking, the flavour quickly vanishes – within a few minutes – and the slices are ruined. To preserve a truffle, place it in a sealed container with rice and eggs – both will absorb the flavour. The eggs have a porous shell the aroma of the truffle will easily penetrate, and you will have the best scrambled eggs of your life. *Bon appétit.*

At Les Quat' Saisons I splashed out on a kilo of truffles and when they arrived from France I removed two of the funghi and kept them in the kitchen. I took the remainder home for safekeeping and put them in the garage, which was nice and cool as it was early in the year. The next morning I opened my eyes, thinking I had woken up in heaven. The famously strong smell of the truffles had permeated the walls of the garage and travelled into the house and into our bedroom. I lay in bed, a smile on my face, inhaled gently and savoured the scent.

Then Jenny woke up. 'What,' she said, in alarm, 'is that rotting smell?'

Oh well. *C'est la vie.*

One of my signature dishes was *truffe de foie gras*. It was foie gras rolled into a truffle shape, cooled, refrigerated, then dipped in Madeira *gelée* and rolled in freshly grated truffle. It looked and tasted delicious.

The problem was that I needed about ten grams of truffle for each serving, and as a kilo cost me £800 each dish contained around £8 worth. And to that I had to add the foie gras and all the other ingredients. It was not too economical.

One dish I always wanted to create was a wonderful Escoffier recipe I had read, *truffe en brioche*, which seemed to epitomize the supreme truffle experience. The truffles are peeled and wrapped up in the finest slices of Bayonne ham which in turn are wrapped up in a brioche pastry (with a little hole to let steam escape), then left to prove in a warm place for twenty minutes or so. Brush with egg yolk, add a pinch of black pepper then into the oven. When it emerges, the brioche is beautifully gold and inside the truffle is barely warm. The sauce was made from Madeira, port and more grated truffle. Many years ago my parents came to Le Manoir and I cooked this dish for them. I wanted to give them the very best, things they had never had in their lives. It was just sublime – my mother said so. (I never told her the price.) The dish is unbelievable. If possible, you must have it at least once in your life. The black truffle season runs from late December to March so order it well in advance.

About fifteen years ago I went to Cahors and visited Jacques Pebeyre, one of the top producers. He had about a ton of truffles in storage, which was some sight, and some smell. We went to the world market for truffles, where paysans and producers lock horns to argue – sorry, barter – with volume and energy about size, quality of scent and the possibility of worms in the funghi. It's a serious business. While in the region I also went for a truffle hunt with a pig called Lily, who was experienced at finding the funghi in the ground. Alas, I didn't come away with a single truffle. Sure, we came across a few, but Lily's snout was too quick for my fingertips and in the course of a hunt she managed to consume a lunch that would have cost her a few thousand pounds in a good restaurant.

All Year Round
Brasserie Blanc
Parfait de Foie de Volaille
Chicken Liver Parfait

Rich, silky, melting and completely delicious. This parfait remains one of the most popular dishes in Brasserie Blanc. A bit rich, but who cares, this will be the perfect treat with a glass of red wine and friends around your table. You can accompany this with pickles, chutney or pickled vegetables, but on its own it will do very well. This dish gains by being made two days in advance. The depth of flavours will improve quite dramatically.

> *Serves (Yield): 8 to 10*
> *Difficulty:* ● ● ○
> *Preparation time: 20 minutes plus 6 hours' soaking time*
> *Cooking time: 1 hour*
> *Special equipment: Liquidizer, terrine mould 23 x 9cm x 8cm*

PLANNING AHEAD

This should be made 2 days ahead if possible to allow the flavours to mature.

INGREDIENTS

For soaking the livers:
400g fresh chicken livers, gall bladder removed
200ml water
200ml milk
4 pinches salt

For the parfait:
100ml dry Madeira
100ml ruby port

60g shallots, finely chopped
2g thyme sprigs, finely chopped
50g cognac
1 clove garlic, puréed
400g butter, diced
5 eggs
10g salt
2 pinches freshly ground black pepper
150g butter, melted, to cover the parfait

METHOD

PREPARING THE CHICKEN LIVERS: (★1)

Soak the chicken livers in the water, milk and salt for 6 hours, then drain.

MAKING THE PARFAIT:

Preheat the oven to 130°C. In a small saucepan (14cm in diameter) over a high heat, bring the Madeira, port, shallots and thyme to the boil, then reduce by half, add the cognac and garlic and boil for a further 10 seconds. Remove the pan from the heat; reserve.

In a small saucepan (14cm in diameter) over a low heat, melt the 400g diced butter for 6–8 minutes; do not colour. Remove from the heat and reserve and keep warm.

In a liquidizer, purée the raw livers, then add the reduction of alcohols with shallots, thyme and garlic, and the whole eggs, and blend for 3–4 minutes until silky smooth. Gradually pour in the warm melted butter. Add the salt and pepper, and taste and correct the seasoning.

Strain the contents of the liquidizer through a fine sieve into a terrine mould and cover the parfait with a piece of greaseproof paper (so a skin doesn't form). Place the dish in a deep baking tray and slide on to the oven shelf, then pour in boiling water until it reaches two-thirds of the way up the side of the terrine mould. Cook for 1 hour in the preheated oven. (★2)

Remove the terrine mould from the oven and allow to cool at

room temperature for 2 hours. Cover with melted butter to prevent the parfait discolouring. Cover with cling film; refrigerate for 1 day minimum, 2 days for a more developed and mature flavour.

SERVING

Dip the terrine mould in a bath of hot water, turn out on to a tray and gently shake to release the parfait from the mould. Dip the blade of a knife into hot water and cut the parfait into thick slices.

Chef's notes:

*1   The water, milk and salt will penetrate the livers and draw out any blood and bitterness, which would affect the finished terrine.

*2   Check the inside of the parfait after 40 minutes with a temperature probe: the temperature must reach 65–70°C. Do not overcook the parfait or it will split and lose its fine, smooth texture.

VARIATION

Some lightly confit chicken livers in the centre of the terrine would be delicious.

In whites for my first holy communion. All that's missing is the chef's hat.

Left: That's me *(far left)* with the lop-sided fringe and posing beside Michel, Françoise and Gérard. Martine came later.

Below: Aged ten and with my classmates in Saône. I'm on the front row, first left, and have been momentarily separated from my tall best friend René (back row, fourth from right).

Right: Sebastien's christening in the early eighties. From left to right. Alain Desenclos, Jenny's daughter Emma, Jenny cuddling Sebastien, me and Monsieur Restoix, the saviour of Maison Blanc, our boulangerie-patisserie.

Far left: My maternal grandparents Alfred and the genius cook Germaine (also known as La Mère Tournier).

Left: Early days at Le Manoir with my parents and Sebastien.

Right middle: Peeling veg (again) for Maman Blanc.

Right: At home in France twelve snails per person is seen as mean – a tray or two is more like it.

Top: Me *(far right)* with my fellow chefs de rang at Le Palais de la Bière. You can tell it was a proper French restaurant as we were given wine to drink during our breaks.

Above: A quick smile for the camera in the tiny kitchen at my first restaurant, Les Quat' Saisons in Oxford.

Below: A visit to the fish market in Lyon with Paul Bocuse, the dreaded logo business long forgotten.

English recip

SOMETHING very surprising is happening behind the scenes at Oxfordshire's leading French restaurant — the English are taking over.

While Monsieur Raymond Blanc still remains firmly in charge of the haute cuisine at the award-winning Les Quat' Saisons in Summertown, Oxford, he now works in the and replaced them with keen as mustard English youngsters.

What's more this Master Chef turns conventional wisdom on its head when he admits that home-grown talent can — and often does — beat the French at their own game.

He fully expects that his present quartet of apprentices — three young men and a girl — will move to top restaurants on the other side of the Channel once their four years' training is completed.

right with the exception recruited by M. Blanc people are they are de them bean why they are or better.

In Fran ognised for brought

Above: There were about thirty in the team at Le Manoir in the mid-eighties. Today the number has grown six-fold.

Right: I saw the hat as a sacred symbol of my great profession. And my hats got taller with each passing year.

Excellence on a plate

— AND THE CHEF MADE IT ALL UP

Left: In the late seventies with the young and gifted team of all-British chefs at Les Quat' Saisons *(from left to right)*: Mark Peregrine, Joanna Craig, me, Robert Brummel and Mark Houghton. Together we won Michelin stars, were voted best restaurant in England by Egon Ronay, and received glowing coverage in the press.

Top: Taking it easy with many chefs who have trained with me. They include *(holding me up, from left to right)*: Benoit Blin, Gary Jones, John Burton Race and Alan Murchison. Heston Blumenthal and Michael Caines are lurking at the back; Eric Chavot is on the far right.

Above: A very special moment with my sons, Olivier and Sebastien.

Right: When I was a child, my father would send me to rugby tackle chickens for the table. Thankfully I still know how to catch lunch (and even wear a rugby top for the job).

In the kitchens at Le Manoir and Brasserie Blanc.

At Le Manoir with the Queen Mother in June 2001. The picture was followed by a rendition of 'La Marseillaise'.

With my fiancée Natalia.

FOURTEEN

LOGOS

The Smiling Apprentice and the Wretched Cockerel

A T LES QUAT' SAISONS WE WERE SERVING CUISINE THAT WAS winning us awards, and what set out to be a bistro had become something of a gastronomic landmark. However, I'd never eaten in a truly great restaurant. It was only after winning our first Michelin star, in January 1979, that Jenny and I reckoned it was time to go to France. There was some work going on in the restaurant – new carpets and a lick of paint; I'd also treated myself to a new oven to replace the bottomless box – so it seemed an ideal moment for a short break. We decided that we would dine at Paul Bocuse's restaurant in Lyon.

By then I'd had a bizarre experience, a minor conflict, with the French master Bocuse, and the story is worth recounting.

When Jenny and I opened Les Quat' Saisons we didn't have a logo. My restaurant must have a logo, I reckoned, and without too much thought I used a drawing of a cockerel, a centuries-old symbol of France, as an emblem on the menus (and, as I mentioned earlier, on the restaurant's frontage). However, I've always had a problem with the cockerel. Why on earth do we French use it as an emblem? It is a brainless animal that clucks around all day. I just can't understand why we feel it is a suitable ambassador for France. Its association with French culture is said to derive from the Latin word *gallus*, which means both cockerel and Gaul. In addition, the bird is a Christian symbol of vigilance, and in the Middle Ages a cockerel was frequently depicted in churches. The French Revolution boosted the animal's popularity. Mind you, Napoleon had a serious problem with it. 'The cockerel has no strength,' he decreed. 'In no way can it stand as an image of a country such as France.' But in 1830 it was emblazoned on the buttons of the National Guard's uniforms. I can understand the English rose, and the Welsh leek, but what are we doing with a picture of the silly animal on our money? Good in a casserole, but ludicrous on our cash.

So while it was our logo at Les Quat' Saisons, I spent spare moments worrying about cockerels and Frenchness and looking around for another emblem my restaurant could adopt, even if my country wouldn't. Late one night I was going through a book of eighteenth-century lithographs when I came across a drawing I knew would be just right for our business. It was a picture of a chef's apprentice. He was about sixteen years old, he wore a cap, he had dreamy eyes that were so large they were out of proportion with his head, and he had the face of a creative, hopeful young man who has stepped into the world of food and fallen in love with it. I saw something of myself in this young man.

I swiftly ditched the cockerel and replaced it with the little apprentice. His dreamy eyes went on to the menu at Les Quat' Saisons and his face also adorned the bills that went to the customers. He was there again, beaming away, at the head of the restaurant notepaper.

Having just won our first star, I was looking for chefs to come and work in my kitchen, so I thought I would write to all the established chefs of France. I must have come across as very eager, but polite. *Cher collègue*, the letter began. I went on to introduce myself and explain that I was on a quest for passionate, committed young people. If the esteemed chefs knew of anyone interested in coming to Oxford then, please, would they be kind enough to send them in my direction? Each

letter was sent on our restaurant notepaper upon which was stamped my special logo of the ever-so-happy apprentice. The letter went to all the one-, two- and three-star Michelin restaurants.

I received a few responses. I was very flattered that one letter came from Alain Chapel and Freddy Girardet, two of the greatest chefs of the time and men who were very much at the heart of the French food revolution of nouvelle cuisine. They said that they would contact me if they came across someone who wanted to come to England, but at that time no Frenchman wanted to come. France was the gastronomic centre.

Then, one day, the postman arrived with a letter from Paul Bocuse, one of the chefs to whom I had written. Bocuse is a legend in the restaurant profession. He is a three-star Michelin chef, today aged in his early eighties, who has a restaurant called L'Auberge du Pont de Collanges, which is a couple of miles north of Lyon, on the banks of the River Saône. Bocuse's name is associated with nouvelle cuisine and he created the era of chef-patron, or chef-proprietor, the chef who owns or has a stake in the business. He helped export French gastronomy across the world, and although I had never met him I had the utmost admiration for him because, running my forty-seater restaurant in Oxford, I considered myself to be a perfect exponent of his chef-patron vision. He seemed to me to be the champion of young chefs who wanted to become their own bosses and were prepared to take the risks. The world of gastronomy owes a good deal to Bocuse, a figurehead who enjoys huge respect. Heavens, the man received the Légion d'Honneur from President Valéry Giscard d'Estaing himself. You get the picture? Bocuse is a great man. He is a food hero.

I opened his letter. *Cher collègue*, it began, imitating the way in which I had started my letter to him. 'I give you two weeks to remove that logo which has been in my family for years. If you do not remove it, I shall instruct my lawyers to deal with the matter.'

My immediate reaction was shock, then fear, then anger. I was convinced I had done absolutely nothing wrong. After all, I had found the lithograph in a book that was about three hundred years old. Aside from that, it is not in my nature to steal. Even if I had wanted to pinch a logo, why would I choose to steal from such a famous person, and then be so foolish as to send him evidence of my crime in a letter?

I did a little research and established that Bocuse's logo was patented in France and the United States, where he also had a business, but it was not patented in Britain. So I thought, 'OK, let's tease the great man.' My next letter to Monsieur Bocuse read something like this:

I am very, very sorry that I upset you. However, in my defence I would like to say that I didn't steal your property. I was simply looking for a logo for my restaurant and I saw that wonderful little lithograph of that particular ouvrage *in a book entitled* L'Histoire de Gastronomie Française.

As much as I respect you, I feel that your letter is quite offensive because you have failed to give me the benefit of the doubt. You presumed that I had seen your brand and copied it, but that is not the case. I actually took it from that particular book, so I thought it belonged to the world and to anyone because it was drawn in about 1780. There was no mention in the book that the picture of the apprentice belonged to the Bocuse family.

Furthermore, should I wish to keep that logo, I could do so because you have no copyright in Great Britain. But with all the respect that I have for you, of course, I would be delighted to stop using it.

I just wanted to let you know that I didn't steal from you.

My letter prompted another from Bocuse. This time it was quite a sweet note. He thanked me for my decision to abandon the ever-smiling apprentice, and added that he had learned some lessons from the episode. Perhaps he had overreacted, he thought. He also wished me well with my little restaurant in Oxford.

A few months later, when Jenny and I were planning our trip to France, it seemed only right to visit Bocuse's famed restaurant. After all, he was the most talked about chef of the time. We didn't have very much money but we booked a room at a small hotel overlooking the Saône. On the day we arrived it was lovely and sunny and we were both happy. Olivier and Emma were being cared for by Jenny's parents; there was nothing to worry us. We were about to discover the delights of a three-star restaurant and taste the food of the reigning king of French cuisine.

Jenny and I arrived at the restaurant all dressed up. My God, pictures of the little apprentice were everywhere – as statues, printed on everything, even etched on to the glass. We ordered aperitifs and clinked glasses. We were toasting that precious feeling of freedom and that unique moment of going to a great master's house, which was a big thing. I had read about this restaurant and accepted that Bocuse was as big as they come.

The menus were brought to us and there on the pages was that wonderful little apprentice again, beaming as he had done, albeit briefly, on my menus at Les Quat' Saisons.

I noticed that Jenny was quiet and pale. She said to me, 'Raymond, oh no, I'm going to have a migraine.' Can you imagine? After all the planning, the expectation and the travelling we had put ourselves through! Even though the restaurant was being refurbished, I felt guilty that I was taking two days off work (two full days off work!). And of course I felt sorry for Jenny. We left. I took her back to the hotel, put her to bed, put some compressed ice in a towel and rested it on her forehead.

'It's silly for us both to miss out,' she said. 'You go back. I know what it means to you.'

I could have kissed her a million times.

I tiptoed out of the room, darted back to Bocuse's restaurant, and was seated at a table at the heart of this temple of gastronomy. For a few seconds I took in Paul's beautiful dining room – cosy and warm. The staff were welcoming and friendly, with no airs and graces. The prices were high but I ordered *consommé de truffes Giscard d'Estaing* followed by pan-fried sweetbreads and casserole of root vegetables. When the sommelier arrived, I ordered the least expensive half-bottle of Beaujolais Julienas, then awaited the meal, although I was missing my companion.

'Excuse me,' said an American accent on a neighbouring table.

I turned to see two large men who clearly had no problem with the restaurant's prices. On their table they had three bottles of wine. The Americans said they'd witnessed Jenny's departure and wondered if I would like to join them for dinner. It was clear they were richer than me and the idea of paying a third of their bill would have been not merely an extravagance but also impossible as I did not have the money. They must have seen the fear in my eyes, and one of them said, 'Please, be our guest, young man.' I didn't need any more persuading.

This meal became a memorable experience, and it all seemed a bit unreal. Once on their table, and as I allowed them to fill me up with glasses of Le Montrachet 1965 and the seriously expensive Richebourg 1952, I learned that they were from Texas, big shots in the oil industry. They told me how they were living a gourmet's dream, working their way through the Michelin-starred restaurants of Europe. For lunch every day they would eat in a bistro, but each evening they would dine Michelin-star standard. They had already eaten their way through sixteen Michelin-starred restaurants. Bocuse was the seventeenth tick on their list of twenty must-do haute cuisine establishments.

At two in the morning we were still at the table and could barely remember the lovely food we had eaten. Now we were singing, and our friendship was sealed. They promised to come to my restaurant.

A week or so later the Texan oil tycoons flew into Kidlington airport, in Oxfordshire. I arranged for a car to pick them up and bring them for dinner at Les Quat' Saisons. The meal would enable them to boast that they had done twenty-one rather than twenty Michelin starred restaurants in Europe.

Paul Bocuse was not at his restaurant on the night I visited. When I had written to him to say that I was coming, he'd responded by saying that he would be in the States so we'd miss each other. Later, I got a letter from him to say that he had heard I'd had a wonderful meal in his restaurant. 'I hope you enjoyed the food . . . and the wine,' he added.

We met, eventually. He came for lunch at Les Quat' Saisons, bringing his family. Paul doesn't criticize food. He likes or he dislikes. At the end of the meal, he said, 'What great food. You do us proud in England.'

It was the start of what has become a long friendship.

Soupe aux Truffes Noires VGE
Elysée Soup with Black Truffles

Created for the Elysée Palace on the occasion of the presentation of the Legion of Honour to Paul Bocuse by French President Valéry Giscard d'Estaing, 25 February 1975.

INGREDIENTS PER PERSON

10g mixture of carrots, onions, celery and mushrooms, finely diced and gently sautéed in butter
10g cooked chicken breast, diced
20g foie gras, diced
25g fresh black truffles, finely sliced
1 tbsp Noilly Prat or other dry vermouth
250ml strong chicken consommé
sea salt and freshly ground pepper
1 x 60g disc of puff pastry
beaten egg yolk, for glazing

METHOD

Preheat the oven to 220°C. In a heat-resistant soup bowl, place the vegetables, chicken breast, foie gras and truffles. Add the Noilly Prat and consommé, and season. Place the pastry round on top and seal the sides firmly so that the soup's aromas are trapped inside. Brush the pastry with the beaten egg yolk and bake the soup in the hot oven for 18–20 minutes. Serve at once.

From the book *Bocuse à la Carte*, published by Editions Flammarion

FIFTEEN

BRASSERIE BLANC

Remind Me How to Laugh

ONE OF THE MOST MEMORABLE GOURMET EXPERIENCES OF MY life came in the spring of 1982, when I was invited to Alsace to do a cookery demonstration. It might never have happened because at first I was reluctant to accept the invitation. The prospect of leaving Les Quat' Saisons filled me with dread. Just a couple of months earlier the restaurant had won its second Michelin star. Great news, but it meant even more pressure, and maintaining high standards in our minuscule kitchen and dining room was an exhausting challenge. It was so strange to see the Bentleys and Rolls-Royces spilling out their well-groomed passengers in front of a tiny little restaurant in a concrete shopping precinct. I wondered if there would be problems if I disappeared to Alsace.

Two factors persuaded me to accept the invitation. One was that the invitation came from Monsieur Marc Beyer. The Beyer family had been making wine since the sixteenth century and they were one of the top houses in the Alsace region. The second persuasive factor was that the Beyer family knew there were strong links between wine and food. The family had associations with the finest chefs in France, and those at the event would include the likes of Alain Chapel, Freddy Girardet, and the Troisgros and Herbelin brothers, all of them three-star chefs. It would have been stupid to turn down the opportunity to be with them, so I accepted. It was incredible. I'd opened this tiny little place just a few years ago and there I was, about to cook alongside some of the most respected chefs in the world.

'I'll do a quick in-and-out,' I thought. 'Fly into Alsace the night before the cookery demonstration, do the demo the next day, then get a car to the airport and fly back to Britain.' It didn't quite work out as intended.

For the demonstration I'd created a dish which became a great classic at Le Manoir – stuffed morels and the first asparagus in a Gewürztraminer *jus* that would certainly please my host M. Beyer as I was using a local wine. I was nervous as I was cooking in front of these great chefs, but it went well. I was complimented on the delicacy of the dish, especially the *jus*. Afterwards, I was ready to pack my overnight bag and head off for the eight p.m. return flight, as planned, when M. Beyer came to me and said, 'Monsieur Blanc, you are in Alsace.'

I nodded. Where was this one heading?

'Alsace people,' he continued, 'take the time to *faire la fête* – enjoy themselves, have a feast.'

I smiled. He was very kind, I said, but, sadly, work beckoned. I had a restaurant to run, and my flight was leaving in three hours.

'We have spoken to your assistant in Oxford,' M. Beyer told me. 'Your diary has been rearranged. You are going to stay at least two days. You need a rest.'

Perhaps it looked as if I needed a rest. I was absolutely knackered. When you are exhausted and burned on your arms and hands, you don't look very nice.

The next thing I knew, I'd accepted I wasn't going home and was with a group of about twenty people, an eclectic mix that included an opera singer, a butcher, the town's mayor, a member of the Académie Française, many other local chefs and a group of journalists. Though it would not be out of place today, this mingling of classes was not something you would have seen in Britain at that time. We went from one bar to another, the crowd increasing in number along the way, and every now and again someone would raise the subject of food and the desirability of sitting down for a meal. It was completely chaotic, as only the French can be. Finally, the rabble was blown like tumbleweed towards a brasserie and that is where we plonked ourselves down.

The brasserie owner – jovial and lardy, in a big blue apron, and with a stonking red nose which showed his love of wine, beer and *marc d'Alsace* – welcomed us and helped to link tables. I glanced around, and saw children on other tables. I remember thinking that it was nineish and back in Britain I'd never seen youngsters in a restaurant so late. Then eight bottles of wine were lined up on the table and the feast started. There was a rowdy atmosphere, voices trying to shout over other voices, people laughing, people talking all at the same time. More wine at the table, more clinking of glasses, more jokes, from the most sublime to the filthiest. Oh my God, that pitch of laughter. Men were ordering before women. The British protocol of the table had been thrown out of the window.

In this blissfully friendly atmosphere I felt completely lost. I had become so absorbed in my work at Les Quat' Saisons it was as if I had forgotten how to enjoy myself. Everyone was ready to grab that little moment and make it very special, except me. I couldn't enjoy the jokes, nor the spontaneous conviviality. I couldn't join in the conversation. I was almost in a state of shock. I tried to join in, but because of my obsession with work I had actually become an introvert. I didn't know how to join in. It was so wild. I had forgotten how to do *la fête*. I had completely forgotten. Me, who considered himself a high priest of the feast. I had completely forgotten.

It was time to reconnect. In front of me lay the answer. I grabbed the bottle of *marc* (60°) and poured myself a large glass. I drank it down in one and suddenly I started to relax and appreciate the glow of the evening and the fact that I was back with my French friends. After a couple of glasses I'd forgotten about Oxford, the kitchen and the whole world.

It was an awesome meal. The food arrived, simple and gutsy: sauerkraut, fat sausages, andouillettes, smoked belly of pork, tripe. The volume of conversation increased a little and so did the tempo. The atmosphere at times became almost electric before breaking down. Suddenly it was eleven p.m. and everyone quietened down. Then the opera singer rose from his chair and burst into a wonderful aria. Red faces were lit up and everyone joined in. It was a lovely evening with that typical flow of the French meal I had known since my childhood: it begins with gentle social interaction, which grows into an emotional maelstrom. Truly the French are the only nation who can speak at the same time as they listen, which invariably causes a few problems. If the meal is allowed to go on long enough – as this one was – then by midnight the French become ridiculously sentimental. Sweet songs from childhood grip their emotions (I must say, including mine). Then there is reminiscence and reflection, nostalgia and tears. By one o'clock in the morning one of the guests, though usually two, will be sobbing.

The mood on this table had died and been reborn twice, and then, just when I thought it would end for good and everyone would get their coats and say farewell, M. Beyer brought life back into us by shouting, 'Let's go into the vineyards and dance!' Why not? What was good for M. Beyer was good for the rest of us. We weren't in a position – I mean, a state – to start questioning. We could sing but we couldn't talk.

Somehow, don't ask me how, we got ourselves to the vineyard. We were ignorant of the dangers of drink-driving in those days. The only thing we could have hit were deer and wild boar, which we didn't (I don't think). The thought of meeting another partying group of French driving in the same state as us on the same road seems pretty scary now.

Once at M. Beyer's vineyard we lit a fire and went on to sing and dance in the snow all night. At one point, I saw the silhouette of a man kneeling, and when I approached him I realized it was the vineyard owner.

'Monsieur Beyer,' I said, 'what are you doing?'

He replied, 'I am praying that the frost and snow will kill the flower of the vine.'

As it was early March, the flowers had just started to appear on the vines. If the flowers died, then there would be no grapes. Trying to be rational, I said to him, 'But why? You want the frost and snow to kill the flowers?'

'No, I'm not mad,' he said. 'I am praying so hard because I have so much wine and I don't know what to do with it. If the frost kills the flower, the government will reimburse me.'

The party lasted two more days and it took me a week to get back to some form of sanity. M. Beyer did not need to worry, as it turned out. First, the flowers did not freeze. It was a great harvest. And his wines sold across the world, as they continue to do.

If you *really* want to have a great party, head for Alsace. Not only do they have the most wonderful wine and the greatest hospitality and warmth, it is also one of the loveliest parts of France.

───────

That evening worked so well because we were in a brasserie rather than a three-star restaurant.

I have always loved brasseries. When I was seventeen and took on that summer job at the brasserie by the bus depot, I fell for the restaurant's simplicity, the speed of service, the preparation, and the room. I loved the feel of the place, its ambience, even how the room slowly filled up, getting more and more busy. I adored the general friendliness of the people, the simple surroundings. At some point café society became brasserie society. Artists, writers and philosophers were drawn to the relaxed and enjoyable atmosphere. If only the food had been better.

Take a seat at a table in a French brasserie and you might be served *poule au pot*, snails, or a beautiful chewy *bavette* of steak, taken from the shoulder and cooked with mustard, tarragon and chives. There will be *boeuf bourguignon* with chunky pieces of beef, and *coq au vin*. There could well be delights from the pig's head, the ear and the cheek. Brasserie cuisine is inspired by home cooking, though it requires more technique, which takes it to a higher level. It is bourgeois cooking at its best – simple, homely and refreshingly unambitious. It is effectively a cross between home cooking and haute cuisine – think Maman Blanc meets Michelin. Traditionally the food is served by waiters dressed in classic black jackets, black bow ties and long white aprons. They look good but in France they tend to be rude and don't stand nonsense.

I'd visited many brasseries – some good, some less good, some exceptional – in search of the finest bourgeois cooking, and I sensed a niche in the market. In the 1990s in Great Britain good restaurants were few and expensive and mostly concentrated around London. Beside the established chefs, young chefs like Marco Pierre White, Alistair Little, Gary Rhodes and John Burton Race were creating a small revolution, preparing London to become a driving force in world gastronomy. But across the country there was a great need for good, affordable quality food, with fewer frills. I saw an opportunity to open a brasserie, or even a small group of them.

Le Manoir had already been up and running for over a decade by this time. I will return to Le Manoir later, but let me just say here that the concept of the hotel was a grand vision that set out to show off the beautiful things in life. Le Manoir is about millions of tiny, seemingly insignificant details: the angle of a light on a carefully chosen painting; the texture or colour of a cloth draping a table; the choice of bed linen. We'll work tirelessly to find the best for our guests. That particular variety of lavender, for instance, does not line the path to the door by chance. It's there to bring a smile to your face, to connect you to the blue skies of Provence. The herbs in the grounds connect you to food. You only see peaceful white and purple in the grounds, no garish yellows or vermilion reds. But if Le Manoir is haute couture, where every stitch, fold and pleat is lovingly created, then a brasserie is like cosy dressing gown. I'm not sure if the analogy is quite right, but you get my drift. A good brasserie is about comfort, informality, warmth and total relaxation. And great, simple food.

The prospect of opening a brasserie was hugely attractive to me and I longed to create wonderful hearty dishes, very much defined by my mother's influence. Actually we had tried it before in the original Les

Quat' Saisons premises the year we opened Le Manoir, with the aim of creating the first brasserie. John Burton Race, a gifted young chef who had worked for me for five years at Les Quat' Saisons, was appointed head chef. He did so well that the 'brasserie' got a Michelin star in his first year. Great achievement, maybe, but I wanted a star as much as a hole in the head: now it was competing with Le Manoir. It did not make any sense. Bruno Loubet took over and for two years led the brasserie and crystallized the concept. Ultimately, however, we sold the brasserie. By now a luxurious conservatory, it didn't really fit the surroundings. As we all know, both John and Bruno went on to achieve great things for themselves.

So by the mid-1990s I was *yearning* to have restaurants where people could come, not once in a lifetime or once a year but once a week, where the rules were different and the fun was different – a Gauloises environ- ment, the type I'd enjoyed in Alsace. In 1996 we opened Petit Blanc in the Jericho part of Oxford. Jericho had previously been the city's red light district and I think it had only one restaurant, which served Indian food. Now there are twenty. We had a swinging launch party with guests spilling on to the street outside, and the brasserie was (at first) hailed as an instant success. It was as if the residents of Oxford had been waiting for something like this. People came for the happy environment and for the *coq au vin*, simple steak, fricassee of wild mushrooms, quenelle of semolina with Gruyère cheese, and for dessert, my favourites, apple tart Maman Blanc and floating islands. Alex Mackay was the chef who opened that first brasserie. He was brilliant, and we succeeded in our aim. From there we opened Petit Blanc brasseries in Cheltenham, Manchester and Birmingham. Each of them had a Michelin bib gourmand, signifying good food and good value for money.

I would love to say that the success continued. But with a certain amount of humility – a trait I did not learn in France but from my friends in Britain – I must admit that I ended up eating the biggest and most indigestible humble pie. A combination of three things led to my downfall. First, the central costs, or overheads, were too high. We found great locations, some not so great, but were paying vast sums in rent for both. Second, the wage costs were too high. When we needed, let's say, six chefs in the kitchen we were employing seven, sometimes eight. I had no idea how complex a multi-site operation could be. I had the right concept and the right business vision but I just was not disciplined enough to control the costs in implementing it.

The third problem was not so predictable. Customers believed they were eating in a Petit Le Manoir rather than a Petit Blanc. Expectations, therefore, were extremely high. 'Can we speak to the sommelier?' customers would ask, or, 'Why can't you fillet the fish in front of me?', not quite accepting that they were supposed to be in a brasserie. They wanted Le Manoir cuisine at brasserie prices. As a result, perhaps the cuisine became more elaborate than it needed to be, and this only confused the people who were genuinely coming for brasserie food. It was like trying to win a Formula One race in a Deux Chevaux.

I set about looking for a managing director for the brasserie business, and I first met John Lederer about four years after Petit Blanc launched. I liked him instantly, for three main reasons. First, he had an immaculate business record and was a highly respected operational director. Second, he understood my vision perfectly so I knew he would be able to implement it and control it. We also had a French connection. John's mother is French, he went to school at London's French lycée and he spent much of his childhood in France, eating good home cooking and savouring the joys of the table. So he understood the true meaning of a brasserie. What's more, he told me that I was his food hero.

I turned John down. I thought I couldn't afford to pay him the amount he could command. It was only a matter of a few thousand pounds so it was a costly mistake on my part, and a foolish one. It would have helped me to avoid so much grief and pain.

Several years later, in 2006, I finally gathered together a new team and set about rebuilding the brasserie business, and as luck would have it John Lederer was available to lead it. We rebranded the business, changing from Petit Blanc to Brasserie Blanc – simple and to the point.

The brasseries' kitchens are overseen by Clive Fretwell, who came to me about twenty-five years ago, when he was eighteen. Clive said, 'I would love to work with you,' so I looked at his CV. I told him to go to France and learn his craft; learn about seasonality and the importance of regional food. So off Clive went. A couple of years later he returned and I took him on as a commis chef, sensing that he would grow and become my head chef. It took him six years to get there. After fourteen years as my head chef at Le Manoir, Clive joined Brasserie Blanc.

The group is now made up of eight restaurants, and Maman Blanc is very much at the heart of our menu. We serve dishes like Roquefort cheese soufflé, Toulouse sausages with the lightest mash and onion gravy, T-bone steak, and maybe flaming baked Alaska to finish. The values and the vision of the brasserie are now obvious to all: it's about good, honest food.

I'm hungry again . . .

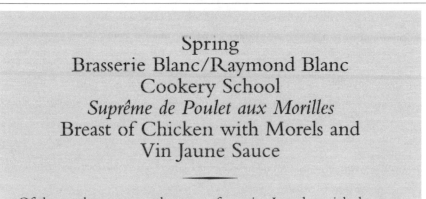

Spring
Brasserie Blanc/Raymond Blanc
Cookery School
Suprême de Poulet aux Morilles
Breast of Chicken with Morels and
Vin Jaune Sauce

Of the mushrooms, morels are my favourite. I used to pick them up in my region of Franche-Comté. Incredibly enough, they can grow in very diverse eco-systems. Their favourite tree to grow by is the ash, but they also grow in odd places like orchards, by the water or near pine trees. This dish is a truly simple and wonderful dish; you must cook it for your family or friends. Morels form a classic association with the Vin Jaune (*1) which comes from the nearby Jura mountains. Fresh morels are very expensive and their season very short (May). But you can buy dried morel in most supermarkets, and they are really excellent. An essential item in your dry store.

Serves (Yield): 4
Difficulty rating: ● ○ ○
Preparation time: 10 minutes
Cooking time: 25 minutes
Special equipment: 20cm sauté pan with lid

PLANNING AHEAD

Soak the morels for 6 hours or overnight.

INGREDIENTS

For the morels:

30g dried morels, soaked in 150ml water

For the chicken:

4 chicken breasts (180g each), skin off
4 pinches sea salt
freshly ground black pepper
30g butter
120g button mushrooms, very firm, washed quickly and quartered
120ml Vin Jaune, boiled for 30 seconds to remove the alcohol (★2)
100ml liquor from the soaked morels
400ml double cream (★3)

For the leeks:

100ml water
1 pinch sea salt
1 pinch white pepper
20g butter
2 leeks, medium size, outer leaves removed, cut across into 1cm slices
  then washed

METHOD
PREPARING THE MORELS:

Pass the soaking liquor through a fine sieve or muslin, then reserve.

Wash the morels quickly under running water to remove as much sand as possible. (*4)

COOKING THE CHICKEN AND MUSHROOMS:

Season the chicken breasts with salt and pepper. In a frying pan on a medium heat, foam the butter. Caramelize the chicken breasts (*5) for 2 minutes on each side and reserve on a small tray. Cook the morels and the button mushrooms in the same pan for 1 minute, add the boiled wine, morel juice and double cream and bring to the boil, then lower the heat to simmering point. Return the chicken to the pan and finish cooking for 6 minutes with the lid on.

COOKING THE LEEKS:

While the chicken is cooking, bring the water, salt, pepper and butter to the boil, add the sliced leeks, cover with a lid and cook on full heat for 3–4 minutes. (*6)

FINISHING THE SAUCE AND SERVING:

Place the chicken on a serving dish and reduce the sauce until it has acquired both texture and richness. Taste and correct the seasoning if required. Pour the morel sauce over the chicken and either spoon the leeks around or serve them separately.

Chef's notes:

*1   Vin Jaune ('yellow wine') is made from the sauvignon grape. The wine is made in an open barrel so that it oxidizes, which gives it its particular character. Vin Jaune can be replaced by dry sherry, which is made the same way and shares some of its characteristics.

*2   See note 2, page 46.

*3   Franche-Comté produces some of the richest milk in the whole of France. A lot of dishes are made with cream and cheese as we don't shy away from either. Not for every day, but for a special occasion you must try it.

*4   The drying intensifies the flavour of the mushrooms; you may lose a bit in texture but you gain in flavour. Morels are honeycombed and may hold bits of sand and forest, and so need careful washing.

*5   The foaming stage is when solid particles of the whey within the butter are browning: about 150°C. It is the perfect stage to caramelize the chicken breast.

*6   Most of our vegetables at Le Manoir aux Quat' Saisons and Brasserie Blanc are cooked this way. You are creating an emulsion with the butter and water. The leeks are not boiled but mostly steamed. By doing so you have more flavour, more colour and retain more of the nutrients, especially the water-soluble vitamins.

VARIATIONS

This dish lends itself to any meat, but pork and veal are best.

Summer
Brasserie Blanc
Clafoutis aux Cerises
Cherry Clafoutis

Clafoutis is one of the great classics of family cuisine. Every house-hold, every family, should know this dessert: it is so easy to prepare. Of course, my mum created the best recipe, which is featured at Brasserie Blanc and is one of the best sellers. Bake the clafoutis right before your meal and it will be at the right temperature at the time you want to serve it to your guests: just warm.

Serves (Yield): 4

Difficulty rating: ● ○ ○

Preparation time: 15 minutes plus 30 minutes for macerating the cherries

Cooking time: 35–40 minutes

Special equipment: Baking dish 20cm across and 5cm deep, cherry stoner

PLANNING AHEAD

The batter can be prepared 1 day in advance.

INGREDIENTS

For the cherries:
400g ripe cherries, best quality, stoned
1 tbsp caster sugar
1 tbsp kirsch (or more!)

For the batter:
4 eggs
120g caster sugar
*1 tsp vanilla purée (*1)*
1 pinch sea salt
30g plain flour
100ml cold milk
150ml whipping cream
finely grated zest of ½ lemon
caster sugar, to finish

For the baking dish:
20g butter, at room temperature
50g caster sugar

METHOD

MACERATING THE CHERRIES: (*2)

Mix together cherries, sugar and kirsch, stir and macerate for 30 minutes. Preheat the oven to 180°C.

MAKING THE BATTER:

In a medium-sized bowl, mix the eggs, sugar, vanilla and salt. Whisk in the flour and gradually the cold milk to create a smooth batter. Finish off with the cream and add the lemon zest right at the end. Reserve.

PREPARING THE BAKING DISH:

Rub the butter inside the dish, add the sugar and shake so it coats the whole dish. This will add a lovely crust to the clafoutis.

MIXING AND COOKING THE DISH:

Mix all the cherries and juice into the batter, stir and pour into the sugar-lined baking dish. Sprinkle with caster sugar. Bake the dish in the middle of the preheated oven for 35–40 minutes. (★3)

SERVING:

Remove from the oven, sprinkle with caster sugar once more and serve warm to your guests.

Chef's notes:

★1   Vanilla purée is made from whole vanilla pods and is a much less wasteful way of using them than opening them and scraping out the seeds. Dissolve 60g sugar in 60ml water, bring to the boil, reduce to a syrup then set aside to cool. Chop up 6 whole vanilla pods and purée them in the cooled syrup using a liquidizer. Now you have your own vanilla syrup to use by the teaspoonful. But if you must use vanilla essence, please use the best available with all natural ingredients.

★2   By macerating the fruit with sugar and kirsch you will have a far better flavour. Kirsch is an alcohol made from cherries.

★3   This recipe is for a fan-assisted oven; if you use a static oven it will take 10–20% more time. The clafoutis is cooked when the surface has become slightly domed. To be sure, place the blade of a knife in the middle and it should come out clean; if you use a probe in the centre, it should read about 92–95°C.

VARIATION

The cherries can be replaced by other soft fruit such as apricots, plums and pears.

SIXTEEN

STOCKS

Taking Stock

IPROMISED TO RETURN TO THE SUBJECT OF STOCK, AND NOW SEEMS as good a time as any. I cannot remember ever seeing my mother use a stock, be it in onion soup or any other dish; in casseroles she would use a bit of flour to thicken the sauce, or use the cooking juices, and there is nothing wrong with that. Instead, for a good taste she relied on the meat in the stew rather than depend on stock for flavour. And who could dispute her culinary skills?

So, what is a stock? What is it for? First, professional kitchens do need stocks, but at home they are usually unnecessary. I'll be simplistic and divide them into two categories. To begin with, the thin stocks, such as clear vegetable stock, or chicken stock, or fish stock. Often they are used to cook a dish, be it a risotto or a soup, or to create the base of a sauce, and also to enrich one. Then there are the richer stocks, cooked for a longer time, which are mostly based on meats such as lamb and veal. Often these stocks will be reduced by half and become 'demi-glace' (giving depth, strength and thickness to a sauce) or further reduced by half to 'glace' (sticky, rich, a bit like Marmite). All of these stocks are used to concentrate the flavour of foods.

I would go so far as to say that stocks (and I am not talking cubes) are often detrimental to a dish because they can overpower other flavours. In a soup, for instance, stock can destroy the freshness of vegetables rather than enhance flavour, so I would never encourage anyone to use it in a soup, at least for home cooking. But there are times when a stock will bring richness, more flavour and depth to a sauce. The cook must think about how it will affect the taste of a dish. Remember, as well, that it will create twice the amount of work because you will have to make the stock before you can make the soup. Will you get twice the amount of pleasure out of doing that? I doubt it.

However, when I was propelled to the head of the kitchen at the Rose Revived, I began to use stocks in my cooking. I understood that stocks were the foundation of the complexity and depth of sauces I had tasted at the Poker d'As and the Palais. At this time only cubes existed, and I despised them (I still do), so I began to experiment with the classic stocks of the great master Auguste Escoffier.

Cooks talk about white stock and brown stock: white when the meat and bones are not browned before being simmered in water, brown when the meat is first caramelized in a pan or in the oven before water is added. Caramelization gives brown stock its appetizing colour and extra flavour. Roast chicken, after all, has more flavour than poached chicken. Escoffier's white stock (with veal as its primary ingredient), or *fonds blanc*, went like this: 'Veal bones and shin of veal, fowls' carcasses, carrots, onions stuck with clove, leeks, celery, faggot of herbs [bouquet garni], water, salt. Allow to boil three to five hours, skim carefully, strain and put aside until wanted.' His white chicken stock is the same recipe but with the addition of 'old chicken and carcasses'. For a brown stock – *fonds brun*, or *estouffade* – he advised: 'Shin of beef (flesh and bone), shin of veal, raw ham, fresh pork rind, carrots and minced onions, browned in butter. Break the bones, and colour in oven in saucepan, moisten with water, add the vegetables and a faggot of herbs, cook slowly for eight hours, strain.'

I am an Escoffier admirer, and unquestionably he was the great modern chef of his time, the first to recognize that a good stock needed meat (which provides flavour), that the bones, connective tissue and collagen provided natural gelatine, and that to extract all that he needed time. But I have issues with his stocks. Maybe in the early twentieth century when food and staff were cheap and plentiful his recipes were appropriate, but everything has changed. I was not happy with the brown sauces. They were thickened with roux, bitter, and laden with gelatine as they had cooked for eight hours, becoming sticky. The *jus* of Escoffier were unaffordable and too complex, taking too long. They didn't fit the modern concept of food at all. I was looking for something cleaner and fresher. I wanted to extract simplicity from the stock. There was also that subject of taste, or rather *tasting*, which is not mentioned by Escoffier. If the cook were asked to taste every fifteen minutes he'd be able to establish for himself the development of flavours. He would then be able to identify when the stock had reached its best and that to cook it any longer would destroy it.

Escoffier's brown stock would be cooked even longer if it were to be incorporated in sauce Espagnole, which is a brown roux, brown stock, tomatoes, mushroom parings, *mirepoix* of carrots, onions, thyme and bay leaves. It is also known as brown sauce, and chefs used to cook it for about two days. I exaggerate, but only slightly. When I was at the Rose Revived I tried to work with sauce Espagnole, but it didn't make any sense to me because after eleven hours of cooking the result was far too sticky. As I said, I like clean flavours, which Espagnole most certainly is not. Stock is there to lift flavours rather than to overpower them.

I began at Les Quat' Saisons by telling myself that Espagnole was from a bygone era, and that it called for too many ingredients – too many ingredients – and it needed massive pots which would take up stove space, as well as the time that was required to cook it. I wanted to create a stock that would be light and rich enough to support the meat without overpowering its own character, an unctuous *jus*, barely coating the spoon, that added a little bit of richness and texture. That's what I was looking for. Chicken just had to be the right protein for my stock. It became obvious. Of all the meats it was the most delicate. So I set to work.

As I said, I wanted a simple stock to which I could add complexity later, so no salt, as meat has natural sodium, and no flour, as there were plenty of cartilages, connective tissues and collagens from which gelatine would leak out, giving the stock richness, texture and taste. To do a good stock, I understood you needed both the meat and the bones. The meat provides flavour, the connective tissues the richness, the bones the texture. There were certain criteria for my meat to do with afford-ability, time-consciousness, simplicity and deliciousness. A whole chicken was too expensive, but chicken wings had everything. They contained half meat and half bones.

I didn't want to cook the stock for long. You simply don't need to. Once the inside of the meat has reached 75°C it is cooked and all the juices and flavours of the meat will have been extracted.

Everyone should be tempted to do this at home, it is that simple. When this stock is added to your sauces it will bring that touch of magic which you have tasted in the sauces served in restaurants.

All Year Round
Le Manoir/Brasserie Blanc/Cookery School
Jus de Volaille Brun
Brown Chicken Stock

Using brown chicken stock as a base for your sauces will give you a delicate and not overpowering accompaniment to your roasted meats and some fish dishes. This is an essential element in retaining a light balance of flavours in my cuisine, and is probably the simplest and least time-consuming brown stock.

Serves (Yield): 1.2 litres
Difficulty rating: ● ○ ○
Preparation time: 15 minutes
Cooking time: 1½ hours
Special equipment: 30cm heavy-bottomed saucepan

PLANNING AHEAD

Once this stock has been made, it can be stored in small containers in the freezer to be used as and when required.

INGREDIENTS

*2kg chicken wings, each chopped into 3 pieces (*1)*
100ml oil, non-scented (such as groundnut or sunflower), plus 1 tbsp
250g Spanish onion, diced 5mm
1 garlic clove, skin on, crushed (to yield 5g)
150g (3 medium) flat mushrooms, halved and thinly sliced
1 bay leaf
1 sprig of thyme
*6 black peppercorns, crushed (*2)*
1.8 litres cold water
*2 tsp arrowroot or cornflour dissolved in 50ml water (*3)*

METHOD

In a large saucepan on a high heat, brown the chicken wings in the oil for 30 minutes, stirring occasionally with a wooden spoon. (*4)

In a medium-sized sauté pan on a medium heat, cook the onions in 1 tbsp oil for 10 minutes until light golden. Turn the heat up high, add the garlic and mushrooms and cook for another 2 minutes. Reserve.

Drain the chicken wings into a colander to remove any excess fat. Return the chicken wings to the large saucepan along with the vegetables and herbs and cover with the cold water. Place the pan over a high heat and bring to the boil for 30 seconds to allow all the impurities to rise to the surface; skim them away with a large ladle. Turn the heat down to a gentle simmer so the bubbles just break at the surface and cook for 1 hour.

Whisk the dissolved arrowroot or cornflour into the stock and bring to the boil to bind the stock lightly. Strain the stock through a fine sieve. Cool, then chill or freeze.

Chef's notes:

*1 By chopping the chicken wings you maximize the surface area, which will translate into maximum flavour and also shorten the cooking time.

*2 No salt is added to this stock as all meats already contain some.

*3 The arrowroot will give a little body to the stock. To create a proper *jus*, reduce the stock by half.

*4 The degree of even, thorough browning of the bones will determine the taste and quality of the stock. If you do not colour enough, both colour and flavour will be lacking. However, if you colour too much the resulting stock might have a bitter edge.

VARIATION

You can use this technique to make a beautiful stock from veal, pork, lamb, etc.

SEVENTEEN

BREAD AND SWEET THINGS

Crazy But True

MY CAREER PATH WAS SUCH THAT I BECAME A CHEF–PATRON overnight, running the kitchen as the head chef and running the business with Jenny in the role of proprietor. If I had been lucky enough to get a job as a chef at Le Palais, I would have worked my way up from commis to the top, which would have taken ten to twelve years. In that case there is one section without question that I would have wanted to run – Patisserie, otherwise known as Pastry.

I love every section, but Pastry is my favourite. Pastry does more than simply make pastry, as its name would have you believe. A restaurant's Pastry section makes all the desserts and sweet delights that give you ultimate joy when you eat out in style.

Actually, I would like to take this opportunity to apologize to my brigade at Le Manoir, especially my chef de patisserie Benoit Blin who has worked with me for the past twelve years, for giving them such incredibly complex dishes. It was all very well for me to make one, but they had to make thousands. (Speak of the devil. Just as I was thinking of him, Benoit dashed into the room with his digital camera, eager to show me photographs of a Grand Marnier soufflé he has just made.

Benoit comes from Normandy and we still fight over whose mother makes the best *riz au bit* – rice pudding – and the best apple tart. We have never been able to resolve it.)

With patisserie I feel most at ease. It is highly enjoyable and richly rewarding because, as we all know, desserts are often the most popular course. To me, it represents a wonderful opportunity to win the heart and soul of the guest. Let me explain. It is the last dish of a celebration so it is the chance not only to create a delicious dish but to stretch your creativity for this final frivolity, to leave them with a smile and a wink. The starter and main course are serious, but a dessert is a chance to tease.

Most of my desserts are founded on these values. Most of them have been inspired by still-lifes. An autumn still-life of ceps in a forest, the tops of the ceps made from chestnut parfait, the feet from hazelnut meringue, on a forest floor of chocolate leaves. A fat Juna Gold apple became the home of a beautiful Calvados soufflé. A painter's palette was made from the finest crispy pastry, the brush was made of caramel sugar, the paints were six quenelles of beautiful shiny ice creams representing all the colours. My daily coffee in the morning became a great dessert called café crème that took me six months to create. The finest leaves of bitter chocolate shaped into a cup and saucer that appeared to be of the finest porcelain, so thin you could see through it. The cup was filled with espresso biscuits, topped with an iced parfait of espresso and finished with the frost of the lightest lemon sabayon, topped by swirls of essence of coffee. The sugar cube was a chocolate ganache rolled in praliné. Detail, detail, detail. *Bon appétit.*

But the best dessert I have designed was inspired by the most wonderful of Maman Blanc's desserts, the floating islands. It was im-mortalized as a *cassolette aux abricots*. The bowl was made of the finest powdered nougatine, filled with a confit of apricots, topped with a poached meringue, the best vanilla cream and threads of hardened caramel. Then it was topped with a beautifully crafted nougatine lid so that you could discover the whole dish for yourself.

Sometimes I wonder if I love patisserie because of my childhood. As a child I had a sweet tooth and treasured Saturday and Sunday afternoons when my mother would make marvellous tarts of wild cherries or pears or apricots. In the winter months she'd make *pithiviers* with almond frangipane in puff pastry.

———

Thoughts of patisserie not only take me back to childhood, they also, inevitably, bring back memories of Maison Blanc, the patisserie I launched in 1981 with Jenny, three years after we opened Les Quat' Saisons.

I have so far avoided mentioning Maison Blanc because its creation was so intense and caused frequent headaches. Even now, the mere thought of those early days sets my temples throbbing. But this book would not be complete without reference to the patisserie, and I have taken the wise precaution of having some Anadin at my side to help me as I dip into the memory bank.

Although Maison Blanc went on to become a thriving business, with outlets across the country serving the best of French patisserie – delicious cakes and pastries – the initial idea behind it was based on something unrelated to sweet food. Les Quat' Saisons was already classed among the three best in the country and was breaking even, but I was seriously preoccupied. I'm talking sleepless nights preoccupied. The reason for my anxiety was bread. The worry nagged away at me, morning, noon and night. In short, we had a French restaurant but no French bread.

If it was difficult to find good food in Britain in the seventies, it was impossible to find good bread. I did not know of a single bakery that served the quality of bread any connoisseur would touch, and certainly nothing I was happy to serve to my guests. In those days the symbol of British bread was a factory loaf, white, sliced and sold in a plastic bag.

The bread was bleached white to make it look appealing, a process that robbed it of nutrients and goodness; the synthetic vitamins would then be injected back in. If brown bread existed it was not much different from the white stuff, but artificially coloured. Its only advantage was that it kept for ages because it was pumped full of preservatives. I had never seen bread that kept for so long without going mouldy. Every television commercial break, it seemed, featured an ad for sliced bread, so imagine the money those companies were making. Factory bread has clever marketing tricks behind it: images of wheat waving in a gentle breeze in a beautiful English valley, accompanied by classical music. We were all fooled. It was marketing at its best and worst. They sold it to us and we bought into it. Still, I am astonished that factory bread remains a massive seller (though the producers of cheap food always benefit from a slowdown in the economy).

Couldn't I make my own bread? Yes, I tried it, but with difficulty. There were a number of serious problems that impeded my success. The restaurant's kitchen, with its corrugated iron roof, had a constantly changing temperature, ranging from scorching hot to freezing cold. Then there was the draught problem: whenever the front door opened a gust of wind swept right the way through the dining room into the kitchen. One night I stood in amazement as that draught came hurtling through the kitchen with such immense power that it took off the fluffy tops of two soufflés. As you know, I had only the one oven, which was tiny and missing its bottom. Could it even be described as an oven? It was more of a three-sided box that was sometimes warm inside. It could never have given me the same results as a special bread oven in which the heat comes from the top and bottom. The cooking process also benefits from an injection of steam, which helps to develop the crust and adds shine to the bread, making it puff up. The steam injection, too, could never have been accomplished in my oven-box. Life later changed, of course. The minute I won my first Michelin star in 1979 I decided to treat myself to a gleaming new oven, which helped me to win my second star. I gave the oven-box to the Oxfam shop above the restaurant. But I still had the draught blowing into the kitchen every few minutes and ever-changing temperatures.

I'd look at what I produced, taste it, then dream of that classic French loaf. This dream turned into an obsession, and then into an imperative. To keep standards high, I told myself, we *needed* quality bread.

I looked into the idea of buying a special baking oven, but the best ones were big and required space. Our kitchen was too cramped. If we'd installed a bread oven there wouldn't have been any room for anyone else in there. It could only have gone on the roof. My research also showed that bread ovens were hugely expensive, and they had to be specially installed. Although I wanted good bread, I had to accept that it would be financially insane to spend an astronomical amount of money solely for a forty-seater restaurant.

Jenny, the businesswoman in our partnership, was convinced that if we opened our own bakery others would buy the bread too, thus making the business worthwhile. And that is where the idea for a bakery came. Originally, Maison Blanc was to have been a bakery serving fantastic bread.

Admittedly, I was seduced by the idea of creating a mini France within Oxford. Oxford was a sophisticated city, and home to many academics who were well travelled. La Belle France was, and still is, one of the favourite destinations of the British, and the Oxford academics were frequent Channel hoppers. I knew the academics loved France, but I was also aware that they loved their money more. Would our mini bakery encourage them to put their palate before their pennies? Would they pay the extra money to replace their anaemic bread with a delicious baguette or *pain de campagne*? Would they give up on their factory bread that could last for a week in a plastic bag and buy into the idea of purchasing freshly baked bread on a daily basis? I loved the thought of the streets of Oxford being filled with academics and professors biking around with our baguettes under their arms.

I didn't visualize just a bakery, but one that sold bread outside, enticing passers-by. If you are going to do it then do it well. And of course it was only a matter of time before we realized that it could not sell only bread; there would have to be more on offer for our potential clientele. So the plan for the bakery developed to take in a confectionery theme. It would sell, we agreed, pastries and cakes, croissants and *pain au chocolat* as well.

Had it remained a pipe dream it would have been a pleasant one, but the period from dream to reality was just a few months.

At this point I need an aspirin. Excuse me.

It was utterly insane. There I was, making a name for the restaurant and at the same time throwing myself into another venture. I had barely mastered the art of brioche-making, puff pastry and choux pastry, and I was making only a kilo or two at a time, unlike the thirty kilos needed for a patisserie. A bakery-patisserie should be overseen by an operations director with experience of both baking and patisserie. Then we needed a chef de patisserie and a chef baker. I was none of these.

The business we were about to engage in was complex, the investment enormous. What's more, I am not an entrepreneur. I don't have the entrepreneur's spirit. Entrepreneurialism clashes with my nature. I saw myself more as an artisan, and the artisan works in his kitchen and at his little business, dealing with the daily problems rather than focusing on the dreadful things that might lie ahead. If I were an entrepreneur I would have at least fifty restaurants by now, but I do not. I was driven to set up Maison Blanc not by business acumen but by a desire to have great bread in the restaurant. I went to London to meet the top quality retailers, such as Harrods and Fortnum & Mason, and the best hotels and restaurants. All seemed excited by the venture and keen to buy our bread – if it was good enough.

I don't mind telling you (now) that I was petrified. I didn't want to build an empire, and although we are only talking about a bakery and a restaurant, it seemed to me like an empire. A few years earlier I had dreamt of having one place. And I had it: it was Les Quat' Saisons. One was great; more than one just didn't seem right. I was also frightened by the prospect of having to split my passion, my resources and my time between the restaurant and Maison Blanc. There I was, working sixteen, seventeen hours a day at Les Quat' Saisons. Three days a week I'd make early-morning drives into London to buy produce from the capital's markets. Come summer I'd be in the pick-your-own fields at dawn, collecting peas, strawberries, raspberries and other fruit and veg.

Jenny and I decided to go ahead with the project.

The next thing I knew we had acquired a property just a few minutes' stroll from the restaurant. Another Oxford restaurant, the well-established Brown's (still there), came in as our partners, thereby lightening the financial burden. They helped us with the accounts and with their general good business sense.

The shop, which was on street level, was in an excellent position, close to busy Brown's and with parking nearby. It was furnished with dark oak and beautiful shelves and was not trying to be fussy and high-tech. Instead it had a country feel about it. The kind of bakery you might have seen in post-war France (a bit like me). We put up a sign that assured customers 'Mangez du bon pain, vous vivrez bien' (Eat good bread and you will live well). Looking at it from the outside, you could have been in the heart of France. Vive la France!

The patisserie was downstairs, and the bread was baked at the back of the shop; the comforting smell drifted pleasantly through and spilled out on to the street. Two ovens arrived, one for the bakery and one for the patisserie. The first was a Pavaillier, a four-shelved beast with four huge rectangular mouths that could swallow vast numbers of baguettes at a time, a monster piece of machinery and the finest when it came to distributing heat. The bread was baked on hot stones, and heat also came from the top, giving it a lovely crust. The patisserie oven, the Pontont le Meunier, although smaller, was ten times heavier. It was made of about five tons of bricks and it took two weeks to build downstairs in the patisserie. It was not the French but the Greeks, skilled bakers, who came up with the idea of brick ovens (though the Egyptians were the first to make bread, some four thousand years ago). Bricks hold the heat and then disperse it gently.

I was in love with both new ovens. Once they were in, I stood in front of them for ages, captivated by their sheer beauty. If Sophia Loren had been on the other side of the room I wouldn't have known which way to look.

Now we had to find staff, the best team, and that was the next problem.

The French are fiercely nationalist, especially when it comes to bread. There is also the traditional enmity between our two countries, based on our shared history. At that time English food, and particularly bread, had the worst reputation in France. It was a long time before the entente cordiale had the success it has now: there are now over 350,000 of us living in London. We needed a French baker and pastry chef because we were selling French bread and pastries, but trying to find a French baker in England was like trying to find a pub in France. We advertised in the British trade press. We believed that if the chefs were based here they would already be used to the standard of food and the weather, but not a single response. Then we advertised in France and – success – we found four commis chefs and a chef de partie. We were still missing the chef de patisserie, the chef baker and the operations director.

Eventually, we got half lucky. We got a French baker, Michel, and a chef de patisserie, Pascal, but the boss eluded us. As far as Michel's CV was concerned, it was frightening. He had thirteen years' experience but, worryingly, had never stayed more than six months in any one place. The CV had book-like volume. Beggars are not choosers, however. At least he was a French baker with a CV.

We carried out taste tests on the food we intended to serve. I remember trying a croissant the chef had baked and saying, 'I am sorry but that is not good enough.' At that point I had no idea how to make croissants but I knew how they should taste. The chefs then created croissants that were out of this world.

Jenny, who did a brilliant job overseeing the shop, found some wonderful staff and set about teaching them how to cash up and charm the customers. Service in those days was often mistaken for servitude. We tried to instil pride in the staff so that we were all working together as a joint venture, each employee as important as the next.

Meanwhile, we went back to see the retailers and hoteliers who'd shown interest in the bread. First of all to Harrods, to see if they would sell it in the shop's famed Food Halls, which are a sort of convenience store for the wealthy inhabitants of Knightsbridge. They said yes. Then we returned to the Intercontinental and other hotels. They all wanted to buy from us as nothing like our new bakery-patisserie existed at the time. The real test would be Le Gavroche, Albert Roux's Michelin-starred restaurant, which was just off Sloane Square, in Chelsea (it had yet to relocate to Mayfair). Albert tasted the bread and agreed to buy it. If Albert, the standard bearer of quality, said yes, it was good enough for anyone.

At this point things were looking quite good.

On the morning Maison Blanc opened I stood on the pavement outside to hear the comments of shoppers who were wandering past this wonderful new bakery-patisserie. I wanted to know their opinions as they glanced through the window and saw the shelves of patisserie that were displayed, looking mouthwateringly delicious – the éclairs, the *tartes aux pommes*, the frangipane-filled pastries.

Soon a little crowd had formed. Some had just taken in the sight of the pastries, tarts and chocolate cakes; others had read about our opening in the local press (yes, I can muster up PR when need be) and had duly come for an inspection. Most of their comments were made in hushed tones I couldn't quite hear. Suddenly, all other voices were drowned out by an elderly, well-dressed but agitated man whose accent

I recognized as belonging to an intellectual or academic. He was pointing with his finger to the sign above the shop – Maison Blanc. 'They claim to be French, but they can't even spell. *Maison* is feminine; it should be *maison blanche*. What a farce!' He became even more agitated when he pointed at a tart in the window and said, 'That's disgusting!' He was not referring to the food itself, but to the price of it. 'Fifty pence!' he told the other onlookers, my potential customers. 'That's unheard of. If you go to the baker's down the road you can buy a doughnut for fifteen pence. And it's three times the size of that tiny tartlet. What's that Frenchman playing at?'

I was mortified and could not stop myself from interrupting his rant. I stepped forward, like the creator unmasking himself, and said to him, 'Sir, maybe you should try it because perhaps it will be very special.'

He clocked the French accent, looked me up and down, sneered and replied, 'My boy, what I want is food, and lots of it.' He then marched off, his parting words delivered loudly from twenty yards down the road: 'I'd never pay that sort of money!'

He was not alone. Other customers, or probably potential customers, grumbled that we were overcharging. I found this confusing. On the one hand there were shops selling factory-produced chocolate éclairs made from chemical-laden pastry, artificial, over-sweetened whipped cream, and finished off with a brick of disgusting chocolate on top. In Maison Blanc, by contrast, our éclairs were made by loving hands. They had a perfect shiny fondant and were filled with delicious creams made, for example, with kirsch and vanilla or caramel. The nasty éclair cost about twenty pence while our magnificent, genuine éclairs sold for about fifty pence each. But in those days the consumer was severely price-conscious when it came to food. The academics of Oxford would happily spend money on the opera, a car or their children's education, but not on food. When they thought of food, quantity meant more than quality, and the nasty éclairs were twice the size of ours.

The truth is, we were making hardly any profit and should have doubled our prices, though heaven knows what that would have done for business.

Then there was the bread. Remember, my dream was to sell French bread, and in order to achieve this I had taken the trouble of ensuring that all the flour we used came from France. Customers would come in and buy a baguette. The next day they'd return clutching half a loaf and complaining, 'It's gone stale.' I found myself in endless conversations with the loaf-clutching complainants, trying to explain to them that *a baguette is a baguette*. 'It is not made with chemicals and conserving agents like most bread that is sold in England,' I'd say. 'The flour has not been bleached. The baguette is crisp and that's it. You buy it and eat it. If you keep it until the next day it is not so good.' Of course, people did not travel the world like they do today. If they crossed the Channel it was for a day trip to Calais, the legendary booze cruise in which food did not feature. So many of our customers did not know France, and as baguettes were not available in Britain they did not realize the French stick does not last long.

Croissants, too, received complaints. No one moaned about their beautiful taste but they wondered why they were half the size of croissants sold elsewhere. I tried to explain that other croissants were mostly made with lots of yeast and flour improvers to puff them up. They also tended to be made with margarine, which was cheap, and didn't have the finesse of butter. 'Which do you prefer?' I'd ask, and I'd receive peculiar looks for daring to introduce the subject of taste into the dialogue. I'd say, 'I can give you a croissant that is filled with cheap margarine and yeast and is massive, but I am not interested in doing that.' And they weren't particularly interested in hearing that.

Food at that time was elitist. For the first few months working-class people would not come into the bakery-patisserie because they considered it to be a place for the rich. It became clear that the British loved the factory-produced, sliced, soft bread, without a crust. That bread had no taste, and because it was mostly white they couldn't understand why mine was sometimes brown (because it had cereal or rye or sours in the flour). Jenny and I were trying to change the eating habits of a nation (oh OK, shoppers in Oxford) by delivering crusty bread which admittedly didn't keep as long but was worth paying extra for because it was handmade and had – here comes that word again – *flavour.*

There were, of course, customers who had travelled all over France and eaten a lifetime's supply of baguettes, and they loved Maison Blanc. They got what it was all about. But for much of the time we were fighting against misunderstandings. It was a completely different world to the way it is now. I wanted to please people, but not at the expense of compromising my own culture.

———

Before launching Maison Blanc my many concerns included this one, which was firmly fixed in the back of my mind: what will happen if there is a problem? What happens if the baker doesn't turn up? I was devoting most of the day to Les Quat' Saisons and I could give only a certain amount to Maison Blanc. But what if there were some sort of difficulty at the bakery that required my time? Where on earth would I find that time? Spare time just did not exist.

Bread, however, fascinates me. It contains just four primary ingredients – water, yeast, salt and flour – but what can happen between those ingredients is amazing. Bread is a mysterious world. To make bread is quite easy to achieve, but to make great bread is a very different story. Rather than beginning to despise bread, my obsession for it deepened. I wanted to try to understand the chemistry behind it.

I would spend nights watching the chefs at Maison Blanc, learning from them and working with them. And what a sight! The speedy movement of the craftsmen; the water flowing into the flour; the live yeast, broken into the dough; the dough starter added to the flour to give flavour and life to it; and lastly the huge hook, plunging and turning and twisting, churning the heavy dough into a homogeneous paste. The salt was always added at the end so as not to kill the yeast.

Then Michel would stop the huge machine. He would pull off a piece of dough and press it between his fingers, evaluating the strength of the gluten, the elasticity, and the humidity content. I watched and learned. He would smell the dough. Then the machine was set on low speed, the arm moving at a gentle pace. A little water would be added, and a bit more salt. Then there would be the satisfied look on Michel's face.

The dough would be divided by a heavy steel machine that would cut through big discs of dough. Michel would pull the steel lever down with his two hands using all his strength and the disc would be cut into perfect fifty-gram pieces for mini baguettes or rolls. Then there would be about fifteen different breads, of course needing fifteen different doughs, all shaped differently. Michel was a good teacher and he showed me how to make and to shape the bread (façonnage), trapping a small ball of dough on the work surface in the cage of your hand, barely touching it with your fingers, and moving in fast concentric circles to make the perfect roll. For the baguette the technique was different, stretching the dough in a V to make the perfect shape. I was mesmerized.

Then the dough would prove for three to six hours. It would double in size and small blisters would appear on the surface. The smell developed and the scent of the fermenting yeast enveloped the bakery. Then, with a razor blade, Michel taught me how to apply the little slashes that add rusticity and sex appeal to bread, and a little flour dusted over by the delicate hand of the craftsman baker. Then hundreds of rolls and baguettes would be swallowed by the gigantic mouth of the oven, with a magnificent *whoosh* to follow as steam burst through and millions of droplets of steam gave the dough a golden crust with the sheen the bread-lover appreciates so much.

Inevitably, the problem I had worried might come did come. Michel, my wonderful baker, liked a drink. Bakers sometimes do; they certainly did in the late seventies. The job is a lonely one and it involves working strenuously through the night in a hot room, and catching up on sleep during the day. A nocturnal existence is not the best for health. When he was drunk he simply didn't turn up. Other nights I would be at the restaurant and I'd get a call from his landlord telling me that Michel had asked him to call me to say he wouldn't be arriving at work.

'Is he drunk?'

The landlord would reply, 'Yes.'

'Can you refresh him?'

'I don't think so. He is liquidized on the floor.'

So where did that leave me? If you have a bakery, its success depends on the quality of the bread. If the baker is drunk and absent, the bread is in danger of not being made, and if you have no bread you will lose your business. That means someone else has to make it. The pastry chef could make it at times but he had his own job to do. On top of that, bakery and patisserie are two entirely different crafts. It is wrong to assume that the brilliant pastry chef can make great bread, and vice versa. Both are specialized in their own craft. So on those nights when Michel was in liquid form on the floor of the Dog and Duck or some such pub, I would leave Les Quat' Saisons at about one in the morning, attempt to restore myself with a couple of triple espressos, and get to work downstairs at Maison Blanc.

Thank God Pascal, our chef de patisserie, had some knowledge of bread. We followed recipes but it was frightening for me. I was not accustomed to the massive proportions and the gigantic equipment. In the tiny kitchen of our restaurant I didn't have much freezer space so I made small quantities of, let's say, choux pastry or puff pastry, and I would have to do that three times a week. It was one up from cooking at home. Actually, most domestic kitchens were larger than mine, so it was more like one down.

Most of the bread we made that first night was good, but at one stage I didn't follow the recipe, to my cost. In my kitchen at the restaurant I always added salt to my dishes at the beginning, so as I made the *pain de campagne* I added the salt at the same time as the yeast. This was a disaster as the salt completely cancelled the effect of the yeast, preventing it from releasing the carbonic gases that would ferment the bread, destroying its flavour and hindering it from rising. Fortunately that was only one of the many recipes. At four in the morning when the bread was ready to go to London we were pale but with smiles on our faces.

We took on a driver to transport the bread from Maison Blanc to the London hotels, Harrods and Le Gavroche. Predictably, there were days when he didn't turn up, so who do you think had to make the sixty-mile journey from Oxford to our prestigious clients in London? Yes, you guessed it.

I'd attach a huge trailer to the back of my car emblazoned with the words 'Maison Blanc' and pack it with about six hundred baguettes, *pains de campagne* and many other breads. Then I'd climb behind the wheel and head for the capital. I have previously talked about my driving skills. You'll recall that my mother gave me a St Christopher because she had once been a passenger in my Renault and knew I'd need lucky mascots to help me. I am so glad she never saw me driving that bread-laden trailer in my Maison Blanc Vauxhall.

Oh, those bread runs! I drove to the sound not of music from the radio but car horns hooting me from all sides. First, I couldn't reverse. There was nothing wrong with the car, the car could reverse, it's just that it couldn't do it very well with me in the driver's seat. I would try to navigate my way through the busy streets of London and I'd frequently get blocked in small spaces by oncoming vehicles. Then I'd attempt a reverse and, bang, I'd hit a car. Have you ever tried to reverse with a large trailer attached to your car? Impossible. Insurance details would be exchanged, then I'd drop the bread at Le Gavroche and head for Harrods. Bang – I'd hit another car. Insurance details would be exchanged. It would have saved time if I'd driven with the insurance details on my lap rather than having to reach across to the glovebox to retrieve them every five minutes. There were times when I was jammed in a space so tightly I just could not see any way of getting out. So I would find a policeman and ask for his help, which, I am pleased to say,

I received. The trailer was much wider than the car, that was another consideration, and I must confess that I have taken out many wing mirrors in the narrow roads of London. Our profits from Harrods and Le Gavroche were eaten up by my ever-increasing insurance premium. Eventually we employed a new driver who never forgot to get up.

I must add a short note on my driving skills. Do not be afraid if you encounter me on the roads now. A leopard can change its spots. Ten years ago I changed completely and became a reformed character behind the wheel. I no longer frighten myself or others.

About six months into the venture we sat down one day and had a good look at the figures. What had been accomplished by those six months of chaos and comedy? Maison Blanc was successful in that it was now popular among the residents of Oxford and had earned a reputation for selling excellent bread. But the figures told a different story. We were not making much money, and the investment, and the worries, had been huge. I swore. Then I said to Jenny, 'We have got to sell up.'

However, Alain Desenclos, the restaurant manager at Les Quat' Saisons (and today the restaurant director at Le Manoir) came to the rescue. 'I think I might know the man who can help you,' Monsieur Alain (as I call him) told me one night as he listened to me groaning about no sleep, my difficulties with Michel and the accidents on my bread runs to London. Alain knew a certain Monsieur Restoix who lived in Périgord, in the Dordogne region in south-west France. He explained that M. Restoix had successfully owned and managed some six or seven shops that sold bread and pastries and had recently taken early retirement. He was a well-known professional renowned in his local area, he knew about bread and patisserie, and he knew about running a business.

Immediately I phoned Monsieur Restoix. 'I don't know you at all,' I said, 'but Monsieur Alain has given me your name.' I explained the problems (missing out the worst bits), then begged him, 'If you could at least come and see us . . .'

There were a number of hurdles – the English weather (he lived in the south of France), he had just retired so why should he take it on, and of course the English food, and as a good Frenchman he did not speak a word of English – but, clearly taking pity, he arrived a few days later with his wife Monique. They were a wonderful couple. M. Restoix was a lovely man, full of smiles, with that wonderful singing accent that identifies the speaker as an inhabitant of south-west France. Monique was elegant with a warmth of personality that made her glow. They were in their late fifties but they looked so young and so happy together.

She had all the experience of the front-of-house part of the business. He told me how he had worked hard his whole life and then had decided enough was enough, 'I am going to hang up my apron'. Not only a craftsman but also self-assured. They listened to my story, which ended with me revealing my fears that the business might have to be sold unless Jenny and I could find someone to help us out. Someone who could manage. He understood that the level of investment had been large, and he seemed to realize that Maison Blanc was in a good location, that the patisserie and bread were of a high standard in England, and that they would have been of a good standard even in France. They asked us lots of intelligent, probing questions and then went away for a few hours. When they came back, both of them with huge smiles on their faces, they said, 'We are with you.'

And thank God, because they saved the business. The day Monsieur Restoix began work at Maison Blanc I knew all my problems would vanish, and they did. I would no longer get any of the two a.m. phone calls telling me that the baker was drunk, or that other staff hadn't turned up, or that the flour had not arrived because it had not been ordered from the supplier, or any of the other daily headaches. It was as if the problems had been sucked out of my mind.

Gone.

For some years now I have been disconnected from Maison Blanc, but as I write this chapter I have been given the opportunity of getting involved with the business once again. Our aim will be to make it the best bakery-patisserie in Great Britain, grow the brand, and reinvigorate the product line. It is the start of a new adventure.

All Year Round
Pain de Campagne
Country Bread

This is a simplified traditional bread recipe that demonstrates the miracle of the action of yeast. Yeast is a living organism, a fungus that feeds on the sugar naturally present in the flour and transforms it into carbon dioxide pockets, creating the rise. It is this activity that, together with the kneading of the dough creating elasticity, produces a light texture and great flavour. This traditional slower proving is in complete contrast to the breads we find in our supermarkets, which rely on flour improvers and rising agents to speed up this process.

Serves (Yield): 2 loaves
Difficulty rating: ● ○ ○
Preparation/proving times: 30 minutes plus 3½ hours
Cooking time: 20 minutes
Special equipment: Electric mixer with dough hook attachment, bread paddle, loaf tin (for creating steam), greaseproof paper, razor blade.

PLANNING AHEAD
Prepare the mother dough 1 day in advance.

INGREDIENTS

For the mother dough:
> 45g strong white organic bread flour (*1)
> 45g rye flour
> 2g fresh yeast (*2)
> 60ml cold water

For the bread dough the following day:
> 400g strong white organic bread flour
> 85g rye flour
> 12g salt (*3)
> 10g fresh yeast
> 260–280ml water at approx. 20°C

METHOD

MAKING THE MOTHER DOUGH:

Prepare the mother dough the day before, mixing all the ingredients together. Cover with cling film and leave to ferment overnight (about 12 hours at room temperature).

MAKING THE BREAD DOUGH:

Preheat the oven to 240°C, placing a baking tray on the middle shelf and the loaf tin on the side.

In the mixer with the hook attachment, mix all the ingredients together including the mother dough for 5 minutes on the lowest speed setting and then for 10 minutes on the second speed setting. (*4) Shape into a ball, cover the bowl with cling film and give a first proving of 1 hour at room temperature. (*5)

Divide in 2 and shape each piece into a loaf. Place each loaf on a piece of greaseproof paper and leave to prove for another 1½ hours at room temperature, covered with a clean cloth to prevent it from drying out. (*6)

It should now be double its volume. (*7) Dust with flour, then, using the razor blade, score the bread in a curve down the length of the loaf but without getting very close to either end. The razor blade goes in about 2mm deep at an angle. (*8)

COOKING THE BREAD:

Pour 50ml water into your preheated tin loaf and close the oven door to allow the steam to be generated. (*9) Then slide the loaves on to the preheated tray using the paddle and bake at 240°C (*10) for 20–25 minutes. Remove from the oven and cool on a rack.

Chef's notes:

*1   The choice of flour is important: we recommend Shipton Mill flour (from Gloucestershire) or the Waitrose flour line. Depending on the time it has been stored, the variety and its nutritional composition, the flour will absorb more or less water when making the dough. Another important factor is its strength. Bread requires a strong flour with a higher protein (gluten) content than regular flour, which will provide better elasticity to the dough and a better texture to the loaf. We use rye flour in this recipe for flavour and for the fact that it ferments easily.

*2   If fresh yeast is unavailable then dried yeast can be used – but use half the quantity. It is important to know that yeast is sleeping at 4°C, best active between 20°C and 40°C, and destroyed at 50°C.

*3   Weigh yeast and the salt separately – the salt will dehydrate and kill the yeast if in direct contact.

*4   The slow mixing process will give the flour the opportunity to fully absorb the water. The faster speed will warm the gluten in the flour, making the dough elastic and creating the right environment for fermentation to happen.

*5   The proving time in a bread recipe is based on a dough's behaviour at a certain temperature. Our recipes are based on a temperature of 20°C (a standard room temperature).

*6   If the dough dries out it will form a crust and not prove properly.

*7   When the bread is proven, you should see some signs of blistering on the surface of the dough. At this stage the dough will be very fragile to manipulate, which is why we have placed the dough on silicone paper to facilitate putting the loaves into the oven.

*8   The sharpness of the razor blade will avoid any drag on the dough.

Ensure the cut is not too deep and is at an angle to create an attractive finish to the bread. The cut also allows the bread to rise during baking; without such a cut, the crust can act like a lid and prevent the bread from rising fully. If the cut is too long or too straight, however, it will cause the bread to open up like a book, which is why you should cut it in a curve and not all the way to the ends.

*9   The steam will create a wonderful crust. Be very careful when opening the oven door, however, as there will be a lot of hot steam. Leave the door ajar for 5 seconds before placing the bread in the oven to avoid burns.

*10   The temperature inside your oven is critical: here it needs to be 240°C. It will decrease significantly when you open the door to place the bread in. You may want to heat your oven to a higher temperature so that the result is closer to what you would achieve in a professional bread oven.

VARIATIONS

You could add seeds for additional texture, such as linseeds, sunflower seeds, poppy seeds. A bread stone will give you better crust and will diffuse the heat better.

For pizza dough, add about 60ml extra virgin olive oil during the mixing and kneading stage. The addition of olives, sun-dried tomatoes, caramelized onions or herbs of your choice would also be delicious.

EIGHTEEN

CELEBRITY CHEFS

Roux the Day

WHEN I OPENED LES QUAT' SAISONS IN THE LATE SEVENTIES, THE
phrase 'celebrity chef' had yet to be coined. Punk rock was the
fashion rather than Food. Delia was around but not yet a household
name, and Keith was yet to arrive on the scene clutching a glass. The
few cookery programmes were shown during the day – this was before
the explosion of daytime television – rather than in the prime-time
slots in the evening currently occupied by Jamie, Rick, Nigella and
Gordon.

The little roost was ruled by Graham Kerr, also known as the
Galloping Gourmet because he charged around the kitchen as he prepared his dishes. At the end of the show, as the credits rolled, he could
be seen clasping the hand of a lady in the audience and bringing her on
to the stage to join him at a table and dine with him. He was brilliant.
Many chefs who are devoted to their craft gallop around their kitchens
– the dashing is commonplace – but Kerr was the first to be seen
publicly doing it.

By then Fanny Cradock's popularity was fading. For many years she
was the face of cooking on British television, trying to teach the

English about French haute cuisine but doing it in a way that bordered on farce. Actually, it went beyond farce: her programmes were in a comic category of their own. Her husband, Johnnie, was her side-kick, passing her kitchen utensils and getting snapped at. Fanny was pompous and condescending, and proud of it. I had seen Fanny on television, trying to imitate the French while cooking turkey or something and trying to place feathers around it. The turkey's neck kept falling over. The memory of it still makes me laugh. As good as *Fawlty Towers*, but she was trying to be serious.

One night Fanny came to Les Quat' Saisons. She was extremely unpleasant to the staff and at the end of the meal when she was presented with the bill she put down her American Express card to pay for it. Like many businesses at the time we didn't accept American Express as it involved paying a 5 per cent commission.

'I'm very sorry, Madame,' said the maître d', aware that he was dealing with one of the world's fiercest women, 'but we don't accept American Express.'

About six seconds later he was standing in the kitchen, ashen-faced, shaky, looking like he'd just been through a wind tunnel, quite clearly a victim of Cradock's rage. I went out to the dining room to see if I could deal with it any better.

'I am so sorry, Madame,' I began, 'but we don't accept American Express. If you have Barclaycard, they charge a smaller commission.'

Fanny looked at me, then pushed her chair backwards and stood up. 'How dare you...?' she started to shout. 'You young people! You want business, and then when you get it you won't take American Express!'

Fanny always liked to take centre stage but I felt it was time to bring down the curtain.

'Please, don't lecture me,' I told her. 'I would like you to leave. Please don't come back.'

She never did.

Although there was no such thing as a 'celebrity chef' yet, chefs had of course long been regarded as famous, though not on this side of the

Channel. Before the French Revolution, the chefs of the royal court in France were renowned regionally, if not nationally, for their talents and they were well rewarded with money, properties and titles. Of course, if it were not for the revolution the dishes created by these cooks who worked with the royal family and for the aristocracy would have remained behind the doors of chateaux. The downfall of the monarchy enabled them to take their food to the masses.

Here, in Britain in the late seventies, apart from the handful of cooks who appeared on television there were also the chefs who did not appear on the telly but who were well known to gourmets and those in the industry. And there was no doubt that the leaders in this field were the Roux brothers, Michel and his older brother Albert.

The sons of well-known charcutiers, they had grown up around food before working as personal chefs to the Rothschild family. They were established professionals, masters of classical cuisine; Michel held the title Meilleur Ouvrier de France (best craftsman of France) – a standard bearer in Pastry. The brothers were great chefs and they were my heroes, partly because they epitomized the French immigrant's dream: they were France's finest culinary export, having arrived here and opened Le Gavroche in 1971 and then, a year later, the Waterside Inn in the sixteenth-century village of Bray, beside the Thames in Berkshire. Albert was chef-patron at Le Gavroche. Michel held the same rank at the Waterside, which drew a wealthy crowd of food-lovers from London to the countryside. I'll say it again: I was filled with utter admiration and respect for them.

One day, shortly after I had received my first Michelin star in 1979, the Roux brothers travelled to Oxford to have lunch at Les Quat' Saisons. What an honour. My emotions were a mixture of happiness and anxiety – that is my nature. The legends were coming for my food, but would my food be good enough?

To begin with, they ordered many of the dishes on the menu. Maybe they were extremely hungry. Perhaps they were curious. But it certainly put a lot of pressure on my little kitchen. The dishes went out, and when the plates returned I noticed that Albert had seemed satisfied but Michel had barely touched his food. Instead, he had pushed my creations to the side of the plate. I was shocked.

'Did he eat any of this?' I asked a waiter at the passe.

'Very little, Chef,' came the response.

Michel was communicating to me via what I suppose we could call 'plate language'. He had ordered, therefore we could assume that he was hungry, but he had barely touched the food. If ever you want to upset a chef and put him in a filthy mood, visit his restaurant, order and then do not touch the food. Did I give him too much? After all, I had been determined to please the brothers and perhaps, just maybe, I had piled too much on to the plates, and this had severely dented Michel's appetite. Had I overdone the portions?

The brothers left that afternoon before I had time to leave the kitchen and have a conversation with Michel. I was in an utter state and for weeks afterwards I shuddered when the memory of those uneaten dishes returned to me.

My worries were for nothing, though. One day I glanced at the reservations book and saw that Michel had booked for lunch again. I was thrilled. This time I promised myself that he would dine well. I told my brigade, 'When Michel leaves today his stomach will be full. We are going to give him the best meal of his life.'

I got it wrong. Again, Michael's plate language was the same and I was hurt by it. He was a fellow countryman. I was a young man starting out, and I had never harmed him – quite the contrary: I respected him for his vast achievements. If there was something wrong with the food, why couldn't he tell me? I would have welcomed his help and advice. Why would he do this? He was a powerful man with the best connections. He had beautiful restaurants while mine was a humble little place. He was an established king and craftsman while I had little experience and was my own mentor.

I felt anger rising within me. I had an archetypal French temperament which could flair quite easily – and it did. Looking back with what I know now, I probably would have made a different decision – it is not wise to take on the establishment when you are a young chef. But wise or not I entered into a seven-year war with Michael Roux.

On Sundays Les Quat' Saisons was closed, and one Sunday I told my team (of about seven) that I would take them for lunch at Michel's restaurant, the Waterside Inn. There is no doubt about it, we were on a mission. We began by playing the same game, minus the gloves. We ordered *every* dish, as well as the day's specialities, knowing that behind the scenes Michel and his kitchen soldiers would be thrown into chaos. At one point I ordered a fish dish – turbot, I think. It was placed in front of me and I began my dissection, prodding and pushing the fish. I could see it was overcooked, and the creamy sauce looked far too rich and heavy, fears that were confirmed when I had a little taste.

I put my knife and fork down on the plate. The maître d' zoomed up behind me, concerned.

'Monsieur Blanc, is everything all right?' he asked.

I leaned back in my chair, looked at him and replied, 'The fish is overcooked. The sauce is so heavy my spoon could stand up in it.' I gave him an explanation that would help the chef, which was more than Michel had done with me.

The maître d' steadied himself before announcing, 'Monsieur Roux cooked it himself.'

Michel and I didn't talk for many years after that. Sure, we would see each other at various functions and gatherings and we'd kiss, French-style, on each cheek, but there was an uneasiness between us. Meanwhile, the gossiping could cross counties, from Berkshire to Oxfordshire, with rumours making their way from his kitchen to mine, and tittle-tattle, in turn, heading from Oxfordshire to Berkshire.

When I opened Le Manoir, my dream was to be part of Relais & Chateaux which stood for (still does) the best welcome, service and experience, as well as some of the best food in the world. I heartily embraced the Relais & Chateaux culture, which is a yardstick for measuring international excellence, and I wanted Le Manoir to be part of it. More vicious gossip implied Michel was not in favour of me joining, though I can't believe that he would have done anything to obstruct me.

When the bosses of Relais came to Le Manoir to check us out they loved the experience. They met me and I was accepted into the group. Two large shiny bronze Relais & Chateaux and Relais Gourmand plaques stand side by side at the entrance to Le Manoir.

There came a time when we were both exhausted by the battle. Warfare is a tiring business. We both thought we should patch things up. There were so few Frenchmen bringing culinary excellence to the country at the time, it didn't make sense for them to be fighting. Enough was enough. In order to seal the new union we decided to organize a football match between the Waterside and Le Manoir on the green at Thame, a few miles from Le Manoir. A friendly game would solve the dispute, though Michel and I would be team managers rather than players. Brian Turner, a fellow chef and friend considered by Michel and me to be independent and without prejudice, agreed to be referee. He had no idea what he was letting himself in for.

I stood with my team, mismatched in moth-bitten T-shirts and frayed shorts, and watched Michel's brigade climb from the minibus. They looked like professional players in gleaming kits with the Waterside motif printed on them. They were a well-known football team with many little Platinis and Zidanes. When Michel stepped from the bus, proud and smiling, I took one look at him and knew that winning meant everything to him. He was looking into a mirror, though: winning meant everything to me too. There was a look in his eyes which told me that while the flames of our dispute might have been extinguished, the ashes were still smouldering. He also knew that his team was well established and had a long history of victories. If Michel's team was the Queen's cavalry, mine was the band of mercenaries.

'Raymond,' said Michel, looking delighted to see me. Then he grabbed my shoulders and gave me a kiss on both cheeks, the way the French do.

Within five minutes the Waterside squad had scored their first goal. By half-time they'd managed to make it 2–0 without getting barely a speck of mud on their kits.

As my team ate oranges, Michel wandered over to me. He was positively beaming. 'Raymond, Raymond,' he said, in a mock tone of commiseration, 'it's only a game.' Those four words sent a rage through me, though I continued to smile as if I genuinely agreed with him that it was only a game. Then he squeezed my shoulders and gave me another kiss on both cheeks.

Of course it wasn't only a game.

I resorted to new tactics. Plan B, if you like. I told my boys, who were bigger and stronger than the Waterside team, 'They've got three dangerous guys on their side: number eight, number seven and number three. Take them out. Take them out or you won't have a bloody job. Don't dare lose.'

That seemed to have an effect.

Brian Turner, who thought he was coming for a nice day out in the countryside, says he has never seen as much blood as he saw in the second half of that match on the green in Thame. Numbers eight, seven and three were swiftly disposed of by vicious tackles. Fists, elbows and knees were put to perfect use. I stood on the sidelines as Brian screamed at my team, 'You can't do that!'

When he blew the final whistle, the score was 3–2 to us. We had won! I raced up to Michel, planted a kiss on each of his cheeks, and said, 'Michel, it's only a game.'

The two teams, along with Michel and me, retired to Le Manoir for post-match drinks and food. But it was not a particularly convivial atmosphere because the Waterside boys were limping and grumbling about Le Manoir tactics. I began to wonder if we had achieved a result, off the pitch.

Looking back on the old days, Michel and I can now have a good laugh about it. Mind you, if ever you're looking for tips on peace-making, don't come knocking on the Roux or Blanc door.

Keith Floyd came for lunch at Le Manoir in September 2007. Of course, if you are British and have the slightest interest in food then you will know of Keith. Perhaps you have one or two of his cookbooks on a shelf in your kitchen. He is a lovely, funny man who should be praised at every opportunity because through his books and compelling television series he encouraged a passion for cooking and eating. My God, how the *bon viveur* made us laugh! It was great TV. Viewers saw him frequently drink wine while cooking and saying things like, 'I'll just have a quick slurp while that cooks.' He inspired a lot of young people to appreciate the joy of food, not to mention entertaining at home.

Keith had finished his lunch at Le Manoir when I caught up with him to say hello. He was at a table in the garden, and at his side he had good company: a packet of cigarettes and a glass of Teacher's whisky with water 'but sans glace'.

'You told me off one day,' Keith began the conversation. 'One day you said to me, "Keith, you know, you are quite good on television, but some of your food is shit." '

'No, that is not true.' It was not true; I never said that. 'What I said was, "You are very good on television. You are extremely good on television. It is refreshing to have someone who is completely drunk, blissfully demystifying food." I thought you were great. You set a precedent. We had a lot of drunken people on television but they were pretty bad. Whereas you were drunk and you were great. And that is the difference. That's number one. Number two, it's true your cooking is not the best.'

Keith looked a little hurt. Hastily, I explained that I was only joking ('Oh, come on, Keith, I thought the English were supposed to have a sense of humour').

Then he said dramatically, *'Je te propose un challenge.'*

Our dialogue continued for a minute or two with Keith, who was raised in Somerset, talking in French and me, the native Frenchman, responding in English. His challenge was this: each of us would cook his own *coq au vin* to see (and taste) whose was the best. A cook-off, I suppose.

He set the challenge because while Keith and I get on well, we disagree about one major fundamental issue: the type of red wine that should be used in the creation of this delicious, comforting Burgundy dish which is, put simply, a casserole of wine with chicken, vegetables and herbs. Keith and I do not dispute any of the ingredients, only the choice of wine. And the success of this dish depends on the wine. Maybe a century or two ago Monsieur Floyd and I would have settled the matter by unsheathing swords and using Le Manoir as the setting for a duel over *le coq*. Of course, you do not need to be a chef to find yourself in such a dispute. People who love food tend to bicker over techniques, ingredients, what is best and what is not. This debate over the wine in *coq au vin* is ancient and frequently fought out.

Keith said he would most certainly use Gevrey Chambertin. Prices for this Burgundy start at about £20 a bottle. I was of the opinion that the best wine was a good plonk from Languedoc costing about a fiver a bottle.

'Let's do the challenge for fun,' I said. 'You live in Provence. Why don't we do it there?'

The challenge has yet to take place, but it raised an interesting point, and one about which I am frequently asked. So it really is worthwhile examining this conundrum, which is not the concern of pairing wine with food, but rather knowing which wines should be used in cooking.

Burgundy, I would insist, is not a good wine to heat up (for reasons I shall come to). Essentially, the trouble with *coq au vin* is that the dish is associated with Burgundy. As previously mentioned, France is a mass of regions not only defined geographically but also by strong and specific food and wine traditions. If you happen to live in Bordeaux you believe that Bordeaux produces the finest cheese and wine. The prejudice is so strong you do not go elsewhere for these products. At some point, *coq au vin* was established as a dish that was invented in Burgundy and therefore the people of Burgundy are convinced it should be cooked with a wine from Burgundy. Many cooks and Epicureans around the world are equally convinced.

However, when you think about it, this dish is really chicken stew made with wine. It is a rustic dish that has been made in every French region. In Burgundy, they make it with Burgundy wine; in any other region, the local wine would be used. At the risk of upsetting the people of Burgundy (which is only thirty miles away from my home town), I really think we need to step away from Burgundy in order to create the finest *coq au vin*.

My mother (and her mother, and probably her mother before her) obeyed this golden rule: never use a great wine to make a dish. They were right, in my opinion. To ignore this rule is silly and expensive. It's a rule that is a blessing from God. I say that because if this dish and other wine-cooked dishes (for instance, *boeuf bourguignon*) could only be made with Gevrey Chambertin then they would never have been made. They would have been an unaffordable luxury. Maman Blanc and millions of other hard-up *mamans* did not have the cash for good Burgundy.

Before even cooking with wine, we should ask, why use it in the first place? We use it as a marinade, to produce extra flavour with more length, flavours that linger for longer on the palate. Like the juice of lemon, orange or grapefruit, wine is a catalyst of flavour and it is there to make the flavour last, to grow the flavour. It also tenderizes the meat and adds a dramatic colour. *Coq au vin* has four main elements – chicken, wine, vegetables and herbs – each of which is as important as the other. The chicken brings proteins, flavour and its distinct character. The vegetables and herbs (bay leaf and thyme) impart their own flavours (and never forget garlic, which you find in most French cooking, thank God). Then there is the wine, which not only provides that length of flavour in the finished dish but also the moisture for the cooking process.

Without dwelling too much on science, when wine is cooked its molecular structure is completely changed. Therefore, a wine that tastes positively delicious in its raw form (i.e. out of the bottle, into the glass, and into your mouth) will begin to take on an entirely new flavour when it is heated. Wines from Burgundy are mostly made from the pinot noir grape. It produces wine that is delicate, almost aristocratic. It has a wonderful, beautiful fruit and is the embodiment of refinement. In a sense, its refinement is the problem when it comes to cooking the stuff. As the wine is heated its alcohol evaporates, its molecular structure changes and what you are left with is a completely different flavour. What started out as a fantastic wine when the cork was removed becomes unrecognizable by the time it reaches the plate. It is thin and a light colour.

Experiments have been carried out on the streets of France. Ten good Frenchmen who really thought they knew about food and drink were asked to blind-taste wines from different regions. Eight out of ten of them got it wrong, and not one of them got it completely right. So if professionals cannot differentiate between claret and Burgundy, let alone Beaujolais or Rhône, imagine how they would fare if they were asked to identify the wines used in dishes.

Actually, there are very few wines you can recognize after cooking. In my opinion they are port, Madeira, Gewürztraminer and Vin Jaune Arbois (the Sauvignon grape). The thing is, the virtues of pinot noir are entirely different to those of the wines from other regions. If I am cooking with red wine, I want something which is big. I might look to Languedoc, or the cheaper rich Shiraz of the Rhône Valley. These wines are spicy, rich, deep and strong in tannins – as big as they come. If you go to Cahors, the wine is even stronger. It is like the blood of Christ: deep red like thick ink, and highly tannic, with lots of wonderful layers of flavour, great for cleansing the arteries. These wines and others from the south-west of France and Provence have sun, sun, sun, and they are the wines you should use when cooking.

My mother would always use a good plonk, most of the time *vin ordinaire*, sometimes from Languedoc, or even Algeria, but never an *appellation contrôlée*, never a Burgundy. The qualities she looked for in wines were darkness, depth, richness and a little tannin.

I would be dispatched to the local farm to get the chicken from its low branch. I was looking for a rooster rather than a hen. Yes, a nice three-kilo rooster who had lived a good life, with lots of great sex, and who had dined on good food from the ground. Once I had captured the bird I would take it home for slaughter and present it to my mother. She'd promptly chop it up into pieces.

First she would hold the chicken over the gas light to burn away the hairs on the skin. Few things are less sexy than being served a hairy chicken. (Of course, all chickens now are waxed.) My mother would then cook the chicken, with vegetables and herbs, in raw wine. That was traditional, but when I became a chef I started to think about the process of cooking with raw wine and how the flavours could be improved. I have mentioned it elsewhere, and I feel it is important if you cook with wine: the flavours are much improved and concentrated if the wine is first boiled.

If I were cooking for four, I would take a litre of one of those wines – something from Languedoc perhaps, or Cahors – and put it into a pan I have already heated. In other words, I am not looking to bring the wine right up to the boil, just to hit it with a high heat from the start. It sputters, it does not simmer.

While it is reducing I taste it, waiting for the alcohol to leave. Once it has reduced by about a third I remove it from the heat. Yes, the reduction process means that a third of the wine will evaporate, which in turn means I have lost money because my wine has joined the air. But it is not a waste of money, believe me (and remember, I have already saved cash by opting for a wine that is a fraction of the price of an expensive Burgundy).

The wine cools, but not so that it is cold. I want it to be up to 40°C, blood temperature, when I incorporate it with the other ingredients. If it were cold, the marinating process would not be so successful. When the warm mass (wine) meets the cold mass (chicken, vegetables and herbs) it produces a far better marinade and facilitates an exchange of flavours. If it is too warm it will begin to cook the chicken, which you don't want.

The warm, reduced wine is poured on to the ingredients: the rooster, which has been chopped into small pieces, and a *mirepoix* consisting of chopped carrots and chopped celery (but not too much because it has a very strong flavour which can instantly dominate and overpower a dish). Add to this some coarsely chopped onion and chopped leek, a few whole cloves of garlic, two or three bay leaves, and a sprig of thyme (my mother would not bother tying them up). This is then left to marinate for between twelve and twenty-four hours, sometimes two days. There ends Step One of the process.

Step Two is simple, and again I turn to my mother's technique. She would drain the ingredients in a colander for two or three hours, allowing the wine and juices to be collected in a bowl. Then she would pat dry the chicken with a towel (these days, of course, it would be a paper kitchen towel) before caramelizing it by pan-frying it in a little butter and sunflower oil on a medium heat. Once the chicken was caramelized she would put it to one side and then caramelize the vegetables before bringing all the ingredients together, along with the wine, and cooking it for about four hours on a low temperature of about 110°C.

Voilà. A traditional *coq au vin*, using the correct wine.

Summer
Le Manoir aux Quat' Saisons
Soupe de Fruits Rouges aux Cabernet Sauvignon, Monbazillac, Basilic et Menthe
Summer Fruits Steeped in Red Wine, Monbazillac, Basil and Mint

---

A great summer favourite at Le Manoir. Many other fruits can be added, such as blackberries, blueberries and peaches. If your fruit isn't ripe enough, marinade it in a little sugar for an hour.

Serves (Yield): 4
Difficulty rating: ● ○ ○
Preparation time: 10 minutes
Cooking time: 10 minutes
Special equipment: Parisienne spoon (melon baller) 2–3cm (optional)

PLANNING AHEAD

This dish must be prepared at least 6 hours in advance or up to 1 day.

INGREDIENTS

250ml Monbazillac or dessert wine
90ml Cabernet Sauvignon
40g caster sugar
5g (1 tsp) vanilla purée (see page 202)
4 turns of freshly ground black pepper (★1)
8 basil leaves
12 mint leaves, roughly chopped
100ml cold water
225g raspberries
150g strawberries, stemmed, halved, and quartered
100g blackberries
¼ Charentais melon, scooped into 12 balls with parisienne spoon
  or diced

40g wild strawberries (optional)

100ml chilled pink Champagne, not optional (the remainder will be
very much appreciated by your guests)

4 sprigs mint, to garnish

METHOD

PREPARING THE RED FRUIT SOUP:

In a small saucepan, mix the Monbazillac, Cabernet Sauvignon, sugar, vanilla purée and black pepper. Wrap the basil and mint leaves in muslin and add them to the pan. Bring to the boil and boil for 1 minute. (★2) Then turn off the heat and add the cold water. Cool down approx to 40°C. (★3) At this stage add all the fruits. Cover and refrigerate for at least 6 hours or up to 1 day.

SERVING:

Remove the muslin bag of herbs. Place the soup and fruit into a large glass serving bowl or 4 individual glass bowls. Pour a little pink Champagne (★4) into each of the individual bowls and add the sprig of mint.

Chef's notes:

★1   The freshly ground black pepper will add a little bit of length and spicy taste to the soup.

★2   This is to burn off the alcohol to give a rounder flavour, and it also means that children will be able to enjoy this dessert.

★3   If the soup is too hot, it will cook the fruits; 40°C is the perfect temperature, just warm, and this will help the exchange of flavours between the herbs, the pepper, the fruit and the wine.

★4   When the Champagne, which is dry, is added to the sweet fruit and juice, it creates a festive foam that will finish this dish beautifully.

NINETEEN

NOUVELLE CUISINE

To Le Manoir Born

'You may accuse me of being a micro-idiot but, as we all know, the devil is in the detail. For me, excellence is the accumulation of seemingly inconsequential, minor and weightless details. Yet, if you gather them together lovingly and patiently alongside your team's intellegence, it is possible to create weight and density. For a fleeting second, one may feel that one has touched excellence.'

R. Blanc

I DIDN'T WANT LE MANOIR. SURE, I WANTED TO PROGRESS FROM Les Quat' Saisons in that shopping precinct in Oxford, and whenever I thought about the next restaurant I had a clear picture in my mind of what it would be like . . .

It was a picture of home sweet home, a lovely little restaurant – a manageable forty- or fifty-seater, so I could give of my best to my customers – within a charming little house which had to be old because I saw England as a kingdom of ancient homes. There would be about ten bedrooms for guests or friends who wished to stay the night after a wonderful meal. A terrace would hold six or seven tables where guests could enjoy an aperitif or digestif on a sunny summer's day, surrounded by a huge garden – and by that I mean a vegetable garden. It had to be huge because I saw it as part of my culture, a necessity for a good restaurant in the countryside.

We spent three years looking for this home sweet home. I viewed lots of houses that were wrong, or in the wrong part of Oxfordshire. 'Why Oxfordshire?' people would ask me. The answers were: Jenny and I lived in Oxford; I loved Oxford; Sebastien and Olivier were at school in Oxford; and our friends were there. We had also established a mutual loyalty with guests who lived in the area. On top of all that, from a business point of view it made good sense to stay as we were in the wealth corridor of Europe. This is where the money was. I just knew it was the right place. I knew that much.

How we came to acquire the manor house of Great Milton, the house that would become Le Manoir aux Quat' Saisons, is a story about how we have no control over our destiny. Oh, how little we know! The moment I laid eyes on the manor house, the dream of that tiny home sweet home vanished.

One Sunday morning in 1982 I was flicking through a copy of *Country Life* when I saw a photograph of the manor house and the words 'For Sale'. Immediately I jumped into the battered green van (Jenny drove the BMW and we couldn't afford a decent second car because we were saving up for the next place) and drove the eight or so miles to Great Milton, whizzing through country lanes and stopping once to ask a villager if he could tell me who owned the manor house. He replied, 'Lady Cromwell.' Then I rattled into the driveway of the manor house. I stopped there and took it all in. I was in awe. It was something from the pages of Lewis Carroll: the mini-grand gravel driveway, the large creaking gates, the immaculate lawns, the old walls, the caramel-yellow Oxford stone, the grand little house topped with four chimney stacks. The house, I was to learn, was built by a Frenchman called Aginscourt in 1356. If anything, it looked a little severe, very masculine; maybe a small statement about the vanity and power of man. I would add the feminine side within the house.

I knocked on the door. I assumed that the woman who answered was a cleaner and I said, 'Lady Cromwell, please.'

'I am Lady Cromwell,' she replied. 'What do you want?'

'I want to buy your house,' I said confidently.

She caught sight of the dirty old banger behind me and looked me up and down.

'But who are you?' she asked.

'My name is Raymond Blanc.'

At that point her expression changed from one of curiosity. She smiled warmly and said, 'Oh, Monsieur Blanc, please come in.' As I crossed the threshold Lady Cromwell added, 'What a lovely meal I had two weeks ago at Les Quat' Saisons with my family. It was a very special moment. Thank you so very much.'

I stepped inside and took in my surroundings. The smell of the fire from the night before, the smell of the old oak panelling. After tea (she left the teabag in the cup) and biscuits we had a lovely chat during which it became clear that she loved the idea of selling the house to us; she could not bear the thought of it being turned into flats. There was an instant bond between us.

I left Lady Cromwell and later learned that after my departure she had climbed on to her horse-drawn carriage and clickety-clacked through the village, stopping off at one house after another. On each doorstep Lady Cromwell told the inhabitants that a certain Mr Blanc, a Frenchman, a cook and a republican, intended to buy the manor house and turn it into a beautiful hotel with a wonderful restaurant. 'I do hope you will support him when he applies to the council for change of use,' she told the villagers.

Who on earth could argue with Lady Cromwell?

We had our own savings, but it didn't amount to much, yet I knew I had value, as I had created a brand. Having achieved two Michelin stars in a few years had given us credibility. Any investor would put their money into this venture. And it was also a good time to invest because

Mrs Thatcher had just created a huge tax incentive to entice entre-preneurs to create new businesses in the UK. That was an opportunity we could not miss. Friends and regulars from Les Quat' Saisons invested in Le Manoir in return for a stake. We also suceeded in getting a government grant, thanks to the genius of M. Lulham, our accountant, because we were setting up a business during a time of recession and would be employing local people. The grant was controversial. 'French chef gets taxpayers' money to serve posh food while miners are dying in the pits' was the gist of public complaints from certain politicians and critics in the press. You can see the argument. However, all publicity is good publicity, and such was the quantity of scathing attacks that we felt no need to pay for a PR company to promote Le Manoir. Everyone was talking about us even before we'd opened.

When we came to hand over the cheque to Lady Cromwell, she said, 'I must warn you, there is a ghost in the house.' She wanted us to know about the spirit, she said, just in case it made us have second thoughts. She explained that the ghost was Lord Cromwell, her late husband, and it occupied the master bedroom. Were we happy to live with a ghost? 'Of course, Lady Cromwell,' I reassured her, adding with a little smile, 'We will look after your husband's spirit. I am sure he will be very happy with us.'

'A ghost?' I thought. 'What bunkum.'

The room became Hollyhock, and it caused one headache after another. When the walls were plastered, the plaster wouldn't dry, and they had to be replastered. Guests would dash to reception first thing in the morning, ask for the bill and talk about the footsteps they'd heard in the middle of the night. When bath taps were turned on, the water ran dirty. Chambermaids felt they were being watched by a ghostly presence and refused to enter the room. Eventually, we called in an exorcist. He stayed for a day, and when he left he said, 'The spirit has been appeased. It will trouble you no more.' He was true to his word. The spirit of Mr Cromwell never came back.

I wish that exorcist could have sorted out the other problems, hundreds upon hundreds of them. We had a lovely, massive house, but one that required so much work it makes me shudder when I think back to those early days. Part of the roof had to be replaced. Some of the foundations had to be underpinned. It had to be entirely rewired and replumbed. All the rooms had to be broken down as wet and dry rot were virulent. It had all the evils of an old building. Once again, we were totally unequipped for the task.

In a way, I had got my home sweet home. After all, I had wanted a forty- or fifty-seater restaurant, which I now had. And there were ten rooms, almost exactly what I had originally dreamt of – *un restaurant avec chambres*. But with Le Manoir I would need a restaurant that catered for seventy or eighty in order to cover the running costs – and the lawn. Commercially, Le Manoir was not viable as it was, so we had to grow it to make it work – we had no choice. That was hard to achieve, but my attitude was not unlike the approach I'd had when we started out with Les Quat' Saisons: the minute we had made the decision to acquire it, I thought, 'Yes, let's make this happen.' Of course, we were now dealing with a massive project so I would have to learn many new skills and surround myself with the best people.

I wanted to create a level of excellence you couldn't find in Britain. I was not just thinking of the cuisine, though I knew that had to be good. I was also thinking about creating a wonderful garden and grounds, which were not in good shape when we moved in. I was thinking of having a cookery school, too, where home cooks could discover the pure joy and creative act of cooking. This had to be a great hotel and restaurant where people could come and celebrate. I wanted the greatest eating place in the world. I wanted conviviality – happy staff and happy guests. People, after all, are at the very heart of a restaurant's success. There is a big leap from starting a restaurant to starting a restaurant as well as a hotel, and aiming to be the best.

As a child, my garden had been a massive vegetable and herb garden with a scrappy piece of lawn, a disgrace by any British standard. At Le Manoir, the contrast was striking. The lawn was large and perfect, but you walked into the *potager*, or vegetable garden, and it was overgrown with ground elder and dead Brussels sprouts. What vegetables there were had been devoured by the rabbits, which were everywhere. A garden that is not cultivated turns into a forest. My heart sank a little when I first saw it, but I recognized it as an opportunity. It took about six months to tidy up that vegetable garden, re-energize the soil and begin planting.

That's when my parents visited. My father became the (unofficial, unpaid) hotel handyman. He was the one who got the rust off the driveway gates – by hand – and painted them. He also arrived with marvellous seeds, and as he is an expert gardener he helped us with the garden. I suppose it was a bit like the old days when we worked together in the garden at home in France, except that this time round I was the one doing the delegating and he was the one getting his hands dirty. Albert Ring, a wise and wonderful gardener, took over, helped by a young apprentice, Anne Marie Owens.

When the first shoots came through the soil I was the happiest man alive. I started to dream of how the vegetables would end up in casseroles, salads and other dishes. Every morning I would visit my beloved young vegetables and herbs and one day I was devastated by the sight that greeted me. Overnight, the entire garden had been chomped by rabbits. I knew the rabbits were a problem, but there was so much damage done in one night that I was convinced Le Manoir's rabbits must have brought their hungry friends and family from elsewhere.

I put a huge pile of cabbage in the grounds and erected a sign on it which read, 'That's for you, rabbits.' It didn't work. They just ate the cabbage, and then everything else. I sent in ferrets. No joy. I sent in men with guns and gas. In the end I had a fence planted around Le Manoir, the type that goes deep into the ground and prevents rabbits from burrowing underneath it. Imagine how long that took, and the expense. But at least I can say I won the Battle of the Rabbits, for a while.

My father went back to France and returned with more seeds,

which he duly planted, and this time the harvest – coco and flageolet beans, Croissy turnips, Nantes carrots, Ratte and Belle de Fontenay potatoes, Marmande tomatoes, you name it, all glorious and plentiful – went into Le Manoir's kitchen rather than the rabbits' bellies. The gardeners, I remember, were surprised that I was growing different varieties for different dishes. 'Potatoes are potatoes,' they tried to tell me when I tried to tell them that one variety is good for salad, another for puréeing, another for roasting, and many are good for nothing.

Now my head gardener, Anne Marie tells an amusing story of her first day at Le Manoir. She was in the middle of something or other when a Frenchman dashed up to her and told her to go with him. He did not introduce himself, and she had no idea who he was, yet five minutes later she was in his car. He drove her to the local pick-your-own farm. 'Fill up baskets with fruit and vegetables,' he told her. 'I'll be back in a couple of hours to collect you.' She obeyed the command, filling the baskets. Then she waited for the man to return. She waited and waited and waited, but he never returned. Eventually she found a phone box (remember the days?) and got in touch with Le Manoir.

'A man has driven me to the pick-your-own,' she explained. 'He said he'd come back, but he hasn't done. I'm stuck here.'

Deadpan, the person on reception replied, 'That'll be Raymond. Don't worry, we'll send a car to collect you.'

Whenever Anne Marie wants to remind me of my poor memory, she brings up this story.

Yes, the establishment of Le Manoir involved much work and many sacrifices, and these included divorce from Jenny. I was devastated, and it took me a long time to recover. I thought I had a partner for life, but it was not to be. I realized, but only through hindsight, that a relationship needs as much love and care and nurturing as a beautiful dish, garden, or hotel. So the cost of Le Manoir was high, for it affected my family, and my early relationship with my sons. It took many years to rebuild the confidence I had lost, because it does affect your confidence. I know my work comes first but it had many far-reaching consequences which I had to deal with. I worked very hard for years to gain back the love and trust of both my sons. Today I stand as a very proud man as my sons, Olivier and Sebastien, are my two best friends.

———

What I was cooking around the time we opened the doors of Le Manoir was modern French cuisine. It was what many would describe as nouvelle cuisine, which inspired me, and is a subject we must address.

In order to understand nouvelle cuisine, we need to go back to the early 1900s and the period of Escoffier. He, as I have previously mentioned, was the great master of his time, a founder of *cuisine classique*. His recipes, his style, influenced millions of chefs around the world, including those in France, America and also in Britain, where he launched the restaurant at the Savoy. *Le Répertoire de la Cuisine*, a compilation of six thousand Escoffier recipes, was a book that was found in most professional kitchens. *Le Répertoire* does not contain photographs or illustrations; it is simply concisely written recipes. The chef, book in hand, would turn to a certain page to see how to cook a certain fish, let's say, and then turn to another page to find out how to create the sauce.

The more I read the book, the more uneasy I felt. Creativity was killed. Chefs did not need to think for themselves as all the recipes were defined, right down to the garnish. No wonder chefs were bored (and sometimes drank a little). If you kill the creativity of food, you kill the life of food. Of course, *Le Répertoire* should still be used. But it should be kept on the kitchen shelf as a good point of reference as opposed to a culinary bible. It should no longer be regarded as imperative to cooking.

Essentially, there came a point when Escoffier's cuisine did not fit any longer. His food was too rich, too creamy, too fattening for restaurant-goers and gourmets. Escoffier was a great master but his bible was killing creativity in restaurants. At times tradition can be a hefty weight to bear. The courageous idea behind nouvelle cuisine was to move away from Escoffier and establish a modern method. It was all about defining that the produce should be local and seasonal. The chef would want to know where the vegetable was grown, or where the fish was caught. Freshness was paramount. And when you have freshness it encourages lightness. Out with the flour and heavy loads of butter and cream, in with delicate, elegant flavours. You didn't want the customer to stand up from the table and fall on the floor, his belly stuffed with richness. The movement dictated that if the chef was cooking an apple he wanted to provide the best apple experience. If he was cooking an oyster, then likewise, he wanted to provide the best oyster experience. Ingredients would be cooked for the less time – again, to retain freshness.Creativity would once again empower the food.

The term 'nouvelle cuisine' was used by Henri Gault and Christian Millau, creators of the Gault Millau restaurant guides, to describe this new style of cooking. (Interestingly, back in the late nineteenth century the term had also been used to describe the food of that revolutionary young chef Georges Auguste Escoffier.) The chefs behind the movement, which began in the sixties, were some of the best in the business, gifted men like Michel Guérard, Jean and Pierre Troisgros, Roger Vergé, Chapel and Girardet, and my dear friend Paul Bocuse. Many of them had worked under one man, Fernand Point, unarguably one of the industry's legends. These chefs were so far ahead of their time. Even before the nutritionists they had seen that food culture had to change. It had to be made lighter to meet the needs of the modern guest.

But there is a problem with revolution, be it political, social or gastronomic: even if it begins in the best hands, a revolution always ends up in the wrong hands, in the hands of people who don't have passion, who don't care, who don't understand. They use it as a marketing tool and the beautiful vision is destroyed. Nouvelle cuisine began as a revolution filled with promise but turned into a nightmare. The philosophy was misinterpreted. They chose the plates before the food itself. The design element seemed to power everything. Taste? Forget it. Anyone who could mix raspberries with turbot was hailed as a genius.

Insane combinations of ingredients were presented on plates to curious customers. Journalists wrote in glowing terms about this new fashion, helping to turn the whole thing into what would become a freak show.

The fashion was embraced by chefs in France as much as anywhere. France had a stronghold on the British restaurant scene (it still does, but its power is diminishing). Pretty soon the whole thing was out of control. This average cuisine worked its way around the world and prospered in countries that didn't have a culture of food. It failed in countries that already had a strong, well-established food culture. You don't see too many French restaurants in Spain, Portugal, Italy, China or India. But 'French food' thrived in countries like Britain and America, who had lost their food culture. Look, for instance, at how chicken tikka masala has become the most popular dish in Britain. Why shouldn't it be wonderful fish and chips, or steak and kidney pudding, or sticky toffee pudding?

I was extremely fortunate that because of my heritage I didn't embrace those excesses. It took about thirty years of mistakes to work through the revolution and arrive at a stage where many chefs now adhere to nouvelle cuisine's original principles. But I knew what good food was and I understood its principles from the outset because I had grown up with it. I already appreciated seasonality and purity of produce. I had a deep understanding of all of these things, and I also accepted the philosophy of the table: it is an act of giving, and an act of love. That is what my mother, and probably yours, did so well. They were brilliant at giving love around the table. So it was this heritage that prevented me from falling into the trap of serving the much misinterpreted nouvelle cuisine.

———

On the face of it, my heritage also caused a problem: I had republican values but was overseeing a restaurant and hotel that apparently catered for the rich. Again, however, I had a firmly fixed philosophy: Le Manoir had to be inclusive rather than exclusive.

I removed the jackets and ties of hundreds of men dining in the restaurant. I wanted children to come and eat in the restaurant so I openly encouraged parents to bring their families. At the time, this confused the Establishment. He doesn't want jackets? He's inviting children to eat in the restaurant? People said to me, 'How do you expect to create a temple of gastronomy?' My response was, 'I don't want a temple of gastronomy, I want a place where people can come and feel relaxed and welcome.' The vision was strong and clear: to create a modern classic. Elegant rather than luxurious. Intelligent rather than clever. And utterly welcoming at all times. To create a place where the ideal defines and drives the adventure. But all times it must correspond to commercial sense. I wanted to prepare Le Manoir so that it would live beyond me, a place of beauty where craft, agriculture and science came together. A place where people came to celebrate life and their special moments.

One Sunday lunchtime I was by the front door when I saw a Mini Cooper come through the gates. There was a young couple inside and they began to look for a space among the Bentleys, Rollers and Porsches. There were spaces, but the sight of these luxurious cars was so off-putting that the couple decided the restaurant would be a little too expensive for them. As the Mini made its way out of the drive, I chased after it and managed to catch up. 'Please,' I told the couple, 'please, come in for lunch.' I managed to persuade them to come inside and we gave them the best VIP treatment imaginable.

Gastronomy has always been exclusive, but we wanted Le Manoir to be different. We wanted to create a place that would be inclusive. And we won. Le Manoir is possibly the busiest Michelin Restaurant and hotel. It is full every day. Among the gourmets, artists and businessmen are people – some 40 per cent – who couldn't afford to come every day or every week, maybe not even every year. They could be my parents. Their visit is a special treat, but when the guests are in the restaurant no one can see the car park. A form of equality is thus created. That is also our true success and it translates to our commercial success.

Autumn/Winter
Le Manoir aux Quat' Saisons
Filet de Barbue, Huitre; Jus au Concombre et Wasabi
Fillet of Brill with Oyster, and Cucumber and Wasabi Jus

This has been a classic dish at Le Manoir for many years. But as with all Manoir dishes, it is about details that are not always easy to duplicate in your own home. I have forty chefs in my kitchen. Maybe the best way to enjoy it is at Le Manoir.

> *Serves (Yield): 4*
> *Difficulty rating:* ● ● ●
> *Preparation time: 20 minutes*
> *Cooking time: 15 minutes*
> *Special equipment: Blender, sieve*

PLANNING AHEAD

It will help speed things up if you have all the ingredients weighed out in advance, and all your equipment to hand. The brill can be brushed with melted butter, etc., in advance: see note ★1.

INGREDIENTS

For the fish:
> 4 fillets of brill (150g each), brushed with a mixture of melted butter, lemon, salt and pepper (★1)
> 50g banana shallot, sliced
> 20g butter
> 120g (6) button mushrooms, washed and sliced
> 1 pinch sea salt
> 1 pinch freshly ground white pepper
> 100ml dry white wine, Chardonnay, boiled for 10 seconds (★2)
> 80ml water

For the sauce:

    200ml strained cooking liquor (see above)
    60g cucumber skin (see note *4 below)
    12g wasabi paste
    1g soya-based lecithin (*3) (optional)
    40g butter
    a squeeze (1g) lemon juice

For the vegetable garnish and oysters:

    20g butter
    30ml water
    200g spinach, washed
    85g (12) cucumber ribbons (*4)
    60g samphire grass
    120g (4 whole size 2) native Colchester oysters, opened and kept in
        their juices in a small saucepan

METHOD
COOKING THE FISH:

Preheat the oven to 190°C. In an ovenproof sauté pan on a medium heat, sweat the shallots in the butter for 2 minutes. (*5) Add the sliced button mushrooms and sweat for a further minute. Add the wine, water and seasoning and bring to the boil. Place the fillets of fish on the mushrooms and cover with a lid. Cook in the preheated oven for 5 minutes. Remove from the oven, spoon out the fish on to a small tray, cover and keep warm. (*6)

FINISHING THE SAUCE:

Strain the hot cooking juices from the fish into a large jug liquidizer, pressing on the shallots and mushrooms to extract as much liquid as possible. To the juices add the cucumber skin, wasabi paste, lecithin, butter and lemon juice, and blitz them. Strain into a small pan and reserve.

COOKING THE VEGETABLE GARNISH AND
HEATING THE OYSTERS:

Divide the butter and water between 2 saucepans. Put the spinach in one, and the cucumber and samphire in the other. Add a tiny pinch of salt to the spinach. Cover both with a lid. Over a high heat, bring the pans of vegetables to a quick boil. The spinach will take 1 minute, the cucumber and samphire 30 seconds. Just barely warm the oysters in their own juices. Place the brill back in the oven for 1 minute. Bring the sauce to the boil.

SERVING:

Place the spinach in the middle of each plate, with the cucumber and samphire around. Top with the brill fillet and oyster, spooning the sauce over and around.

Chef's notes:

*1   This can be done a few hours in advance. The melted butter mixed with the lemon juice and salt and pepper will season the fish. Then as the fish is refrigerated, the butter will solidify and prevent the salt from curing the fish.

*2   I like to boil wine to remove the alcohol before cooking with it (see page 46). Here, however, the wine is boiled very briefly to remove only some of the alcohol, not all of it.

*3   Lecithin is an emulsifier that you can find in many vegetables, seaweeds, eggs, etc. Here we are using a natural extract of soya beans in powdered form. Once emulsified with liquid, it produces a light airy sauce. It is optional.

*4   Peel the cucumber, reserving the skin, then use a mandolin or a sharp knife to cut ribbons from the cucumber, turning as you go, until you are left with the seeds, which can be discarded.

*5   This converts starches in the onions into sugars; it's not so much 'sweating' as 'sweetening'.

*6   Once the fish has been taken out of the oven, it is rested for 3 minutes. This will allow the residual heat to finish cooking the fish perfectly, and also some of the juices to escape. This will be used to enrich the sauce. The fish will then need to be flashed in the oven before serving.

VARIATIONS

The fish could be portioned on the bone and cooked, which would provide more flavour to the sauce. Tomatoes, mustard, basil and leek could also be used as the vegetable garnish. The brill could be replaced by fillets of turbot, plaice, lemon sole, etc., but the cooking times will vary. Scallops can be used in place of the oysters. A few cockles and clams would also be nice.

TWENTY

●━━━

MOLECULAR GASTRONOMY

The Professor

Agnes B. Marshall in *The Book of Ices* (1885) let guests at a dinner party prepare their own ice cream by putting the mixture of ingredients into a bowl of liquid nitrogen. 'Its powers are astonishing,' she said, 'and persons scientifically inclined may perhaps like to amuse their friends as well as feed them when they invite them to the house.'

A MONG THE CUSTOMERS AT LES QUAT' SAISONS WAS A WELL-DRESSED elderly man who from time to time came for dinner with his wife. One night we said hello, and he introduced himself as Nicholas Kurti.

Chances are you have never heard of Nicholas Kurti, and back in the late seventies his name meant nothing to me either. He was not a chef or a restaurateur but a Hungarian-born recently retired professor of physics at Oxford University. Although I got to know him well, as a mark of respect I always addressed him as Professor Kurti rather than Nick, as I think I'll continue to do for the purposes of this chapter. He steered my life, and not just mine. Indirectly he played a significant role in defining the sort of food that is now served in the world's best restaurants. Right or wrong.

Although Professor Kurti's name might not ring any bells, I'm sure you are familiar with the term 'molecular gastronomy'. It was Professor Kurti who coined the phrase way back in the mid-eighties when he founded the discipline that examines the science behind food – the physics and chemistry of cooking. Even further back, in 1969, he gave a lecture at the Royal Society of London on the subject, entitled 'The Physicist in the Kitchen'. 'I think it is a sad reflection on our civilization,' he told his audience, 'that while we can and do measure the temperature in the atmosphere of Venus we do not know what goes on inside our soufflés.' By the time I met him he had reworked this observation. 'Isn't it incredible,' he said to me, 'that we can put a man on the moon but we don't know what's happening inside a soufflé?'

Hundreds of years before Professor Kurti was born there were chefs, gourmets and scientists who looked at the science of food, but he was unquestionably the father of the movement in the twentieth century. The professor was the best in his field, and a kind person who provided me with a fantastic insight into food. He was himself a keen cook, and like all Hungarians he loved to eat, he appreciated good produce and he understood the joy of the table. He was precisely what you'd want in a professor – eccentric, excitable and curious – and he was also always happy.

Professor Kurti came into my life at just the right time. As a self-taught chef, I suffered the insecurities that come with being untrained. Though if I had been trained then possibly I would have been just a reflection of my mentor, with that mentor's knowledge and philosophy. Sure, I would have acquired the knowledge of technique, but maybe not the freedom to challenge established views. I might have lacked curiosity. But I think that as I was self-taught I always wanted to know why ingredients reacted in certain ways when steamed, baked, emulsified . . . I wanted to be in control. I also wanted to be a better teacher. I had an overwhelming desire to pass on my knowledge to my chefs, but also to touch and enrich their lives. I knew that science was one of the building blocks of good cooking, so I needed to learn. In fact I felt compelled to establish what was happening chemically during the cooking process.

I encourage every chef to acquire curiosity when he comes to work with me. Curiosity will inevitably lead to knowledge. If you are a chef who is not curious then you may as well pack up now and go home. Home cooks know that when they have done a dish countless times they start to lose their love for it. They are no longer curious. This is even more obvious in a restaurant, where you might be cooking the dish many times every day. If you've lost that interest, then suddenly that dish which was once beautiful will lose its colour, its character and its beauty. So I always look at a dish with curiosity. The moment you stop doing that the dish is bound to die a little.

Professor Kurti, it transpired, could answer my questions but he was more than a teacher. I think I was really looking for a mentor, someone who could listen to my culinary problems and provide the solutions. Opening Les Quat' Saisons and then taking it forward had been tough. Perhaps I wanted a culinary agony uncle. He was also looking for someone, a pupil, who could ask him questions, and I was a chef asking questions − a rare beast, because at the time chefs didn't ask many questions about the science of food.

Professor Kurti's mistake was to give me his phone number. I phoned him day and night, bombarding him with questions about cooking. I wrote pages of essays about bread-making and then sent them to him and awaited his comments. Twenty pages was nothing. The ingredients of bread are yeast, water, flour and salt. *C'est tout.* Yet a million words could be written about why it sometimes goes right and why it sometimes goes wrong.

I dispatched essays about jam-making too. Again, there are only four ingredients in jam: fruit, pectin, citric acid and sugar. But if you don't understand your pectin and your fruit, you might soon be in trouble. A cookery book might tell me to add two ounces, let's say, of pectin in a powdered form, but it wouldn't necessarily tell me that pectin is the substance that makes jams set, or that pectin starts off as pectose in the cell walls of fruit and that it is converted, as the fruit ripens, into pectins. If the fruit is overripe then the pectin begins to turn into pectic acid, and that will cause problems with jam-making. If the fruit is underripe there will not be enough pectin. And there are varying levels of pectin in different fruits: lemons, oranges and apples have stacks of it; straw-berries and raspberries have pectin at low levels so they won't set particularly well; cherries and peaches don't contain much pectin at all. When the fruit is boiled, the pectin escapes and mingles in the mixture. Cooking is, indeed, an inexact science. The water from the fruit starts to evaporate. In goes the sugar. All the molecules begin to become entangled, creating a gel. Then the citric acid will further help the jelly set. Some pectin is reversible, some is not.

Inconsequential stuff to many people, but I wanted to know why all these things were happening. The professor was always happy to help solve my problems. The more I learned about the chemistry, the more I discovered it was a wonderful tool to understand the cooking process. It was hugely important. As a schoolboy I hated chemistry, but when I applied it to cooking it became exciting and magical.

At the time few books delved into the science behind cookery, and when they did they were like unhelpful textbooks written for people with a scientific background, not for chefs. As a cook I found these works totally unreadable. Professor Kurti was one of those gifted academics who had the ability to talk simply about complex issues, thereby appealing to the layman like me. He made me feel more assured about my cooking, and made me a more knowledgeable craftsman and a better teacher. In short, he improved my food.

Although he was retired, Professor Kurti gave a lecture at the 1985 Oxford Symposium on Food and Cookery. The symposium takes place annually at St Antony's College in Oxford and brings together historians, sociologists, anthropologists, scientists, writers and others who specialize in the study of food in history, its place in contemporary societies, and related scientific developments. I was the only chef there back in 1985, when the symposium's subject of debate was 'Kitchen Lore and Science'. Harold McGee was the keynote speaker. (It was at one of these symposiums, incidentally, that I was introduced to Alan Davidson, who had retired from the Diplomatic Service in the mid-seventies to pursue a career as a food historian – and highly knowledgeable on the subject he was too. It was Alan who in 1981 co-founded the Oxford Symposium. Like Professor Kurti, Alan enriched my life and helped me to sort out a number of little problems. I would also wake him up at three in the morning. The only time I had to write was between one and four a.m. so of course that was when I needed to speak to him.)

At the time, as I related in the previous chapter, I was striving to make food lighter and more flavoursome. I couldn't bear the thought of people celebrating with a great meal and leaving so stuffed they couldn't move for days. Food should be delicious and it shouldn't punish you. I remember looking at how lightness could be achieved with the classic sauces, one of them being hollandaise. Escoffier recommended whisking four egg yolks with about five hundred grams of butter, and some lemon juice. It creates a lovely sauce but it is so rich and indigestible. This quantity of ingredients may have been OK years ago when people were less stressed, did a lot of walking, and manual labour was much more common, but I felt that in our modern world the sauce just didn't fit. It didn't make any sense.

During his lecture, Professor Kurti covered the issue of oil and water. They do not mix, as we all know. Bring the two together and the oil will sit on the surface. His words went right to the heart of my hollandaise sauce dilemma. If you whisk oil and water, you create an emulsion. But this emulsion is not stable and it will soon separate, the oil once again heading to the surface, above the water. But what if you can find a medium, a third ingredient, that can bind the oil and water?

I kept looking at hollandaise, and then one day, eureka! I had it.

I took three egg yolks and whisked them with a hundred millilitres of water in a bowl over a saucepan of simmering water. The egg yolk contains lecithin, a natural emulsifier. It also has the ability to coagulate when heated, becoming a natural thickener. The whisking introduces millions of bubbles of air, which are captured in the mixture. The foam will increase to about three times the original volume, but at this stage it is not stable and the foam will collapse as the egg yolk around the bubble is uncooked and the air will leak out. Partly cooking the egg yolk makes the mixture more stable, coagulating the bubble around the air. (The protein of the egg yolk starts to denature at around 47°C and then to cook at around 60–65°C. However, as you have the constant movement of the whisk, you must raise the temperature to 80°C.)

I added eighty grams of melted butter rather than the suggested five hundred. I used just a pinch of salt, as the sauce is so delicate. Then I added a touch of cayenne pepper and a few drops of lemon juice to lengthen the flavour.

The sauce will serve about eight people and is exceptionally light. It keeps its structure for two to three hours, long enough for your guests to enjoy it.

To many this may seem a small triumph, but to me it was another little breakthrough, which I called a lemon sabayon (not hollandaise).

In 1992 I was invited to attend the first molecular gastronomy workshop in Erice, Sicily, which was presented by Professor Kurti. I did a small presentation on emulsions. It sounds pompous, but I can assure you that I was the happiest young man as I had finally begun to understand a few secrets inside the saucepan, so to speak.

Shortly after that we did a programme with the BBC. They liked the unusual idea of the chef/scientist double act. In 1994, the professor and I filmed *Blanc Mange*, which aimed to make both cooking and science accessible and show how they complemented each other. By that time the professor was in his mid-eighties but he was still fit: he could be seen at the beginning of the programme cycling from his home in Oxford to Le Manoir with a great big smile upon his face. *Blanc Mange* was directed by a lovely and brilliant man called Robert Oakland, who was himself a scientist. I did the cooking and Professor Kurti was there to help explain the chemistry and physics of the processes. We even proved in front of the camera that the flavours of an organic chicken are so much better than those of an intensively reared chicken. Both were roasted in ovens from which the molecules of flavour escaped through copper tubes. A gas was released into the tubes to break down all the flavour molecules into groups. It was incredible. The accompanying graphs showed the results — dramatic peaks for the organic chicken, mild undulations for the intensively reared one — but it was the nose that told the real story. The organic chicken had wafts of coffee, almonds, citrus, hazelnuts and vanilla that came in waves. The intensively reared chicken smelled fishy, of rancid fat, with no complexity or depth.

We also wrote a book to accompany the series, and I was helped in this by the wonderful French chef Hervé This. He has a great knowledge of both food and chemistry and was invaluable.

After the series, Professor Kurti asked me to become his champion. He wanted a chef on board, a professional cook who could promote the principles of molecular gastronomy.

I took stock. I was concerned that I was beginning to put science before food, which did not feel right. Sure, I wanted to use chemistry to better understand the behaviour of food, but I simply couldn't put it before food. To me, chemistry is just as important a building block of cuisine as nutrition, purity of ingredient, seasonality, tradition, the skill and knowledge of the chef and thousands of years of observation. No more, no less.

Let us imagine that we are watching a rainbow which all of us agree is magical and beautiful. Let us also say that the physics and chemistry behind the rainbow have been explained to you. Will that devalue your appreciation of the beauty of the rainbow? I don't think so. The miracle will not be undermined. If anything, it will make the experience even more glorious. But if while I am watching the rainbow somebody deconstructs it in scientific terms, that will undermine the experience, my powers of imagination, my sensibilities and my ability to get emotionally involved. Let me enjoy the miracle of a rainbow or a sunset. Let me enjoy the food. In my opinion, that is where molecular gastronomy could go badly wrong, if the chemistry is put first.

The programme we made was interesting because it aimed to demystify both food and science. Then came debates with people along the lines 'Is food simply a science, or is it an art, or is it a craft?' I'd say, 'It is a science, an art and a craft. It is all of these things, and more.' But after *Blanc Mange* I felt I didn't want to go beyond that. So I made a decision not to put science in front of food, even though I still feel that every chef requires a basic knowledge of chemistry if he wants to be a better craftsman. Quite simply, he needs to have a good understanding of what he is doing, to know what is happening in his pan. Then he is in control.

Molecular gastronomy also addresses old wives' tales and many misunderstood myths. Most old wives' tales have been found to be true, but not all. For example, we always thought that searing meat kept the juices in and thus added to flavour, but this isn't true. What enhances the flavour is the Maillard reaction: sugars and proteins in the meat, when cooked, produce the colourful and flavourful molecules that give seared meat its brown colour and delicious taste.

Something else we have discovered to be a myth, during tests here at Le Manoir, is that adding oil to butter during frying prevents the butter from burning by making it stable at higher temperatures. It is not so. In fact, with the addition of oil, the butter seperates and burns at a slightly lower temperature.

Likewise, it was long considered correct that when making a savoury soufflé salt should be added at the start, because it was thought that salt assisted the coagulation of the egg white. It doesn't. Quite the opposite, in fact: it delays the coagulation. Far better to put in a bit of citric acid

– in other words, a splash of lemon juice – at the start. This ingredient will help the binding of the egg-white proteins and the acidity will also bring more flavour to the dish. The salt should go in at the end. (I will return to the subject of the soufflé in detail shortly.) When you know these little things, when you start to understand why you are doing something, you will win all the way.

Having said that, culinary tradition has the major advantage of having been established after a process of trial and error a thousand times over; techniques have been proved to be correct. We rely on the experience of cooks before us who have tested and tasted and achieved perfection. So I said no to the ambassadorial role. Professor Kurti understood my concern, and we remained good friends until his death in 1998. I think of him very fondly. He was my first mentor.

The British chef most associated with molecular gastronomy is Heston Blumenthal. Back in the early eighties, Heston came to Le Manoir for a couple of weeks. He found himself working alongside a French chef, and then a big Yorkshireman with long hair said to him, 'Why are you working with the French? Come over here and work with the English.' That man was Marco Pierre White, who had forgotten that *he* was working for a Frenchman. Heston did what he had to do and followed his own passions. He remains a friend to both Marco and me.

I have the greatest respect for Heston and consider him to be a creative genius, totally true to himself, with an incredible knowledge of food and chemistry. But, sometimes I wonder if he is misguided.

Fundamentally, what both Heston and Ferran Adrià at El Bulli in Spain do is right. They are top professionals with the best understanding of gastronomy and chemistry. As I have said, chemistry should be part of our food world because it can give you the weaponry to be a better chef and to understand what's going on. They are also keen advocates of using seasonal produce and regional suppliers. But I worry about the effect they will have on up-and-coming young chefs. I don't like the prospect of young chefs coming along thinking that food is all about test tubes, Bunsen burners and liquid nitrogen. I worry that while they meddle in science labs they will forget about the core values of food. Molecular gastronomy can unleash a flood of creativity in the hands of an imaginative, forward-thinking chef. It can also easily be bastardized by a lesser chef. Already in my own kitchen I see that young chefs are mesmerized by gadgets and novelties. Gadgets should be used only to confirm what a chef's senses have already told him, but more and more young chefs rely on them and cannot tell whether any food, for example a chicken, is cooked by touch, the way it looks or the way it smells, only by sticking a probe up its arse. There is no substitute for basic knowledge and skills. You need to have them first. I am concerned that these young chefs will forget about food and misuse that wonderful knowledge of chemistry.

It seems inevitable that people will embrace molecular gastronomy. And as it falls into the wrong hands – of the trendsetters, the people who don't really care for food, the people with no passion – we may have to live through a nightmare the way we did with nouvelle cuisine, but worse.

More and more, people go to a restaurant to relax, and I wonder if molecular gastronomy's expression of cuisine is slightly flawed. If you arrive at a restaurant and then feel you have to watch a show and you have to be clever, the conversation is either killed or it centres on what is happening around you. For me, a table is a place where you can sit down with your friends, celebrate, and enjoy food. I want to be in an environment that is utterly comfortable, rather than one where you feel you are being told to observe little tricks and make some intelligent comments.

Professor Kurti was always surprised that the world seemed so excited by food science. He died before he could see its true global impact, but he didn't want science to be the central component of good cooking. He wanted to show that science is one of the building blocks of great food; he just wanted to know what was happening inside the soufflé. Professor Kurti respected food too much to let science control it.

Of course, if you think that molecular gastronomy was invented recently you are misled. For the last fifty years our food chain has been manipulated by processors, in their ugliest form in the supermarkets. Mix intensive farming with agro-chemistry and follow it with heavy processing, and there you have it. Put it in the ready meals shelves. Oh, and don't forget the marketing and shiny packaging. The food is more than tampered with, it is completely changed. It is broken down and reinvented, with emulsifiers and colourings and textures. Food processors have been using molecular gastronomy for decades and we are only just discovering the consequences.

By the way, Gary and I have thrown out all pipettes, syringes and test-tubes from the kitchen.

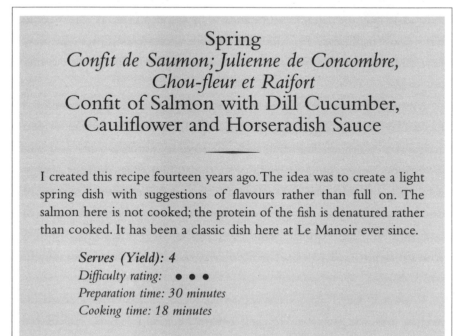

Spring
Confit de Saumon; Julienne de Concombre, Chou-fleur et Raifort
Confit of Salmon with Dill Cucumber, Cauliflower and Horseradish Sauce

I created this recipe fourteen years ago. The idea was to create a light spring dish with suggestions of flavours rather than full on. The salmon here is not cooked; the protein of the fish is denatured rather than cooked. It has been a classic dish here at Le Manoir ever since.

Serves (Yield): 4
Difficulty rating: ● ● ●
Preparation time: 30 minutes
Cooking time: 18 minutes

Marinating time: 1 hour
Special equipment: Mandolin, thermometer, smoker

PLANNING AHEAD

The salmon can be marinated 8 hours in advance and cooked to order. Freeze the cucumber ribbons at least 1 day in advance. The horseradish sauce and lemon oil can be prepared 1 day in advance.

INGREDIENTS

For curing the salmon:
240g salmon, filleted, boned, skinned and cut into 4 portions
1 tsp chopped dill
finely grated zest of ½ lemon
6 pinches sea salt
4 pinches caster sugar
2 pinches white pepper

For smoking the salmon:
400g oakwood chips

For the cucumber salad and white wine vinegar dressing:
3 pinches sea salt
½ cucumber, peeled and cut 12cm x 2mm ribbons (*1)
1 tbsp chopped dill
2 tbsp extra virgin olive oil
2 tsp white wine vinegar
1 pinch caster sugar

For the lemon oil:
400ml extra virgin olive oil (*2)
zest of 3 lemons

For the horseradish sauce:
12g fresh horseradish, finely grated
35g yoghurt
1 tbsp crème fraîche

1 pinch sea salt
1 tiny pinch cayenne pepper
2ml lemon juice

For the cauliflower florets:

80g cauliflower florets, boiled for 5 seconds and refreshed in cold water
20g horseradish sauce

For garnish:

warm flakes of salted cod
salmon eggs
caviar
micro sorrel leaves

METHOD

MARINATING AND SMOKING THE SALMON:

Put the salmon in a dish. Mix all ingredients for curing and evenly distribute them over the salmon. Marinate in the fridge for 1 hour. (★3) Wash off the marinade, pat the salmon dry and reserve.

In a purpose-built or home-made smoker, place the chips on a high heat and let the harshness of the smoke die down. (★4) Smoke the fish for only 4 minutes, 2 minutes on each side. Reserve and refrigerate.

MAKING THE CUCUMBER RIBBONS:

Salt the cucumber strips and marinate for 25 minutes; wash off the salt. Freeze the strips overnight. (★5) Defrost at room temperature, taste and wash any excess salt off. In a bowl, mix together the cucumber ribbons, dill, olive oil, vinegar and sugar; taste and correct the seasoning. Reserve.

PREPARING THE LEMON OIL:

Heat the olive oil gently to about 50°C. Add the lemon zest and infuse for 30 minutes, then strain the oil through a fine sieve and reserve.

PREPARING THE HORSERADISH SAUCE:

Mix all the ingredients and strain through a sieve. Taste and correct the seasoning.

PREPARING THE CAULIFLOWER FLORETS:

Mix the cauliflower florets with the horseradish sauce, taste and reserve the remaining sauce for the plate.

PREPARING THE SALMON:

Heat the lemon oil to 42°C. 'Cook' (*6) the salmon, maintaining the temperature, for 15–18 minutes. Lift the salmon out, drain and place on absorbent kitchen paper.

SERVING:

Warm the salmon and salted cod under a low grill for 1 minute. (*7) Place the salmon in the middle of the plate; arrange the flakes of salted cod, the cucumber ribbons and cauliflower florets around. Spoon over the remaining horseradish sauce, top with the salmon eggs and caviar, and the micro sorrel leaves. (*8)

Chef's notes:

*1   Peel the cucumber, then use a mandolin or a sharp knife to cut ribbons from the cucumber, turning as you go, until you are left with the seeds, which can be discarded.

*2   Use the best and most delicate extra virgin olive oil.

*3   It is only a light curing to firm up and season the flesh of the salmon.

*4   A common mistake is to use the harsh, first smoke of the chips, which is too bitter and too hot, and will lend its properties to the fish. What we want to achieve is a light smoky flavour.

*5   There are two processes involved here: a light curing, followed by freezing. The light curing seasons the cucumber and draws out the moisture. The freezing breaks down the cell walls of the cucumber and gives it a much brighter colour.

*6   Here I use the word 'cook' quite loosely. 42°C will not cook the salmon fillet, but will denature the proteins lending it a different, special texture and flavour.

*7   The fish must be barely warm and certainly not cooked as this would spoil the dish.

*8   We are lucky at Le Manoir to grow our own herbs. Micro sorrel is a beautiful leaf with a delicate acidity. Mr Richard Vines is probably the very best and most creative grower in this country.

TWENTY-ONE

JAPAN

The Search for Kobe

ONE OF THE MOST EXCITING MOMENTS OF MY LIFE CAME IN 1993, when I received an invitation to do a promotional tour of Japan, cooking and doing demonstrations. I was in my early forties and had barely travelled. There was that family holiday to Switzerland when I was seven years old and I looked around for green cows and was disappointed when there were none, and there had of course been trips back to France, but apart from that I had not left Britain. I'd rarely ventured beyond Oxfordshire's borders. Come to think of it, I'd hardly left Le Manoir. It seemed as if I had just worked, worked, worked. So the prospect of flying off to Japan for three weeks seemed highly attractive, even though I worried about leaving because I had never previously left my business.

I was seriously curious about Japan too, its cultures and, of course, its food, which of all the world's cuisines seemed to me the most exotic and mysterious. This tour would give me the opportunity to acquire a substantial knowledge of their cooking techniques, styles and ingredients. And I wasn't the only one who would learn: accompanying me on the trip would be a mini brigade including Gary Jones, who was a sous chef then but today is Le Manoir's executive chef, my pastry chef Nicolas Lambert (who is now the head of the Cordon Bleu cookery school in Tokyo), and Nicholas Dickinson, my then general manager.

Clive Fretwell, who was my head chef at the time (he is now executive chef at Brasserie Blanc), urged me to go, saying, 'Just have a break, Chef, you deserve it. I know how much you want to go. You must go.' But what a break! I would be cooking for about a hundred people every day and spending the rest of my day doing demonstrations and media interviews. I also knew it made good business sense to get on that plane because we had a nucleus of Japanese guests who visited every year and I saw the trip as a fantastic opportunity to increase that client base.

I accepted the invitation.

Before heading off, I read up on Japan in order to prepare myself. I went from being curious to being completely mesmerized by the country's refined culture. It was a world where food seemed to play a central role. During that period of research I came across a book that contained a few paragraphs about an extremely tasty type of beef much prized and loved by the Japanese. The meat was divine because it came from the cattle in Kobe which were specially pampered to produce succulence on the plate. The cows were apparently massaged by beautiful geisha girls, one geisha being assigned to every beast. And that's not all: the cattle drank sake and beer. The idea was that the booze would relax them and the geishas' nimble fingers would then redistribute the fat within the muscle tissue.

I could not quite understand how this would happen. How would the fat be spread through the muscle? It just seemed odd. Yet I bought the story completely. It was just too good to question. I was even more impressed when I read that the cattle were chosen for slaughter by a trusted adviser to the emperor. This adviser alone picked out the finest cows.

Today, Kobe beef is well known around the world and features on the menus in some of the finest restaurants (it does not come cheap). The meat is well marbled, which creates an unarguably buttery flavour, and it is adored by the gourmets of the twenty-first century. But in the early nineties few in Britain had heard of it, let alone tasted it or served it. Quite simply, the beef was unavailable in this country. My trip would enable me to taste this delicacy, which is to Japan what foie gras and truffles are to France, because Kobe was on the tour schedule. If I was really lucky I would be able to visit a farm, see the cows, meet the geishas, have a beer, and maybe get a massage myself.

The visit took us to five different parts of Japan. We created large banquets where we served the best gourmet food, as well as doing cookery demonstrations in the best restaurants, one in each region. My name was known in Japan and chefs were just as eager to learn about my cuisine as I was to learn about theirs. The Japanese are the most inquisitive of people, ready to pick up every little idea to increase their knowledge.

My God, what an experience. Let me start with the bullet train. First, it was beautiful and elegant, and then I met the conductor, immaculately dressed in a white starched shirt and tie and white gloves. The magnificent machine arrived at the very second it was due. It was the most incredible train experience I ever had – such a contrast to Britain! It was travel at its best.

We began in Tokyo, which set the scene for the rest of the tour. A limousine was waiting at the airport to drive us to the Seiyo Ginza Hotel, home to one of Japan's finest restaurants. The entire hotel management was waiting to greet us on a red carpet. We stepped out of the car, and flashbulbs flashed. First I was treated to head bowing, and there was a ceremony in which I was given presents – huge, ornate dolls in the finest silk dresses. More cameras flashed. While I felt like royalty, my chef Gary received little acknowledgement. I understood that the level of treatment was proportionate to your standing. Nicholas Dickinson, who was in the party to drum up business and meet travel agents, is tall and blond, the sort of Englishman who would choose well-done roast beef and Yorkshire pudding as his final meal, so he struggled with Japanese food. He may have been hungry, but because of his blond mane he was adored and had geishas swooning around him. For me it was a different story with the ladies in Japan. My French accent didn't have the success it has in England, nor did my dark hair. You cannot always win.

We were shown around the hotel and then led into the kitchen where some twenty Japanese chefs were lined up waiting to meet us. The kitchen was spotless and the chefs were immaculate in white, their aprons tied at the front with a beautiful bow, the same sort of bow that is used for karate and judo belts. More cameras flashed as I worked my way along the line, shaking hands. In advance of the trip, Gary had sent over my recipes. Being a good artist, he had also sent immaculate drawings of the dishes to illustrate their design and content. When we were led to another part of the kitchen I was flabbergasted by what I saw. There in front of me were all the dishes, all twelve of them, I intended to cook for the first banquet. They had been prepared by the Japanese chefs working from my recipes and drawings Gary had sent.

I wanted to taste each dish, to see if they were as good as they looked. The recipes must have been accurate because most of the dishes hit the mark. Most were very good, some excellent, but there were ones I felt could do with improvement and I said so. I might say, 'Mmm, it's OK, it's fine, but put in a little bit of lemon juice, we need a little bit of sourness here.' That caused problems. As you know by now, I am inclined to change a dish almost every time I do it. But the Japanese chefs would look at me with confused expressions on their faces. They could not understand how I could suggest changes within an established recipe. In Japan, a recipe is cast in stone. You simply don't meddle with it. Flexibility is rare. The recipe is the recipe.

Normally when you work abroad it's a nightmare trying to get hold of ingredients and to come to terms with the kitchen. It can often be a place you have to share with many other chefs, and they hate you for it. This work was arduous for different reasons: with every step in the kitchen there were three chefs photographing me. I would lift a spoon to taste something and I'd hear 'Camera,' and I'd have to look up and smile for a trio of young Japanese cooks with their lenses fixed on me. At one stage I was very tempted to tell them to get lost, but I didn't. The shadowing was constant.

In between the work, travel and media interviews there were also some feasts, some of which were the most divine of my life. I discovered the incredible Japanese obsession with seasonality and the wonderful symbolism behind food, service and every detail of the china. It was so beautiful, refined and elegant. I discovered that the Japanese food culture is certainly as strong as the French, maybe even stronger.

One night we were being entertained by various dignitaries who took us for dinner at an elegant restaurant. I love the ritual of eating in Japan: the elegant and discreet service; the intricate flavours; the extra-ordinary layering of textures from crunchy and rubbery to melting, glutinous and slimy, and the mixture of temperatures – warm, cold, hot, tepid. I couldn't help noticing that there were even textures on the walls, and on the plates too. As we sat at the table, a geisha arrived with a glass bowl that at first glance seemed to be filled with water. She gracefully placed the bowl on the table, and I looked a little harder. I noticed that within the water there were scores of little silver lights. On even closer examination I realized that these lights were tiny electric eels. I thought, 'That's a very nice table decoration. How clever.'

As I was admiring the sight of these minute fish, the geisha produced a little net, plunged it into the water and collected some of the eels. She then put them in another small bowl. As they wriggled furiously she poured some sake on to them. They wriggled even more furiously, as you might do if you were doused in alcohol. Then she poured some rice vinegar on to them. Now they were really jumping.

The bowl was then handed to me. I looked at my hosts, who were nodding cheerfully at me, telling me to drink. Drink and don't chew. I have that never-say-no rule, as you know, so I drank the drunken eels. Somewhere between my chest and my stomach I could feel the fish merrily dancing. The sensation lasted for a few seconds, then they reached my stomach where they met their fate. As far as food experiences go, it was one of the weirdest. I suppose it was a bit like the culinary equivalent of sado-masochism: you go to any lengths to find a new sensation, a fresh adventure, and in this case it was achieved with tiny drunk eels rather than bondage and whips. But that is Japan for you. It can be extreme.

Gary and I then went to a restaurant and were ushered into seats beside the chef and his counter. There was a large tank of water which contained some fish and Gary and I sat there for a moment admiring their beauty. Suddenly the chef put his hand into the tank and pulled out one of the fish. It was plonked on to the counter, and with lightning speed, as it wriggled for its life, the chef sliced away one side of it; then he turned it over and sliced away the other fillet, leaving its head, tail and the triangle of the belly containing the organs intact. He rapidly chopped the fillets sashimi style, placed this flesh on to a platter of evergreen leaves, and there you had it. We ate the fillets while watching the remains of the fish on the board in front of us, still rhythmically moving its mouth, gasping for air. One minute earlier it had been swimming in the tank. Yes, it was fabulously fresh, but we all felt uneasy.

At another restaurant I was treated to the same technique, though this time applied to octopus. The octopus was in a tank of water one minute and the next it was on a board in front of me being chopped up. A chopped tentacle was put on to a plate in front of me where it squirmed. It got a squirt of lemon juice and squirmed even more. It was in spasms. I was given the nod to eat it and duly obliged. It may have been dead by the time it went in my mouth, but only just. The sinews, strong and chewy, seemed alive. If you can imagine eating a freshly chopped finger, you'll get my drift.

At one banquet Gary arrived late, was seated, and a dish was placed in front of him. He looked at the food but could not identify it. Others at the table stared at him as he started to eat. Our hosts were keen to gauge his reaction, which he tried to make as positive as possible, but he paled a little when told that he was eating sea slug intestines, a

Japanese version of the French andouillette, but uncooked. 'It was so big you had to chew it before swallowing it,' he told me. Nicholas, our roast beef lover, stood up, ashen-faced, made his excuses and rushed to the toilets (which is where he spent much of his time in Japan).

Our last stop was Kobe, home to the pampered cattle. At the hotel I asked the manager if it would be possible to organize a car to take me to a farm to see the cows and geishas. 'Of course, Mr Blanc,' he said, but the next day nothing had been arranged. I made the same request and again he said, 'Certainly, Mr Blanc, I will arrange a car.' This went on for five days. The Japanese, in my experience, will always say yes. Eventually enough was enough and I told him firmly, 'Please, sir, I would like you to organize a car today. I want to see the Kobe beef.' And I wanted to see the geishas. The car appeared, and Gary and I made the journey to the farm. The sight that greeted us was terribly shocking. The cattle were not grazing lazily, they were being kept in wooden boxes. I come from peasant stock and I know what a clean cow looks like. These ones were dirty. Their rumps were covered in excrement. I had been expecting to see shiny, beautiful, fattened cows that had been well groomed. And geisha girls? Not even the fragrant scent of one. Beer and sake? Neither a bottle nor a drop.

As Gary and I tried to hide our disappointment it was explained to us that things were about to get exciting because the cattle were going to be slaughtered. We had arrived just in time for the killing of some fifteen cows.

The abattoir was like a large pen divided in two. The cows were herded into one half of the pen, then one by one they were taken for slaughter into the adjoining area which had a gutter into which the blood ran. What I found bizarre was that the cows could see from the safe side of the pen into the annexe where death awaited them. You could see the fear in their eyes. I couldn't understand why they should want to scare the cows as the meat wouldn't be so good: fear causes a blood rush to the liver, kidneys and muscles, creating little blood clots in the meat as the capillaries explode, which results in poor beef.

The slaughterman got to work. The noise of the machinery was drowned out by the stomping. The air was invaded by the stench of blood, guts and cattle excrement. I was filled with disbelief. Nothing made sense.

Then Gary and I were summoned to one end of the pen. The slaughterman was holding a plate upon which was a piece of meat freshly cut from one of the cows that a few minutes earlier had been alive. The meat was still twitching and warm. I was given the nod to eat it. I was already trying to cope with the surrounding stenches, and as I lifted the meat, which was warm and steaming, I caught its unappetizing pong. I ate. I didn't want to give them the pleasure of not eating it. It was a terrible experience, but I couldn't throw up. I found myself saying, 'Thank you, delicious' – as you do. When Gary was offered a slice, he smiled warmly and declined. But he held a piece of the steaming flesh close to his mouth and I took a photo of him – for what purpose I cannot tell you.

We left the abattoir and were whisked off for lunch – a lunch of Kobe beef cooked on a hot stone. It was good, but I did not fall in love with it as I'd imagined I would back in Oxfordshire when I was reading up on Kobe. The stench of the slaughterhouse had seeped into our clothes. The experience had left us shaken.

Later I found out that there was some truth to the legend of the pampered Kobe cattle. At some point the emperor of Japan had his own herd which received the geisha-and-sake treatment. Yet this left the question, how was the famed succulent taste acquired? To begin with, Japan is almost entirely vertical so there are few flat spaces for cattle to graze. The cows are kept in confined areas, have little exercise, and so get fat. Add to this their diet, which is mostly grain and cereal rather than grass. These protein-rich foods increase the fat content. Apparently they are indeed fed beer, but this is to help the digestion process rather than improve the flavour of the beef.

The cattle are Wagyu, a cross-breed, which might partly explain the meat's unique look and taste. There are successful Wagyu breeders in

America and Australia, but 'Kobe beef' comes from Wagyu cattle raised within the borders of Hyogo, which includes the city of Kobe. Go back a couple of hundred years and the Japanese were not beef eaters. They kept the beasts as working cattle only. It was only after the Meiji Restoration in the nineteenth century that things changed. The Japanese discovered that their cattle were not only strong, they tasted pretty good too. They had stores of intramuscular fat for energy, and that same fat meant well-marbled meat.

That visit to Japan was to prove highly influential on my life, my outlook and approach. In food, design and textures, the Japanese are masters of refinement, from cuisine to the design of a beautiful plate to the arrangement of flowers. My greatest food experience there was a kaiseki meal: an offering of twenty tiny dishes, all exquisitely presented, a succession of minute masterpieces, each one a burst of flavours and textures. And alongside this their uncompromised approach to the seasons and to freshness. In Europe we consider a fish to be good to eat if it has been out of the water for a day or two. In Japan they like their fish to go on to the plate straight out of the water. I like chopsticks too. I liked the way the chefs worked with them, allying speed and elegance with perfect hygiene as they never touched the food with their hands. I was good with chopsticks too. So good that I felt I could take on their chopstick champion in a pea-eating competition. (I beat him.)

I returned to Britain with eighty sets of chopsticks. Why do things by halves? I handed a set to each member of the brigade and told them, 'From today, guys, you are going to use these to handle the food.' Initially, they thought I was joking. I was serious. Soon they were moaning, 'Chef, I can't do this.' I'd try to reassure them that if they persisted they would get the hang of it. One chef started to cry and I had to tell him gently that chopsticks were the way forward. Meanwhile, Gary was spending much of his time giving chopstick lessons. My hopes were smashed one day when I walked into the kitchen and spotted a couple of chefs using spoons and forks. When they saw me they quickly picked up chopsticks as if they had been using them all the time. It transpired that the entire brigade was doing this, secretly using cutlery rather than sticks. I was forced to abandon the idea, but I may well try to reinstate it one day.

My trip to Japan also enabled me to fall in love with Japanese tea-gardens – the epitome of purity. I decided there would have to be one at Le Manoir, that I would create a Japanese microclimate within our own French potager and English ponds. A Japanese tea-garden is reflective and introspective, quite different to the beautiful and colourful gardens of the rest of Le Manoir. The tea-garden at Le Manoir, Fugetsu-an, was opened in May 1995, and it coincided with a Japanese Food Festival, a week-long extravaganza that cost £700,000. We flew over one of Japan's greatest chefs, Hiroshia Koyama, and he came with his family and a mini brigade of six chefs. We also flew in Japanese artists, sculptors, kimono-makers and opera stars. Geisha girls were on hand to explain the symbolism.

The festival was opened by the Japanese ambassador, His Excellency Hiroaki Fujii, and I took him to the tea-garden where together we planted an amelanchier tree. Then I took him to the tea-house. We followed the tradition of removing our shoes before going in to crouch (so that everyone is the same height) and drink tea. I removed my shoes and made my way in, but as the tea was being served I felt a draught on my big toe and looked down to see a massive hole in my sock. This sent me into an inner panic. The ambassador and his wife were immaculate, as is the Japanese way, and there was I with a hole in my sock, which they had spotted. You know that you have a few seconds to retrieve the situation.

'I am so sorry, sir,' I piped up. 'I do not have a wife.' (This was not a lie: Jenny and I had been divorced for some time.)

Today you could not get away with such a joke about wives being sock-menders, but in the tea-house beside the pond that day it got a smile of approval from His Excellency and his wife. It was just the right answer – at least it was thirteen years ago – and I drew sympathy from both of them. 'Poor man,' they were thinking, 'he hasn't got a wife so that's why he's got holes in his socks.'

In the hotel world, we were the first to honour their culture, and we reaped the benefits. Tens of magazines covered the event. Our Japanese market increased by 6 per cent. Both the trip and the Fugetsu-an garden made sense. I could have opened dozens of restaurants in Japan, but I declined.

Le Manoir aux Quat' Saisons
Anguille à la Gelée; Mooli Aigre Doux
Eel in Teriyaki Jelly, Soured Mooli

This dish was inspired by my visit to Japan, where I truly discovered new flavours and textures. This dish used to feature on our menu up to five years ago, but eels are now endangered. You can replace the eel with monkfish or salmon, or best of all mackerel. However, I wanted to show you the classic Manoir recipe, complete with eel. And, as a Manoir recipe, it is complex and time-consuming, but it is a fine example of how textures and flavours from elsewhere can enrich a repertoire.

> *Would serve: 48 Manoir guests as an appetizer*
> *Difficulty rating:* ● ● ●
> *Preparation time: 30 minutes*
> *Cooking time: 40 minutes*
> *Special equipment: 4 terrine moulds 25 x 4 x 4cm (★1), tray of crushed ice*

PLANNING AHEAD
The terrines need to set for at least 8 hours, or overnight.

INGREDIENTS

For the mooli for the terrines and the garnish:

400g ribbons of white mooli, 2mm thick, 25cm long
35ml sake, boiled for 30 seconds (*2)
400ml water
50ml mirin
40ml rice wine vinegar
4g bonito flakes, in a muslin cloth
5g kombu seaweed
2 pinches sea salt

For cooking the eel:

200g eel bones and 100g trimmings, chopped into 2cm pieces
20ml rapeseed oil (*3)
20ml sesame oil
30g ginger, finely chopped
1 tsp dark brown sugar
200ml sake
150ml mirin
100ml dark soy sauce
350ml clear fish stock
1 pinch Japanese Szechuan pepper
900g (1 medium) eel, skinned, filleted and trimmed to fit terrine
    moulds

For the jelly:

7 gelatine leaves
750ml eel cooking liquor
20ml lime juice
salt and pepper, to taste

For building the terrines and garnish:

the eel jelly
20g dried wakame seaweed, soaked in 200ml warm water
half the cooked mooli ribbons
the cooked eel fillets

METHOD

COOKING THE MOOLI:

In a large saucepan, bring all the ingredients to the boil, skim and simmer for 20 minutes until soft. Leave the mooli ribbons to cool in the liquid. Reserve.

COOKING THE EEL:

On a medium heat, in a large pan, caramelize the eel bones and trimmings in the rapeseed and sesame oil for 5 minutes until golden. Add the ginger and cook gently for 1 minute, then spoon off the oil before adding the sugar and cooking for 1 more minute. Add the sake, mirin, soy, fish stock and pepper, bring to the boil and simmer for 15 minutes. Strain through a fine sieve and reserve.

Add the eel fillets to the strained cooking liquor and cook for 20 minutes just under simmering point. (*5) Lift out the eel fillets, cool down and refrigerate. Refrigerate the cooking liquor, too, so that you can remove the solids to produce a clear stock with which to make the jelly. (*6)

MAKING THE JELLY:

Soften the gelatine in plenty of cold water. Drain. On a low heat, bring the clear cooking liquor to blood temperature (40°C). Transfer 100ml of the liquor to a separate pan, add the gelatine and bring to the boil. (*7) Mix both together, taste and adjust the seasoning with the lime juice, salt and pepper. Place on ice and stir until the cooking liquor thickens.

FOR BUILDING THE TERRINES:

Place the terrine moulds in a tray of crushed ice to help speed up the setting of the jelly. Layer each terrine first with a fine layer of jelly, then a thin layer of seaweed, then a little more jelly; next come the mooli ribbons, then an eel fillet in the middle, covered with a fine layer of jelly, then repeat the pattern all the way to the top. Do the same for the other 3 terrines. Leave to set overnight for best results. (*8)

TO SERVE:

Slice each terrine 1cm thick, place 2 pieces on each plate, arrange the seaweed and mooli ribbons around the plate. Serve to your guests.

Chef's notes:

*1   You could make this in individual tiny moulds or espresso cups. I prefer the terrine as once cut it will reveal all the textures, colours and layers.

*2   See chef's note 2 on page 46.

*3   Rapeseed oil is neutrally flavoured and has a high burning point. (Sesame oil, in contrast, has a lower burning point and can be toxic when it reaches around 170°C.)

*4   Using cold water and bringing it to a gentle boil forces any impurities to the surface, making it easier to skim and giving you a clear stock.

*5   The eel fillets are huge muscles and need gentle cooking to prevent them retracting and toughening.

*6   During refrigeration, the solids will sink to the bottom and the fats will remain on the surface. Once cold, you can easily remove both, leaving you with a clear stock.

*7   Boiling the gelatine in a small amount of stock facilitates mixing with the rest of the stock.

*8   The jelly needs a minimum of 8 hours to firm up perfectly. This also makes it easier to slice.

TWENTY-TWO

TEXTURE

The Return of the Chew

YES, JAPAN CHANGED SOME OF MY LIFE. I RETURNED HOME INSPIRED in many ways, and the country's uplifting effect on me is reflected in the food, gardens and design of Le Manoir. OK, so I couldn't push my chefs into using chopsticks when plating up, but they happily embraced one element of Japanese cuisine, which seemed new and exciting. In a word, it was *texture*.

Today, chefs and foodies talk incessantly about texture. They debate the crunch of one ingredient perhaps, contrasting with the softness of another. Switch on to any cookery programme or pick up a recently published cookery book and you will see texture mentioned as if it has always been an essential requirement of our cuisine: 'The texture is not quite right . . . the texture is perfect . . . what you are looking for in this dish is texture . . .' Now in the dictionary of Western cuisine it sits comfortably somewhere between 'taste' and 'tongue', but it was only a few years ago that 'texture' entered the parlance of most professional kitchens. Two of my protégés, Xavier and Aguar Rousset, have opened their own restaurant in Portman Square in London called Texture.

Even if it is not yet embracing ethics and environmentalism, the fast food and confectionery industries are also embracing textures. Note, for instance, McDonald's mixing crunchy chocolate pieces with ice-creams, or think of a Topic bar, or Ferrero Rocher chocolates. Textures have also moved the world of design.

Food is connected to everything else in our lives and that's why we see texture playing a role in food, but also a role in interior design and art, the way we dress and the clothes we wear. The minimalist period of food – the nouvelle cuisine revolution – coincided with, or even led to, the minimalist period in design. It was a style that worked against joy and comfort, two luxuries the modern consumer craved. We had to go through that minimalist period . . . and now look at design. Sure, there is modernity, but now design takes into consideration the ideas of comfort. It is friendlier, less pretentious, less fashionable. Feeling good about oneself is hugely important today, though a few years ago it was not there. Texture has become a significant part of design. It has embraced creativity, not only in the culinary world.

The trip to Japan in 1993 encouraged me to give a good deal of thought to the subject of texture. It is a supremely important characteristic of Japanese cuisine, and it is equally valued in the cuisine of Asian countries like China, Cambodia, and North and South Korea.

We all have textures we do not like. For me, it is the viscous texture – sticky and glutinous – which was the texture of a number of dishes I tried in Japan. However, I found that once I had overcome the shock of what was going into my mouth (I put it in quickly), I was willing to taste again and again. While I was writing this book, tonight for example, I decided to cook for myself some tripe, to my grandmother's recipe. It is both slightly viscous and rubbery, and an acquired taste. But the smell you will never forget. Natalia complained bitterly as the smell invaded the whole house.

In Japan there were countless dishes of raw fish with raw vegetables, providing a contrast of textures as well as contrasting flavours. The bite size counted. Apply this to Western food and suddenly you can begin to see the potential. The way the meat, for instance, rectangular, square or finely sliced, will not only affect the texture but also the flavour. Also, whether you cut the meat with or against the grain will alter your experience. Take carving the Sunday roast, or just a sirloin steak. Cut across the grain and you'll find that the flavour will be magnificent and the texture will be succulent as the fibres are short; cut along the grain and the meat will not be so good because you'll be biting into the wrong texture. The fibres are longer, not allowing the juice to ooze out, so it will also be much tougher.

There was a time when you could rarely make an Englishman eat a piece of fried skin. Now it is possible because of our new-found love of texture. That piece of fried skin will be beautifully cut and magnificently cooked. It could be a piece of crispy duck or pork fat that has been ground down and seasoned with paprika or cayenne pepper. On the plate, it will also act as a design element. Quite simply, it will look appetizing. When eaten, it will bring flavour and texture to the dish. All of this is second nature to the well-trained sushi chef.

Then there is the ever-present *gelée* of today's haute cuisine, forever melting and fresh, incomparable to the jellies (including aspic jelly) that used to stand up on their own. These *gelées* are delicate and refined. A teaspoon of *gelée* meets the heat of your mouth and melts in a second or two.

Every dish now, whether dessert or savoury, is guided by texture. It is an integral part of the experience.

Even simple stews can benefit. But first get to know your meat and the factors that will influence the tenderness and flavour – age, length of hanging, whether or not it is marinated, which marinade has been used, how thinly it is cut, with or against the grain . . . so much will define your experience. When I think about it, my tripe was good, but there was something missing in the texture. If I add a little pig's trotter, cut two centimetres across, to the tripe and cook for about six hours at about 110°C (which gives about a 90°C temperature inside – strong enough to break down the skin and transform it into a delicious, melting thickness) it will be just right.

Once upon a time we used to bang a stew in the oven where it would bubble away nicely, and that was it. It emerged from the oven and the meat was grey and dry and not at all nice. Now we can look at stews using a better understanding of basic food science. By cooking at the right temperature the meat in that same stew will be a beautiful pink and it'll melt in the mouth. Cooking for a long time at a temperature of about 70°C will bring a better flavour and also a much improved texture because most of the collagen breaks down or becomes gelatinous. The meat is not dry but moist and appetizing.

And let's look at roast chicken. For decades in Britain we have been told that when you cook chicken it should be tender and melt in the mouth. And it does, for a good reason. The majority of chickens bought in this country are battery-farmed. Still today, 80 per cent are intensively reared. They have never run around or eaten worms from the ground. They have lived in confined spaces and not enjoyed a good life. The breed has also been carefully selected so it grows as much as possible, with no consideration for flavour. As a result, for years we have associated the texture of chicken with tenderness, whiteness and tastelessness, the bone spongy and brittle. This means that when the finest chicken from Bresse or Laverstoke Park is presented on a plate it is not quite right for many people. The leg is grey and the meat does not melt in the mouth; it requires a chew. My God, when you eat it you have to chew it, but that is a good thing. I have so many complaints about proper free range organic chicken. At one stage I was concerned that my British friends were losing the muscle structure around their jaws because they didn't have to chew their food. If it wasn't the battery-farmed chicken, it was the supermarket ready meal, which likewise does not require too much chewing. Thank God the free range chicken is back on the menu. By 2018 I do not think that battery chickens will be legal.

Intensively farmed fish often has that same easy texture because the fish has not done much swimming. It also has a totally different muscle structure from a wild fish, which has covered ten times the length of Britain before it reaches your plate full of flavour and texture. The texture of intensively farmed food simply does not compare to the texture of the real thing, and thankfully we are now rediscovering the real thing.

For me, a great dish has a juxtaposition of different textures. But too many is not good because it will confuse the palate. Sometimes I have had dishes with ten different textures. I think it's all wrong. It's like having ten different flavours in your mouth: it will mess you up. When I see a dish overpainted on the plate I always worry a bit because I know there will be too many textures and often too many flavours, and no dish needs that much. The hardest thing for a chef is to extract simplicity out of complication. You don't need stacks of colours, flavours and textures to make a great dish. A good chef, a wise chef, knows that. And that's where the good chef, the honest chef, the authentic chef, will look for truth and ultimate pleasure by combining just two or three textures, rarely more.

A wise old chef learned this a long time ago.

Autumn/Winter
Ballotine de Queue de Boeuf, Braisée au Vin Rouge
Braised Oxtail, Red Wine Jus

When I introduced this dish, nobody liked me in the kitchen, and I'm sure you wouldn't have either. Boning an oxtail is like trying to complete Rubik's cube, only worse – you have a knife in your hand. The sharp blade has to find its way through the complex network of bones that makes up the tail, minimizing waste and scraping the rich meat clean from those little vertebrae. Marco Pierre White worked with me and, as we all know, became a hugely talented chef, but not everyone knows that in the oxtail business he was the true champion: he would attack the oxtail in the most deadly manner, and won any challenge he was put up to. You should ask the butcher to prepare the oxtail for you!

Serves (Yield): 4 x 150g portions
Difficulty rating: ● ○ ○
Preparation time: 30 minutes
Cooking time: 6 hours
Special equipment: Medium flameproof casserole with a lid, string for
   tying the oxtail

PLANNING AHEAD

You can braise the shallots 1 day in advance.

INGREDIENTS

For the braised shallots:

   400g banana shallots
   30g butter
   1 pinch sea salt
   1 pinch freshly ground black pepper

Cooking liquor for the oxtail:

   800g (1) oxtail, boned (★1)
   20ml groundnut oil
   50g white onion, cut into 2cm dice
   2 cloves garlic
   25g carrot, cut into 2cm dice
   25g celery, cut into 2cm dice
   400ml red wine reduced by half (★2)
   400ml brown chicken stock (see page 206)

METHOD

BRAISING THE SHALLOTS:

Preheat the oven to 100°C. In a large ovenproof pan, sweeten the shallots in the butter for 3 minutes, (★3) season with the salt and pepper, cover with a lid and slow-cook in the oven for 40 minutes, stirring occasionally. Taste and correct the seasoning. Cool down and reserve.

TYING THE OXTAIL:

Preheat the oven to 100°C for the oxtail. Place the oxtail on a chopping board, skin-side down, and roll out flat. Season well with salt and pepper. Down the middle of the oxtail, place the braised shallots in a line. Roll up the oxtail, starting at the thicker end, and tie a piece of string in a knot at this end, then wind the string all the way round to the other end, keeping the tension throughout. Tie off at the other end to secure.

BRAISING THE OXTAIL:

In a flameproof casserole on a medium heat, caramelize the oxtail in the oil for 8–10 minutes until golden brown all over. (★4) Remove the oxtail and caramelize the vegetables for 4–5 minutes until lightly browned, then strain off all the fat, add the reduced wine and the brown chicken stock, and bring back to the boil. Return the oxtail to the casserole, cover with a tight-fitting lid, and cook in the preheated oven for 6 hours. (★5)

Allow the oxtail to cool in the liquor, then strain and pass the cooking liquor through a fine sieve. Remove all the string and slice the oxtail into 4 portions. Reserve.

FINISHING THE SAUCE:

In a medium saucepan, on a high heat, reduce the cooking liquor by half. Taste and correct the seasoning with salt and pepper if required. (★6) Reserve.

SERVING:

Place the sliced oxtail back in the oven for 5 minutes to heat through, and serve with the red wine *jus*, and potato mousseline and pot-roasted vegetables. Do not put knives on the table: a spoon and fork will do fine.

Chef's notes:
★1   You need a skilled butcher to prepare the oxtail for you.
★2   Choose a rich, full-bodied wine, but don't spend more than £4–5.

Many interesting tests have been carried out on the French, who are meant to know their wine, and 9 out of 10 could not recognize the top seven regions. So when you cook the wine, what chance have you got? And to use an expensive Burgundy or Claret is plainly wasteful. A good local wine from the south-west of France might be just right. You are looking for depth of colour, rounded tannins, good fruit and a heady flavour. That will do perfectly.

*3   The shallots should be just cooked – that is, still firm – as they are to be cooked again in the oxtail.

*4   The slow caramelization will give a better flavour and colour to both the meat and the sauce.

*5   The worst thing that could happen is if the cooking juices were boiled during cooking. The meat will toughen and be inedible. The base temperature in the pot needs to be about 85°C for this type of meat. This is sufficient to break down the collagen to a melting gelatinous texture, and also to have a melting quality and enhanced flavour to the meat.

*6   Braising requires a long cooking time, so the sauce will lose a little bit of its freshness. If it is so, reduce 100ml red wine to about 2 tbsp and add it to the sauce. This will revive it and add depth of colour.

VARIATION

Of course this method could be applied to any other meat that requires slow cooking, such as beef cheek (unfortunately this magnificent piece is not available to us due to the lack of trust in our practices), blade of beef, silverside and shin of veal (which, thank God, are available). A fricassee of wild mushrooms would be a wonderful accompaniment to this dish.

TWENTY-THREE

LE SOUFFLÉ

Rise Above It

O F ALL THE DISHES THAT CREATE ANGUISH FOR COOKS, THE soufflé has to be way up there, somewhere at the top of the list of so-called kitchen conundrums. Again, it is all about texture and flavour: the light crunch of the outside crust combined with the fluffiness inside, and full-on flavours.

For a couple of centuries this egg-based dish, savoury or sweet, has been the subject of myth and confusion. It is the cause of dinner-host horror stories: 'I got the soufflé to the table but then it collapsed and my guests sniggered'; 'I opened the oven door to take a quick peek and that's when it deflated'; 'I thought I'd give it an extra ten seconds, and it collapsed!'

The soufflé, it is believed, was the invention of Antoine Beauvilliers, who was chef to the Count of Provence (later to become King Louis XVIII). Beauvilliers is recorded as the world's first chef-patron, having opened La Grande Taverne de Londres in Paris in the 1780s. It was the first restaurant to serve what we know as haute cuisine. At some point in the late eighteenth century Beauvilliers created soufflé for his customers (whom he would greet, incidentally, wearing a spotless uniform and a dress sword). When the mixture was removed from the oven it had risen, increasing in height by about a third. It had *soufflé*.

With the puffing up came the huffing and puffing of cooks. The soufflé saga began. Some fifty years later the world-renowned French culinary master Antonin Carême wrote about the dish in order to help cooks who were fretting because of their collapsing soufflés. But things have moved on since the days of Beauvilliers and Carême. Today I can say with confidence that soufflés are in fact simple to make successfully. Unless, of course, you try to cook the Soufflé Rothschild that Albert and Michel Roux created, with three different flavours; that might be too much of a challenge. As with most dishes, there are principles that need to be observed, but the fear must be dispelled, otherwise there won't be a cook left in Britain who feels courageous enough to make these puffed-up delights.

I was raised, so to speak, on soufflés. My mother often made cheese soufflés, or a cheese tart soufflé, both invariably made with Comté. A special autumn dessert was a baked apple and semolina soufflé, which was always a treat. All my mother's soufflés were served in a wide shallow dish so all the members of the family could help themselves. One of my favourite soufflés is made with Roquefort, which is twice baked. This saves the possibility of embarrassment as it never collapses. It has been on the menu at Brasserie Blanc for the last ten years and is still hugely popular. Crumbs of the blue cheese are hidden in the middle of the dish. When cooked they become little pockets of cheese, bursting in the mouth. English Stilton is also good in soufflé, but for my palate Roquefort does it. Made with sheep's milk and matured in the limestone caves of Les Causses, it has an unrivalled salty, acid flavour.

So let's try to remove the complexities of soufflé-making. To do this, I want to try to simplify the process, which I hope that you, the food lover, will appreciate. If you have already mastered this dish then by all means skip to the next chapter.

There are four elements to the soufflé. By recognizing and understanding the importance of each element the cook can progress with confidence and, fingers crossed, ease. The process for both a sweet and savoury soufflé is quite similar, but for the moment we will talk only of the sweet.

The four elements are the buttering and sugaring of the dish or ramekin; the base; the flavour; and what I shall call the lifter. Think of these four elements separately, though eventually if they are done correctly they will come together to make a perfect soufflé.

First, the **butter** and **sugar**.

Brush the inside of all the soufflé dishes with melted butter, right to the top, and then add sugar to the first one and shake it. Pour the excess sugar into the next soufflé dish and repeat so that each soufflé dish is coated with butter and sugar. If the mixture goes into an unbuttered soufflé dish it will stick to the side and fail to rise to a good height. However, some scientists have told us that we do not need the butter. If you are curious, try it. The butter acts as a lubricant.

The sugar also has a specific role to play: it creates that prized crust. Although in a small soufflé for one the crust doesn't quite have time to form. That is why I love a large soufflé for four or six guests where the cooking time is longer and the textured sweetness of the crust has time to form. The larger soufflé is the most delicious, in my opinion. When you come to eat it, you work your way from the crusty outside before reaching a more firm texture, and then you hit the creamy, melting centre. Because of that I will give you a recipe for a large soufflé, for both the crust and the conviviality.

There are so many variations and textures and flavours you can add to the soufflé, particularly in the coating. To the coating of sugar you could add powdered nuts, unsweetened cocoa powder or cinnamon, dried vanilla seeds, zest of lemon . . . the opportunities are endless. A chocolate or vanilla soufflé could include grated cocoa bean, or nougatine, or crunchy crushed-up pieces of biscuit or fudge, or fragments of chocolate which melt when cooked. One of my classic soufflés at Le Manoir was a pistachio soufflé with a little surprise: nestling in its centre was chocolate ice cream.

Then there is the **base**.

The base acts a bit like cement, though never, I hope, in terms of taste. It holds together the structure and gives density and creaminess to the dish. It will also give viscosity to the egg-white protein around the bubbles of air as the starch in the flour strengthens during the cooking. This base is called *crème patissière*, also known as confectioner's custard or pastry cream. You might never have made pastry cream but undoubtedly you will have tasted it because it is used in many desserts, cakes, pastries and tarts. If you tried to cook a sweet soufflé without pastry cream then the egg white would be overly spongy and would fail to win you praise.

The pastry cream should be quite thick; too thin and runny and the mixture will be too wet. Worse, the result will be dramatic: your soufflé will rise but it will not transform into a fluffy texture. It will run over the edge of the dish, like lava erupting from a volcano. You will suffer embarrassment in front of your guests. No applause.

Next, there is the **flavouring** element.

This goes into the pastry cream (the base) and it can be whatever you wish it to be. For instance, it could be caramel or chocolate, praline, pistachios, coconut – any of your favourites; or a fruit: raspberries, blackberries, gooseberries, apricots, passionfruit, mango; and of course any type of liqueur you can think of. The number of flavourings is countless, so some thought needs to be applied to the flavouring element.

Let's say, for example, that you want a raspberry soufflé. If you made a raw coulis of raspberries by puréeing and straining the fruit you would have a problem because when the time came to add it to the base it would make the base too runny. Which, remember, you certainly don't want. You need to cook down the raspberry purée with a little sugar to a light jammy consistency (taste it first as it might not need it: the fruit might be sweet enough, and remember that you will add some sugar to the egg white). Now warm the base of the soufflé and whisk in the raspberry purée. It should have the consistency of crème fraîche, not runny and not firm. Most fruit purées need to be cooked down, thickening but also intensifying the flavour and colour. Most fruit has skin or pips (sometimes both), so strain them. The fruits I can think of at the moment that don't need to be reduced are lemon and lime; they are reinforced by their zest, grated into the base. Bananas are used as they are.

For chocolate soufflé, the chocolate is melted in the hot pastry cream, and the chocolate should be bitter with a minimum cocoa content of 70 per cent. If you wish, the chocolate could be strengthened with unsweetened cocoa powder.

One of my favourites is caramel soufflé. First, keep your base warm in a bain-marie. The caramel should be cooked to a dark and handsome colour, almost to burning point. You will have some smoke, but don't panic, you will get there. It will have a tinge of bitterness and be rich in caramel taste. Undercooked caramel will be beige, overly sweet and boring. It is always better to whisk the caramel into warm pastry cream. If it goes into cold pastry cream the caramel is likely to solidify.

This brings us to the fourth and final element, the **lifter**.

The lifter is of course egg white. Albumen protein, which is made up of many other proteins, helps the viscosity. These are wonderful proteins because of their ability to expand when whisked. I add a little lemon juice before whisking to reinforce the structure of the foam.

They must be whisked in a very clean bowl, and egg yolk should not be allowed to sneak in with the whites. Yolk is partly fat, and the fat content will prevent the whites being whisked to the maximum volume. In fact, the slightest trace of yolk or any other fat could lose you about a quarter of the potential volume.

When you whisk, millions of bubbles of air get wrapped up within the albumen and a foam structure begins to form. Add sugar little by little but not at the start or you will have less volume, less lightness and less rise.

Sugar and lemon juice assist with the binding process. They prevent what is known as graining, which is when the water content of the egg white separates from the solid of the protein and you are left with a pool of liquid in the bottom of the mixing bowl. Of course, sugar and lemon juice help build up the flavour too.

What you want to achieve is a perfect foam which has density but also lightness. The peaks should be soft, not stiff. This will give lightness to the soufflé as you have larger bubbles. Be careful, though: if the peaks are too soft the soufflé will collapse. On the other hand, if the peaks are too stiff you have overwhisked the egg white and divided the bubbles into tens of millions which will create a denser soufflé with less rise and a more rubbery texture. We want a soufflé that really melts. Practice makes perfect.

The mixing of the base and flavour can be done up to a day in advance. When you are about to prepare the soufflé, though, warm the mixture up. If the pastry cream and flavour comes straight out of the fridge it will be too firm, it will be difficult to incorporate the egg white, and you will lose more volume. The base should also be warm because if you are making fresh soufflé it will cook a little faster than if it were cold and you will achieve a better rise.

Mixing in the egg whites is simple, but there is a procedure to follow. Understand that you are dealing with a light-structured foam made of millions of bubbles of air wrapped in uncooked egg-white protein and sugar. They are utterly delicate, and the more you fold the more friction is created, causing the bubbles to burst, and you will lose volume and lightness. Not so good!

To achieve the best result, don't just mix in all the foam at once. Instead, take about a quarter of the foam and whisk it into the warm flavoured pastry cream. Do this with speed and with strength and without any form of pity. This lighter base will help to incorporate the remaining egg white.

Next, use a spatula to fold in the remaining three-quarters of the egg white/sugar foam. First with one quick turn, and then continue to fold in very carefully. Try to think of it as damage limitation: you know you have to mix in the foam but at the same time you want to retain as many bubbles of air as possible so that the soufflé can rise when cooked. Lift the mixture from the base in a circular motion. Overmixing is a classic mistake, and you will lose volume and lightness. I would prefer to see little traces of white foam in the soufflé. We all would.

So there you have the elements together, and the soufflé is ready to be cooked.

The mixture goes into the soufflé dish, which has of course been buttered and sugared. The mixture can fill to the top of the dish. Run a palette knife across the surface of the mix so that it is level and the surface smooth. Sprinkle with icing sugar and let it melt. Sprinkle again with more icing sugar. This will develop a delicious crust when cooking.

Now that the mixture is in the dish, we come to what is known in the business as 'thumbing up'.

The aim of thumbing up is to create a tiny gap between vessel and mixture. In a circular movement, run the tip of your thumb around the inside of the top of the ramekin. You want to push away the mixture from the side of the dish; just a millimetre will do it. I suppose it is a little like a moat running round the top. Unlike the best moats, however, it should be neither too deep nor too wide. Be warned: some cooks are laughed at if they make a large moat which results in a lop-sided soufflé that looks as if it is wearing a silly little hat.

Soufflé likes a little help and a little kick. It should always go on to a hot tray in your preheated oven and this will give it the desired kick. It should never go on the top shelf because it is likely to burn, especially from the reflected heat from the roof of the oven. Soufflé is best positioned about one third up from the bottom of the oven. It can be cooked in any oven, but be aware that today's ovens are mostly fan-assisted, which has consequences: they force the heat in and shorten the cooking time by about 15–20 per cent.

How long in the oven, and at what temperature? My small soufflés are ten centimetres in diameter and seven centimetres high and take about eight minutes. I must have made thousands of them, every time testing the temperature, and I have found that 200°C is just right. The large soufflé will cook at the same temperature but for twenty-five minutes in a fan oven and thirty-five in a static. If you open the oven door it's all right. A few times is still all right, but too often and for too long the temperature within the oven will decrease and this may affect the soufflé. After three or four minutes for a small soufflé and five or six for a large, check if they are rising well. If they are lopsided, release the soufflé from the edge of the dish by sliding the tip of a knife between the soufflé and the dish.

Soufflé can be deceptive. You see it rise and a large smile comes on to your face. You think it is ready and that if it stays in the oven any longer it will collapse. You remove it, serve it, and then discover that inside it is uncooked. So use a timer and observe the cooking time. Yes, they might look good on the surface, but they are uncooked inside. So please, follow the recipe, at least the first time.

To establish whether the thing is cooked or not, insert a skewer into the middle of the soufflé, withdraw it, and lightly touch the centre of the skewer against the skin just above your top lip – or just below your bottom lip – for two seconds. The skewer should feel quite warm, bordering on hot. Then you know the soufflé is cooked inside. Alternatively, and if you want to get high tech, insert a cooking thermometer or probe right in the middle of the soufflé; when it reads '67°C' it is ready to serve. Of course, if you don't want to do either of those you could bring it to your guests to see if it is cooked.

We should always bear in mind that cooking is an inexact science. Your oven, your cooking dishes and your ingredients will all be different (if only slightly different) to mine. So get to know your oven, think about the ingredients you are using, and think (in this instance) about the dish in which the soufflé will be cooked. For example, if you are making a large soufflé and you cook it in china which is thick, the conduction of heat will not be as strong as if you were to use thin china. In silver there will be even more conduction, likewise copper. But for a soufflé I think china is best. It is good to experiment and test for yourself. After all, as is said, practice makes perfect.

———

Savoury soufflés have the same four elements – butter, base, flavour and lifter – but they are slightly different. As it is a savoury soufflé, the coating cannot be sugar; instead it is butter and breadcrumbs. The base is béchamel sauce or white sauce which is made of butter, flour for the roux, milk infused with cloves, a bouquet garni and black pepper. Often this base is enriched with egg yolks and sharpened with mustard. At all times the base must be the same consistency as the pastry cream – thick and not runny. It is very much just a savoury version of pastry cream.

The most familiar flavouring for savoury soufflés is cheese, whether it is Comté, Gruyère or Stilton (as I said, as far as I'm concerned, Roquefort is the best). Purée or grate the cheese and add two or three lovely chunks of it to the centre of the soufflé so they melt when cooked. Add some pieces of walnut for extra flavour and texture. Gruyère soufflé can be enriched with a splash of kirsch, the liqueur distilled from cherries and their stones. Taste, taste, taste as you cook. Think how you can make the flavours bigger, stronger, sharper. Remember to add lemon juice, and black pepper, which will lengthen the flavour and can be used in both sweet and savoury soufflés.

Of course you can do savoury soufflés with meat and fish protein, but personally I am not keen on that. I find puréed meat or fish grainy. I much prefer to do a beautiful soufflé with whole flakes of fish. Smoked fish – cod, salmon, haddock – goes brilliantly in soufflé. Just put the flakes of the smoked fish in the ramekins before pouring in the mixture. Sea urchins are wonderful too – a real flavour of the sea.

The lifter, of course, is still egg white. Add lemon juice at the very beginning. You will have exactly the same volume of whisked egg white as you would have with sugar. The difference is that you need to whisk the egg whites a little bit more to make them a bit firmer. Lemon juice will prevent graining, sharpen the flavour and help to strengthen the structure, but it does not add the density and viscosity achieved by the sugar. Because savoury soufflés don't have sugar you will never achieve quite the same rise during cooking as is accomplished with the sweet soufflé because the foam structure isn't supported by sugar. Ignore recipes that tell you to add salt at the beginning of the whisking of the egg whites: salt will delay the binding process rather than speed it up. Season with salt and pepper or even cayenne, Worcestershire sauce or Tabasco towards the end of whisking to add a little kick.

Follow the same principles as if you were making a sweet soufflé: the flavour element is mixed with the warm base element, and this is then mixed with the egg-white foam.

———

I think I have kept the best for last. I would like to give you a little technique that will allow you to prepare a sweet soufflé in advance, not just the base and flavourings, but the whole thing. First make the base, then whisk in the egg whites and sugar, pour the mixture into the dishes and store them either in the freezer or in the fridge for up to three hours.

The cooking time will be different, according to whether you put the soufflés in the fridge or freezer. I will assume that you have a fan oven and that your soufflé would have taken ten minutes to cook from fresh. Here is a table of new cooking times depending on how long you chill your soufflé:

Chill time	1 hour	1½ hours	2 hours	2½ hours	3 hours
Cooking time from the fridge	10 min	10 min	11 min	12 min	14 min
Cooking time from the freezer	12 min	14 min	16 min	19 min	24 min

You will notice that with the freezer the cooking time more than doubles over three hours, but with the fridge it is an increase of less than 50 per cent. When refrigerating fruit-based soufflés there will be a tiny bit of degradation, but you will not notice it; in the chocolate and caramel versions there is almost none. When taken from the freezer there will be a little less volume to your soufflé when it is cooked, but again, it's not really noticeable. So, unless you are a masochist like me, this is very good for the cook at home.

Imagine your dinner party, then. You have finished the main course. Make sure that everyone is listening and say, 'I am sorry to leave the table but I must make my Grand Marnier soufflé.' When you leave the table of course your guests will be impressed. Some might smile. You may add another little sprinkle of icing sugar, then slide the soufflé into the preheated oven. Make a little noise in the kitchen so people know you are working. After a few minutes you rejoin your guests with a beaming smile and not a single smear on your face, just oozing confidence. Twelve or fifteen (or whatever) minutes later you rise again and announce that the soufflé is ready. Then you make a grand entrance with your perfectly risen soufflé. Take all the applause and enjoy the moment.

All Year Round
Crème Patissière
Pastry Cream

One of the easiest and safest creams to make, and used in so many desserts. And, of course, as a base for the soufflé.

Serves (Yield): 600ml
Difficulty rating: ● ○ ○
Preparation time: 10 minutes
Cooking time: 10 minutes

PLANNING AHEAD

This can be made up to 2 days in advance and kept covered in the fridge.

INGREDIENTS

500ml milk
6 egg yolks
50g caster sugar, plus extra for sprinkling
1 tsp vanilla purée (see page 202)
80g plain flour (*1)

METHOD

In a medium-sized saucepan, bring the milk to a simmer. Meanwhile, in a large mixing bowl, whisk the egg yolks, caster sugar and vanilla purée; then, whisk in the flour. Gradually add the hot milk and continue to whisk.

Now we need to cook the pastry cream. Pour the mixture back into the saucepan and, on a medium heat, bring to the boil, whisking constantly (*2) for about 1 minute until you obtain a smooth consistency. Pour immediately into a bowl and sprinkle with caster sugar to prevent a crust forming. Cool down. Once cool, cover with cling film and refrigerate.

Chef's notes:

*1   The use of flour prevents the curdling of the egg yolks. Through the process of boiling, starch, egg yolk and milk thicken and bind together to create a homogeneous cream.

*2   The whisking will distribute the heat and prevent the cream from burning at the bottom. The short boiling is enough to cook and bind the cream.

All Year Round
Soufflé au Grand Marnier
Grand Marnier Soufflé

One of the great classic soufflés. Try it first on your long-suffering family or trusted friends.

Serves (Yield): 4
Difficulty rating: ● ○ ○
Preparation time: 15 minutes
Cooking time: 8 minutes
Special equipment: 1 large soufflé dish: 15cm across x 6cm deep,
*   electric whisk, pastry brush*

PLANNING AHEAD

The pastry cream (see page 307) can be kept warm in a bain-marie. The egg whites can be kept in a mixing bowl ready to be whipped. The soufflé dish can be buttered and sugared.

INGREDIENTS

For the soufflé dish:

1 tsp butter, at room temperature
20g caster sugar

For the souffle:

100g warm pastry cream for soufflés (see page 307)
30ml Grand Marnier
finely grated zest of ¼ orange
175g (5) egg whites
60g caster sugar
icing sugar for dusting

METHOD

FOR THE DISHES:

Preheat the oven to 170°C with a baking tray on the middle shelf. Using a pastry brush, butter the inside of the soufflé dish. Sprinkle the sugar inside and rotate it until completely coated. Shake out the excess.

FOR THE SOUFFLÉ BASE:

In a bowl mix together the pastry cream, Grand Marnier and orange zest, and keep warm in the bain-marie. (*1) In a separate bowl, whisk the egg whites to soft peaks, then gradually add the sugar and whisk until firm but not too stiff. Whisk a quarter of the egg whites into the warm pastry cream until smooth. Using a spatula, briskly fold in the remaining egg whites by cutting and lifting with large circular movements.

FILLING THE DISH:

Fill the soufflé dish to the top. Smooth off the surface with a palette knife. Sprinkle the top with icing sugar, leave to melt for 1 minute and repeat. Thumb the edge (see page 302).

COOKING THE SOUFFLÉ:

Place the dish on the pastry tray in the preheated oven and bake for 20 minutes.

Chef's notes:

*1   This is the point at which you would use other flavourings of your choice.

VARIATIONS

These soufflés can be cooked in individual soufflé moulds. Follow exactly the same method; only the temperature and cooking time will change. Individual soufflés need to be cooked at 200°C for 10–12 minutes. Over a shorter cooking time, the temperature is higher in order to give enough lift, to cook the centre and to leave a nice crust.

TWENTY-FOUR

THOUGHT

The Salt Tests

I WAS ON MY OWN IN LOS ANGELES A COUPLE OF YEARS AGO AND WENT to a restaurant for lunch. I did not have a book to read so I entertained myself with the next best thing: pricking up my ears to listen to the conversation on the neighbouring table. It was occupied by two American women somewhere in their fifties, and they were chatting away happily. Suddenly one of them pointed at the kitchen with a horrified look on her face, so I stretched my ear sideways (which is never easy, especially when you are eating). 'Oh my God!' she announced, and clasped her hand to her mouth. 'That chef just used salt!'

Life is strange. It's even stranger if you happen to spend time in LA, where salt is considered the most vulgar of four-letter words.

The episode took me back to the opening day at Les Quat' Saisons when I cooked for my first two customers, a middle-aged couple. He had ordered gateau of Jerusalem artichokes with a chervil *jus*, she went for the salad of duck liver, with its crunchy skin and confit of stomach, in walnut oil dressing. They were the first two dishes I served in my new restaurant. They meant something to me. I was proud of them, particularly the Jerusalem artichokes as that was my first signature dish.

The dishes were collected by a waiter at the passe and I followed them as far as the kitchen door. How would my first guests react? I held the door ajar and watched.

The couple stopped their conversation and looked at the plates in front of them. So far, so good. Then came the reality check for me: the man lifted the salt cellar and shook its contents furiously on to his food. The speed of movement was a blur. I gasped. Once he was done, he passed the salt to his wife and she too shook with all her might. I gasped again. When the man reached for the pepper mill I closed the door.

They murdered my food in front of me. But that was Great Britain in the seventies, when people really worked hard to get their palates hooked on salt and sugar and the processors and retailers were helping the consumers in their addiction.

What is a palate? It is the roof of the mouth, and it helps us to eat and to taste. But the word is used in other ways. Chefs sometimes talk about colleagues having a good palate, by which they might mean he has a natural flair for combining ingredients, sometimes unusual ones, that lift the flavour. If a chef serves his guests ghastly mixtures of ingredients we would probably say he has a bad palate, or no palate whatsoever. And we'd be right. We talk also of people having 'a good palate' when we want to say they have the ability to detect flavours or little undertones in a dish, the sorts who would do well in a blind tasting. It's a form of reverence.

We can go even further. We can look at how the palate is messed around. If you draw on a cigar then put a mouthful of smoked salmon into your mouth as the smoke is emerging from your nostrils . . . well, you get my point. On that subject, when I stopped smoking many years ago, in terms of taste I was expecting a miracle, but it didn't happen. My palate seemed slightly less salty, but as I have never had a salty palate it didn't have a huge effect. But I found that my sense of smell was revolutionized. I could smell a storm coming many miles away and could pick up the slightest scent of a flower. That was lovely.

If you go to any of the great cellars of France, you'll be greeted by tasters with berets on their heads and cigarettes in their mouths, so I think we are either born with a good palate or not. But if your diet consists mostly of salty, sugary, fatty processed food then your palate will degrade and come to depend on such food. You'll crave salt and sugar. The health effects of this are well documented; you will be a likely candidate for a heart attack, or at least cardiovascular problems. Your palate will tell you to avoid anything that does not have the required sugar or salt level. It will tend to guide you away from the fresh flavours of, let's say, fruit and vegetables or perfectly seasoned food.

There will be the cook who adds a little salt, then tastes and nods approvingly. This might suggest his palate is good, not too salty. Then there is the cook who adds salt, tastes, but is unable to taste enough salt so he chucks in a few more pinches, and then some more. So establishing the saltiness of your palate can help tremendously when you cook. Whenever a chef started in my kitchen I did this test to measure the saltiness of his palate. It is a strange aperitif, but it is quite fun, so try it yourself. Of course, the yardstick of measurement was my own palate.

Take six glasses, and on the bottom of each put stickers numbering them from one to six. Pour into each glass 150 millilitres of water at room temperature, as coldness affects the flavour. Put glass number one to one side – this is the glass with no salt. Now, into the five remaining glasses put varying degrees of salt, from one pinch to five pinches. Stir to dissolve the salt. Make a note of the numbers and how much salt is in each glass. One of them should be perfectly salted, or seasoned. (If heated, incidentally, it would taste more salty.)

Along the way, he must identify the saltiness of each glass, ranging from very salty to no salt. Allow others to try the test. You will be amazed to discover that what tastes repulsively salty to you might be perfectly acceptable to someone else's palate. So when you have thirty chefs in your kitchen, you'll see what I mean.

The aim of this test in my kitchen was to measure the saltiness of my chefs' palates. If one had a very salty palate I knew that he was dangerous and I had to watch him. Perhaps he would be placed in the dessert section. If you are the cook of the house and through this experiment find that your palate is the saltiest then you might like to question the amount of salt you use when you are serving up for others. On the other hand, if you have a good palate – not too salty – don't be surprised when your family and friends reach for the salt cellar, just like my first customers at Les Quat' Saisons.

It is currently accepted that adults require about five or six grams of salt in their daily diet. Though now it's as if we are going from one extreme to another: after eating food loaded with salt, we now believe we shouldn't have any salt at all in our diets. The no-salt brigade wants us to follow the new fashion, but there is nothing wrong with a little salt.

How many people know what that quantity of salt looks like, though? A cook is following a recipe that instructs him to use, let's say, two grams of salt. Does he reach for the kitchen scales and measure it out? If three pinches are required, how does the cook know that his pinch is the same size as the pinch that is required? And are you using flakes of sea salt or the more dense ground salt? My preference, incidentally, is always *fleur de sel*. Unfortunately, by 'salt' we usually mean granulated table salt. Two per cent of its total weight is chemicals to prevent moisture from being absorbed. Those additives include aluminium and silicon compound, silicon dioxide (which ceramics are made from) and magnesium carbonate. There are also anti-caking additives. So, please, try to use more natural salt from the earth or the sea.

I use salt purely as an example to illustrate a point. The best chefs, like Gary, are the ones who think and question. Gary and I ask Le Manoir's new chefs to conduct another short experiment . . .

You have a box of sea salt and your kitchen scales. Take ten pinches of the salt and put them on the scales. What is the weight? If it is not ten grams then carry out the experiment again. And do it again, if necessary. Conduct this experiment until you know that each pinch is one gram. You have now successfully told your fingertips the weight of a gram of salt. Looking at it another way, you have told yourself that one pinch equals one gram. Your life in the kitchen has improved significantly, maybe the lives of your guests as well. From now on, if you are cooking a dish that needs three grams of salt, you can give it three of your unique pinches. You have saved the time of searching for the scales and you can tell yourself that you are beginning to question. In addition, you can begin to assess how much salt you are taking in on a daily basis, though take into consideration the fact that most food already has its own sodium content.

The only problem comes when you ask the question, which salt should I use? One gram of flaked salt will be a very large pinch, while one gram of refined salt will be a smaller pinch.

You can apply the same logic to other ingredients, measuring them with a spoon or a cup. Remember, cooking is simple.

The purpose of this salt experiment is not only to show the chef how to save time, it also encourages him to use his senses as well as common sense. It's not just about taste. I do not teach my chefs to cook, I teach them to reconnect all of their senses with their intelligence, and also to be curious and ask questions.

Our eyes and ears should tell us what stage the cooking is at. You arrive at a friend's house for Sunday lunch. The door opens and the scent of the perfumed hostess is closely followed by the welcoming scent of roasting meat. There is another smell when it is undercooked, and when it is overcooked there is a sharp whiff of overcaramelizing. But somewhere in between is the smell of perfectly cooked meat, that smell that makes you go, 'Wow.' If you are roasting meat at home, notice the smell when it is correctly cooked and make a nasal note of that aroma.

There is a common misconception that salt is one half of seasoning and pepper is the other half. Season, says the recipe, so the cook throws in some salt and then does a few turns of the pepper mill. We tend to forget all the other forms of seasoning — put simply, ingredients that enhance and improve the flavour of the finished dish. Bitter or sour ingredients such as mustard, ginger, galangal, cocoa beans, chicory, radicchio, horseradish and onions lift flavour. Astringent ingredients like teas, coffee, wine, and acids such as orange and lemon will work. All the spices of the world are also there. And what about the garden of herbs? These are also true catalysts of flavour, and their addition minimizes the amount of salt I put in a dish.

Be warned, however: it is easy to spoil food by overusing herbs and spices.

Then we have temperature, which again is a catalyst of flavour and deserves consideration. There was a time when you would go to a restaurant and order a cognac at the end of the meal. The sommelier would approach the table with the bottle and a lamp. The glass was placed in a wire frame and the sommelier would heat the alcohol to bring out the flavour. In the grandest restaurants, the cognac would be heated to room temperature, 21°C — not too warm, just perfectly conditioned. In the not-so-grand places it was a different story. The sommelier would manage to burn the glass and then the balloon would be passed to you. While you were losing several layers of skin from your fingertips and lips, your nostrils were filled with the vapours of boiling alcohol. You'd leave the restaurant scorched and poisoned.

The law tells us to store cheese at 4°C, which we do. We serve cheese at 14°C. We have had a special fridge built which stores the cheese at 4°C, and has a 14°C section into which we move the cheese before service. However, we all agree that even at 14°C it is like eating a piece of cold fat, but for the sake of hygiene and safety we do it. Better to be safe than sorry. Then when we serve the cheese - because our guests are so discerning – we ask them to wait a few minutes before eating it.

So temperature is as much a catalyst of flavour as salt, pepper, lemon and any other seasoning. You do not want to drink vodka warm; it will kill you, and the food as well: your caviar will become boiled eggs in your mouth. You want it to come from the freezer. That essence of tomato mentioned in chapter one must be chilled; it would be too acidic, too sweet, too aggressive if eaten warm. Think of tepid coffee . . .

And beware when adding ground pepper at the start of cooking. As you add salt, suddenly the pepper, which was innocuous, will jump to the roof of your mouth. That is why I mostly add a little salt followed by herbs, then spices, and lastly the acid. I find that this order is the least likely to be dangerous. A little salt needs time to permeate vegetables and meat. If cooking, salt added right at the end will create an aggressively salty taste on the outside and an unsalted flavour within.

By adding the herbs in the same way you will create an exchange of flavour. To bring out the flavour I usually add spice and then, for length, some acid (a dash of red wine or lemon juice, or even a bitter herb), or a tiny dash of sweetness. Always a combination. I want flavours that are layered and grow. A good flavour will stay for about six or eight seconds (a bad one too), but a mediocre flavour will just disappear, for there is no roundness, no length.

Also, give some thought to the choice of peppercorn. Do you use green, white or black? It defies logic, in fact. The different colours tell you so much but not what you might at first expect. Black peppercorns are harvested when they are unripe and green. Then they are left to dry for up to ten days, and as they dry they shrivel and change in colour to dark brown and black. Green peppercorns, as you will have guessed, are picked when green but are usually canned, brined or now sometimes frozen. White peppercorns are the berries that are allowed to ripen almost completely on the vine. Once picked they are soaked in water so that the outer skin can be easily removed, and what reaches the consumer is the grey-white seed.

Green and white peppercorns bring acidity and coarseness to the dish; black or dark peppercorns will provide a rounded, more mature flavour. Disregard the rule that white pepper goes in a white sauce while black pepper goes in a darker sauce. Adding a few twists of black pepper to a white sauce is something I can live with because the taste is more important than those dark specks.

Summer
Brasserie Blanc
Canard Confit; Haricots Tarbais
Duck Leg Confit with Flageolet Beans in Persillade

This dish represents what the nutritionists call the French paradox. The people in the south-west of France are known to be the most ferocious carnivores. In this region, mountains of fat, foie gras and meat are eaten and enjoyed. Yet here you have the fewest cardio-vascular problems and illnesses, and a long lifespan. Maybe this is due to the quality of life in this part of the world: the fact they eat the very best fruit and vegetables and, of course, drink a fair amount of best local red wine . . . and enjoy a quieter life.

Serves (Yield): 4
Difficulty rating: ● ○ ○
Preparation time: 15 minutes, plus 12 hours' curing
Cooking time: 3 hours
Special equipment: Temperature probe

PLANNING AHEAD
You can cook the duck legs 2 days in advance and keep them in the duck fat. If you use dried beans, soak them for 12 hours (★1) in advance.

INGREDIENTS

For the duck legs:

    4 large duck legs (200g each) (*2)
    30g rock salt
    1 tbsp black peppercorns, crushed
    4 cloves garlic, finely sliced
    4 sprigs thyme, leaves picked
    2 bay leaves, finely sliced
    800g duck fat, melted (*3)

For the beans:

    400g fresh flageolet beans (*4)
    ½ onion, chopped
    4 cloves garlic, halved
    100g smoked streaky bacon, finely chopped (optional)
    1 bay leaf
    4 sprigs thyme
    1 clove
    800ml water
    1 tsp freshly ground black pepper
    2 pinches sea salt (*5)

To finish the dish:

    4 tbsp extra virgin olive oil
    2 tbsp chopped flat-leaf parsley

METHOD

CURING THE DUCK LEGS:

Lay the duck legs on a small tray, flesh-side up, and distribute the rock salt, crushed pepper, garlic, thyme and bay leaves evenly over. Cover with cling film and cure overnight or for 12 hours. (*6)

COOKING THE DUCK LEGS:

Wash off the curing mix and pat dry with kitchen paper. Pack the duck legs in a saucepan and cover with the melted duck fat; bring the temperature to boiling point for 30 seconds, skim the impurities, then lower the heat to about 80°C – check with a probe. Cook for 3 hours at this temperature. (★7) Cool down in the duck fat, and reserve.

COOKING THE BEANS:

Whilst the duck legs are cooling, mix the beans and all the other ingredients in a saucepan. (★8) Bring to the boil for 2 minutes and skim, then lower the heat to the most gentle simmer, one single bubble breaking the surface. Cook the beans for 50–60 minutes. Taste to see if they are perfectly cooked. The beans should be soft and melting – the signs are tiny little blisters in the skin – but always taste.

SERVING:

In a non-stick pan, over a medium heat, crisp up and colour the duck legs on the skin side for 5–7 minutes. Transfer the beans and cooking juices into a shallow serving dish, add the extra virgin olive oil and parsley, top with the confit of duck legs, and serve.

Chef's notes:

★1   If you are using dried beans, especially red kidney beans, be careful as they hold a toxin within. They can be neutralized in two steps: first soak the beans overnight for 12 hours; discard the soaking water as many of the toxins will have leached into it. Secondly, cook the beans: the cooking process will kill the toxins and make the food safe. If you don't do these things, badly cooked beans may cause illness, such as vomiting and nausea. With the correct precautions, dried beans are an excellent addition to your dry store.

★2   Use the best ducks available. I prefer to use the French varieties of Challan and Barbary, from the Bresse area, but now we have some excellent English varieties of Gressingham duck, or Trelough ducks from Trelough House in Herefordshire.

★3   Duck fat contains a lot of monounsaturated fat. This dish is not an unhealthy one.

★4   Of course you can get dried beans all year around, but fresh is best. My favourites are coco, flageolet and tarbais. They are at their best during the months of July and August; they grow very well in the British climate.

*5   People say that salt toughens up the skin of the beans and lengthens the cooking time. I have not found that to be true, unless you put 30g salt into 1 litre water.

*6   Salt has been used as a means of preserving food for thousands of years, and man has depended on it for his survival. During curing, salt permeates the meat or fish, extracting the water, and by doing so, killing the bacteria. What the cook gets excited about, however, are the changes in the texture and flavour of the meat or fish.

*7   This method of cooking the duck legs or confit can be used for any other meat. Once cured the meat is immersed in duck fat and cooked at a low temperature which will give a succulent richness to the meat as well as a very much loved flavour. Some people love their duck completely overcooked and falling off the bone; personally I prefer it medium. Adjust the cooking time accordingly. In the past the meat was preserved in the duck fat. Today, to be on the safe side, you should only keep the duck legs in the fat for 3 days.

*8   If you don't use the bacon, add a little more salt, so the quantities of salt in the recipe are not high.

TWENTY-FIVE

THE F WORD

The Lost Secrets

FUSION IS A HORRIBLE WORD. IT BRINGS TO MIND AN IMAGE OF ghastly combinations, dressed up as one cuisine meeting another, or even two cuisines meeting two others, or more. Usually the meetings are not happy. Fusion can too easily become confusion. It reminds me of terms like 'nouvelle cuisine', the original meaning of which has been obscured through misuse and abuse by trendsetters. What we are witnessing is a complete meltdown of cultures. In trying to incorporate other cultures into our own we have lost sight of the secrets and mysteries of both. We have lost all authenticity. On the one hand it is exciting and enriching, but on the other, one feels one may have chewed too much and not digested properly.

Take, for example, European cuisine. Most foodstuffs in Europe are not European at all. They were originally imported from elsewhere. But they have been introduced to Europe ever so slowly and elegantly. Each of the foods, be it the bay leaf or basil, tomato, chocolate or coffee, right down to the humble potato, each of them enriches our culture and what is simmering in the pot. All these new foods and techniques were slowly integrated into our culture and our recipes to become part of our food heritage. This process took hundreds, even thousands of years. Then in the last few decades we have become a global village where everything is fair game and available. Even more so here in England as the food culture is less strongly rooted. Without much food culture of our own, it seemed obvious that we should embrace that of others. In many ways we wanted to respect and understand other cultures, and in doing so we have created the world of fusion. Countries like Spain, Italy and France with a stronger food culture have not turned so much towards fusion food. They have protected their agriculture and small producers better, as they understood their importance. Right down to the local *coq au vin* or *spaghetti vongole*.

But perhaps fusion is what we are all about today, and will be even more so in the future, as cuisines move across the world, accompanied by a global crossover of technology, political ideas and philosophies. My God, I remember the days when the French used to sneer at the British for putting mint sauce on their lamb. Now the French can't get enough of the sauce. Once upon a time my countrymen laughed at that classic British dessert the fruit crumble. Now it is being cooked throughout France.

With my French culture I try to embrace responsible gastronomy. At the cookery school at Le Manoir we have a course which might be 'fusion' in other people's minds, but is described as 'Tastes and Textures from Elsewhere'. Fusion, for me, is all about exchanging ideas, and in the case of food it should be about enrichment rather than a clash of ingredients and cultures. Some countries, like France, Spain, Portugal, Italy and Greece, have always fought against globalization. But how can you fight something that is natural and inevitable? I like to think I know exactly who I am. I am a Frenchman, but a better Frenchman for having lived in Britain for many years. I came with my own baggage, my own tradition. I've enriched it with the British openess to other cultures and cuisines. As a person, I've moved on. In the old days I was a bit too tempestuous. Nowadays, I can laugh about myself. (Not too much, mind you.) I have learned just to listen rather than speak at the same time as I listen. I am more thoughtful, more reflective. This has also played a part in my cuisine. I feel I have not only retained and passed on tradition, I've modernized it and enriched it, mostly through being in Britain, where people are open to new ideas. I also like to think I have always integrated my French culture responsibily.

My first true taste of Thailand nearly blew my head off, but it turned into an experience that inspired many dishes, sweet and savoury.

I visited Thailand about ten years ago, and on my first day there I decided to go for a stroll in the street market, which was heaving with people and food stalls. I stopped at the first stall for a bowl of tom yum soup. It is a clear soup whose character is largely defined by chilli peppers – many of them are used and the heat can take you by surprise – lime juice and galangal. As I said, it blew my head off. The dominating flavour of the chilli is made all the more powerful by the acidity of the lime juiceand the bitterness of the galangal. Most tastes in south-east Asia are based on sweet and sour, sweet and acid or sweet and bitter. Tom yum soup is bitter, acid and sour. Its spice is so intense it can strip your tongue. Once I'd drunk it I looked like a fish with a hook in its mouth.

Most people think that a beer is the best way to cope with hot (as in spicy) food, but that is not so. Starch or carbohydrate will dampen the heat (a bit), so for my next course I thought I'd have rice to put out the fire in my mouth. I wandered along to another stall and had chicken bang bang with rice. It felt like great food, and good medicine after the hook.

I fancied something else, and that is when, a little further down the street, I chanced upon something that at the time seemed out of this world in terms of taste. The stallholder handed me a bowl of sticky rice and mango. The mango, deep orange, was unlike any mango I had ever eaten in Britain, or anywhere. British supermarkets buy most of their mangoes from intensive farms in Australia and New Zealand and they are large, so hopelessly average; the shopper ends up with more flesh but at the expense of flavour and texture. In Thailand the mangoes were oval with caramel skin and incredibly dark orange flesh which was sweet and sour and heavily perfumed. There are as many varieties of mango in Thailand as there are potatoes in England – a huge range, with many different flavours. They are nothing like the bland and flavourless mangos generally available in England. (If you can, please try an Alphonso mango from western India and Pakistan, which is one of my favourite varieties. Its skin is yellow and inside the flesh is deep orange and wonderfully sweet.) The rice had been steamed and the stallholder had then added coconut milk so that the rice absorbed it. It was served with a slice of lime and mango on the side. I felt that the dish was essentially Thailand in cuisine. It was simple, but one of the greatest food experiences of my life. Sticky rice and mango is to Thailand what chocolate mousse and floating islands are to France and crumble and sticky toffee pudding are to the British.

During that trip I also tasted red rice, which was unrefined so it was more starchy and as a result more chewy.

When I returned to Le Manoir I brought with me sculptures and paintings that would find their way into the guests' bedrooms. (In the north of Thailand I saw an incredible mountain which inspired one of the most beautiful rooms at Le Manoir, Lemongrass.) And I set about creating a dessert, *brochette de fruits exotiques*, inspired by the sweet dish I tasted at that stall in Thailand.

I marinated mango, papaya, lychees and bananas with Vietnamese mint, Thai basil, lime syrup and green peppercorns, which are soft, unripe and mellow in terms of heat. Once marinated, the fruit was threaded on to a brochette, or skewer. This was served on sticky rice. A peppery guava sabayon went on top of the fruit, and to finish, the pulp of a passion fruit for tartness and acidity.

The thing about this dish is that while the fruit comes from far away – they are tastes and textures from elsewhere – it is transformed into the perfect French dish because of the *brochette* and sabayon. (Of course, it had the sticky rice. What it didn't have, sadly, was that incredible mango flavour as it just was not available here.) The ingredients are Thai and south-east Asian but the concept is entirely French. This is how I like to interpret fusion cuisine.

———

You will encounter many micro-climates from elsewhere in the garden at Le Manoir, be it in the form of the Japanese tea-garden, Fugetsu-an the south-east Asian garden, the mushroom valley where we grow shi-take and King Oyster mushrooms, or the vegetable garden inspired by my childhood home in France. These micro-climates are also reflected in the concept of the rooms at Le Manoir: Lemongrass, Jade, Opium, Sandalwood; and, of course, there's the French influence in Provence, Manon, Le Rouge et Le Noir. The ensemble is elegant.

I find travelling very enriching; it fills me with so many new ideas. In northern Thailand and Malaysia I walked up a mountain to a height of a thousand metres, where the temperature dropped from 50°C (at sea level) to a more temperate 22°C. There I was surrounded not only by all the usual tropical fruits but also by trees bearing European fruit. 'Well,' I thought, 'if European fruits can grow in Thailand, can Thai fruits grow in England?' After seventeen years of experimentation, we now manage to grow lemongrass all year round, which serves as a constant reminder of the tom yum soup I tasted in that busy street market in Thailand.

We even took our south-east Asian garden to the Chelsea Flower Show, sponsored by a Malaysian airline. We were delighted to win a silver gilt medal, with Newington Nursery as our partner. At Le Manoir we now grow thirty varieties of south-east Asian produce. The various gardens have been integrated into the landscape of Le Manoir. And we are continuing to work with the University of Bangkok to introduce more Thai herbs which have never previously been grown in Europe.

Summer
Le Manoir aux Quat' Saisons
Gratin de Fruits Exotiques; Riz à la Noix de Coco
Exotic Fruit Gratin with Coconut Rice

This dish was inspired by the sticky rice and mango I first tasted on a Thai street, which is to Thailand perhaps what *îles flottantes* are to France.

>*Serves (Yield): 4*
>*Difficulty rating:* ● ● ○
>*Preparation time: 30 minutes plus 2 hours to soak the rice*
>*Cooking time: 45 minutes*
>*Special equipment: A mixing machine with whisk attachment, grill or blowtorch, bamboo steamer lined with muslin cloth, sugar thermometer*

PLANNING AHEAD
The coconut rice and the sabayon can be prepared 1 day in advance.

INGREDIENTS
For the coconut rice:
>160g Thai glutinous rice, (*1) soaked in cold water for a minimum of 2 hours
>500–600ml unsweetened coconut milk
>40g palm sugar
>8ml lime juice (about ½ lime)

For the exotic fruit:
>120g ripe mango, cut into 2cm pieces (about 1 whole mango, peeled and stoned) (see pages 324–5)
>80g ripe but firm papaya, cut into 2cm pieces
>80g banana, cut into 2cm pieces
>6 lychees, peeled, stoned and halved

1 tbsp palm sugar (optional)
8ml lime juice (about ½ lime)
pinch of cayenne pepper

For the guava sabayon:

50ml water and 90g caster sugar, for the syrup
3 egg yolks
150g guava purée (*2) or mango
10ml lime juice
50g whipped cream, soft peaks

To finish:

icing sugar
1 passion fruit, seeds and pulp

METHOD
MAKING THE COCONUT RICE:

Drain the rice, place in a bamboo steamer lined with muslin and steam for 20 minutes with the lid on. (*3) Taste to see that it's done – it should be soft and sticky with no bite – then transfer to a mixing bowl. Separately, simmer the coconut milk and the sugar for 1 minute. Add the milk to the cooked rice, cover the bowl with cling film and leave for about 5 minutes to absorb. (*4) Stir in the lime juice and taste. Reserve.

PREPARING THE FRUIT:

In a bowl, mix all the fruit and macerate with the palm sugar, lime juice and cayenne pepper. (*5) Reserve.

MAKING THE GUAVA SABAYON:

In a small saucepan on a medium heat, boil the water and sugar to 120°C. Meanwhile, in a mixing bowl, whisk the egg yolks until they turn a pale straw colour and increase four times in volume. (*6) Lower the speed and gradually pour in (*7) the hot syrup between the side of the bowl and the whisk. Then, on a medium speed, whisk until cool. Pour the guava purée and lime juice into the sabayon; last, fold in the whipped cream. Taste and reserve in the fridge.

TO SERVE:

Place a spoon of the rice in the centre of a dessert bowl or plate, arrange the macerated fruits neatly on top and spoon the sabayon generously over. Dust liberally with icing sugar and flash under the grill or caramelize with a blowtorch until golden brown. Sprinkle with passion fruit seeds and pulp, and serve immediately.

Chef's notes:

*1   This variety of short-grain rice with a high starch content is mostly grown in the northern part of Thailand. During cooking it develops a prized glutinous texture and clings together, and that is why it is called sticky rice. Many other varieties can be found in Thailand, among them a red glutinous rice which is steamed with its own husks. It has a bit of a chew, but I find it delicious.

*2   You can increase the flavour of a purée by cooking and reducing it by 20%. The guava purée can be replaced with other purées, such as mango and passion fruit from any good supermarket.

*3   Traditionally it is first soaked in water overnight, then steamed. Boiling would deprive the rice of its character, flavour and, of course, much of its stickiness.

*4   You must add the coconut milk to the rice while both are hot. This process will allow the rice to soak up the milk, and give it its sweetness. According to which variety of rice you have used and how long you have steamed it, it may require a bit more coconut milk. (Maximum 100ml extra.)

*5   Cayenne pepper may sound out of place, and might be if you add too much: just a little pinch will add length and a tiny spice in your mouth.

*6   This is not a classic sabayon, where both egg yolk and wine would be whisked over a bain-marie to partly cook and to make a delicious, stable foam, but the principle remains the same. First, whip the egg yolk at a high speed: air will be introduced and it will lighten and expand. But the foam is not stable, you need to partly cook it. So while the egg yolks are being whipped, the syrup is being cooked to 120°C. At this stage, lower the whisking speed and carefully pour the boiling syrup into the base. This will partly cook the egg yolk and make it stable, reaching a core temperature of 63–65°C. This will also sterilize it.

★7   Syrup at 120°C could burn you badly, so lower the speed of the whisk and ensure you pour the syrup between the edge of the bowl and the whisk so it doesn't splash up.

TWENTY-SIX

THE SMILE

The Marseillaise with Ma'am

A MONG THE FRAMED PHOTOGRAPHS IN THE DRAWING ROOM AT Le Manoir there is a shot of the Queen Mother and me, taken as we walked in the hotel's grounds. Her Majesty appears to be listening patiently to me, while I am open-mouthed, doubtless enthusing about the asparagus or potatoes in the vegetable garden.

Guests often ask me about my acquaintance with the Queen Mum, who died in 2002, and I happily tell them the unusual story behind our association. It dates back to a period long before the photograph was taken.

I was at Les Quat' Saisons, and one of my best customers was a well-mannered gentleman by the name of Captain Charles Radclyffe, and his wife Ellen, who lived in the Oxfordshire village of Lew and would come to eat with their friends. The captain trained racehorses for the Queen Mother. She had some 450 winners during her fifty-year career as an owner; in 1949, when Montaveen won at Fontwell, she became the first Queen of England to see her horse win a race in Britain since Queen Anne in 1714. One day the captain told me that Her Majesty would be coming to his home and she had asked him if I would cook lunch for them. Even though I am a republican, I readily accepted the invitation. I was delighted and enthusiastic about the prospect.

The event seemed promising because of the season. It was late spring (early June), which for me is the perfect time of the year, when fruit and vegetables are at their best. As spring meets summer there is an abundance of choice.

The captain requested that the meal begin at 1.30 p.m., which would mean I would have to be in his kitchen, prepping up, by ten in the morning at the latest. With my young English commis chef Mark as my assistant, I loaded up the restaurant's green van and began the twenty-mile journey to the captain's home, setting off late because . . . well, because I always set off late. At half-past eleven we were still driving through Cotswolds lanes, hopelessly lost. I began to worry that we would never reach our destination and my panic only made me drive more insanely than usual. Young Mark clung to his seat as we careered around hairpin bends and zoomed over hump-backed bridges. Every so often he would let out a yelp as his life flashed before him. He wasn't the only one in the van who was frightened. I was scared to death too, not only because of my driving but also because I was late for a royal appointment.

At about noon we found Captain Radclyffe's home. I say home, but it was not the sort you and I know. It was a sprawling old country pile set in acres of fields and woodland with a long driveway, thick with gravel that had been lovingly raked, akin to a road leading from the property's gates to the front door. I veered on to that driveway at twenty miles an hour, and skidded. As the tyres sank into the shingle our van, with the French cockerel imprinted on its side, was engulfed in dust. Hundreds of tiny stones flew up; it was as if we were being fired upon. The captain must have piled about twenty centimetres of gravel on his driveway.

Eventually we got moving again and headed at speed towards a line of stately cars beside which stood a group of beefy men – the Queen Mother's security team. They looked on as we raced towards them in our battered green van with the chicken on the side. I think I managed to attract more attention than the royal guest of honour's arrival. When it comes to ways of disturbing stillness, that green van on deep gravel takes some beating.

In short, I have made better entrances.

We were greeted in the kitchen by the head butler and helpers, all of them tense because I was so late. We had one hour to prepare the feast, which was daunting because I had only seen the kitchen once, and I knew that Her Majesty was on schedule and had to leave at a certain time. We hurriedly prepared a five-course meal which would be complimented by beautiful wines from the captain's magnificent cellar. The star of the meal was *turbot rôti*.

This turbot dish is one of the great fish dishes, and one of the simplest to make. It came on to my menu after family holidays in Provence with Jenny, Sebastien and Olivier. We used to drive to that part of France because it was cheaper than flying. As the Blanc family zoomed through the country lanes of France I would frequently stop the car suddenly and dash to the roadside to pick from the hedgerows. Wild fennel, thyme and lavender went into the boot of the car and accompanied us on the return trip. Jenny wasn't too keen on all this wild gathering but she was keener on the fennel than she had been on truffles. I particularly treasured the wild fennel because I had never seen it in Britain. We'd arrive back in Oxford, the car packed with herbs and flowers plucked from the lanes of Provence. Hay fever sufferers would not have wanted to be in that car. Subsequently I grew it at Le Manoir, where I'm pleased to say it flourishes.

Back at my restaurant, I'd dry the fennel and then use it in the turbot dish, which is inspired by a classic Provençal dish. When I cooked it for the Queen Mother, I served it with *beurre blanc* (butter sauce). I have modified the recipe to serve four, and it only takes about forty-five minutes to make.

Leave four strips of orange zest to dry in a warm place one day in advance of cooking the dish. The turbot and bed of fennel can also be prepared in advance. Order the turbot well in advance and ask your fishmonger to gut them and cut off the fins and gills. You can buy farmed turbot, but I would not recommend it. Try to get a line-caught fish.

Autumn/Winter
Les Quat' Saisons
Turbot Roti au Fenouil et Huile d'Anchois
Whole Turbot Roasted on a Bed of Fennel

This recipe goes right back to Les Quat' Saisons. Cooking fish on the bone gives the very best results in both taste and texture. This recipe has wonderful heady flavours from Provence, and makes a magnificent dish to serve to your friends. Do not be daunted by carving; it is easy enough as the bones are well structured and run flat on each side of the fish. Cooking fish on the bone will give a better texture and flavour. A better texture because there is less retraction; a better flavour because the bones themselves add flavour and, at the same time, through holding the fish firm, prevent the loss of precious juices.

Serves (Yield): 4
Difficulty rating: ● ● ○
Preparation time: 15 minutes
Cooking time: 30 minutes

PLANNING AHEAD

The fennel and orange can be dried up to 1 week in advance and stored in a sealed container. (Either cut the sticks off from the top of a fennel bulb, or go to Provence and cut the fennel wild from the side of the road.) The red wine sauce can be made 1 day in advance. The *beurre blanc* sauce can be prepared 1 hour in advance and kept in a warm bain-marie (50–60°C).

INGREDIENTS

For the beurre blanc:

30g banana shallots, finely diced
1 tbsp white wine vinegar
20ml dry white wine
50ml cold water
125g butter, cold, diced (★1)
1 pinch sea salt
1 pinch freshly ground white pepper
5ml lemon juice

For the red wine sauce:

60g banana shallots, finely sliced
30g butter
100g button mushrooms, finely sliced
250ml red wine (★2)
350ml brown chicken stock (see page 206)

For the turbot:

20 dried sticks of fennel
4 dried strips of orange zest
6 sprigs thyme
½ bay leaf
2 star anise
1.2kg turbot, trimmed (for baby turbot, use 2 x 450g and cook for
    17 minutes, with 5 minutes' resting)
300ml olive oil
50ml anchovy oil
salt and freshly ground white pepper

METHOD

MAKING THE BEURRE BLANC:

In a small heavy-bottomed saucepan, combine the shallots, vinegar and wine and boil until you have about 1 tablespoon of syrupy liquid. (★3) Add the water, then, over a gentle heat, whisk in the cold diced butter, a little at a time, until completely amalgamated. (★4) The finished sauce will be creamy and homogeneous and a delicate lemon yellow. Season with a tiny amount of salt and pepper and enliven with a squeeze of lemon juice.

If the sauce separates, bring 2 tablespoons water to the boil in a clean saucepan, then slowly whisk in the separated sauce.

MAKING THE RED WINE SAUCE:

Soften the shallots in the butter on a medium heat for 2–3 minutes, add the mushrooms and soften for a further 2 minutes. Pour in the red wine and reduce by half. Add the stock and continue to reduce by half. Taste and correct the seasoning if required. (★5) Strain and reserve.

PREPARING AND ROASTING THE TURBOT:

Preheat the oven to 180°C. Line a roasting pan with the fennel, orange, thyme, bay leaf and star anise. Lay the fish, white skin side up, in the pan on the bed of dried fennel, and pour over the olive and anchovy oils, then season with salt and pepper. (★6) Roast the turbot in the preheated oven for about 25–30 minutes, basting frequently. (★7) Remove from the oven, cover with foil and rest for 7–8 minutes. (★8)

FINISHING AND SERVING THE DISH:

Present the turbot as it is to your guests and, if you feel confident enough, fillet it in front of them. (★9) Serve with the warm *beurre blanc* and red wine sauce.

Chef's notes:

★1 The success of the sauce depends greatly on the quality of the butter. Use the very best unsalted butter you can find; salted butter often contains more whey, which has a farmyard flavour. The butter must be cold. If too soft, it will melt too quickly and not emulsify.

★2 Choose a rich, full-bodied wine, but don't spend more than £4–5. (See note 2 on page 294–5.)

★3 If the liquid is not sufficiently reduced the sauce will be too sharp – a classic mistake which kills the dish, the wine and your guest.

★4 This extra liquid will help the emulsion. Fat and liquid do not mix, so in order to make an emulsion, you need two things: the first is warmth, followed by a speedy whisking movement. You can make this sauce without the reduction of shallot and vinegar and it will become a *beurre monté*. To create a more lasting emulsion, use a hand-held electric blender.

*5   A pinch of sugar may be required, depending upon the strength of tannins in the wine. Taste and season.

*6   For an added visual impact, heat a large griddle pan until very hot. Then place the washed and well-dried turbot, brushed with a little oil, on the pan, white skin side down, for 40 seconds. Very carefully lift the turbot and place at a different angle so that you create a criss-cross marking on the skin. Then place in the roasting pan.

*7   The length of time for roasting the fish may vary according to its weight and freshness. Do not be tempted to roast at a higher temperature as the delicate flesh will shrink and flake. It is important to baste the fish frequently; this moistens it, and reinforces it with the flavours of the oils, herbs and spices.

*8   The resting time is equally important. At this stage residual heat will gently complete the cooking, leaving the flesh still firm. The problem with cooking a whole fish is you don't know if it is cooked until you cut into it. So use your knife to open up the thickest part of the fish to be sure. It should just pull away from the bone and still be firm.

*9   Turbot is one of the easiest fish to fillet after cooking. Make an incision down the central bone, round the gills and down the sides of the fish so you have a triangle shape. Loosen the fillets from the central bone, sliding the knife down beneath the fillet, and lift on to a serving plate.

VARIATIONS

Turbot – you could replace the turbot with a baby brill, john dory, sea bream or your favourite fish.

Beurre blanc – once you have finished the sauce and it is still warm, place it in a jug liquidizer and blend with the skin of a cucumber. Add ¼ tsp wasabi paste (enough to taste), which will really enhance it.

Red wine sauce – for a more refined sauce, you could add some caramelized bones and then pass the sauce through a fine sieve.

Chicken stock – if you want to replace the brown chicken stock, bring 30g butter to foaming stage, add 60g chopped shallots, 1 sprig of thyme and ¼ star anise, and cook the butter to hazelnut stage, by which time the shallots will be slightly brown. Meanwhile, reduce 250ml wine to 90ml, then add to the hazelnut-stage butter along with 20ml water.

If I recall correctly, I brought the turbot into the dining room to carve in front of the guests. It was a big fat turbot line-caught in Devon that had barely fitted into the oven. It had to be big as it had to feed eight guests (who, as you would expect, included ladies-in-waiting). I served the fish with the latest purple-sprouting broccoli, the first broad beans of the season and, fittingly, Jersey Royal potatoes. The skills I had acquired as a waiter were very useful and the guests were suitably impressed.

After the meal and before departing, the Queen Mother came into the kitchen and spoke to me in fluent French, but with a delightful English accent, saying, 'Oh, Monsieur Blanc, you made such a wonderful meal.' She reminisced about France and I was highly impressed by her — but not nearly as impressed by what she then did. She moved around the room shaking the hands of every member of the kitchen staff, as well as my young commis and the washer-up. The foundations of my republican spirit were severely shaken. Her Majesty was a people's person.

The lunch was successful, and every year, when summer approached, Captain Radclyffe would be in touch to see if I was available to cook for his annual get-together with the Queen Mother. I never said no. I felt honoured that my services were required.

Every year the event followed the same pattern. I'd arrive late, gravel flying, cook for the captain, the Queen Mother and her ladies-in-waiting, and later on she would come into the kitchen for the ritual handshake and our chat in French. 'I very much look forward to seeing you next year,' were her parting words, delivered in French. And so it continued. Sometimes the Queen would come too. Although she was very nice, she was more distant than her mother.

One year, after I had cooked for her about a dozen times, the Queen Mother said to me, 'You have done a lot for me, but I have done nothing for you. What should I do for you?'

I was slightly taken aback. What does one say when the Queen Mother asks what she might do for one? She interrupted my nervous laugh by saying, 'I know exactly what I will do. I am going to come to Le Manoir and I am going to bring *The Times*.' In other words, she was going to make public our friendship and display her patronage. As PR puffs went, it would be a coup. I was already imagining the wonderful plaque – 'By Appointment to Her Majesty the Queen' – over the entrance to Le Manoir.

Sure enough she came, with her ever-present ladies-in-waiting and miscellaneous consorts, and a journalist and photographer from *The Times*, which had somehow pulled off a scoop by securing a day-in-the-life piece with the much-loved matriarch of the royal family. I have a vivid memory of the Queen Mother and her entourage arriving up Le Manoir's driveway in a parade of smartly polished stately cars; capped chauffeurs opening doors; ladies in lemon pastel dresses and well-groomed gentlemen in exquisite suits climbing out.

It was a glorious summer's day, and in the shadow of the garden's aged cedar tree we had set up a table for our royal guest and her companions. I showed her around the house and gardens, then we sat and had an aperitif by the tree. She had her favourite cocktail, Dubonnet and gin, with soda water to dilute the alcohol content.

She had insisted that she wanted to eat with 'my people', i.e. the other guests. So we had prepared a lovely table in L'Orangerie – the conservatory part of the restaurant. Picture the scene: you are in a restaurant and the Queen Mother strolls by, her entourage in tow, and they take their seats on a table beside yours. The other guests were delightful. They didn't stare, or leave their tables to ask for autographs, or sing 'God Save the Queen'.

The Queen Mother had a lovely meal and then, with her guests, adjourned to a spacious suite to watch the races on television. One of her horses was racing, you see. The gathering, perhaps twelve or fourteen of them, stood with the Queen Mother as she excitedly watched the horses come into the paddock, and then make their way to the starting line. A few minutes later they were racing towards the finishing post. It was the 3.30 at Epsom. Or was it Sandown, or York, or Aintree? The point was that if the horse won it would be a colossal win because it would be its twentieth victory. Or was it the thirtieth, or five hundredth?

It won. There were cheers in the room and that wonderful sense of accomplishment that comes, or that must come (I can only imagine), from seeing your horse first past the finishing post. By this point the Queen Mother was a little bubbly and certainly very happy. The world, for her, was perfect. She'd had a great day, a lovely lunch, the sun was shining and her horse had won. You'd be happy too. And of course if she was happy then I was thrilled. For the Queen Mother to visit and find contentment was a restaurateur's dream come true.

The television was muted, I sat down beside the Queen Mother and she talked to me (again in perfect French) about her fondness for General de Gaulle and French things in general; she also reminisced about enjoyable times she'd had in Deauville and Monaco. 'Oh, I do love France,' she said. She turned towards me and her expression turned mischievous. 'Monsieur Blanc,' she asked, 'what might be your greatest achievement?'

With a question like that, and when it comes from a lady like that, you struggle. I opened my mouth like a fish as I searched for something clever or intelligent to say. I ummed and erred before replying that it was cooking for her, but she wouldn't accept that for an answer so I said, 'Actually, Ma'am, my greatest achievement has nothing to do with the culinary world. It came two years ago, when I got a hundred Englishmen to sing the Marseillaise.'

I was referring to a night at Le Manoir when we celebrated Bastille Day, the symbolic uprising of the modern French nation during the French Revolution (the storming of the Bastille took place on 14 July 1789). For the event I had dished out lyric sheets and encouraged (I mean coerced) all the guests to stand, clasp a fist to their hearts and sing 'La Marseillaise'.

'As you will know, Ma'am, Bastille Day was all about the bringing down of a monarchy, the creation of *les droits de l'homme* – the rights of the common man.'

I suddenly became aware that the other guests had stopped talking and were now listening with alarm and consternation as I shared my views on monarchy with the Queen Mother. But I had started, and I could not stop.

'As you know, Ma'am, the motto of the French Republic is *liberté, egalité, fraternité* . . .'

When my monologue about republicanism finally drew to a close, the room was eerily silent. I glanced around to see lots of white anxious faces. The Queen Mother did not seem upset by my views. She took her cane and, no, she did not whack me with it, she used it to help her get to her feet. The rest of us stood too.

'Monsieur Blanc,' she said, 'if I had been here, I also would have sung the Marseillaise.'

She then put her fist on her heart and began to sing the rallying call of the French Revolution: 'Allons enfants de la Patrie / Le jour de gloire est arrivé / Contre nous de la tyrannie / L'étendard sanglant est levé . . .' (Arise children of the Fatherland / The day of glory has arrived / Against us tyranny's / Bloody banner is raised . . .'). By the chorus the room was swaying to the sound of about fifteen of us, led by the Queen Mother, singing out against monarchy. 'Aux armes, citoyens! / Formez vos bataillons / Marchons, marchons / Qu'un sang impur / Abreuve nos sillons' (To arms, citizens! / Form your battalions / March, march / May tainted blood / Water our fields'). (If you're looking for a song to sing while cooking, this one takes some beating.)

Oh my God, it was great. That day was the closest I ever came to becoming a royalist. To think, the same conversation with a member of the royal family in a different era could have lost me my head.

'I have had such a splendid day,' she said to me. 'The food was out of this world and you have made me feel wonderful. I would like to say thank you to all of your staff.'

Getting the Queen Mother to sing the Marseillaise was one thing; bringing together Le Manoir's staff seemed impossible. Mostly I was concerned that it might be too much for her. 'There are too many of them,' I said, 'and they are all working. Some of them will be in the kitchen, others will be in the garden, and others will be cleaning rooms. I have about eighty staff. I don't see how I could do it.'

There followed a few seconds of silence.

'Monsieur Blanc, I would like to say thank you to everyone who has made this day so special.'

Translation: Just do it, Monsieur Blanc. You don't say no to royalty.

So the staff were rounded up, eighty of them – the kitchen brigade, the front-of-house team, cleaners, gardeners, porters – and they stood in Le Manoir's driveway. The Queen Mother walked along the line, shaking the hands of each and every one of them and having a word with each employee too. It was a lesson in humility. The lady had class. I was impressed to see that the story even made it into her biography.

Many years ago Captain Radclyffe invited me to join him and the Queen Mother in the royal enclosure at Ascot. The event, held annually in June, is a must in the diary of any horse-racing lover, as well as ladies (and many men) who go to parade their classy (sometimes not so classy) wardrobes. In my own case, I had to hire a morning suit from Moss Bros (republicans don't own such attire, especially cooks).

I was watching the ladies in their beautifully designed, expensive outfits and colourful, sometimes outrageous hats when suddenly I caught sight of a hat that was particularly fascinating. It was silky black, like a small bowler hat, with a lightly curved, elegant rim that was so broad it seemed never-ending; you could hardly see the face of the young woman who was wearing it. In a split second that hat transformed itself into the most magnificent plate. Immediately in my mind I pictured it turned upside down. And not just any plate, but the most modern style of plate. Gastronomy was heading towards lighter food and smaller portions and I just knew the plate's design would fit the way we'd be eating in restaurants in the future.

I was overwhelmed by a sense of urgency to create the plate; I could see food framed by it in the most dramatic way. When I said farewell to Her Majesty and thanked her for a lovely day I ran to the car park and whizzed back to Oxford to see my friend Richard Hamilton, the man behind the British Pop Art movement.

Unlike me, Richard can work a computer, and I knew he had all the technology to help me design my special plate. He was a wizard at it. I explained the concept and he set about turning it into something visual on the computer screen, adding detail after detail. What had been the rim of the hat would become the wide lip of the plate; the bowl part of the hat, obviously, was where the food would sit. But what I particularly liked was the contrast in textures: the small bowl would be smooth and shiny, while the lip would be rough. For centuries the plate had not changed, had not progressed in terms of shape. As the design developed on the screen, Richard and I became more and more excited.

We worked through the night. I left Richard's home with my plate on a disk. I returned a couple of days later for a copy, after losing the disk (you know me by now). Then I went to see Villeroy Boche who had been my partners since the seventies, when Jenny and I opened Les Quat' Saisons. They said, 'Wow!' I would love to be in a position to tell you that the design made me the world's richest restaurateur. Alas, nothing came of it because Villeroy Boche did not have the machinery to create the plate and the new technology would have called for too large an investment.

Some nine years later my plate was produced by another company, a French company as well. There had been no skulduggery behind the scenes. No one had passed on my idea or anything like that. I always felt it was only a question of time before someone else came up with it. Oh well. *C'est la vie.*

Summer
Fleures d'Ananas; Parfait Glacé au Kirsch
Iced Pineapple Parfait with Pineapple Sunflowers

This is a dessert I created for the Queen Mother when she visited us at Le Manoir.

Serves (Yield): 4

Difficulty rating: ● ● ○

Preparation/drying time: 40 minutes/3 hours

Cooking/freezing time: 10 minutes/3 hours

Special equipment: Food processor with blade attachment to slice 1–2mm thick; 2 non-stick baking trays 30 x 40cm; 1 tray 30 x 20cm and a piece of greaseproof paper the same size; pastry cutter, 6cm in diameter; sugar thermometer, jug blender

PLANNING AHEAD

The dried pineapple can be prepared 1 day ahead and kept in an airtight container. The parfait and the sauce can also be prepared 1 day ahead.

INGREDIENTS

For the dried pineapple slices:
400g (1 small) pineapple, peeled
juice of ¼ lemon
100ml water
15g caster sugar

For the candied pineapple:
50ml water
50g caster sugar
200g (½ small) pineapple, peeled, core removed, cut into 5mm cubes

For the parfait:
   100g caster sugar
   40ml water
   70ml (2) egg whites
   juice of 1 lemon
   75g candied pineapple
   100ml whipped cream in soft peaks
   60ml kirsch

For the pineapple sauce:
   400g (1 small) pineapple, peeled and diced small
   50ml coconut milk
   15ml Malibu
   1 small pinch black pepper

For the cherry garnish:
   25 black cherries, pitted
   20g kirsch
   30g caster sugar
   1ml lemon juice
   1 small pinch ground black pepper, ground cloves and ground
      cinnamon
   4 stalks and petals made from sugar (*1)

METHOD
MAKING THE DRIED PINEAPPLE SLICES:

Cut 8 thinnest possible slices of pineapple, no thicker than 1mm. Place in a bowl and sprinkle with the lemon juice. Bring the water and sugar to the boil together in a small pan, then pour this boiling syrup over the slices. Spread with the back of a spoon to allow the syrup to coat all the slices, then cover the bowl with cling film and allow them to marinate until the mixture has cooled.

Preheat the oven to the very lowest it will go: about 80°C. Drain the syrup from the pineapple slices and place them next to each another on the 2 non-stick trays. Place both trays in the preheated oven and dry slowly for 2–3 hours until the pineapples have dried.

Check occasionally to make sure they do not darken. Remove the trays from the oven and, while still hot, use a palette knife to slide the pineapple slices off the trays. Leave to cool, place in an airtight container, cover and reserve.

MAKING THE CANDIED PINEAPPLE:

Bring the water and sugar to the boil in a suitable pan. When the sugar has dissolved, pour it over the pineapple cubes in a bowl. Allow to marinate for a few hours. (*2)

MAKING THE PARFAIT:

Place the sugar and water in a small pan and cook to 120°C. Check using a sugar thermometer. While the sugar syrup is cooking, whisk the egg whites to soft peaks. Reduce the speed of the machine and pour the cooked sugar syrup in between the side of the bowl and the whisk (this will prevent spitting). Whisk until incorporated, then allow to cool by constant whisking, before adding the lemon juice.

Drain the candied pineapple cubes and discard the syrup. In a bowl mix together the pineapple cubes, whipped cream and kirsch. Add a quarter of the egg-white mixture to the cream mixture, then the remaining three-quarters of egg white, and carefully fold together.

Line the 30 x 20cm tray with the sheet of greaseproof paper. Spread the parfait mixture evenly over this. Place in the freezer for about 3 hours, until it has hardened.

PREPARING THE PINEAPPLE SAUCE:

In a jug blender, purée the pineapple pieces, pour into a small pan, add the remaining ingredients and bring to the boil. Pass through a fine sieve and reserve.

COOKING THE CHERRY GARNISH:

Place all the ingredients for the cherry garnish, except the stalks and petals of sugar, in a saucepan, cover with a lid and simmer on a medium heat for about 3 minutes. Remove the lid and carry on cooking for a further 5 minutes. Remove from the heat and leave to cool.

Pour the pineapple sauce on to the plate. Scatter the warm cherries around and spoon around their spiced juices. At the top of the plate, arrange 2 discs of iced parfait and top with a slice of dried pineapple. Finish with the stalks and petals of sugar.

Chef's notes:

*1   I have not given the recipe for pulled sugar as it is far better and safer to receive professional instructions at Le Manoir.

*2   Marinating the pineapple cubes for the parfait allows the hot sugar syrup to penetrate the pineapple flesh. The sugar will stop the pineapple cubes freezing hard in the parfait.

TWENTY-SEVEN

THE COOKERY SCHOOL

A Perfect Coulis

A FEW YEARS AFTER OPENING LE MANOIR, WE SET UP THE COOKERY school. It adjoins the restaurant's busy kitchen, and it has been a tremendous success. Through the cookery school I wanted to teach the joys of simple home cooking. My mother is not there, but she drives that school as it is her philosophy that we teach. Cooks young and old, good and maybe not so great, come to acquire knowledge, have some fun and enjoy the lunch they have cooked with the tutor. I think it is the only cookery school in the world with two chefs, Nurdin and Vladimir, who are also fully qualified nutritionists. They have worked with me for seven and nine years respectively so they share the Blanc philosophy.

Few things give me greater satisfaction than to pop in to the class, boast about France's recent victory in football or rugby, and then recreate some of the dishes they are just about to learn how to cook.

Not so long ago, Kylie Minogue came to do a day-long course. Ordinarily there are about ten students on the course, but Kylie booked the cookery school for herself and a friend, which was probably a clever move because otherwise all eyes would have been on her. The night before she was due to do the course, she was in the bar having a drink with her friend when my fiancée Natalia spotted her. Natalia's wonderful daughter, Natasha, is a big fan of Kylie so Natalia thought she would ask for an autograph. Kylie obliged. In fact she went further, wandering over to have a chat with Natasha.

Once this was done, Kylie left the bar to have dinner and I walked in. Natalia said, 'We were just talking to Kylie Minogue.'

I said, 'Coulis who?'

'Not Coulis, Kylie. You must have heard of her.'

I shook my head. I thought long and I thought hard. No, the name meant nothing. I swear to you now, it did not. I had never heard of her. Kylie, pretty and talented, has been splashed all over newspapers and magazines for the last twenty years and is constantly on television and on the radio, but for some reason or other I was the only person on planet Earth who did not know of her. Guests on nearby tables were listening in, giggling at my baffled expression.

Kylie had gone into the restaurant, so I thought I would go and say hello. On the way into the dining room I asked the maître d', 'Do you know who Coulis Minogue is?'

He said, 'You mean Kylie. Yes.'

He gave me her table number and I went over to her. She was utterly charming, and said she was very much looking forward to the following day's course, which would be one-on-one tuition with the school's supremely gifted head tutor Nurdin Topham.

During our conversation Kylie mentioned that she was a vegetarian who loved fish. I thought no more about her dietary preferences until the next morning, around about elevenish, when Kylie would have been an hour or so into the course. Her comment suddenly popped back into my head and I was filled with fear that Nurdin might not know she was vegetarian and might at that very moment be teaching her how to braise beef or slice chicken. I raced to the cookery school, and sure enough there was Nurdin demonstrating how to slice kidneys. However, it turned out that he had already discussed the day's dishes with her and she'd said she wanted to learn how to do a roast chicken for her meat-eating friends and family. I joined in, and we were there for the next six hours.

Kylie was keen, clever, and picked things up quickly. If only everyone was such a delight to teach. Normally I don't like to talk about my guests, but she was so wonderful this little book will be sweetened by the mere mention of her name.

I ended the day showing off, not my cuisine but my dancing steps. We put some music on in the school's kitchen and I showed Kylie how I dance. She didn't give me any advice. For some reason my sons' faces turned crimson with embarrassment when I boasted that I'd showed a few of my moves to Kylie. Maybe you should know that I am an OK dancer. I was invited to do *Strictly Come Dancing* but I refused because I don't want to be remembered as a ballerina. Well, not yet, anyway. Maybe when I am eighty, God willing.

———

Not all guests have been as easy to please as Coulis – sorry, Kylie – and the Queen Mother. Shortly after opening Le Manoir I was in the restaurant one day chatting to my guests when suddenly I became distracted. Out of the corner of my eye I could see a pair of hands reaching for the pepper mill. One hand then held the mill above a plate of food while the other hand twisted and twisted. And twisted. A stunning chicken dish was being killed twice over.

I was alarmed that anyone would wish to put so much pepper on their food and looked at the man who was doing the milling. He was in his mid-seventies, he had a handlebar moustache and he wore a herringbone jacket, all spick and span. He looked like a field marshal. I stood up and went over.

'Sir,' I said, 'is there anything wrong with the food?'

'It's just not spicy enough,' he said.

He looked like the sort of man who had served thirty years in India and was used to spicy food; I would never have a chance to convert his palate. If there was no hope, I proposed to cook a new dish for him.

'Could I give you a spicier version of the same dish?' I asked.

When he agreed, I dashed off to the kitchen and prepared a dish that incorporated all the ground spice such as cardamom seed, cayenne pepper and ginger. Any spice I could find went into that dish. I pan-fried the chicken and added a dash of lime juice at the end. It was a dish to take the roof of your mouth off, a fearful concoction. You and I would not have been able to eat it. Yet when it was presented to him he buried his fork into the food and proceeded to wolf it down. 'Young man,' he told me, 'that is just how I like my food. I am very grateful.'

Initially I was annoyed that the man had objected to the original dish. I could not see how he could find a problem with my food. I could have reacted by chucking him out – a fate that would have been his in many other restaurants. I could have taken it personally and allowed it to upset me, as well as my team, not to mention the customer himself. Equally, as I said, I knew that this man and his palate could not be saved, and by tipping a barrowload of spice on to his food I had made that man extremely happy. I'd had fun with the dish too. Was he right to want so much spice? No. The man was a delightful specimen of an age-ing eccentric, perhaps with the palate of a camel. But that was what he liked, and you have to accept that everyone is different.

We are not in the business of scaring the guests into submission. If you like salt, take salt. More pepper? Here is the mill, help yourself. If I kick up a fuss and throw someone out, who is the loser? I am here to give joy rather than to educate. If I educate by giving joy, all the better, but it is not my primary aim. Such guests are always welcome.

There are times, however, when guests come simply to cause trouble. I remember one group of students arriving for lunch. They were looking forward to breaking up and their end-of-term celebrations included a meal at Le Manoir. It was a very busy day, and as soon as the waiter started to take their order he realized he was

dealing with difficult customers. He came to see me, looking concerned.

'I think we've got a problem,' he said. 'They want to start with
dessert.'

'They want to do what?' I asked, and he explained that the students
had decided that their meal would begin with chocolate mousse and
soufflé.

I recognized these young people as rich Oxford students. Most of
them are wonderfully appreciative, but sometimes they are trouble.
These ones were trying to be a little cocky, a bit clever, perhaps to call
my bluff. I also felt in a wicked mood. I must warn you that this little
episode could easily have belonged to *Fawlty Towers* – one of my
favourites.

I dashed over to their table. They were thinking, perhaps, that I
would ask them to leave. Nothing of the kind. 'Gentlemen,' I began,
'I understand that you would like to begin your meal with dessert.' They
all nodded. 'I think that's a great idea. Why not have the cheese after
your dessert? Then have the main course, and finish your meal with the
starter.' Each of them ordered the courses in this ludicrous reverse order.
For good measure I added two mini courses, with the compliments of
the chef: they were a Roquefort sorbet and a salad with Worcester sauce
loaded with chilli. I wished them '*Bon appétit, messieurs*' and walked away
from the table.

They drank wines in the appropriate order with each course: a sweet
Sauternes followed by a glass of port with their cheese, progressing to
claret with their main course and white Burgundy with their starter.
The meal finished the way other people might begin their meal, with
a glass of champagne.

I am sure that these students had set out to upset me, but I was not
at all upset. They provided me with entertainment and helped my profit
margins. By the third course I observed with some amusement that one
of them had turned a nausea-induced white colour and was heading
towards grey. By the end of the meal they were all the same colour.

Some were even green as they headed for the front door and the fresh air of Oxfordshire. That is what it costs you if you ignore the basics of gastronomy – the rule of the stomach! Maybe it was a good lesson in their young lives, not to take the mickey out of the chef.

As I said, 99.5 per cent of our guests come to enjoy themselves and to appreciate the service and environment. But there will always be a few, and thank God it's only a very few, who like to create a nuisance. We all have them. They come to my restaurants. They come to your home. You know them well. They are members of your family, dear friends or work colleagues. They are united in their quest to irritate the hell out of you. When thrown into social occasions, their role is to make demands that are tough to meet. These are not necessarily impossible demands, just *très difficile*. They are the fussy guests in your home, the difficult customers in my restaurant. They do not like what is on offer – the delights of our kitchen – and wonder whether it would be possible for you to 'rustle up' something, something you know will take hours to prepare and will bring down the service. Perhaps they turn their nose up at something you have slaved away at, explaining that they have just turned vegetarian. Or they are on a diet which means they cannot eat this or that. Or they have tasted wine in a sauce and are outraged because they are on the wagon. Everybody has allergies these days too, which puts huge pressure on the kitchen, even though we are prepared.

How does one deal with these wretched people? Smile, I say. Simply smile and give them what they want. In general, it is nice when you smile at people because they smile back at you. I have found that if you growl at people, they often growl back. Mind you, rude or drunken guests must not be tolerated.

In the eighties there was a group of miscreants called the Assassins Club. It was made up of rich students who behaved atrociously. This club of evil young men was feared by every restaurateur and hotelier in the land. One day they came to Le Manoir. The maître d' came to see me and said, 'I have a problem here.'

I said, 'OK, try to contain it.'

'I can't,' he replied. 'They are simply terribly rude. They have already drunk three bottles of Montrachet and one bottle of cognac. They are absolutely unbearable, and very difficult to deal with.'

I was particularly bothered that this group of rich yobs was being rude to my team. That is when I break my never-say-no rule. I asked Clive Fretwell, my head chef, and two muscular chefs to stand behind me and then I wandered up to the Assassins Club.

'Right,' I said, 'you've got to get up and you've got to get out. Do your show outside.' They sat and stared, so I added, 'If you think I am just a little Frenchman then just wait, because I have about ten other chefs who are ten times the size of them. Nobody is rude to my team. Never. My guys work very hard, they are professionals, and I don't want them to be insulted and diminished by you lot. Now get lost.'

Behind me, Clive flexed a bicep, and the Assassins scarpered. As they left, I thought that they did not resemble assassins so much as little brats.

Then I remembered that I had forgotten to give them the bill. They'd had three bottles of Montrachet and a bottle of cognac on the house. I kicked myself. *C'est la vie.*

Later I thought, 'Why am I kicking myself when I could kick them?' So I commissioned a bronze sculpture from the artist Lloyd Le Blanc, who does all the sculptures in the garden. It depicted the Assassins' pack leader, a slender little rich boy, drinking champagne as he looks down on the world; I named the boy Max after him. (It is still here, by the old entrance gate by the Belle Epoque private dining room.) Every time I passed Max holding his champagne flute I gave him a good kick on the arse. Kicking Max not only brought me immense joy, it also reminded me that the pay-the-bill rule is just as important as the never-say-no rule.

TWENTY-EIGHT

THE FUTURE OF FOOD

It's All in the Past

IT WAS ONE OF THOSE LOVELY EXPERIENCES IN LIFE. MY SON OLIVIER and I packed the car on a gloriously sunny Friday morning in May this year and drove off to Haddon Hall, a twelfth-century manor house in Bakewell, Derbyshire. It is home to Lord Manners and his wife Saskia, and has been in the family since 1567. The house and its grounds are spectacular. Actually, there's every chance you would have seen Haddon Hall: it is open to the public and it is the first choice when television location scouts want a beautiful setting for costume dramas.

Olivier and I stayed in a cottage on the grounds, and on the Friday night we ate well and drank well. Our giddy heads hit the pillows at three in the morning. A few hours later I was up and re-reading material for this book, outside in the garden, as it was another beautiful day. Then Olivier and I took our fishing rods and wandered down to the River Lathkill. There, some of the best specimens of wild trout were supposed to be waiting. We spent a few hours on the banks but the weather was so warm the fish stayed on the riverbed where it was cool. Alas, we caught nothing. Not even *goujons*.

As all fishermen know, *c'est la vie*.

Although there was nothing happening in the calm waters in front of me, there was plenty whizzing through my mind.

In my life as a chef I've always connected food to the soil and ethics and people; that was what I was taught. After reading about my own childhood in the draft material, I found myself thinking about the future of food. I promised myself that there would be something not quite right about devoting chapters to what has happened without giving consideration to what may lie ahead. Food issues have always been upper-most in my mind as a chef, and as far as possible I have acted on my concerns. But this book has enabled me to crystallize those thoughts.

The fishing expedition was magical because I was with my son, and that quiet day made me reflect on how we lead our lives in this day and age. We have breakfast meetings, lunch meetings and dinners, most of them rushed and uncomfortable. We have been conditioned to feel that life must be lived at breakneck speed, dashing and rushing from A to B. It is rare for the whole family to sit down for a meal because, well, because we don't have time. What time we have is devoted to the television screen because we are exhausted by the pace of our lives. We live in a culture of winning at any cost. And there is a cost.

When it comes to the subject of missing the family meal, then I, the chef, would be first to put my hands up. You have read my story. When I started out at Les Quat' Saisons, then built up Maison Blanc, Le Manoir and Brasserie Blanc, there was very little time for family meals. I had to break away from my culture, a culture that had taught me to spend time with my children. I could either make a success of the restaurant by putting my talent to good use or I could swap time in the restaurant for time at home. I wanted to be able to provide my sons with the very best of everything in life. I wanted my businesses to be a success for all of us.

Was it the right choice? I think it was. Sure, there are things I would have done differently. I might have tried to temper my passion, but how can you do that and catch up at the same time?

I was a slow learner and always used to place work before family.

Now I have learned that there needs to be space for both. Even if you have to squeeze it in! A day on the banks of the Lathkill with Olivier made room for a bit of maintenance work.

The story of my childhood in post-war France might seem ancient and simplistic, and we may have lacked the science or high-tech values and sophistication we have today, but we had one great asset: common sense. Information was passed on from one generation to another. We had a deep understanding of seasonality, provenance and purity. We loved the soil and respected what came from it. We understood the sub-story of food, that it connected with everything – the table, the family, environment, society, health.

I am convinced that the future of food will have to incorporate at least some of those values.

When I crossed the Channel in the seventies the nation was in economic turmoil and the quality of the food supply chain was not questioned; it had become an irrelevance. We had embraced intensive farming, and we held it as a triumph. Indeed to grow four times as much produce in the same field is a great achievement. But food connects with every single part of our lives, a truth that has been ignored over the last fifty years. Successive governments and consumers chose to look away. The future of food was guided (still is, to some extent) by a failure to recognize the potential consequences of our choices. After all, we all know that, as it is, our food chain is not sustainable.

Indeed, it is actually harmful. Agribusiness and agriculture have combined to create one massive intensive garden which is completely dependent on fossil fuels. Intensive farming is followed by heavy processing, dependent on molecular chemistry, manipulating poor-quality food and mixing in hundreds of E numbers and synthetic vitamins to replace the nutrients that have been processed away. On top of that, throw in transfats, excess salt and an overdose of sugar to compensate for the poor quality of the food itself. Then the heavy retailing comes into play. Everyone understands that companies have a duty to make money for their shareholders, but in doing so, are they a bit overzealous? It seems that their priorities for their products are mostly concerned with shelf life and driving down prices. Next comes the marketing, with beautiful pictures on our TV screens and in our magazines, along with glittering packaging. Right at the end of this chain are the consumer and the environment. Meanwhile, the independent farmer has become a small player, either ignored or abused by the system.

This model is based on seed selection, the criteria for which are immunity to any known disease (we paint these seeds with all the anti-everything chemicals known to ensure they are 'healthy'), how big it will grow (size is money) and how fast it will grow (time is also money). Never mind about taste or nutrients. Both have become irrelevant. The direct consequences of this are a loss of biodiversity, a loss of our own agricultural heritage and a loss of our sense of taste.

Director of the Soil Association Patrick Holden has illustrated to me the importance of biodiversity. In autumn 2008 the Soil Association is launching a major new campaign on the theme of feeding Britain. It will be a call to action to every citizen to play a part in building a rich and diverse food culture, and will be based on their philosophy that the health of soil, plants, animals and people is indivisible. This principle of biodiversity, of the life in the soil, of plant varieties, of native breeds of livestock, lies behind a rich regional food culture. All I can say is bravo.

The old system of agribusiness has no future.

We have reduced food to a mere commodity, the only values and virtues of which are speed, cheapness and convenience. Successive governments, which were elected to lead us, chose to look away from these problems. Every decision was based on the short term and for the sacrosanct 'national interest' and commerce. Never mind that our system has not only polluted the West but the whole planet. We were so dizzy with our success that we conveniently forgot about the consequences, that we were polluting and slowly taking life out of the sea and the earth, disproportionately affecting the poorest countries of the world. In today's world, with its rapidly increasing population, half of us are overfed and half of us are hungry. It is an international problem and it needs to be dealt with at this level.

But on a smaller level, the life of the modern-day consumer is not easy. Every time you choose a steak or an apple it's almost as if you need a degree in politics, food ethics, farming, socio-economics, environmental science and nutrition. Choice is only going to become even more confusing. How can I as a consumer decide whether or not to buy those lovely-looking Kenyan beans in the supermarket?

There are two separate problems to be taken into account. The first is, in principle, decidable. What is the carbon footprint of air-freighting the beans here, then trucking them from a central depot to the supermarket? Then add the carbon emissions represented by the packaging of the product. All this can be represented by a single numerical value. Then calculate the carbon emissions saved by growing these beans in a sustainable way, *not* under glass (if it's out of season here) and *not* using chemical fertilizers and pesticides. You can weigh these two numbers against each other and make a rational environmental decision based on the difference between them. (Some supermarkets already put a carbon emissions rating on the label.) This, of course, only applies when beans are not in season in your locality.

However, that still leaves the second ethical problem. If you are a Western consumer affluent enough to buy these beans in the first place, you have to think about whether it might not even be your *duty* to buy Kenyan beans. This exported crop is probably the largest cash-earner for a poor farmer who uses honest and sustainable means to grow it. By buying his beans you are contributing to the welfare of a farmer's family in one of the world's poorer areas. Unless you have made a decision never to buy food when it is not in season locally, you may feel that it is virtuous to buy Kenyan beans and help some of the world's poorest farmers. Unfortunately, you can't assign the same sort of numerical value to this.

One thing is for sure: we will pay more for our food, which might force us to respect it more. These last few years we have been engaged in a process of reconnecting with our food, from producing it to cooking it and eating it. The choices we make will define the kind of society in which we live, what kind of food supply chain we have, what colour and character our regions and villages will have. I certainly don't think any of us can single-handedly change these highly complex problems we have created for ourselves. But as consumers, we all have a responsibility for what we choose.

So, what will be the food supply chain of tomorrow? You can put scientists, farmers, environmentalists and politicians in a room together and they will all disagree. To compound the problem there is the dilemma about the energy of tomorrow. A great deal of land is being sacrificed to growing biofuels, which seems so illogical. In May 2008, an ITV documentary claimed that the crops needed to fill a tank in an ordinary car with biofuel would feed a family of four for three months. So I must invite the speculators to speculate with me. What will happen?

One thing is for sure: there are four models. Maybe five, if we decide to do more of the same.

First, GM technology. Billions of pounds have been invested and the technology is ready to be deployed. The lobby's argument is powerful. They claim they are able to save the world from malnutrition. But as a consumer, would you be prepared to feed your family with genetically modified food, or worse, transgenetically modified food? (Spinach genes implanted in pigs to produce lower-fat bacon?) And what about the consequences of cross-pollination and creating an irreversible process? What about the long-term safety of it?

Second, there is a big, fully integrated commercial food supply chain which produces, grows, transports, processes and sells all its own food on a huge scale. It has large efficiencies of scale, making it cheap, but it comes with huge consequences, social, economic and environmental.

Third, there is organic farming, championed by the Soil Association. The total amount of organically managed land now accounts for 3.5 per cent of the UK's agricultural land area. The area of in-conversion land in the UK is fast increasing (by 40 per cent last year). Of all methods of agriculture it is the only sustainable way to grow food.

Fourth, there is the more integrated model of intelligent farming which encourages biodiversity, soil and water management, and management of the land as a valuable resource, the type of agriculture that the Slow Food movement's president, Carlo Petrini, has always promoted: 'a type of agriculture which is good, clean and fair'. Of course, there will be new technologies, engineering innovations and new preserving techniques that will allow us to grow more produce at a faster pace and more safely. This will produce a sustainable system of agriculture less dependent on fossil fuels and make us more self-sufficient and less reliant on food from abroad. Could it even ally itself with organic farming?

Every part of the food supply chain has lost its craft and needs to find it again. From the farmer to the consumer, we need to reconnect in order to make responsible choices. We are currently rediscovering all these crafts, and it is an exciting time. As consumers we have been quite disengaged. We have been manipulated into buying cheap food, not knowing how it was produced. We are now, at last, engaged in a true revolution but it is going to take some time. We cannot overturn fifty years of abuse in a five-year miracle. But we must change our ways.

One person with whom I agree is wine-maker Anne-Claude Leflaive, who said of her beloved Burgundy, 'Our earth is our gold.' Not only that, it is the gold of future generations. The point she was making is that by putting more pesticides and nitrates into our soil we are burning it out and every year we need more and more chemicals to keep it going.

And what about the gastronomy of tomorrow?

The famed nineteenth-century gourmet (and Frenchman) Jean-Anthelme Brillat-Savarin pondered the definition of gastronomy.

In his book *The Physiology of Taste*, he wrote, 'Gastronomy is the reasoned comprehension of everything connected with the nourishment of man. Its aim is to obtain the preservation of man by means of the best possible nourishment.' He went on to add that gastronomy 'is the motive force behind farmers, vine growers, fishermen and huntsmen, not to mention the great family of cooks, under whatever title they may disguise their employment as preparers of food'.

In other words, gastronomy could be that foie gras dish in a Michelin-starred restaurant as much as it could be that sandwich made at home using the finest bread and the best ingredients.

Gastronomy defines us. It is central to our lives. It differentiates man from beast. In Britain and America we have made the gravest mistake over the past fifty or sixty years. We have separated food from all of the connections to which Brillat-Savarin referred. We have ignored the fact that it is linked to nutrition, science, chemistry, the environment, the tradition of craft. So, gastronomy does not belong to Michelin-starred restaurants. It is not exclusive to what we think of as haute cusine or fine dining. No, gastronomy is nothing of the sort.

Gastronomy means the 'rule of the stomach', but it should mean so much more than that. The word 'companionship' derives from the Latin for sharing bread. Food is inextricably linked with culture, and even the soul. Now in Britain, at last, we are reconnecting with gastronomy. It makes sense, for instance, to use a local producer. His food will be fresh, plentiful because it is seasonal, cheaper because there is a glut, and more nutritious because it is fresh; it will also have a smaller carbon footprint because it does not have to travel thousands of miles to get to you.

The British gastronomic scene, led by London, is thriving. It has a proud place among the best in Europe, some say even the best. And it is wonderful to witness the change, the creative power, the dynamism and entrepreneurial might of the restaurant scene. But gastronomy has also lost its roots, in Great Britain more than any other nation in Europe. What if I were to ask a young chef now what the MSC is (Marine Stewardship Council) or the MCS (Marine Conservation

Society), or Sustain? What about the seasonality of sole, its provenance (most of them would say Dover), its sustainability? Which fisheries you might get it from, the minimum size, its spawning time (and the meaning of this), and availability? Ordinarily I'm not a betting man, but I'd wager 100/1 against that they would look at me incredulously, as if I had lost my marbles.

Where can you get the best lamb in England? Which are the best breeds? Is the lamb best from high land or low land? What are the different breeds of pig in England and which regions do they come from? What is the best pumpkin variety? What are the best potatoes for deep-frying and for salads? There is a moral imperative for gastronomy to examine its relationship with food, the soil and where it comes from.

Last year (2007) the increase in food prices was 12 per cent. In some ways this puts lots of pressure on our industry, and on consumers, but it may also give us an opportunity to reconnect with our craft. Today meat arrives boned, filleted and portioned. Using the whole animal from nose to tail makes a great deal of sense. Tasty offal and the cheaper cuts of meat might well go back on our menus. Fillet steak may become less common, replaced by braised slow-cooked oxtail, or shin of beef. Interestingly enough, because meat already commands a large premium, this shift towards cheaper cuts is already beginning to happen. We have to deliver a good food cost to remain in business. No doubt chefs and domestic cooks will use less protein, becoming more creative in the use of vegetables and pulses. Meat production represents a huge strain on our environment (18 per cent of CO_2 emissions).

Like the consumer, we chefs have eaten through the world's produce and discarded our own responsibilities. For chefs, gastronomy has too often been more about the look of the dish and its complexity. We have failed to look deeper than that.

I can understand some of it as I have worked with the Soil Association for twenty-five years. I am well aware that it has been difficult to find great produce (not just good or OK, but great), so much so that it was sometimes easier to import it. To some extent that is no longer true. We have better produce in Britain than we have ever had. Even so, although we talk so much about food and local issues, when you go to the supermarket, what is there that is local? Why can't we have local food selling in the supermarket, as they do in Italy or France? Maybe one of the reasons is that our growing season is so short – May to November. In France, spring lasts from January in the south to June in the north. We are still net food importers.

But today there is a growing awareness of our responsibilities. Chefs and gastronomy have a huge role to play to help reinvent each region, rediscover our heirloom varieties and help keep their characters. This can be done in beneficial partnership between chefs, local farmers, consumers and local schools, and pass on knowledge to customers and young chefs alike. For example, at Le Manoir, we are aiming for total traceability on all ingredients. We began two years ago and it is a hard task as most suppliers are not always keen to reveal their secrets, whether breed, feed, antibiotics or whatever. Haute cuisine makes this process even more complicated due to the complexity of what is offered. We use so many products, but we know now where our chicken has come from, its breed, its age, what it has eaten, whether it has ever been given antibiotics. Everywhere in the world, chefs have played a significant role, and their influence has filtered down the food chain. American chefs embraced the French model and created the modern farmers' market across America – the nucleus of a food culture. In England, this process has started in our towns, villages and cities these last few years.

———

We will also have to teach our children about the value of a meal. We need to instil in them that sense of place, of region. We need to show our children what flourishes near their homes. We need to reconnect with the simple act of cooking and how rewarding it can be, both at school and in the home. We need to learn to make our own bread and grow our own vegetables in the garden. If that's not possible we can grow leaves and herbs in window boxes and teach our children the miracle of the little grey seeds that contain the life force. If you decide to grow your own healthy vegetables and cook them once a week, twice a week, or even once a month, it will have consequences: life will feel better and you and your family will feel better. You will be part of gastronomy, too – 'everything connected with the nourishment of man', as Brillat-Savarin said. When it comes to imported food, children, I pray, will learn to regard it as a treat, not as a birthright. In doing so, what they will gain is their true birthright: the food of their own regions and a sense of their own gastronomy.

As Caroline Drummond of LEAF once told me, 'The issue is a balance between what we might get and what we want. The difference between the two is our ability as citizens to take our own responsibilities seriously.' It is our responsibility to empower our children by teaching them about basic nutrition, that counting calories is not the basis of good health. Diet-peddlers have taken us hostage, using our lack of interest and sometimes ignorance to sell us their newest fads, with terrible and lasting consequences. Instead of enjoying our food, we fear it. If we have knowledge, if we understand basic nutrition, simple cooking and our individual needs, we will take away their power.

Good nutrition is uncomplicated – a varied diet of fresh seasonal ingredients cooked simply. No more, no less. We must understand that every molecule of food we eat has a short- and long-term effect on us, positive or negative. All we need to do is reconnect with the simple craft of cooking and show our children how our food is grown, and I'm happy to say we are starting to make more responsible choices, and the regions are being reborn. Allotments, which were once the vegetable gardens of the lower classes, today have three-year-long waiting lists.

One of the agricultural triumphs of recent years is cheese. There are now as many varieties of cheese in Britain as there are in France. Many of them are excellent, so much so that the French cheese industry has lost a large slice, so to speak, of the market. Having as many cheeses as the French may be a good thing, but as General de Gaulle said, facing his citizens on strike, 'How can you rule a country which has as many cheeses as there are days in the year?' Perhaps England will soon become ungovernable.

But of course the future of food is not just a British or French problem, it is a world problem that we all need to address. We need a body of apolitical wise men – scientists, environmentalists, politicians, farmers, processors – to create cohesive worldwide policies. But, sadly, it seems as though we are far away from that. My old friend Jody Scheckter truly understands earth. He told me, 'Scientists think they know, but they know little compared to nature. An example is a handful of good soil. In this soil there are more living things than people on Earth.' Jody and a group of scientists – ones who are appreciative of soil – are trying to track the minerals as they pass through the earth and into the food chain, and even the people who eat the produce. They are hoping to discover a way to grow food that is highly valuable in nutrients and also helps the biodiversity of the land.

Food is a big issue, and it will only become bigger. We have had the Stern Report, the Kyoto Report, the Bangkok Report and numerous others, and documentaries, informing us about the dangers that await us. It took the best scientists on the planet to tell us what was blindingly obvious!

Meanwhile, fast food outlets benefit. I recently had drinks with one of the bosses of a main fast-food outlet, who told me that turnover for the business during the 'credit crunch' has so far increased by 20 per cent. Olivier once took me for a burger, at McDonald's, the fast-food chain that can claim no connection with gastronomy. I was not repulsed by the place. In fact, I became aware of why it is so successful. The staff are quite cheerful (because they are told to be), the burgers taste OK – some would say good – and they do the job of filling you up, and it is all about cheapness: its food has a price tag that defies any form of competition. But McDonald's remains a fuel station, albeit a clean one.

Following their 'McLibel' difficulties a few years ago, the business claims to be aware of its social responsibilities in the communities in which it operates.

I may have my doubts about the global community, but I have no doubt that Britain is engaged in the process of reconnecting with its food culture by increasingly encouraging seasonal and regional produce. This is bound to have a beneficial impact on our towns and villages and how the supermarkets work. The government has more power than any individual and eventually the public will demand that it legislate on the things that worry us about our food supply, from pesticides to fertilizers, from proper labelling (so consumers can at last have the power to choose) to giving the carbon footprint of food and precise information about nutrition, whether our food has been produced by intensive farming and whether animal welfare has been respected. We have to hope that those we elect to govern us will also reintroduce domestic science and basic nutrition to the school curriculum, and see that future generations know something about farming and how our food reaches the table.

There is currently a huge amount of creative activity within the food supply chain – farms, shops, markets – as many people and parts of the industry engage in a spring clean. We are discovering that while it might be painful, the process may not be as painful as we thought it might be. The future must be established by us taking from the past. Only then will we rediscover the values we used to cherish, not least respect for food, the environment and farming.

And there is something else. When I look back on my childhood stories in the early chapters of this book, it brings a smile to my face. Aside from the sentimentality and the fact that it was fun, I know that these stories reflect a culture that was based on respect of food and its production, and the family.

The purpose of *A Taste of My Life* – and thank you so much for taking the time to read it – was to share stories, share a knowledge of food, share the excitement of food. Perhaps it has enticed you back into the kitchen, or to spend longer there, so that you can make simple or more beautiful meals for your loved ones and then sit with them at the table and celebrate life and family . . . and tomorrow.

I feel very privileged to be part of the food revolution. Cheffing is looked upon as a demanding profession, but a wonderful and extremely rewarding one at that.

I am often asked, 'Do you feel British?' No, never. But I feel a far better Frenchman for being here.

What next for me? Natalia, who is as beautiful in spirit as she is in looks, tells me the Russians have a saying: 'If you want to make God laugh, tell him your plans.' Very wise. What's more, he has had enough laughs at my expense.

Voilà. C'est tout.

All that remains is a call to Olivier. We'll fix a date to return to the river and see if we can catch something this time. My father taught me to fish, and I taught Olivier to fish. We have to pass on knowledge, don't we? And on those iron gates at Le Manoir, the ones my father painted back in the mid-eighties, I'll hang a sign: 'Gone Fishing'.

SELECTED READING

Achatz, Grant, *Alinea* (New York: Ten Speed Press, 2008)

Adria, Ferran, *A Day at El Bulli* (London: Phaidon Press, 2008)

——, *El Bulli 2003–2004* (New York: Ecco, 2006); *El Bulli 1998–2002* (New York: Ecco, 2005); *El Bulli 1994–1997* (New York: Ecco, 2006); *El Bulli 1983–1993* (Barcelona: Rba Libros, 2005)

Barham, Peter, *The Science of Cooking* (Berlin: Springer-Verlag Berlin, 2000)

Barr, Ann and Levy, Paul, *The Official Foodie Handbook* (London: Ebury, 1984)

Blumenthal, Heston, *The Big Fat Duck Cookbook* (London: Bloomsbury, 2008)

——, *In Search of Perfection: Reinventing Kitchen Classics* (London: Bloomsbury, 2006)

Blythman, Joanna, *Bad Food Britain: How a Nation Ruined Its Appetite* (London: Fourth Estate, 2006)

Brillat-Savarin, Jean Antheleme, *Physiologie de Goût* (France: 1825; new ed., trans. Anne Drayton, London: Penguin Classics, 1994)

Coultate, T. P., *Food: The Chemistry of Its Components* (4th rev. ed.,

London: Royal Society of Chemistry, 2001)

Davidson, Alan, *The Oxford Companion to Food* (2nd ed., ed. Tom Jaine, Oxford: Oxford University Press, 2006)

De Pomaine, Edouard *Cooking in Ten Minutes* (London: Serif, 1993)

Dinesen, Isak, 'Babette's Feast' in *Anecdotes of Destiny* (London: Penguin, 2001)

Driver, Christopher, *The British at Table, 1940–1980* (London: Chatto and Windus, 1983)

Drummond, J. C. and Wilbraham, Anne, *The Englishman's Food: A History of Five Centuries of English Diet* (London: Cape, 1939)

Food Standards Agency, *Manual of Nutrition (Reference Book 342)* (London: Stationery Office Books, 2008)

Hannsen, Maurice and Marsden, Jill, *E for Additives* (rev. ed., London: Thorsons, 1987)

Harris, Joanne, *Chocolat* (London: Doubleday, 1999)

Kafka, Barbara, *Vegetable Love: A Book for Cooks* (New York: Artisan Division of Workman Publishing, 2005)

Keller, Thomas, *Under Pressure: Cooking Sous Vide* (New York: Artisan Division of Workman Publishing, 2008)

——, *The French Laundry Cookbook* (New York: Workman Publishing, 1999)

Lawrence, Felicity, *Not on the Label: What Really Goes into the Food on Your Plate* (London: Penguin, 2004)

Levy, Paul (ed.), *The Penguin Book of Food and Drink* (London: Viking, 1996)

——, *Out to Lunch* (London: HarperCollins, 1987)

McGee, Harold, *McGee on Food and Cooking: An Encyclopedia of Kitchen Science, History and Culture* (London: Hodder & Stoughton, 2004)

Paxman, Jeremy, *The English: A Portrait of a People* (London: Michael Joseph, 1998)

Pollan, Michael, *In Defence of Food: The Myth of Nutrition and the Pleasures of Eating* (London: Allen Lane, 2008)

—, *The Omnivore's Dilemma: The Search for a Perfect Meal in a Fast-food World* (London: Bloomsbury, 2007)

Roberts, Paul, *The End of Food* (London: Houghton Mifflin Company, 2008)

Royal Society of Chemistry, *Kitchen Chemistry* (London: Royal Society of Chemistry, 2005)

Steingarten, Jeffrey, *It Must've Been Something I Ate: The Return of the Man Who Ate Everything* (London: Headline, 2003)

—, *The Man Who Ate Everything* (London: Headline, 1999)

Tannahill, Reay, *Food in History* (new ed., London: Crown Publications, 2002)

This, Hervé, *Molecular Gastronomy: Exploring the Science of Flavor (Arts & Traditions of the Table: Perspectives on Culinary History)* (New York: Columbia University Press, 2006)

Wilson, Bee, *Swindled: From Poison Sweets to Counterfeit Coffee – The Dark History of the Food Cheats* (London: John Murray, 2008)

INDEX

abattoir at Kobe 280–1
Abel, Tom 150
Adrià, Ferran 268
aïoli 70, 77
air-freight 359
allotments 365
Alphonso mango 325
Alsace 189–93
animal rights activists 173–4
Apple Tart 'Maman Blanc' 18–20
apples 44
Ascot 342
asparagus 35, 43, 71
Assassins Club 353–4
L'Atelier, London 173
L'Auberge du Pont de Collanges,
    Lyon 184, 185–7
Aylesbury ducks 129–30

baked Alaska 197
baked apple and semolina soufflé
    297
basil 84

Bastille Day 340–1
basting 90
bay leaves 84
BBC
    Blanc Mange 265, 267
    The Restaurant 150
Beauvilliers, Antoine 296–7
béchamel sauce 304
beef 91, 135, 148, 295
    from Kobe 276–7, 280–82
Besançon
    brasserie at the bus station 97–100
    Le Palais de la Bière 15–17,
        101–6
    Poker d'As 95–7
beurre blanc 333, 335–6
Beyer, Marc 189–90, 192–3
Billingsgate 150
biodiversity 358, 366
biofuels 360
Bitter Chocolate Mousse 32–3
black pepper 316, 317, 318
blackcurrant gelée 11

Blanc, Anne-Marie (mother) 8, 49,
    94–5, 147, 203
    Christmas 49–50, 51, 53, 55, 59
    cooking with wine 239, 241
    desserts 211
    fish 63, 65
    rabbit 39–40
    soufflés 297
    soups 88–9
    steak 25, 26–8
    tomato salad 5–7, 8
    wild foods 25, 36
Blanc, Françoise (sister) 49, 94
Blanc, Frederick 173
Blanc, Gérard (brother) 49
    dismantles toy 52–3
    grasshoppers' legs 21, 22
    hunting and fishing 56–7, 63
    summer camp 65–6
Blanc, Jenny see Colbeck, Jenny (ex-
    wife)
Blanc, Martine (sister) 49, 94
Blanc, Maurice (father) 5, 166
    fishing 63–4
    gardening 34, 48–9, 249–50
    hunting and gathering 34, 36–7
Blanc, Michel (brother) 49, 63, 65
Blanc, Olivier (son) 119, 246, 252,
    333, 350, 366
    fishing 355, 356, 357
Blanc, Paul 173
Blanc, Sebastien (son) 119, 246, 252,
    333, 350
Blanc Mange (TV series) 265, 267
Blin, Benoit 163, 209–10
Blumenthal, Heston 267
Bocuse, Paul 181, 183–5, 187, 188,
    253
Bordeaux 168
bouillabaisse 70

bourgeois cooking 194
Braised Oxtail, Red Wine Jus 292–5
Braised Rabbit with Mustard 45–7,
    147
Brasserie Blanc 196–7, 274, 361
    M. Bernard 107
    menu 120, 175, 297
brasseries 193–5
    Alsace 191–2
    Besançon 97–100
    Petit Blanc 195–6
    see also Brasserie Blanc
bread 211–13
    Country Bread 226–9
    deliveries 223–4
    making 220–1, 222–3, 262
    ovens 215–16
    popular attitude to 219–20
Breast of Chicken with Morels and
    Vin Jaune Sauce 197–200
brill 256–9
Brillat-Savarin, Jean-Anthelme 362,
    365
Britain
    in the 1970s 112, 357
    catering industry 116–17
    cheeses 54, 366
    farming practice 129–30, 147,
        175, 357–9
    gastronomy 362–3, 367
    popular attitude to bread 219–20
    RB's first impressions 111–14
brochette de fruits exotiques 325–6
Brown Chicken Stock 206–8
brown stock 204, 205
brown trout and rainbow trout 66–7
Brown's restaurant, Oxford 215
bûche de Noël 55
bullet train 275
Burgundy, coq au vin 238, 239, 240

butchery craft 363
butter sauce 333, 335–6
butternut squash soup 88

café crème 210
Cahors 177
    wine 241
Calabrese, Salvator 15, 17
calorie counting 365
calves' heads 2–3
Cambodia 288
caramel soufflé 300
caramelization
    meat 26–8
    onions 83–4, 85
    stock 204
carbon footprints 359, 362
career choice 95, 97–107
Carême, Antonin 297
Carpenters (vocal group) 114–15
cassolette aux abricots 210
cattle
    Kobe 274, 280–82
    Montbeliarde 22–3
caviar 165–8, 317
celebrity chefs *see* television cookery
character of ingredients 14
cheese soufflé 197, 297, 304
cheeses 54, 366
    making 23–4
    storing and serving 316–17
Chelsea Flower Show 326
Cherry Clafoutis 200–2
chicken 38, 89–90, 197, 266
    Breast of Chicken with Morels
        and Sherry Wine Sauce
        197–200
    coq au vin 238, 239, 240, 241–2
    farming 175
    roast 291

soups 89, 91
stock 205–8
chicken bang bang 324
Chicken Liver Parfait 178–80
chicken liver paté 173
childhood
    alcohol 41–2
    battles 24
    Christmas 49–50, 51–5
    fishing 63–6
    fuel gathering 51
    gardening 48–9
    grasshoppers' legs 21–2
    home 50–1
    hunting and gathering 24–5, 34–7
    meals 5–7, 37–9, 42–3
    starting to cook 93–5
    values 357, 367
    village life 22–3
children and food 365
China 289
chives 84
chocolate
    Bitter Chocolate Mousse 32–3
    lobster with chocolate sauce 72–5
chocolate soufflé 300
chopsticks 282–3
Christmas 49–50, 51–3
    lunches 44, 53–5, 56
Christmas log 55
cleaning 103, 145
clothing factory 101
cockerel as emblem of France 181–2
cocktails 131
cognac 15–17, 316
Colbeck, Mr 115–16
Colbeck, Mrs 115–16, 118, 119, 124
Colbeck, Jenny (ex-wife) 116, 117,
    118–19, 333
    divorce 251

Les Quat' Saisons 143, 144, 148, 149, 163, 181
Maison Blanc 211, 213, 217
truffles 177
visit to L'Auberge du Pont de Collanges 185–6
commis at Le Palais 105–6
commis debarasseur at Le Palais 104–5
Le Comté cheese 23–4, 54, 297
Comté Cheese Soufflé 28–31
Cona coffee 115, 118
confectioner's custard *see* pastry cream
Confit of Salmon with Dill Cucumber, Cauliflower and Horseradish sauce 270–3
Constance Spry Cookery Book 127
consumers 358, 359–60, 361
cookery demonstrations
    Alsace 189–90
    Japan 275
cookery school 249, 323, 348–50
coq au vin 238, 239, 240, 241–2
coriander 84
Country Bread 226–9
Covent Garden 150
crab 147
Craddock, Fanny 230–1
crayfish
    freshwater 34, 63, 125, 126
    saltwater 70–2
crème patissière see pastry cream
Crêpes 107–9
Suzette 93–4
croissants 219
Cromwell, Lady 246–7, 248
cross-contamination 141–2
crows 24–5
crudités 53
crumbles 120–1

curiosity 104, 260–1, 273–4
curried mouse 136–8
customers
    Besançon 98–100
    Le Manoir 73–5, 254–5, 350–4
    Petit Blanc 196
    Les Quat' Saisons 151, 247, 260, 311–12, 331

dancing 350
David (chef) 118
Davidson, Alan 264
Desenclos, Alain 164, 224
designer cuisine 253, 290
desserts 55, 110
    starting with 352–3
    see also patisserie
Dickinson, Nicholas 275, 276–7, 280
difficult customers 350–4
Dijon mustard dressing 6
distillation 41–2
Dorchester Hotel 152–3
driving 110–11, 112, 223–4, 332
Drummond, Caroline 365
duck 129–30
duck à l'orange 130–1
Duck Leg Confit with Flageolet Beans in Persillade 318–21

education 365
Eel in Teriyaki Jelly 284–7
eels 63–4, 167
    electric 278–9, 281
egg whites 268
    in soufflés 300–1, 305
Elizabeth II, Queen 338
Elizabeth, Queen Mother
    at Ascot 342–3
    RB cooks lunch for 331–3, 338
    visits Le Manoir 339–42, 344

Elysée Soup with Black Truffles 188
emulsions 172, 264–5
English language 112, 126–7
escargots 54
Escoffier, Auguste 125, 177, 204–5,
    252, 263
Espagnole sauce 203
L'Esperance, Burgundy 62
Essence of Tomato 8–9, 10–12, 317
ethical issues
    foie gras 169, 173–5
    see also future of food
European cuisine 254, 322–3
Exotic Fruit Gratin with Coconut
    Rice 327–30

family meals 356
fast food 91–2, 366–7
fennel 333
Fillet of Brill with Oyster and
    Cucumber and Wasabi Jus 256–9
fish and chips 111–12, 113
fish farming 291
fish soufflé 304–5
fish soup 70, 76–9
Fish Soup with Aïoli 76–9
fish supplies 125, 148, 150
fishing 62–6, 355, 356
Floating Islands 'Maman Blanc'
    121–3, 210
Floyd, Keith 237–8
foie gras 168–72, 177
    ethical issues 169, 173–5
    terrine 172–3
food poisoning 136, 139–40, 141–2
food safety rules 140–2
food traceability 364
football matches 235–6
Franche-Comté 67–8, 70
French beans 171

French bread 211–12, 219
French regional produce 67–70,
    168–9, 239
    see also cheeses
freshness 128–9, 148
    in Japan 278, 281
    nouvelle cuisine 253
freshwater crayfish 34, 63, 125, 126
Fretwell, Clive 196–7, 275, 354
frogs 36–7
fuel gathering 51
fusion 322–4, 325–6
future of food 356, 357–67

gadgets and basic skills 269
gardens 48–9
    at Le Manoir 249–50, 283, 326–7
gastronomy 362–4, 365
    molecular 260–70
gâteau de foie gras 146, 173
Gault, Henri 253
Gault Millau restaurant guides 253
Le Gavroche restaurant, Chelsea 217,
    223, 232
geishas 275, 277, 281
gelées 11, 289
    of oysters 138
Gérard, Michel 172–3
ghosts 248
gin and tonic 131
goujons (gudgeons) 34, 63
government grant 248
Grand Marnier Soufflé 308–10
La Grande Taverne de Londres 296–7
Great Milton manor house 246–7
    see also Le Manoir aux Quat'
    Saisons
green peppercorns 317–18
Grigson, Jane 127, 128
Grigson, Sophie 128

Gruyère soufflé 304
guests *see* customers
Guigol, Côte rôti 96

Haddon Hall, Derbyshire 355
Hamilton, Richard 343
hand washing 141
hanging meat 25–6
Harrods 217, 223
haute cuisine 96–7
health and safety rules 140–2
Henri IV, King of France 89
herbs 84, 316, 317, 327, 333
Hiroaki Fujii 283
Hiroshia Koyama 283
Holden, Patrick 358
hollandaise sauce 264–5
horse racing 331, 339–40, 342
Hôtel de France, Wiesbaden 119
hunting and gathering 24–5, 34–7,
    56–7
    see also fishing
hygiene 136–42

Iced Pineapple Parfait with Pineapple
    Sunflowers 344–7
îles flottantes 43, 121–3, 210
intensive farming 147, 174, 175,
    357–9

jam making 262–3
Japan 274–84, 288, 289
Japanese Food Festival 283
Jerusalem Artichoke Mousse with
    Chervil Sauce 157–9
Jerusalem artichoke soup 88
Jones, Alan 168
Jones, Gary 148, 163, 274–5, 281,
    314–15
    in Japan 276–7, 279–81

joy of being a chef 160–2
Jura mountains 65–6, 197

Kenyan beans 359–60
Kerr, Graham 230
kidneys 95, 96, 147
kitchens during service 160–3
Kobe beef 275–6, 280–2
Koffmann, Pierre 156
Kurti, Nicholas 260–1, 262, 263, 264,
    265–6, 269–70
    Blanc Mange 265, 267

lamb 147, 148
    shoulder 132–5
Lambert, Nicholas 275
Lanesborough Hotel 15, 17
Languedoc wine 240
Larousse Gastronomique 93
Lathkill, River 355–6, 357
Laverstoke Park Farm 90, 291
Lawson, Michael 156
Lay, Mr (gardener) 124–5
Le Blanc, Lloyd 354
LEAF (Linking Environment and
    Farming) 365
Lederer, John 196
Leflaive, Anne-Claude 361
lemon grass 326
lemon sabayon sauce 264–5
lemon sole 258
Lily (pig) 177
Little, Alistair 194
liver 173, 175, 178–80
    see also foie gras
lobster with chocolate sauce 72–5
local produce 128–30, 362, 364, 365
    nouvelle cuisine 253
    see also French regional produce
logos 181–5

Los Angeles 311
lotte 69, 70
Loubet, Bruno 195

McDonald's 289, 366–7
Mackay, Alex 195
mackerel 284
Maison Blanc 162, 211, 213–20, 226
    bread deliveries 223–4
    bread-making 220–1, 222–3
    M. Bernard 107
    saving the business 224–5
maîtres d'hôtel 151–2
Malaysia 326
management 162–3
    Petit Blanc 195–6
mangos 324–5
Manners, Lord and Lady 355
Le Manoir aux Quat' Saisons 146,
    194
    cookery school 249, 323, 348–50
    early days 247–9, 250–1
    foie gras 174–5
    gardens 249–50, 326–7
    guests 73–5, 255, 350–4
    Japanese influence 282–3, 288
    Keith Floyd visits 237–8
    M. Bernard 106–7
    philosophy 72–3, 254–5, 364
    Relais & Chateaux 234–5
    searching for home sweet home
        245–7
    Thai influence 325
    vegetable trials 9
    visit from the Queen Mother
        339–42, 344
margarita (cocktail) 131
marinades 239–40, 242
marjoram 84
markets 69, 70–1

London 150
Marmande tomatoes 6, 10
Marseillaise 340–1
medaillons de veau, ses beatilles et
    amourettes 147
memory and taste 14–15
Meneau, Marc 62
Michel (baker) 216, 221–2
Michelin Red Guide 156–7
    bib gourmands 195
Michelin stars 156, 195
    Les Quat' Saisons 152, 157
Millau, Christian 253
minimalism 253, 289
Minogue, Kylie 348–50
Le Mitre, Oxford 114
molecular gastronomy 260–70
monkfish 284
Montbeliarde cows 22–3
morels 190, 197–200
mushrooms 35–6, 326
    drying 84
    morels 190, 197–200
    seasons 44

Napoleon, Emperor of France 182
Natalia (fiancée) 167, 289, 349, 368
Natasha (daughter to Natalia) 349
Newington Nursery 326
Normandy onion soup 87
North Korea 288
nouvelle cuisine 252–4
nursing 100–1
nutrition 363, 365

Oakland, Robert 266
octopus 279
offal 147, 363
old wives' tales 267–8
olives 68

onion soup 80–7
onions 80
    flatulance 72
    varieties 81–2
Oonagh Fawkes's Apple Crumble
    120–1
oranges 43–4
ovens 212–13, 215–16
Owens, Anne Marie 9, 250–1
Oxford 114, 144, 195, 213, 245–6
Oxford Symposium on Food and
    Cookery 263–4
oxtail 292–5
oysters 127, 138, 139–40, 256–9

packaging 358, 359
Le Palais de la Bière, Besançon
    15–17, 101–6, 147, 175–6
palate 312–14, 351
pancakes see Crêpes
parfait de foie gras 173
parsley 84
parsnip soup 88
Pascal (patisserie chef) 216, 222
pastry cream 299, 300, 307–8
patés 54, 173
patisserie 209, 210–11
    see also Maison Blanc
paysans 22–3
Pebeyre, Jacques 177
pectin 262–3
pepper 316, 317
Peregrine, Mark (commis chef) 62–3,
    332, 338
Périgord truffles 175
Petit Blanc 195–6
petit gris de sapin mushrooms 35–6
Petit San Marzano tomatoes see
    Essence of Tomato
Petrini, Carlo 361

philosophy 72–3, 150, 151, 254–5
Phoebus (hunting dog) 56, 57, 59
pick-your-own 150, 171, 251
pike 65, 125–6
pineapple 344–7
Pink Roscoff onion 82
pistachio soufflé 299
pizza dough 229
plaice 259
plate design 342–3
ploughing 42
plum spirit 41–2
Point, Fernand 253
Le Poker d'As, Besançon 95–7
polishing glasses 103
pork belly 91
Postgate, Raymond 112
potato varieties 9
Potiron Muscade de Provence
    pumpkin (Iron Bark) 87–8
poule au pot 89, 91–2
poultry supplies 89, 148
price and quality 218–19, 359, 360,
    363
processed foods 270, 357–8
Provence 68–72, 333
puff pastry 153
pumpkin soup 87–8

quality produce, search for 128–30,
    147–8, 165
Les Quat' Saisons 43, 143–6, 148–52,
    163–4, 214–15
    bread 211–13
    customers 151, 248, 260, 311–12,
        331
    foie gras 169–73
    logos 181–5
    menu 146–8, 153–6, 165–7
    Michelin stars 152, 157, 189

stock 205–6
truffles 176–7
visits from the Roux brothers
 232–4
quenelles of pike 125–6

rabbit (*lapin*) 38–40, 45–7, 147
rabbits at Le Manoir 249, 250
Race, John Burton 194, 195
Radclyffe, Charles 331–2, 338, 342
rainbow trout and brown trout 66–7
rascasse 69, 70
raspberries 44
raspberry soufflé 299–300
rats 145
raw food 279, 282, 289
red rice 325
Relais & Chateaux 12, 234–5
Le Répertoire de la Cuisine 252
The Restaurant (TV series) 150
Restaurant of the Year 152
Restoix, M. 224–5
Restoix, Monique 225
retailing of food *see* supermarkets
Rhodes, Gary 194
Rhône valley wines 240–1
Rhug Estate, Wales 90
Ring, Albert 250
risotto, tomato 12
roast chicken 89–90
Robert (maitre d'hôtel) 115
rock-fish 69, 70
Ronay, Egon 152
Roquefort cheese soufflé 197, 297
Rose Revived, Oxfordshire
 RB as chef 124–6, 128, 130,
  136–8
 RB as waiter 106, 114–19
rosemary 84
rouille 70

Roux, Albert 156, 157, 217, 232–3,
 297
Roux, Michel 156, 232–7, 297

sage 84
Saint Cyr-sur-Mer 69
salmon 270–3, 284
salt 311–15
salt beef 91
saltwater crayfish 70–2
Saône, Besançon 5, 22–4
scallops 259
Scheckter, Jody and Clare 120, 366
science and food 260–70, 366
sculpture 354
sea bass 146–7
sea slug intestines 279–80
sea-fish 69–72
seasonal produce 43–4, 138, 362
 Japan 278, 282
 nouvelle cuisine 253
seasoning 311–18
seed selection 358
Seiyo Ginza Hotel, Tokyo 276–7
service 98–100, 151
shallots, soused 170–1
Simon, Mme 64, 70
Simon, M. 69, 70, 71–2
Simon, René 21, 22, 35
 fish 64, 67, 68–70, 72
slicing onions 82
slow cooking 92
Slow Food Movement 361
Slow-roasted Shoulder of Lamb,
 Braised Summer Vegetables and
 Roasting Juices 132–5
smell 315
 fish 125
Smith, Delia 230
smoked fish in soufflés 305

snails 54
Soil Association 358, 360, 363
Soufflé Rothschild 297
soufflés 28–31, 197, 267–8, 296–8,
    308–10
  base 299, 304
  cooking 302–4
  flavour 299–300, 304–5
  lifter 300–1, 305
  mixing the elements 301–2
  preparing in advance 305–6
  preparing the dish 298–9, 304
soups 88–9, 188, 324
  chicken 89, 91
  fish 70, 76–9
  onion 80–7
  pumpkin 87–8
  stock 204
sousing 170–1
South Korea 288
spices 316, 317, 350–1
spinach 172
Spitz, M. 16, 102–3, 104
Spitz, Bernard 16, 106–7
Spry, Constance 127
steak 25, 26–8
steak, kidney and oyster pudding
    127–8
stews 290
sticky rice and mango 324–5
Stilton soufflé 297
stock 203–8
stock rotation 141
strawberries 44
sturgeon 165–6, 168
summer camp 65–6
Summer Fruits Steeped in Red
    Wine, Monbazillac, Basil and Mint
    243–4
supermarkets 270, 358, 359, 364

sushi chefs 290
symbolism 278

table salt 314, 315
tarot (card game) 50, 52, 64, 81
taste 13–17, 130–1
  caviar 166
  foie gras 169–70
  stock 205
  truffles 176
tea-gardens 283
television cookery 150, 230–1, 237
  Blanc Mange 265, 267
temperature 316–17
tench 64
terrines 54, 284–7
  Chicken Liver Parfait 178–80
  foie gras 172–3
testing the palate 313–14
texture 278, 288–92
Thailand 324–6, 326
Thame 235–7
This, Hervé 266
thumbing up 302
thyme 84
The Times 339
Tokyo 276–7
tom yum soup 324
tomato salad 5–7, 8
tomatoes 6, 9–10, 14
  see also Essence of Tomato
Topham, Nurdin 348, 349–50
Toulouse sausages 197
Tournier, Alfred (grandfather) 42
Tournier, Germaine (grandmother)
    40–1, 42
  chicken and duck liver 175
  raspberry jelly 11
  tripe 53, 59
training staff 162–3

Tripe with Calvados 53, 59–61, 289, 290
trout 65, 66–7
truffe en brioche 177
truffe de foie gras 176–7
truffles 175–8, 188
turbot 146, 259
turbot rôti 333–8
turkey farming 175
Turner, Brian 235, 236

University of Bangkok 327

varieties of vegetables and fruit , 6, 9–10, 81–2, 87–8
veal kidneys in Hermitage sauce 95–7
veal (*veau*) 91, 147, 148
Villefranche-sur-Mer 71
Villeroy Boche 343
Vin Jaune 197

Vines, Richard 273
Vladimir (chef) 348
vodka 167, 317

Wagyu cattle 281–2
waiting at table 97–100, 116–17
washing up 103
Waterside Inn, Berkshire 232, 234
    football match 235–7
White, Marco Pierre 194, 268, 292
white peppercorns 317–18
white stock 204
Whole Turbot Roasted on a Bed of Fennel 334–7
Wiesbaden 119
wild asparagus 35, 43
wild boar 56–9
wild fruit 25
Wimpy bars 113
wine in cooking 85, 238–42
wine lists 149–50